Core Concerns in Indian Defence and the Imperatives for Reforms

Core Concerns in Indian Defence and the Imperatives for Reforms

Editor

Vinod Misra

idsa

INSTITUTE FOR DEFENCE STUDIES & ANALYSES
NEW DELHI

PENTAGON PRESS

Core Concerns in Indian Defence and the Imperatives for Reforms
Vinod Misra (Editor)

First Published in 2015

ISBN 978-81-8274-818-7

Published by
PENTAGON PRESS
206, Peacock Lane, Shahpur Jat,
New Delhi-110049
Phones: 011-64706243, 26491568
Telefax: 011-26490600
email: rajan@pentagonpress.in
website: www.pentagonpress.in

Branch
Flat No.213, Athena-2,
Clover Acropolis,
Viman Nagar,
Pune-411014
Email: pentagonpresspune@gmail.com

In association with
Institute for Defence Studies and Analyses
No. 1, Development Enclave,
New Delhi-110010
Phone: +91-11-26717983
Website: www.idsa.in

Printed at Aegean Offset Printers, Greater Noida

CONTENTS

	Foreword	*vii*
	Contributors	*ix*
	Abbreviations	*xi*
	Overview	*xix*
1.	India's External Security Environment and its Impact on Indian Defence *Kanwal Sibal*	1
2.	The Conundrum of Indian Defence and Civil-Military Relationship *Shekhar Dutt*	9
3.	Roots of Civil-Military Schism in India: The Need for Synergy *Arun Prakash*	19
4.	India's Defence Organisation: A Re-Orientation and the Need for Change *Srinivasapuram Krishnaswamy*	38
5.	Higher Defence Organisation and The Pursuit of Jointness *Deepak Kapoor*	52
6.	Defence Planning in India at Crossroads *Amiya Kumar Ghosh*	74
7.	Defence Planning, Programming and Budgeting: An Agenda for Reform *Narendra Singh Sisodia and Amit Cowshish*	101
8.	Defence R&D *A Sivathanu Pillai*	121

9. Acquisition in Defence 143
Vinod Misra

10. Strengthening the Defence Industrial Base in India 156
Ravindra Gupta

11. Defence Budget: Constraints and Capability Building 172
Vinay Kaushal

12. Financial Management in Defence 208
Amit Cowshish

13. Defence Manpower 231
Satish Nambiar

14. Logistics and Supply Chain Management 245
Pramod Vasant Athawale

15. India's Offset Policy: The Way Forward 270
Satya Narayan Misra

16. Arms Trade Offset: Global Trend and 'Best' Practices 289
Laxman Kumar Behera

17. Oversight in Defence 310
Vinod Rai

18. Oversight for Defence: Mechanism, Objectives and Methodology 323
Pratyush Sinha

Annexures 335
Vinay Kaushal and Laxman Kumar Behera

Index 368

FOREWORD

We are living in an uncertain global and regional security environment. The nature of conflict is changing; terrorism, cyber threats, pandemics, economics, financial instabilities, migrations, etc., endanger global, regional and national security. Our responses have to be tailored to meet these new challenges.

The Kargil war in 1999 and the Mumbai terror attacks in 2008 were reminders of the changing nature of conflict. In 2001, on the recommendation of the Kargil Review Committee, a Group of Ministers (GoM) came up with a set of recommendations for a comprehensive reform of the Indian security management system. Since then, the debate on the role of defence forces in the nation's security and on the need for defence reforms has intensified. Although a number of measures have been taken, the debate remains unstoppable and inconclusive.

Taking note of the growing and justifiable public interest in defence issues, the IDSA in 2013 embarked on a project to identify the core issues of defence reforms debate. Several knowledgeable experts, who have had intimate knowledge of the issues involved, were invited to contribute. Most authors had earlier occupied senior positions in the government and participated in policymaking processes. They were also involved in the implementation of reforms at different times. Their contributions in the present volume provide fascinating glimpse and diverse perspectives on the evolution and complexities of Indian defence reform process. The issues covered in this volume range from a discussion on India's security environment and higher defence management to critical aspects of defence reforms like defence planning, jointness, R&D, budgets and India's defence acquisition policies.

I am confident that the book will be found to be useful by the strategic community. The volume will hopefully enrich the debate and also provide useful ideas to policymakers. I congratulate the IDSA, and particularly the editor Shri Vinod Misra, for bringing out this edited volume at a useful juncture of time.

New Delhi
October, 2014

ARVIND GUPTA
Deputy NSA &
Former Director General, IDSA

CONTRIBUTORS

Vinod Misra, a former Secretary Defence (Finance), Ministry of Defence, Government of India, is presently Distinguished Fellow at the Institute for Defence Studies and Analyses.

Kanwal Sibal is former Foreign Secretary, Ministry of External Affairs, Government of India.

Shekhar Dutt, a former Governor (Chhattisgarh), was Deputy National Security Advisor and Defence Secretary, Ministry of Defence, Government of India.

Arun Prakash is former Chief of Indian Navy.

Srinivasapuram Krishnaswamy is former Chief of Indian Air Force.

Deepak Kapoor is former Chief of Indian Army.

Amiya Kumar Ghosh is former Financial Advisor (Defence Services), Ministry of Defence, Government of India.

Narendra Singh Sisodia is former Secretary (Defence Production), Ministry of Defence, Government of India and Director General, Institute for Defence Studies and Analyses.

Amit Cowshish, a former Financial Advisor (Acquisition), Ministry of Defence, Government of India, is presently Distinguished Fellow at the Institute for Defence Studies and Analyses.

A Sivathanu Pillai is former Chief Controller of Research and Development, Defence Research and Development Organisation (DRDO), Ministry of Defence and former head of BrahMos Aerospace.

Ravindra Gupta is former Secretary, Department of Defence Production, Ministry of Defence and Ministry of Civil Aviation, Government of India.

Vinay Kaushal, a retired Indian Air Force officer, is presently Consultant to the Institute for Defence Studies and Analyses.

Satish Nambiar, a retired Lt General of Indian Army and a former head of the United Service Institution of India, is presently Distinguished Fellow at the Institute for Defence Studies and Analyses.

Pramod Vasant Athawale is former Air Officer Commanding-in-Chief, Maintenance Command, Indian Air Force.

Satya Narayan Misra is former Joint Secretary (Aerospace), Ministry of Defence, Government of India.

Laxman Kumar Behera is Research Fellow at the Institute for Defence Studies and Analyses.

Vinod Rai is former Comptroller and Auditor General of India.

Pratyush Sinha is former Central Vigilance Commissioner.

ABBREVIATIONS

A&N	Andaman and Nicobar
ADGWE	Additional Director General Weapons and Equipment
AEW	Airborne Early Warning
AFLC	Air Force Logistics Command
AFMC	Air Force Material Command
AFSC	Air Force Systems Command
AG	Adjutant General
AGPL	Actual Ground Position Line
ALH	Advanced Light Helicopter
ANC	Andaman and Nicobar Command
ANURAG	Advanced Numerical Research and Analysis Group
AoB	Allocation of Business
AOC	Army Ordnance Corps
APC	Armoured Personnel Carrier
ARC	Administrative Reforms Commission
ARF	ASEAN Regional Forum
ARTRAC	Army Training Command
ASAT	Anti-Satellite Weapon
ASEAN	Association of Southeast Asian Nations
ATF	Aviation Turbine Fuel
ATM	Anti-Tank Missile
BAFO	Best and Final Offer
BCA	Budget Control Act
BDL	Bharat Dynamics Ltd
BEL	Bharat Electronics Ltd
BIS	Bureau of Industry and Security
BRDB	Border Roads Development Board
BRDs	Base Repair Depots
BRO	Border Roads Organisation
BSc	Bachelor of Science
BUR	Bottom-Up Review

C&AG	Comptroller and Auditor General
CAPF	Central Armed Police Forces
CBGA	Centre for Budget and Governance Accountability
CBI	Central Bureau of Investigation
CBP	Capability Based Planning
CCPA	Cabinet Committee of Political Affairs
CCS	Cabinet Committee on Security
CCV	Canadian Content Value
CD	Conference on Disarmament
CDM	Chief of Defence Material
CDS	Chief of Defence Staff
CEP	Circular Error Probability
CFA	Competent Financial Authority
CFD	Computational Fluid Dynamics
CGE	Central Government Expenditure
CIDS	Chief of Integrated Defence Staff
CII	Confederation of Indian Industry
C-in-C	Commander in Chief
CISC	Chief of Integrated Staff to the Chairman, Chiefs of Staff Committee
CJS	Chief of Joint Staff
CKD	Completely Knocked Down
CNS	Chief of Naval Staff
COSC	Chief of Staff Committee
COTS	Commercial Off The Shelf
CPI	Consumer Price Index
CPWD	Central Public Works Department
CSP	Customer Supplier Partnership
CST	CENTRAL SALES TAX
CVC	Central Vigilance Commission
CVD	Countervailing duties
CVO	Chief Vigilance Officer
D&E	Designed and Engineered
DAC	Defence Acquisition Council
DAD	Defence Accounts Department
DAPA	Defence Acquisition Programme Administration
DBMS	Database Management Systems
DCC	Defence Committee of the Cabinet
DCP	Defence Capability Plan
DDG	Demand for Grant
DDP	Department of Defence Production

DDR&D	Department of Defence Research & Development
DE&S	Defence Equipment and Support
DESW	Department of Ex-Servicemen Welfare
DG	Director General
DG OL	Director General Op Logistics
DGAFMS	Director General Armed Forces Medical Services
DGAQA	Directorate General of Aeronautical Quality Assurance
DGFT	Director General of Foreign Trade
DGMO	Director General Military Operations
DGWE	Director General Weapons and Equipment
DIA	Defence Intelligence Agency
DIB	Defence Industrial Base
DIPP	Department of Industrial Policy and Promotion
DLA	Defence Logistics Agency
DoD	Department of Defence
DOFA	Defence Offset Facilitation Agency
DOMW	Defence Offset Management Wing
DOTMLPF	Doctrine, Training, Material, Leadership, Personnel and Facilities
DPC	Defence Planning Committee
DPG	Defence Planning Guidance
DPM	Defence Procurement Manual
DPMs	Draft Presidential Memorandums
DPP	Defence Procurement Procedure
DPS	Defence Planning Staff
DPDOs	Defence Pension Disbursement Offices
DPSUs	Defence Public Sector Undertakings
DRDO	Defence Research and Development Organisation
DSE	Defence Services Estimates
DSIEP	Defence and Security Industrial Engagement Policy
DWP	Defence Works Procedure
ECHS	Ex-Servicemen Health Scheme
EDA	European Defence Agency
EEZ	Exclusive Economic Zone
E-in-C	Engineer-in-Chief
EME	Electrical and Mechanical Engineers
EPTL	Enhanced Priority Technology List
ERP	Enterprise Resource Planning
ERV	Exchange Rate Variation
EU	European Union
EW	Electronic Warfare
FDI	Foreign Direct Investment

FGFA	Fifth Generation Fighter Aircraft
FMCT	Fissile Material Cut-off Treaty
FMS	Foreign Military Sales
FOO	Forward Observation Officer
FPA	Focal Plane Array
FRBM	Fiscal Responsibility and Budget Management
FRBMA	Fiscal Responsibility and Budget Management Act
FYDP	Five year Defence Plan
FYP	Five Year Plan
GDP	Gross Domestic Product
GNP	Gross National Product
GoI	Government of India
GoM	Group of Ministers
GPA	Government Procurement Agreement
GT	Gross Tonnage
GWOT	Global War On Terror
HAL	Hindustan Aeronautics Ltd
HDI	Human Development Index
HDM	Higher Defence Management
HQs	Head Quarters
IAF	Indian Air Force
IAS	Indian Administrative Service
IC	Industrial Cooperation
ICA	Industrial Cooperation Authority
ICG	Indian Coast Guard
ICT	Information and Communication Technology
ICV	Infantry Combat Vehicle
IDS	Integrated Defence Staff
IDSA	Institute for Defence Studies and Analyses
IED	Improvised Explosive Devices
IFA	Integrated Financial Advisor
IFS	Indian Foreign Service
IGA	Inter-Governmental Agreement
IGMDP	Integrated Guided Missile Development Programme
IIFT	Indian Institute of Foreign Trade
IIT	Indian Institute of Technology
ILMS	Integrated Logistics Management System
IMA	Indian Military Academy
IMD	Indian Meteorological Department
IMMOLS	Integrated Material Management Online System
INA	Indian National Army

IOP	Indian Offset Partner
IOR	Indian Ocean Region
IP	Industrial Participation
IPR	Intellectual Property Rights
IPS	Indian Police Service
IRB	Industrial and Regional Benefits
ISI	Inter-Services Intelligence
ISPPL	Itemised Spares Parts Price List
ISRO	Indian Space Research Organisation
IT	Information Technology
ITC	Indian Trade Classification
J&K	Jammu and Kashmir
JAKLI	Jammu and Kashmir Light Infantry
JFC	Joint Forces Command
JIEDDO	Joint IED Defeat Organisation
JLE	Joint Logistics Environment
JSPD	Joint Strategic Planning Document
JV	Joint Venture
KIP	Korean Industry Participant
KRC	Kargil Review Committee
LAOs	Local Audit Officers
LCA	Light Combat Aircraft
LCC	Life Cycle Cost
LCH	Light Combat Helicopter
LoAC	Line of Actual Control
LoC	Line of Control
LPD	Landing Platform Dock
LPP	Last Purchase Price
LTIPP	Long Term Integrated Perspective Plan
MAP	Married Accommodation Project
MBT	Main Battle Tank
MDL	Mazagon Dock Ltd
MEA	Ministry of External Affairs
MES	Military Engineer Service
MGO	Master General Ordnance
MHA	Ministry of Home Affairs
MIC	Military Industry Complex
MIS	Management Information System
MMRCA	Medium Multi-Role Combat Aircraft
MoD	Ministry of Defence
MODVAT	Modified Value Added Tax

MoF	Ministry of Finance
MoS	Minister of State
MRAPS	Mine-Resistant Ambush Protected
MRC	Major Regional Conflict
MRO	Maintenance Repair and Overhaul
MSME	Micro, Small and Medium Enterprises
MTBF	Mean Time Between Failures
MTCR	Missile Technology Control Regime
MTEF	Medium Term Expenditure Framework
MTTR	Mean Time to Repair
NADI	National Association of Defence Industries
NATO	North Atlantic Treaty Organisation
NBC	Nuclear, Biological and Chemical
NCC	National Cadet Corps
NCNC	No Cost No Commitment
NCO	Network Centric Operations
NDA	National Defence Academy
NEFT	National Electronic Fund Transfers
NFS	Network for Spectrum
NIC	National Industrial Classification
NMS	National Military Strategy
NMZ	National Manufacturing Zone
NPOL	Naval Physical and Oceanographic Laboratory
NSA	National Security Advisor
NSAB	National Security Advisory Board
NSC	National Security Council
NSCS	National Security Council Secretariat
NSG	Nuclear Suppliers Group
NSS	National Security Strategy
OBC	Other Backward Caste
OEM	Original Equipment Manufacturer
OFs	Ordnance Factories
OIC	Organisation of Islamic Cooperation
OP	Observation Post
OR	Operations Research
OSD	Office of the Secretary of Defence
OTA	Officers Training Academy
P&A	Pay and Allowances
PAC	Public Accounts Committee
PAT	Profit after Tax
PBL	Performance Based Logistics

PBOR	Personnel Below Officer Rank
PCDA	Principal Controller of Defence Accounts
PE	Peace Establishment
PESC	Public Expenditure Survey Committee
PET	Peace Equipment Table
PLA	People's Liberation Army
PM	Prime Minister
PMO's	Prime Minister's Office
POK	Pakistan-occupied Kashmir
POL	Petrol, Oil and Lubricants
POM	Programme Objective Memoranda
PoV	Professional Officers' Valuation
POW	Prisoners Of War
PPBS	Planning, Programming, and Budgeting System
PPO	Pension Payment Orders
PPP	Public Private Partnership
PSAs	Pension Sanctioning Authorities
PSUs	Public Sector Undertakings
PT	Physical Training
PV	Price Variation
QA	Quality Assurance
QDR	Quadrennial Defence Review
QMG	Quarter Master General
QR	Qualitative Requirement
R&D	Research & Development
RE	Revised Estimate
RFI	Request for Information
RFP	Request for Proposal
RIAF	Royal Indian Air Force
RIN	Royal Indian Navy
RM	Raksha Mantri (Defence Minister)
RMA	Revolution in Military Affairs
ROH	Repair and Overhaul
RR	Rashtriya Rifles
RTGS	Real Time Gross Settlement
RUR	Raksha Udyog Ratna
SAARC	South Asian Association for Regional Cooperation
SC	Scheduled Caste
SCM	Supply Chain Management
SDSR	Strategic Defence and Security Review
SEZ	Special Economic Zone

SFC	Strategic Forces Command
SHQ	Service Head Quarter
SKD	Semi Knocked Down
SME	Small and Medium Enterprises
SOA	Service Oriented Architecture
SRI	Self-Reliance Index
SSKP	Single Shot Kill Probability
ST	Scheduled Tribe
TAT	Turn Around Time
TBO	Time Between Overhaul
TCS	Tactical Communication System
TDP	Technology Demonstration Project
TEPID OIL	Training, Equipment, Personnel, Information, Doctrine, Organisation, Infrastructure and Logistics
TF	Task Force
TFC	Twelfth Finance Committee
TFP	Total Factor Productivity
ToB	Transaction of Business
TOC	Theory of Constraints
ToT	Transfer of Technology
TPCR	Technology Perspective Capability Roadmap
TTL	Total Technical Life
UAE	United Arab Emirates
UAV	Unmanned Aerial Vehicle
USAF	United States Air Force
VAT	Value Added Tax
VoP	Value of Production
VoS	Value of Sales
WE	War Establishment
WET	War Equipment Table
WMD	Weapons of Mass Destruction
WPI	Wholesale Price Index
WTO	World Trade Organisation
WWR	War Wastage Reserves

OVERVIEW

Vinod Misra

The defence realm in India has largely remained shrouded in secrecy notwithstanding a considerable spurt in recent years in activities such as seminars, roundtables, conferences, symposia and publications which have essentially catered to the needs of the relatively small body of the already initiated. With core concerns in defence essentially the domain of the political executive and the civilian and military bureaucracy, there has been a conspicuous absence of informed debate in the public space encompassing the entire range and depth of issues which require richer discerning public awareness and focussed and purposeful debate, which could potentially generate the necessary momentum for ushering in long overdue reforms.

With current practitioners preoccupied, as always, with day-to-day fire fighting and decision making, it is apparent that the essential groundwork for identifying a package of reforms and suggesting an implementation roadmap would have to be done by past practitioners, academics, think tanks and other stakeholders with appropriate domain awareness. This book seeks to draw upon the wealth of experience and domain knowledge with several apex level past practitioners and others on the full spectrum of key challenges and concerns in Indian defence ranging from an appropriate world view of the geopolitical environment and the part diplomacy can play, perspective and medium range planning, higher defence organisation and civil-military relations, defence R&D, defence industrialisation, acquisitions, offsets and Public Private Partnership (PPP) to budgeting, financial management, oversight, logistics and manpower. These structural changes and policy reforms brook no further delay if the outcome of lean, mean and efficient forces, capable of a potentially two-front war, a near cold start with an optimal capability basket rooted in the concept of jointness, capabilities to handle out of area contingencies and an adequate blend of strategic and conventional/non-conventional war fighting capabilities against a nuclear backdrop are to be realised in a reasonably short span of time. These alone can lay a sound foundation for long-term, sustainable and affordable defence capabilities which could meet the imperatives for India's emergence as a strong regional/world power.

Higher Defence Organisation and Civil Military Relations: It is necessary to briefly dwell upon some of the major facets of the various themes covered in this book. On the aspect of higher defence organisation and civil-military relations, it should be noted that the three defence services are not necessarily on the same page in so far as the proposal concerning the creation of a Chief of Defence Staff (CDS) as a single point of military advice to the government is concerned. Some of the other expectations of the three Service Chiefs concern free and ready access to the PM/RM/Members of the Cabinet Committee on Security (CCS), manning of senior level jobs in Ministry of Defence (MoD) and full and effective integration of the Services Headquarters with the MoD. There are inherent challenges in altering the essential Indian system of governance based on checks and balances. There are also major responsibilities by way of inter-ministerial consultations and approvals, handling of Parliamentary Questions and Parliamentary Committees such as the Standing Committee, PAC, Consultative Committee and the like. It is pertinent to note that quite naturally the defence services operate on the basis of carrying out the writ and directions of the respective chiefs with very little scope for dissent and divergent viewpoints. In any event, most of the proposals emanate from the respective services Hqrs. with the MoD playing only a reactive role and the occasions where MoD chooses to adopt a pro-active stance are few and far between. In any event, there is no dearth of challenges before each of the defence services which require sustained attention and application internally. These include an abiding concern for serviceability/readiness levels of weapon platforms and diverse capabilities, adequacy of ammunition and armaments (War Wastage Reserves (WWR)), a more determined and focussed pursuit of jointness in areas such as planning, acquisition, logistics, training/exercises and finally moving towards joint operations. There are also capabilities to be rapidly put in place for handling the emerging challenges in domains such as special operations, cyber warfare and space. Separately, the services have to rise up fully to the challenges of cost efficient formulation of Qualitative Requirements (QRs) and also for generating appropriate choices for meeting various mission/war objectives optimally – a situation conspicuously absent in the current decision making landscape. With a significant package of delegated financial powers, the services currently have near full authority over resource management in the matter of revenue expenditure while capital spending powers have also been enhanced to Rs.150 Crores in each case at present. Among the significant delay-prone activities entirely within the control of the services is the persistent inability to undertake time bound trial evaluation of systems on offer and the uncomfortably large number of cases in which an effectively single source situation emerges. Services could also well buttress their in-house capability to constantly track emerging defence technologies and new state of the art weapon systems which would enable them to work in close concert with the Defence Research and

Development Organisation (DRDO) for updating the technological capability development roadmap.

It would appear advisable to adopt a somewhat different approach in the initial years in so far as the creation of a CDS entity is concerned. In a situation where we are far removed as yet from the concept of theatre commands/joint operational commands, the CDS could, in the early years, be tasked only with certain equally compelling responsibilities such as joint long/medium range planning, joint acquisition, joint logistics, development of joint doctrines, joint training and responsibilities concerning the on the anvil cyber command, space command and special operations command. This apart, arrangements need to be formalised for structured interaction/meetings between the three Chiefs/proposed CDS with the PM, RM and CCS with the participation of all the secretaries in the MoD. This could well be by way of formal meetings with the RM every week, a monthly meeting with the PM and a quarterly presentation before the CCS.

Defence Industrial Base: Rapid defence industrialisation is quite clearly the most formidable challenge facing Indian defence given the current import orientation and its deleterious consequences for sustainable and cost efficient defence. With life cycle costs towards operations, maintenance, refurbishment and upgrades being significantly higher than the initial acquisition cost and the readiness/ serviceability levels seriously affected in an import setting, resource management efficiency in defence demands a whole range of domestic capabilities covering research, design, engineering, manufacturing, Maintenance Repair and Overhaul (MRO), infrastructure, training/simulation and human skill development enhancement and sustainment. Domestic capability for critical value addition and final system integration has to be the hallmark of a strong defence industrial base in the country. There are also corresponding benefits for the Indian economy by way of technology acquisition/upgradation, dual-use technologies, manufacturing skills and excellence, project management efficiencies, skill development, significant job creation in R&D/manufacturing/logistics supply chain management and a promising export potential. The present situation is absolutely ripe for providing a strong fillip for rapid defence industrialisation given the magnitude of our current and foreseeable needs for defence goods and services. Yet, we would require a significant quantum of policy correctives in order to attract the necessary domestic and foreign investment inflows. The long term business case has to have necessary clarity before any worthwhile investment inflows occur. This would require sharing of the long term potential order book for the specific defence goods and services and nurturing of a long term relationship with the professionally short listed entities (tiers 1, 2 and 3) and based on transparent and verifiable criteria governing the long term pricing basis. Adequate competition would have to be created among two or three entities wherever possible. It is apparent that greenfield capacities would be needed in several areas and consequently there would be no further merit in continuing with the system of nomination of Defence Public Sector Undertakings (DPSUs)/Ordnance Factories (OFs) for undertaking manufacture in essentially a single source milieu. Separately, DPSUs/OFs would also have to resort to far more significant levels of outsourcing to tiers 1-3 entities even if it is essential for them to retain final system integration capabilities. There are also reforms required in the matter of setting up joint ventures among Indian entities in the public and private sectors on the one hand and the best in class manufacturing/R&D entities worldwide. Given the formidable cost of infrastructure, plant and equipment, material, testing/evaluation/certification and the like, there is an imperative for realising the full potential of public private partnership as well. Efforts are also called for to encourage innovation, entrepreneurship and risk taking among Indian entities in the Micro, Small and Medium Enterprises (MSME) space or otherwise through setting up of a venture capital fund to finance such initiatives. There are also urgent correctives needed by way of the current FDI norms which restrict investment inflows from foreign entities to 26 per cent with higher inflows requiring a case by case approval. The fact of the matter is that this has contributed to an insignificant FDI inflow of less than US $ 5 million in more than a decade. If we are to succeed in our efforts to capture key technologies, design excellence, manufacturing know-how and know-why and target logistics supply chain management efficiencies, this FDI ceiling would need to be enhanced to at least 49 per cent across the board with higher inflows being considered on a case by case basis. Separately, concerted efforts would be needed to secure appropriate exemptions from the rather strict export control regime in place in the US/Europe governing export of key technologies and process know-how. There is also great merit in dismantling the highly restrictive and delay-prone licensing regime for undertaking manufacture in defence. The Joint Venture (JV) norms and guidelines too require focused correctives urgently in order to optimise both resources and efficiency.

Planning: Planning for the long and medium term is among the most daunting tasks in Indian defence. A Long Term Integrated Perspective Plan (LTIPP) spanning three Five Year Plan (FYP) periods is of recent origin (2002-17 being the first) while a FYP process, co-terminus with the national plans, has been in place nearly all along. It should be recognised that the plans form the fundamental basis for formulating a balanced basket of capabilities and infrastructure against the backdrop of force level comparisons with potential adversaries, defence objectives and threat assessments, defence technology outlook and the likely duration and intensity of potential wars. It is only through a rigorous planning process that a cost efficient blend of capabilities can be formulated and the roadmap for acquisitions, life cycle support, defence industrialisation and defence technology development/acquisition can be enunciated. Another key ingredient would be the resource requirements for meeting the plan objectives based on which conscious decisions would need to be taken either to augment resource availability or appropriately stagger the plan fulfilment timelines. Resource allocation efficiencies also come to the fore in this process. The emphasis has naturally changed from threat based planning to the more holistic effects based/capability based planning. Choices are required to be made between acquisition of new platforms vis-à-vis upgrade of existing platforms with the modernisation effort focused on new weapons and sensors. The planning process is also required to capture the full potential for optimisation based on the compelling concept of jointness. The plans must necessarily be comprehensive in nature encompassing not just the weapon system but all related aspects such as manpower, infrastructure, life cycle product support, utilities and Information and Communication Technologies (ICT)/networking challenges. A key aspect is to preserve the sanctity of an approved plan whether long or medium term whereby changes with change in incumbency of key functionaries particularly at the level of Service Chiefs are brought about only as an exception and that too based on a rigorous appraisal of alternatives. Unfortunately, the plans are not getting formally approved at the highest political executive levels such as the PM/CCS. It is also critical that the defence plans are a subset of comprehensive national power required to be articulated in a national security doctrine. In the absence of either a national security strategy document or a defence security doctrine, all planning in the defence context is currently carried out against the backdrop of RM's operational directives laying down the broad defence security imperatives. The plans could also form the basis for a planning, programming and budgeting system which would contribute to rapid and resource bound attainment of stated objectives within the envisioned cost and time ceilings. It would be for consideration if a separate Planning Commission type of permanent structure could be put in place comprising representatives from the defence services, civilian bureaucracy, finance professionals, system analysts and the like in order to do fuller and continuing justice to this vital task. Once the plans have been formally approved, the emphasis must necessarily focus on project management efficiencies in the matter of implementation of individual schemes/projects enumerated in the plan document with the necessary mix of financial and administrative empowerment on the one hand and accountability, transparency and probity on the other.

Financial Management: The principal focus of financial management in defence is optimal resource management designed to achieve the objective of rapid capability build up even while ensuring that the task is achieved through economy, efficiency and effectiveness. Generation of cost effective choices for meeting a stated objective, ensuring minimum need based QR formulation, minimising possibilities of a single source situation in procurement/acquisition, rigorous commitment/liabilities control, imparting an outcome orientation to the budgetary outlays and ensuring full and efficient utilisation of revenue and capital funds are some of the key tasks in this behalf. There are also significant challenges yet to be met by way of full exploitation of the ICT/networking potential and data base management concerns. There is also considerable potential for application of Operations Research (OR) tools and techniques towards optimising resource allocation and utilisation. In so far as documentation is concerned, it is noteworthy that Indian defence has in place very comprehensive procedures and guidelines covering revenue and capital procurements. While oversight through the institution of the Comptroller and Auditor General (C&AG) and the Central Vigilance Commission (CVC) has been extremely robust, the same, unfortunately, cannot be said about the range and depth of internal audit activities in defence. There is no gainsaying the enormous benefits of a vibrant internal audit set up as a near online correction mechanism based on comprehensive ICT capabilities.

Acquisitions: Defence acquisitions have attracted considerable public and media attention in recent years. Yet, public perception on the complex range of the acquisition tasks has been inadequate in the absence of clarity in the public realm of the processes, procedures and roadblocks encountered during weapons acquisition. First and foremost, major infirmities can get embedded in this process in the event the task of cost efficient QR formulation has not been handled with utmost professionalism. It is this stage which would determine whether a competitive setting would eventually emerge or, in extreme cases, whether the envisioned weapon system has even been proven fully and operationally deployed elsewhere in the world. Given the challenges of the acquisition process and the fact that everyone's hands are tied once a Request For Proposal (RFP) has been issued based on a two bid (technical and commercial) system, it is important that full understanding of the system under acquisition is achieved at the preceding Request For Information (RFI) stage. The single most delay prone activity in the acquisition process is the trial evaluation of the offered systems in different terrains, climate and environmental conditions. A new dimension has got added in recent years by way of life cycle cost evaluation of competing offers which could be prone to errors based on assumptions and assertions far in excess of proven performance much later. Another major challenge is to benchmark prices for proposed acquisition in as much as commercial bids get influenced by a variety of considerations such as design and development cost, whether adequate numbers have already got sold whereby lower prices could be offered, the timing of induction in as much as prices could vary steeply between a newly developed product at one end of the spectrum and a fully matured product moving towards technological obsolescence at the other. Securing a comprehensive and price stable life cycle product support over the potential life time of 20/30 years in a reliable and sustainable manner also adds to the difficulties in targeting high serviceability levels for the weapons platform on a continuing basis. It has been the endeavour of the government to secure an umbrella of Inter-Governmental Agreement (IGA) for all major acquisitions in order to secure the strong backing and support of the government in the country of origin of the foreign OEM. For strategic and other reasons, single source acquisitions have also been regularly resorted to with Russia, USA, Israel and others, which inevitably throw up the challenge of efficient price discovery.

Offsets: The provision for direct offsets to the extent of a minimum of 30 per cent for contracts higher than a threshold value of Rs.300 crores designed to leverage our formidable buying strength was expected to be a transformational step towards strengthening of the defence industrial base, infrastructure development, Maintenance, Repair and Overhaul (MRO) capabilities, training/ simulation facilities development, integration with the global supply chain, project management strengths and realising the enormous potential of defence exports. Even while nearly US $ 5 billion worth of offset contracts are currently in place, none of the key expectations have yet been fulfilled. While several corrective steps were taken such as elongating the offset fulfilment period, permitting multipliers and technology inflows through this route, the current policy frame has thus far failed to act as the catalyst it was expected to be. Several steps are still necessary to exploit the full potential for defence offsets. These include a prioritised roadmap for technology inflows, RFP specific offset choices, easing of the FDI norms (from 26 per cent to 49 per cent at the least), changes in the joint venture norms, which currently require one single Indian entity to hold 51 per cent of the equity base, full clarity on the export policy which would provide economies of scale apart from serving our strategic interests and setting up a fully empowered body to guide offset bidders, monitor offset contracts and suggest corrective measures whenever warranted. The important point is to transparently convince the foreign OEMs that offsets would bring a competitive and fair return on their investments and that the business case in the short and medium term as well as potentially in the long term is well established.

Oversight: It would be patently inappropriate and unfair to lay the blame for any 'policy paralysis' in defence decision making on the doors of the three 'Cs', namely, the C&AG, the CVC and the CBI. These agencies, together with the Parliamentary oversight committees such as the Standing Committee on Defence, the Consultative Committee, the Public Accounts Committee (PAC), the Estimates Committee and the Committee on Public Undertakings, have been performing a vitally needed oversight function, analysing in the process, inefficiencies, inadequacies, wastages and the like in key decision making areas such as planning, acquisition, project implementation, logistics, training and manpower. In so far as the C&AG is concerned, their principal task has been to look at adequacy of internal control mechanisms, time and cost bound attainment of targets and the efficacy of internal audit. The CVC have, in recent years, taken determined steps to plug loopholes and reinforce transparency, probity and accountability in important areas such as acquisitions, construction projects and life cycle cost assessment methodology. None of their initiatives and specific inputs can be construed as fresh stumbling blocks in the way of time bound decision making. If at all, several systemic corrections have been possible in the light of feedback and advice forthcoming from these entities. There is also considerable stress at present on collective and collegiate decision-making in defence which is also intended to harmonise as well as speed up the process. Indeed, the real challenge is in enforcing accountability in situations of slow/non-decision making for which the necessary impetus has to perforce come from the political executive. It is thus important that all the key decision making areas in defence affecting rapid capability build up and war preparedness must continue to be adequately commented upon by the C&AG as well as the CVC and the Standing Committee on Defence from time to time. These include resource allocation/utilisation efficiencies, the pace of important acquisitions, logistic supply chain management efficiencies, planning process, attainment of the full ICT potential, infrastructural deficiencies, WWR levels and readiness levels for major platforms.

PPP: As commented upon earlier, PPP in defence offers rich avenues for rapid defence industrialisation. It has to be recognised that the wherewithal for domestic defence manufacturing by way of land, manpower, infrastructure, raw material, machinery, test equipment, quality assurance, inspection and certification are extremely expensive and certainly beyond the reasonable capacity of tier three entities for sure and may be some tier two entities as well. On the other hand, several of these assets lie significantly underutilised with defence PSUs, OFs, DRDO, army base workshops, base repair depots in the IAF and naval dockyards and repair depots with the Indian Navy. Consequently, permitting the use of many of these facilities at a reasonable fee which has been professionally determined, could provide the much needed impetus to defence industrialisation in the country. The private sector would also expectedly contribute substantially towards productivity enhancements, lower fixed overheads, more competitive manpower costs as well as project management efficiencies.

Diplomacy: Diplomacy has a major role to play in meeting the defence security objectives. While India has had extremely close military ties with Russia which have stood the test of times, the time has come to secure a long term strategic relationship with the US in the defence sector. There has been significant augmentation of the Indian defence capabilities through Foreign Military Sales (FMS) from the US. However, the full potential of a strategic tie up with the US is waiting to be realised. It is noteworthy that the kind of defence technologies, manufacturing excellence, supply chain management efficiencies designed for optimal readiness levels and project implementation skill sets that are available with the US entities could have a transformational impact on defence preparedness in India. Fortunately, at this juncture, there is considerable identity of security and strategic interests with the US. It would be in our interest to build upon this rich potential in as rapid a timeframe as realistic. The US on its part would have to take a number of corrective steps to address the stiff arms technology control regime in place there.

The Ministry of External Affairs (MEA) has been extremely reluctant to permit export of Indian defence goods and services to the large number of countries in Asia, Africa and Latin America, where considerable potential exists for development of a vibrant arms export market. Quite apart from providing the much needed economy of scale to Indian manufacturers and consequent lower prices for supply to Indian Defence Services, exports would also serve a vital strategic interest in nurturing closer ties with these countries.

MEA would also have to work actively towards India's integration with countries of the WASSENAAR agreement/Australia group in order to facilitate the inflow of critical defence and dual use technologies and get around the strict arms control regimes in place in the US and the Western countries.

For obvious reasons, India also needs to develop strong, deep and lasting economic, military and strategic reciprocities and interdependencies with several countries such as Japan, Indonesia, Vietnam, Central Asian Republics, Brazil, South Africa, Israel, Germany, UK and France. Military diplomacy has to get deeply embedded into the overarching diplomatic architecture. There is also a compelling need for developing a medium and long term Defence Cooperation Framework and Roadmap for targeting surefooted and realisable expansion and consolidation of military ties with the countries of strategic interest to India. This would be in sharp contrast to the highly reactive and case by case responses that have largely guided our relationships so far.

Manpower: It is noteworthy that revenue outlays towards pay and allowances of army manpower comprising both combatants as well as non-combatants/civilians aggregate to over 60 per cent of the army's revenue budget. Though lower at around 38 per cent and 46 per cent for navy and air force respectively, they are equally significant nonetheless. In the aggregate, in so far as the entire defence outlay is concerned comprising both revenue and capital funds, over 30 per cent is the contribution of the manpower costs. This is without reckoning the manpower related costs towards rations, clothing, medicines, single/married accommodation, utilities (water/electricity) and personnel transportation, which are directly related to the manpower base of the three Services. We should also take note of the fact that defence pensions, which form part of the civil estimates of the MoD and not the defence estimates, account for around two-third of the aggregate allocations for pay and allowances of the serving defence personnel. The rising requirements of funds on this score has had a serious impact on fund availability for the rest of the defence needs including critical requirements such as revenue stores for keeping readiness levels high and funding the significant training tasks, infrastructure creation and upkeep, meeting the WWR for ammunition and armaments and attaining the capability acquisition targets. All this should establish the compulsions for taking a hard look at the potential for right sizing defence manpower. In so far as fighting forces are concerned, it is possible to target a more agile, modular, rapidly deployable and adaptable force level and force mix which would also underscore a more youthful profile of the combat forces. More importantly, it is possible to explore comprehensively the current imperatives for improving the teeth to tail ratio in the defence services. This would require outsourcing of many of the tasks which can be more cost efficiently done in the private/public sectors without compromising operational preparedness instead of continuing to retain expensive in-house capabilities. It is important in this context to undertake an exhaustive one time in-house review of the currently authorised Peace Establishment (PE) and War Establishment (WE) on the concepts of zero based budgeting and outcome orientation to determine the continued validity of many of the organisations, establishments and tasks which have long ceased to have relevance in the current operational environment. Some determined steps also need to be taken towards multi-skilling, multi-tasking, trade rationalisation, enhancing man hour availability norms and improving productivity standards as reflected in the man hour content of multifarious tasks. The introduction of Performance Based Logistics (PBL) would also have a significant impact on captive defence manpower with responsibility for ensuring a desirable level of serviceability cast on the OEM. Significant benefits are also expected to flow from a more focused and purposeful thrust towards jointness among the defence services in areas such as training, logistics, infrastructure, acquisitions, maintenance & repairs and eventually operations. The emergence of a strong and vibrant defence industrial base and benefits which could accrue from a well directed offsets policy would also contribute to the manpower right sizing effort. However, the most decisive impact on manpower costs could arise only as a consequence of a review of the current terms of engagement/colour service in respect of PBOR whereby the existing 15/17 years of minimum service which also entitles them to long lasting pensionary benefits could be lowered to five to seven years which would also bring down the pay and allowances costs and eliminate pensionary entitlements. This, of course, is a very serious issue requiring sustained debate on it implications in terms of enhanced training effort and retention of core capabilities.

Logistics: Along with strategy, technology contemporariness and capability creation, logistics is one of the key pillars of comprehensive national power in the realm of defence. Life cycle costs towards operations, maintenance, repairs, overhaul and upgrade could potentially range between three to five times the initial acquisition costs. Without focused logistics, there could be no assurance about the required serviceability levels of major weapon platforms even while considerable outlays are there for meeting the logistics needs. It is a major challenge to attain satisfactory readiness levels over the entire (20/30 years or even longer) life of major platforms and ensure acceptable levels of stock towards first line/ second line/WWR needs of ammunition and armaments. This is rendered even more complex in the light of prescribed shelf life, storage condition, adequacy of storage accommodation and supply side constraints whether in respect of domestic manufacture by ordnance factories/DPSUs or ex- imports.

With a significant proportion of the weapon systems inventory being of Russian/erstwhile Soviet Union origin, the defence services have faced a recurring challenge of sourcing spares supplies from the OEMs in Russia, who, in turn, have to depend on an extremely large number of sub-suppliers. Stable and long-term spares pricing basis and achieving economies of scale in their production runs vis-à-vis the modest annual consumption requirements of the defence services, are some of the other problems affecting spares availability. There have also been issues pertaining to fulfilment of warranty obligations, relatively low life of sub systems/major components in terms of time between overhaul, total technical life/calendar life, turn around time for spares which have to be sent back to the OEM for repairs/restoration and non-attainment of guaranteed Mean Time Between Failures (MTBF) guarantees. It has also not been possible for the Russians to establish the much needed service support centres in India for fulfilment of their long term product support obligations.

Among some of the other reform measures which are needed in the area of logistics are:

(i) OEMs should be asked to share with the Indian side the feedback concerning operations/maintenance needs from the other major customers using the same weapon system.

(ii) A one time exhaustive review on an in house basis of the War/Peace Equipment Tables (WET/PET) which determine the current entitlement for the entire range and depth of stores and where several redundancies have come to light.

(iii) A review of the necessity for milspecs vis-à-vis the option for Commercial Off The Shelf (COTS) specification which is significantly cheaper and also more readily available in the global supply chain.

(iv) Developing optimal ICT capabilities for tracking life cycle costs on operations and maintenance and for capturing actual performance vis-à-vis guaranteed MTBF for major parts, assemblies, sub-systems and systems.

(v) Sustained application of operations research techniques and capabilities for determining logistics efficiencies particularly in areas such as centralised stocking, transportation model, productivity standards and allocative efficiencies.

Defence R&D: Before attempting a critique of the defence R&D effort in India as spearheaded by the DRDO, it is important to recognise their lasting contribution to the cause of achieving significant strategic deterrence in the spheres of nuclear capabilities, development and deployment of an array of potent missile systems and the considerable progress in the area of ballistic missile defence. This has resulted in India's undoubted emergence as a strong regional power and potentially an important world power.

However, many of the other significant programmes of the DRDO such as the Light Combat Aircraft (LCA), Kavery Engine for the LCA, Arjun Tank, EW capability acquisition, Airborne Early Warning (AEW) and Unmanned Aerial Vehicles (UAVs) have suffered from considerable delays and cost overruns. For India's true march towards self-reliance, acquisition of key technologies which are prone to denials/bans/embargos, critical value addition and final systems integration capabilities for major weapon systems and the like, there has to be a far more focused and intensive R&D effort to develop the requisite blend of strengths in research and development, concept and detailed design, engineering and free flow production. In recent years, DRDO has targeted a collaborative R&D and manufacturing effort with some of the best in class foreign entities to step up the pace of realisation of the necessary capabilities. However, this effort requires significant expansion whereby DRDO would be able to collaborate with the best in class R&D entities worldwide for co-development and co-production. Even here, the emphasis would have to be on attaining capabilities for build to specifications rather than the current situation in which only build to print capabilities are yet in place.

Some of the other initiatives to provide a fillip to the defence R&D effort would be the following:

(i) Firming up of a long term technology development and acquisition plan in concert with the defence services' needs as reflected in their LTIPP and based on professional evaluation of the trends and possibilities in the evolution of military technology and future weapon systems. Conscious decisions could thereafter be taken on the specific initiatives required for each of these technologies whether through the domestic development route or by way of co-development or even through a well directed offsets policy. In certain situations, even a sharply focused Transfer of Technology (ToT) arrangement seeking to capture both know-how and know-why as well as full scale raw material based manufacturing may have to be targeted.

(ii) The courage to carry out independent peer reviews at regular intervals in respect of sanctioned projects. In extreme cases, a call may have to be taken to foreclose R&D effort where cost and time overruns and progress on attainment of intermediate milestones have been unsatisfactory.

(iii) Thin spreading of resources on a large number of programmes has to be severely controlled. In the same context, it would be important to ensure, in letter and spirit, the concept of milestone linked funding.

(iv) There has to be full assurance from the defence services as well as the MoD that successful R&D progress would lead to placement of firm orders as originally envisaged and thereby there would be the necessary ownership by the customer as well as the production entity of successful R&D projects.

(v) DRDO would also have to be freely allowed to associate tier-1/2 entities in both the private and the public sectors from the prototype development stage in order that production efficiencies get built in from the very beginning and there is a clear business case in all situations of successful R&D.

(vi) There has to be an efficient arrangement for the formal association of the user service for the entire duration of the R&D and manufacturing effort till the capability gets operationally deployed.

(vii) Much closer and lasting linkages have to be established between the R&D and manufacturing clusters.

(viii) A well honed export policy would also go a long way in establishing a strong defence R&D capability in the country whereby adequate re-affirmation of the domestic R&D and the consequent manufacturing strengths is reflected in meeting the defence needs of foreign countries.

1

INDIA'S EXTERNAL SECURITY ENVIRONMENT AND ITS IMPACT ON INDIAN DEFENCE

Kanwal Sibal

India faces formidable security challenges. Most major countries have settled borders, but ours are not. Our entire northern border is unsettled and we have a Line of Control (LoC) and not a border in Jammu and Kashmir (J&K). This means that while it is the normal responsibility of any state to protect its frontiers and its territorial integrity, the responsibility of the Indian state in this regard becomes that much more onerous. The defence burden on our resources becomes even heavier than might be the case if we had friendly neighbours with no outstanding territorial issues plaguing our ties with them.

What makes our security situation particularly tough is the nature of the countries contesting our borders. If our border differences were confined to Nepal or Bangladesh, our concerns would be more manageable. But it is China that either occupies or, what is even more problematic, claims large parts of our country still. China has become a formidable economic power in the last three decades or so, outperforming India decisively. With the massive financial resources at its command, it has developed its military muscle to a degree that now gives it confidence to advance or assert its territorial claims more aggressively than ever before, even in areas of great sensitivity to a large number of its neighbours in the Western Pacific and to the US.

China has developed its military infrastructure in Tibet dramatically, far more than it needs to control Tibetan resistance to its rule. The military infrastructure on the border with India is clearly directed at us. In recent years, after some lull, China has started laying claims to Arunachal Pradesh more openly and offensively, calling it South Tibet, which implies that it looks at Arunachal Pradesh not as "disputed" territory subject to a negotiated settlement over sovereignty, but as part of Tibet (and therefore China) that India is occupying illegally. In other ways too it is trying to unilaterally consolidate its territorial claims, as, for example, by shortening the length of the India-Tibet border, issuing stapled visas to those belonging to Arunachal Pradesh, affixing revised maps of China's borders that show parts of India as Chinese territory on newly issued Chinese passports or distributing such maps to the People's Liberation Army (PLA).

Despite the latent dangers of an untoward incident occurring if such a large border is left undefined, the Chinese side shows no serious interest in either resolving the differences in a practical way or, at least, defining the Line of Actual Control (LoAC) on the ground. The last is important because incidents of transgressions across the LoAC continue to occur at regular intervals, which India tries to downplay officially so as to prevent the atmosphere of India-China relations deteriorating to a point that engaging China becomes even more problematic. The Depsang incident of May 2013 is a reminder of the perils of the present situation, which cannot be eliminated entirely by entering into yet more agreements on border management. The fact that the Special Representatives of the two countries have held numerous rounds of talks since 2003 did not prevent the Depsang incident or others less frontal.

We need to pay more heed to the import of statements by the Chinese president about the determination of China not to make any concession on territorial issues and the country's aggressive conduct in the South China and East China Seas on territorial and maritime boundary issues, even when all this entails challenging US power and its defence commitments to countries threatened by Chinese claims and actions. It is the same Chinese leadership with its newly assertive mind-set that is devising a strategy to deal with India. It is another matter that China is showing a scowling face in the western Pacific and a smiling one to us. China can time the nature of its offensives as it suits it politically and militarily, eastwards or westwards, with its current charm offensive towards us being tactical and not strategic in nature. Our defence planning has to take cognisance of this.

The irony is that the 1993, 1996, 2005 and 2013 agreements on maintaining peace and tranquillity, confidence-building and ensuring peaceful management of the border have, instead of allaying mistrust and bringing some sort of a peace dividend, resulted in enhancing the defence burden on India. We have decided to improve our military infrastructure on the border, entailing a sizeable outlay of resources. The decision to raise two mountain divisions, a strike corps and an independent mountain brigade is the fruit not of enhanced confidence in China but mounting distrust of its medium to long term intentions. We have stationed our most advanced aircraft in the east and opened up advanced landing grounds in the north, all indications of increased military preparedness. Our strategic programmes, especially the development of Agni missiles and undersea capabilities are directed at countering the Chinese threat. China, however, has already developed impressive military capabilities for countering US power, and these can simultaneously address the challenge of steadily increasing Indian military strength. Yet, it remains unclear why China has goaded India into steadily developing capabilities to strategically threaten it, when it could have lessened the incentives for such Indian efforts by resolving outstanding issues with us. Its policies are, in fact, helping to reduce the military power differential between us and its ability to browbeat us.

Beyond its own capacities to pressure us militarily, China has indirectly raised huge problems for Indian security by helping build up a nuclear Pakistan and endowing it with missile capability. This has served the strategic interests of both countries vis-a-vis India. Pakistan too contests India territorially in J&K. Unlike in China's case where the effort is to avoid military incidents on the border that could result in casualties on either side, Pakistan has actively sought to disturb the status quo by direct military action, infiltration, cease-fire violations, inciting violence across the border, encouraging separatists in J&K to keep the situation continually on the boil politically and using the instrument of terror against us. It declares openly its "political, moral and diplomatic" support to "freedom fighters" in J&K, seeks external intervention on its behalf against India and works tirelessly to target India at international forums and at the Organisation of Islamic Cooperation (OIC), besides seeking to otherwise play the Islamic card to undermine our political relations with other Islamic countries.

In this, Pakistan's conduct differs from that of China on border differences with us where the latter seeks to control tensions even while maintaining its claims. The Chinese strategy is to encourage Pakistan in its confrontation with India by giving it the political, military and moral support it needs. As part of this strategy, China has insidiously questioned India's sovereignty even over J&K by denying a proper visa to our Army Commander there even when he was to travel to China for official defence level talks. While it opposes any assistance from international financial institutions to projects in Arunachal Pradesh because it is "disputed" territory, it is engaged in major strategic and other projects in *Pakistan-occupied Kashmir* (POK), even though Pakistan harps that Kashmir is "disputed" territory whose sovereignty should be decided through a plebiscite in accordance with relevant UN resolutions. It suits China to have India bogged down in simmering conflict with Pakistan and confront us with a potential two-front situation, though it is unlikely that in the perspectives of a limited conflict between India and Pakistan or India and China we will be faced with an attack on two fronts. The nuclear dimension that now exists also argues against any such adventurism by China and Pakistan in tandem, though our military planning cannot ignore such a possibility. In any case, our military's pre-occupation with Pakistan makes us exceedingly cautious towards China. Pakistan's hostility towards

India also keeps SAARC weak and prevents us from playing any significant role in Central Asia, a situation that also suits China's interests. Even if we become stronger militarily, we will not have a solution to easier connectivity to Central Asia or an upsurge in the strength of SAARC. That solution will depend on India's economic rise and Pakistan's political evolution.

Pakistan has used its nuclear capability as a cover to continue its terrorist depredations against us, dramatised by the staging of the 2008 Mumbai carnage. India is unable to retaliate militarily because of the risks of escalation, especially in a nuclear background. Pakistan is aware that limited activity on the LoC and on the terrorism front will not provoke an Indian military strike. In the event that a major terrorist attack was to compel India to think of a limited but potent strike across the border, Pakistan is threatening to use tactical nuclear weapons in riposte. The Indian army's Cold Start doctrine is the target of this Pakistani threat. In actual fact, rather than the West coming down on Pakistan heavily for its nuclear adventurism, its aggressive conduct in stoking tensions with India is actually cynically used by western non-proliferation lobbies to create scare scenarios of a nuclear stand-off in the Indian sub-continent and lobby for imposing nuclear restraints on India by calling for strategic stability in the region. While it is true that India is not hampered in developing its credible minimum nuclear deterrent because of external pressures, our security situation is not helped because of lack of any pressure on Pakistan's nuclear policies,. including the rapid expansion of its nuclear arsenal, the plutonium reprocessing capability it is developing and its obstructionism in the CD at Geneva on Fissile Material Cut-off Treaty (FMCT) negotiations.

Despite international concerns about the increasing radicalisation of the Pakistani society, the proliferation of the jihadi groups in the country, many nurtured by the Pakistan state itself, and the spread of terrorism within because of the deterioration of the internal situation and compulsions of having to cooperate with the US to exercise some control over terrorism from Pakistani soil targeting Afghanistan, Pakistan is escaping pressure from the West on its nuclear policies. Whereas the West led by the US has put enormous pressure on Iran on the nuclear question, even threatening military action and, indeed, suffocating Iran financially through stringent sanctions, Pakistan is being treated benignly. Some western think tank elements have begun advocating a nuclear deal with Pakistan on the lines of the agreement with India, indicating a strong political nuclear bias in favour of Pakistan. China has, of course, decided to give Pakistan a nuclear deal of its own to parallel the one given by the US to India. It is buttressing Pakistan's nuclear capability in violation of its Nuclear Suppliers Group (NSG) obligations, without any opposition from the US. The high level of international tolerance of Pakistan's nuclear policies suggests that considerations of strategic checkmating of India and creating a nuclear balance in the sub-continent are not absent from the calculations of even our "friends".

Outside the terrorist threat and that of Islamic radicalism emanating from Pakistan, India has to contend with a mounting danger of a wider religious radicalisation of West Asia eventually spilling over into India. The politically misconceived policies of regime change followed by the US and some of its partners in West Asia have veritably generated the threat of extremist Islamic forces spreading their sway across the region. The western military intervention in Iraq has spawned today the Islamic State in parts of Iraq and Syria. That Syrian territory has been captured by these elements is the result of the backing the West has given to extremist forces in Syria in a bid to topple the regime of Bashar al-Assad. Libya has descended into lawlessness with extremist forces fighting each other for control and fuelling the spread of Al Qaida in sub-Saharan Africa. The Gulf states have fuelled these extremist forces—not to mention Turkey's pernicious role in Syria contributing to this—both in collaboration with the West and also independently to bolster Sunni extremism against the Shia threat embodied by Iran and its allies in the region.

The collapse of the Iraqi army in Sunni-dominated western Iraq creates concerns about the robustness of the US trained Afghan army to withstand a potential Taliban onslaught in Afghanistan, some factions of which are now combating the Pakistani state. If Afghanistan were to get seriously destabilised by these forces post 2014 or 2016, Pakistan itself could be threatened with an extremist take-over of sorts, with security consequences for India. Pakistani democracy, such as it is, is already threatened by street movements which could well invite a military take over. If the US can politically digest a military take over in Egypt, it will make peace with such a take over in Pakistan, with consequences for Indian security. Beyond that, India's ties with Afghanistan will be ruptured and those with Central Asia will remain underdeveloped. US sanctions on Iran will continue to hamper a stronger Indian-Iranian collaboration to deal with Taliban inroads into Afghanistan and use Iran as a transit country for our relations with Central Asia. China will, of course, have no difficulty with a military take-over in Pakistan or increased tensions between it and India as a result. China may be concerned about terrorism in Sinkiang getting sustenance from safe-havens in Pakistan, but that does not make it more cognisant and critical of Pakistan's involvement in terrorism in India. It is not surprising that the Chinese special envoy to Afghanistan should have very recently dismissed the charges against the Pakistani ISI for truck with terrorism. The problem for us is that the spectre of these threats cannot be dealt with militarily. The only practical solution will be to strengthen the defences on our borders and handle our internal situation with greater vigilance.

Our immediate security environment is also threatened by Chinese inroads into Nepal, Bangladesh, Sri Lanka and Maldives. These countries play the Chinese card against us to a lesser or higher degree, or are being wooed by the Chinese politically and economically, at the cost of our ties with them. Our capacity to influence these countries to align themselves with our legitimate interests, or at least, not damage our interests, is impaired by the Chinese presence and influence. In Nepal our problem is especially acute as we have an open border with that country and the Chinese are developing road and rail links across Tibet to the Nepal border. Besides this, the Chinese presence encourages the traditional anti-Indian forces in Nepal to continue nourishing a sense of alienation in the country towards India. China has already made strong inroads into Myanmar, though of late the Myanmarese are trying to limit this penetration. By pushing proposals like the Bangladesh-China-India-Myanmar corridor, China aims at bringing the areas bordering it in the south into China's economic orbit, which in turn will facilitate its political penetration in these countries even more. This would imply allowing our north-east, which is underdeveloped and inadequately integrated with the rest of India to fall into China's economic orbit. The security dangers of this are evident and therefore India should have little reason to encourage the Chinese strategy until such time as China's territorial claims on us in this area are withdrawn or amicably settled. Meanwhile, India would be well advised to build east-west connectivities, linking it increasingly to Myanmar and Thailand and further on to south-east Asia up to Vietnam. We need a better alignment between our political attitude to such Chinese proposals and security-related consequences that can flow from wanting to remain diplomatically open to Chinese overtures.

China's maritime strategy requires a strong Chinese presence in the Indian Ocean littoral, whether in the Bay of Bengal or the Arabian Sea. In this, ports in Myanmar, Bangladesh, Sri Lanka, Maldives and Pakistan become important. India of course dominates the Indian Ocean geographically as well as militarily because of its strong navy. The Andaman and Nicobar islands give us the capacity to control the Straits of Malacca. For the time being the Chinese naval presence in the Indian Ocean is limited, though with the development of its nuclear submarine fleet we will be faced with a challenge in the future. China has cleverly tried to disarm our security concerns about its strategy in the Indian Ocean by proposing our participation in what it calls the maritime silk route extending from the Pacific to the Indian oceans. By this it is seeking legitimisation of its increasing presence in the Indian Ocean and drawing attention away from its muscle-flexing in the western Pacific, all this by covering its strategy with a peaceful cloak. India has to find an answer to China's clever diplomacy of roping Asian countries, including our neighbours, into its grand strategic design of extending its influence throughout the region backed by its huge economic and financial strength, in a way that relegates India into a secondary role, as a large piece in a larger Chinese jigsaw puzzle, ousting or weakening US's role in large parts of Asia in the process. As a counter India needs to strengthen its overall ties with Japan and continue to collaborate with US in the Indian Ocean. For a better balance that would serve our security interests, we should be willing to strengthen trilateral India-Japan-US cooperation in not only building east-west connectivities in Asia but also in maritime cooperation in the Asia-Pacific region.

We often say that our security horizon extends from the Straits of Malacca to the Straits of Hormuz. For us to be able to exert our weight adequately in this expanse we need to keep strengthening our naval power. For one, a decisive growth of naval power in the Indian Ocean will act a deterrent to any Chinese adventurism in the Himalayas. Hence, the internal debate one hears at times that we would be better served in countering the security threat from China by spending more money in strengthening our navy rather than expending huge sums in raising additional army units for combat in the Himalayas. A powerful Indian navy can subtly change the security environment in the Gulf in our favour from where we get 70 per cent of our energy and where our 6 million expatriates remit a large part of the $70 Billion remittances that India now receives annually from abroad. This large Indian dependence on the Gulf in terms of manpower, energy and financial resources is not backed by any security architecture in which we participate. The Pakistan dimension is a huge handicap for us in this. The US has a strong military presence in the Gulf but US policies in the region are also the source of the instabilities ravaging this larger region, and this includes the partisan US role in the emerging Shia-Sunni conflict pitting Saudi Arabia against Iran. We have no control over this dynamic which can potentially cause enormous problems for our interests in the region. If with the shale gas revolution the US strategic interest in the region relatively declines, the current levels of security provided by the US for ensuring the flow of oil into the international market could go down. A robust Indian navy gives us increased options in forging required political arrangements and dealing with a potential crisis.

Asia encompasses some of the world's largest countries; it is contributing increasingly to global growth; economic power is shifting gradually from the Euro-Atlantic region to Asia. Russia has the larger part of its territory in Asia and many of the resources of this vast region lie untapped. The US, through its network of military alliances, is a formidable force in the region. No Asia-wide regional security architecture exists, though ASEAN has built an architecture to protect its security—the ASEAN Regional Forum (ARF)—which has spawned the East Asia Summit which is a forum of 18 countries for discussing larger Asia-related security issues. However, as the name indicates, the focus of the summit remains on East Asia or Asia-Pacific, with India alone being represented there from our region. This emerging Asia-Pacific security architecture deals with the interplay of forces in that region, with China's South China Sea claims in focus, but with India's security challenges remaining unaddressed. Curbing China's assertiveness in the western Pacific collectively by member countries aids India's security indirectly, even though this will still not affect our issues with China over Tibet or China's growing influence in our neighbourhood.

Finally, no country can ensure its security at required levels unless its military strength emerges from an autonomous indigenous base. A truly independent policy can be followed only if a country has a capacity to defend itself by relying on its domestic resources. Our external security apparatus suffers from a major weakness because we are almost 70 per cent dependent on import of arms. It does little honour to India and how we manage our defence that India should be the world's largest importer of arms. Vested interests have developed in the country in favour of import of arms rather than domestic manufacturing. Even as regards arms imports our dilatory and corruption tainted procurement procedures have led to inordinate delays in acquisitions and gaps in our military preparedness. The new government is stressing the need for indigenous manufacture of arms for which the FDI ceiling for investment in the defence sector has been raised from 26 to 49 per cent. Even this is unlikely to lead to transfer of needed technologies. India has to use the lure of its market and, hopefully, its return to a high growth trajectory to press for technology transfers. Despite western arms embargoes on China since 1989, China has succeeded in developing its arms manufacturing industry in an impressive way. We need to emulate its example in whatever practical way available.

Our external security environment is almost unique in that we have two powers on our borders that claim our territory; both are nuclear and cooperate with each other against us. Both are in their own way dominated by the military and are either not democratic or dubiously democratic. We face terrorism and the dangers of Islamic radicalism from Pakistan, threats that cannot be fought with conventional military means, which aggravates our security problems. Pakistan is unrelenting in its hostility towards India despite the elapse of 67 years and radical changes in the international environment. China is seeking hegemony in Asia; it is encircling us strategically by implanting itself in our neighbourhood and curtailing our influence there. An India-China rapprochement can change the geo-politics of Asia and beyond, but this does not seem to be part of China's long term vision of its international role. We have to live with these realities. Which means that we have no choice but to build up a robust defence capability with self-reliance as our goal.

2

The Conundrum of Indian Defence and Civil-Military Relationship

Shekhar Dutt

Setting the Context

The issue of the higher defence organisation in India, the state of civil military relations, or more specifically, the structure of the Ministry of Defence (MoD) comes up for attention quite often. It has been a part of the deliberations of a group of ministers as also some task forces set up at different points. Despite changes that have been made because of such examinations, the issue still remains unsettled and comes up for regular debate. My views on the subject are tempered by four tenures in the MoD and an opportunity of a life time that allowed me an active participation in the 1971 Indo-Pak war where I was the Forward Observation Officer (FOO) and the authorised Observation Post Officer (OP) of the 11 Infantry Division in their operation in the Western Sector (Rajasthan/ Sindh). This has allowed me abiding friendship both with those in uniform and the much maligned bureaucracy. My assignments as Director (Navy), Joint Secretary (MoD), Secretary Defence Production and Defence Secretary and later as the Deputy National Security Advisor (NSA) allowed me an experience that needs to be shared. I mention these not as credentials but because I am oft reminded of President Kennedy who said "*Too often...we enjoy the comfort of opinion without the discomfort of thought*". In India, all of us, in any case, seem to be quite attached to our opinions. I will attempt to initiate the required '*thought*' so that this vital subject moves beyond issues of emotions and turf.

It is interesting to note that one does not hear much discussion on the higher organisation and management of the Railways, Indian Space Research

Organisation (ISRO), or for that matter any other government concern such as the ministries of petroleum, agriculture or industry. In contrast, shape and contours of higher defence organisations are a subject of constant and intense debate, in India and in most major powers across the world. Reasons for this could be the disproportionately larger impact that the armed forces of a State have in the shaping of its self-image. Military as its intrinsic character is expected to possess the ability to *assert* itself, and this creates a behavioural peculiarity within the armed forces. I need to qualify by calling it the armed forces *bureaucracy*. At levels of Service HQ the function is quite akin to implementing the policies of the political leadership and providing them professional advice. The attitude grows from a life time of accomplishing a mission, regardless of the costs or methods and means. As opposed to this the civilian counterpart are expected to implement policies without any cause for confrontation or conflict. The uniformed fraternity the world over follows norms and customs that are a little different, to say the least, and peculiar to the uninitiated. This poses no challenge to structures at lower levels of the organisation which do not require external interface. But it becomes discomforting, to say the least, at higher organisational levels, where such interface with civilian bureaucracy and political leadership is required. It needs mention that even amongst the three services; whenever a common platform is needed, minor issues of form and protocol assume complex dimensions. In essence, a democratic society would demand that policies *represent the will of the people and therefore should never be the cause of internal conflict or confrontation.* '*Assertion*', which is an intrinsic military characteristic, is alien to this democratic construct. The political and bureaucratic side is quite open to a system of debate to accommodate various hues of opinion and perspective to preclude subsequent conflict or confrontation. In the military, the senior is always right—but this is how it should be. Neither side can be considered at fault because such an attitude is part of their charter and growth. It is this democratic and participative need that is getting reflected in the public mood that we see around us in the election year. It is therefore obvious that the political vector has shown preference for a layer of civilian bureaucracy between them and the military. This is the default position of the structure. In terms of any civil-military structure we cannot ignore this reality notwithstanding other factors of competence and specialisation.

Concern for the security of a nation is as old as the birth of a nation-state itself. In a way, it can even be traced to the evolution of civil society when man transformed himself from the state of nature to a civil society, where he could seek collective security for himself and his fellow beings. However, academic interest in national security developed only in the interregnum of the two world wars. The aftermath of World War II led to de-colonisation and emergence of a host of new nations. This obviously brought with it an awareness of issues involved with independent existence and underlined the problems of a modern state.

Territorial integrity thus became a concern. Growth of military hardware and military doctrines was therefore axiomatic. These were born out of the experience of long drawn campaigns, yet, they did not remain contextual. A more comprehensive view of National Security developed due to the Cold War era that simultaneously followed. National Security got linked to a more sophisticated usage of National Power as an element of a more comprehensive construct. Change in our structure, if any, has to come based on this larger view of synergistic aggregation of power, security and defence.

Dynamics of the Construct

Managing Defence is a complex business and ministers, military officers and civilian officials have to work together to provide effective direction. Today, Pakistan does not need great research or invest in covert operations to discover what goes on in terms of capability building or the voids that can be exploited. Our friction between the existing structures allows the proverbial dirty linen to be brought before the public. This is happening at a time when India is confronted with all instrumentalities of asymmetry abetted and sponsored by Pakistan, an assertive China imposing a long term challenge and Indian Ocean Region (IOR) is becoming an arena of contest. Can India avert being pushed to a mere sub regional context or can it become a global player that has a say in all international platforms? Our geography, history and the geo-politics of the day demand that we prepare ourselves for this role. For this, our structures need to be agile, synergistic and somewhat nimble. Instead of quoting from the *rules of business* there is a need to identify what national defence has to deliver. The fundamental aspects of Defence policy and planning include Strategy and Leadership. It implies providing the strategic vision for defence and top level leadership of the three Single Services. The next level requirement is about Setting Policy. This calls for providing long term strategic planning; defining requirements e.g. force levels, and the formulation and dissemination of departmental level perspective. What is often ignored and covered by our obsession for security is Corporate Planning and Image. We need to put out to the public clearly the procedures and methods for the management of MoD's planning processes including the development of outputs and targets that are covered in any annual planning and monitoring process. Finally there is a need for Setting Targets, Allocating Resources and Measuring Performance. It is evident that these basic drivers cannot be purely civilian and obviously neither can these be purely military. The situation becomes far more complex when defence is linked to the umbrella considerations of national security.

Any consideration of a country's military capabilities or its military effectiveness must begin with an examination of the resources—financial, human, physical, and technological. The national leadership has to make these available. These resources are clearly a function of the larger national-level assets or resources. The dynamics that impinge on this rest on the imperatives emerging from national performance when weighted against the pressures levied by external threats, the power of the state vis-à-vis its society and the ideational acuity with which both state managers and society as a whole can perceive problems and develop satisfactory solutions. These aspects operating interactively, then define the kind of resources transferred to the military. The implication is that while the military can generate a wish list of professional capability required but what it finally gets will depend on national level iteration of resources and priorities. The military will need to function within this constraint and deliver through an internal prioritisation, rebalancing and re-strategisation. The so called civil supremacy is about this. Those familiar with the function within the MoD will know that while there is a perpetual sense of dissatisfaction about resource allocation, there is little done by way of rebalancing or re-stratigisation. In fact, even re-prioritisation happens by default because the effort is somehow to spend the allocated budget within the financial year instead of deciding on the priority. Therefore while each service debates on the changing battlefield and modernisation within itself, there is a great reluctance towards complementarity and maximising on combined strengths in the immediate areas of logistics, intelligence, training, cyber and operational domain. Combining elements of two or more services is phenomenally more effective than simply tallying numbers. Integration does not imply linear increase and on the contrary the philosophy builds on diversity and draws strength from competing ideas. Concepts that emerge need to be pluralistic and based on discussed and experimented alternatives so that interests of each stake holder are incorporated. The basic issue is that much can be done in-house instead of awaiting a political decision and seeking an overhaul.

Defence as a structure, as a process or even as a constituency has never been a major political issue. For that matter National Security is more in the domain of rhetoric than substantive debate. This is apparent in an election year. Unfortunately, India has many other priority areas that concern the daily lives and livelihood of our people. The problem is not that Security and Defence have been kept out of the National Perspective Matrix, the gravity lies in the fact that a disconnect between National Power and Military Power has come about in our 'thought'. Strategy has become the responsibility of separate and transient holders of offices in different disciplines of politics, administration, diplomacy, military, intelligence, sciences and economics. They have expertise in their own fields but the understanding of national power and security as one complete entity is missing. Unfortunately there is no dearth of platforms or institutions that can look into this synergy but the process is not institutionalised.

To prevent this, an articulated position in the public domain is mandatory and this needs to be updated regularly through a National document. Without the cloak of undue secrecy, public debate is possible and this will bring about transparency. Transparency in an established and structured manner, can in turn institute accountability. It is obvious that however professional the military maybe and however democratically committed it remains, it cannot compensate for the value of civilian bureaucracy as an interface with the political leadership. If there is harmonious synchrony between the two, adequate resources can be apportioned and priorities will be based on essentials instead of ownership and expediency. The criticality is an open mind, mutual faith and understanding.

There are numerous arguments against the present structure. Lack of civilian expertise, strong but competing bureaucratic control over the military and considerable autonomy granted to the military to compensate for the previous two factors is an oft expressed sentiment. K. Subrahmanyam used to call it the "*absent dialogue*" that directly translated into a system where "*politicians enjoy power without any responsibility, bureaucrats wield power without any accountability and the military assumes responsibility without any direction.*" It is felt that our present structure ensures that single point of views prevail, without the benefit of research enabled alternatives. This suits everybody because the enablers have neither any commitment or accountability and the actual decision makers need not be encumbered with even legitimate dissent. Each issue, in reality, gets treated as a stand alone agenda; without synchrony with a long term perspective that is both imperative and mandatory at the highest level of decision taking. There is little doubt that economic and social progress cannot take place in an environment that is not secure. A fortuitous combination of factors (economic, demographic and geo-political) has created a "critical mass" and placed the country on a trajectory which generates its own security compulsions. We cannot afford turf distribution and creation of fiefdoms, and thereby deprive ourselves of the benefits of holistic thinking and synchronised action. There organisational process is seen as a zero sum game, where the increase in the influence, domain, resources or stature of one is at the cost of the others. The easiest recourse under such circumstances becomes status quo, particularly in a situation where the political leadership of the day is not inclined to assert itself in pursuing a particular path.

The arguments by the military or on behalf of the military have sought a larger participatory role and greater say in the department of defence. Strategy and Leadership aspects involve synergy with overall human resource policies and overarching perspective on National Security. The functions are therefore coordinative, implementative and conceptual. There is a scope for a civil-military mix. Level at which the military component operates will depend on aspects of continuity and understanding of national level policies. Setting of policy calls for providing long term strategic planning; defining requirements e.g. force levels, and the formulation and dissemination of departmental perspective. This involves resource optimisation, synergy and alignment with trends and national interests. This is a somewhat inter-ministerial function and requires coordination between all departments of defence and the three services. Levels of integration between the three Services however need to be very high before some areas of this responsibility are entrusted to them.

Unfortunately the career graph of the military and the civilian staff are different. The military has to move between command and staff assignments and every officer needs to be given an equivalent opportunity to prove his comparative potential in a pyramidical structure. Such a career design dos not ensure adequate time to learn the job requirements of an assignment at the MoD. The Army is the worst off and this is reflected in the tri service resource optimisation and consequent acrimony. Within the Service there are numerous specialisations that preclude intimate knowledge of all issues being dealt with. A way out should be found. My personal experience convinces me that as a Joint Secretary with a tenure of five years, in the nineteen nineties in the MoD, I had a far more detailed, current and intimate knowledge about equipment and platforms than the officers of the concerned military directorates who were to push the cases of acquisition. During this tenure of five years I had worked with four different Additional Director Generals Weapons and Equipment (ADGWE) of the Army Head Quarter. Therefore, how can one expect a DGWE/ADGWE of the Army to acquire cross cutting knowledge about all issues being dealt by him except for the critical cases. He is given a limited tenure and institutional memory through our files is not the best answer. Similarly the civilian bureaucracy has little knowledge about the connectedness of diverse arms and services to combat and operational readiness. An effort has been made to bridge the gap in some manner through the creation of Integrated Defence Staff (HQ IDS) but mindsets have not changed. An episode will place the issue in perspective. The Chief of Integrated Defence Staff (IDS) (of the rank equivalent to Army Commander) and the Chief of a certain service were from the same batch. The differences in their turf and personal issues came up many times where my personal intervention was needed to iron things out. On one such occasion when the value of IDS came up for discussion, the Chief told me in no uncertain terms that he would provide his worst human resource to HQ IDS because that is what they deserve. The actual language is beyond being quoted. With such mindsets there is little that structures can change in terms of performance.

Organisational Parametres

Force application has never been a default option for India. It has always been in our interest to retain peace and encourage the conditions of economic growth.

Progress and stability not only in India but even in its periphery has been an article of faith for us. India's response to these multiple threats and challenges has always been restrained, measured and moderate. While skilful diplomacy is seen as the prime answer to various threats, it can work only if it is backed by credible military power. The three military services are vital but remain a lower order response rung of the National security construct. Yet they are the most difficult to de-conflict and finally integrate despite the professional imperatives. Integration or Jointness touches aspects of individual identity and the services draw the critical bonding from this very emotion for their cohesion and performance. Pyramidical structures are inherently resistant to lateral linkages as a design deficiency and this creates greater emotive issues. Areas of partnership get viewed through partisan positions of 'them and us'. Correctives, therefore, have to be forced into the system and cannot be expected to emerge despite their own professional imperatives. Expecting changes to flow from the operational level upwards is flawed due to the core and ingrained mindsets based on fraternity considerations. Therefore, while each service debates on the changing battlefield and modernisation within itself, there is a great reluctance towards complimentarity and maximising on combined strengths. Not only is change internally resistant even the MoD as a functional construct has not been able to promote or initiate a change.

Various initiatives have been taken in the past but these have not been able to address the essentials of establishing a coherent and comprehensive picture of totality of operational capability that is in synchrony with political objectives. This includes the cumulative capability of the entire range of weapon systems, logistic support inventory, manpower availability and training status. Neither has a requisite mechanism been established to guide the means and processes to optimise the existing potential of the military and priorities for modernisation. The problem of the day is also that security is getting a far more comprehensive connotation than a purely military construct. Today, the individual human being and civil society is conceiving itself as an equal and complementing matrix of National Security.

Technology has removed the comfortable distinctions between 'External and Internal', between 'Front and Rear' and even between 'War and Peace'. Yet the structure of governments allocates neat and distinct areas of responsibilities. Concerns of the moment, do not allow the time and the energy to devote themselves in sufficient measure to matters in the domain of the possible, the probable and even the improbable. It is here that speculative but structured thinking demonstrates its relevance and helps bridge the gap between the worlds of ideas and action.

The structure has to be seen holistically. An approach based on fault finding and incremental change will prove as ineffective as all our efforts so far. We might increase the establishment, create peripheral structures, bring about some improvement but will never be able to create a structure that delivers military effectiveness and political confidence and assurance. For this, we will have to move out of the rules of business approach.

Possible Structure and Functions

If Defence has to be a function of diplomacy, military capabilities and above all the Political will, the structure needs to be cross attached at various tiers. Brigadiers/Colonels and equivalents is a reasonable first level of cross postings. The tenures, however, need to be reasonably long. Since it is in the interest of the Armed forces to have competent people to take care of their interests, there should be no problem with regards to the standard of the human resource. Similarly the War Establishment and equivalent directorates can have civilian officers from the director level onwards. There is no reason similarly for denying the Services the billet of Secretary Ex-Servicemen Welfare. The Ministry of External Affairs (MEA) should similarly earmark a Secretary level post to a military officer to provide competence for strategic military balance with respect to our adversaries. The details can be worked out easily as long as the Higher Defence Structure concerns itself with the following areas:

(a) Resource Optimisation
   (i) Resource provisioning including all aspects of finance, defence industry, manpower and other national infrastructural and industrial resources including those concerning space, cyber and atomic energy.
   (ii) Policy guidelines and long term planning to establish the structure, objectives and processes for resource allocation and utilisation. This should include prioritisation between competing demands and establishing linkages between trade and industry.

(b) Qualitative Guidance and Monitoring
   (i) Development of human skills in specialised areas like aeronautics, R&D, production engineering, identification of attributes for formulation of product specifications as also trials and testing.
   (ii) Profiling of inventory to include aspects of interoperability, maintainability and sustainability. Commonality of equipment and technology.

(c) Responsiveness
   (i) Contingency planning based on a systems approach with a long term perspective. Increase of options and alternatives.
   (ii) Agility of structures and processes. Synergising of all instruments of power through a whole Government approach. Diffuse single power centres in pyramidical structures.

(d) Integration
 (i) Linkage of military force application with national security objectives and perspective.
 (ii) Development of Joint and integrated strategy in areas in contingencies of probability, possibility and improbability.
 (iii) Agility of policy modification and policy implementation.
 (iv) Ability to draw from common resource, multiple usages of single resource and drastic reduction in overheads.
 (v) Strengthen civil-military interface and relationship.

The Way Ahead

There is a need to highlight that there are obvious benefits in a structure that has intrinsic role-based characteristics of the military with the comfort zone of a layer of civilian bureaucracy between itself and the political layer. Integration is about a changed mindset instead of changed structures or nomenclatures. Transparency in an established and structured manner, can institute accountability. For this, an articulated position in the public domain is mandatory. Synchrony with a long term perspective is both imperative and mandatory at the highest level of decision taking. It also needs reiteration that there is no substitute to knowledge and experience on the work assigned to the billet. Methods and means have to be found to overcome limitations of tenure compulsions of the military and improve the basic functions carried out by the civilian bureaucracy of the MoD. Mindsets have to change before any change of structure becomes effective. Once this happens, cross postings and joint responsibilities and widened authority will become a reality.

I would like to explain the aforesaid issue in this manner: if a sufficient tenure (of four to five years) is provided to a competent military officer of the rank of brigadier/colonel (and equivalent), certain director/deputy secretary level posts in the MoD can be manned by such military officers. It is necessary that these officers be such who are assessed to have a potential to take on higher command in their respective military services after the tenure in the MoD. A selected few from the same bunch, after a tenure or two in their respective services, having been promoted to the rank of Major-General and equivalent, could then be posted to the MoD as Joint Secretary or equivalent. The Military would need to ensure a tenure of four to five years to such officers to enable them to effectively handle the responsibility in the MoD. This should not be at the cost of their promotion to the next rank.

The problem of the day is that huge sums of money are involved in military capability building and that makes people vulnerable to unsubstantiated allegations and the threat to their honour, good name and professional future besides the pain of being left to defend themselves. There is no denying that it is an area where personal greed can take priority and indiscretion cannot be allowed. What makes matters worse is that time imposes a big penalty in costs and leads to preventable and huge wastage of public money. Not taking a decision is at times a bigger crime than taking a well deliberated decision through consensus. The answer lies in making finance as a tool of planning instead of a means of accounting. Instead of an audit post a decision, finance has to be concurrently supportive as also corrective. This should bring about changes in price discovery and factor in the cost of time.

Similarly the comfort of security of a government job should be linked to productivity both in terms of innovative research and development and product improvement. It is a change that will have to be reflected in the entire spectrum. This will include those who set Qualitative Requirements (QR), those who accept these, those who develop these, those who produce these and those who assure the quality. Higher Defence Organisation is not about protocols and egos; it is about delivery of assurances and matching capabilities with political objectives.

In my view, the change cannot come about internally because of inherent characteristics of the constituent players involved. Unlike other countries where a CCS decision (Goldwater Nichols Act as an example) can bring about a functional change, it cannot happen in India because of our fractured polity and dissenting orientation. The change not only has to be initiated, it has to be monitored, enforced and institutionalised along with modifications as required. There is a need to establish a standing body to look into all aspects of force application within the umbrella domain of National Security. A Military Commission will be able to fill this void. This will have to be empowered adequately and will need expertise from all areas that concern capability building and constituents of force application.

3

ROOTS OF CIVIL-MILITARY SCHISM IN INDIA: THE NEED FOR SYNERGY

Arun Prakash

Introduction

It is a well-known fact that in India's short but eventful existence as a modern nation state, civil-military relations have remained a vexed issue; with many deleterious consequences for its security. A key feature of the prevailing situation is its contrived asymmetry, which gives rise to suspicion and disharmony that have become the hallmark of civil-military relationships in New Delhi. A clear indicator of this is the fact that while the military seethes with dissatisfaction at perceived imbalances, the political establishment and civilian bureaucracy are quite content with the way things are, and remain staunch upholders of the *status quo*.

While this topic does, from time to time, attract public attention and forms the subject of sporadic media discourse, this generally happens at the onset of a security crisis or disaster, and remains a short-lived phenomenon. Moreover, discussions relating to civil-military relations are based on empirical observations and thus remain ill-informed and superficial.

The civil-military equation is a complex dynamic which has roots, not only in political science and sociology but also in many other fields including history, philosophy and psychology etc. This essay will make a modest attempt to examine a few of these factors in order to, firstly; obtain a better understanding of the nature of civil-military relations in India, including its flaws, and secondly; to identify the consequences of the existing discord. The concluding section contains some options and recommendations, in this regard, for consideration of the decision-makers.

The Concept of Civilian Control

War is Now Amidst the People

National security, in the larger context, denotes the ability of a state to withstand military threats and political coercion and to ensure protection of its interests and ideals. While today, the concept has been expanded to encompass a range of factors including economic, diplomatic, political and even environmental; the original notion of national security, born in post-WW II USA, had focused, largely on the use of military force in the belief that 'if you want peace, you must prepare for war'.

The concept of mobilising the whole nation to participate in war was first practiced by Napoleon, and inter-state conflict has evolved, thereafter, into a 'peoples' war'. In the most common form of conflict today, non-state actors tend to make civilians the exclusive targets of terrorist violence. At the other end of the scale, the very essence of nuclear deterrence is to hold the lives of millions of ordinary citizens to ransom, in order to compel forbearance on the adversary's part. Thus, instead of being fought between armies on a battlefield, wars are now fought, in the words of Lt Gen Rupert Smith, 'amongst the people', because civilians have become as much 'targets to be attacked', or 'objectives to be won', as any military force.[1]

Acquiring an insight into the nature of war, understanding the compulsions of national security and evolving strategies for achieving security objectives has become the *sine qua non* of the security establishments of major powers. In this endeavour, the distinction between 'civil' and 'military' components of the security establishment becomes blurred, and post-WW II experience shows that the evolution of nuclear and other strategies owes more to civilian scholars and analysts in academia and think-tanks, than to military institutions.

The civil-military relationship has, in fact, come to form the keystone of national security. According to social-scientist Samuel Huntington, in his classic work *The Soldier and the State,* "Nations which fail to develop a balanced pattern of civil-military relations squander their resources and run uncalculated risks."[2] Huntington has undertaken an in-depth examination of the military's role in society, and subjecting civil-military relations to a historical analysis, in the context of major wars, he evolves a general theory of civil-military relations. While, at present, his discourse is only marginally applicable to India, as this country gathers the economic and military trappings of power, and matures politically, it will have much to learn from Huntington.

Despite its frequent mention in discourse, the term 'civilian control' lacks a satisfactory definition. Huntington proceeds on the hypothesis that this concept is based on 'relative power' and that the key to establishing civilian control is to minimise military power vis-à-vis civilian power. Given the large number, varied character and conflicting interests of civilian groups it is impossible to maximise civil power as a whole, and the inevitable question that arises is; which civilians are to do the controlling?[3]

The answer to this conundrum can vary widely. Whereas 17th century England witnessed a struggle between the Crown and Parliament for control of the military, present day US sees continuous sparring between Congress and the President for influence over the armed forces. Debunking the popular thesis that civilian control is associated with democracies and military control with authoritarian regimes, Huntington cites the case of USA where, during WW II, the armed forces acquired immense political power through legitimate democratic processes and institutions. In Hitlerian Germany and Soviet Russia, on the other hand, measures such as infiltrating the officer corps with political commissars, creating rival armed militias and deploying instruments of state surveillance and terror, including bloody purges, were used by civilian autocrats to keep the military in check.[4]

Whether or not Huntington's detailed study has current relevance to India, we need to take note of: (a) his observation that civilian control is sought by all dispensations, and is not the monopoly of any one political system, and (b) of his dual prescription for minimisation of military power and retention of civil control; firstly, professionalise the military and secondly, render them politically neutral and sterile.[5]

Civil Control in the Indian Context

From the above, it is obvious that the question: 'which civilians are to do the controlling?' can have multiple answers. In the unique system of democracy, evolved by India, a layer of civilian bureaucracy has interposed itself between the political leadership and an isolated military establishment, and the term 'civil-military' here implies a three-cornered relationship encompassing political and bureaucratic players on one hand and the military on the other. This relationship has, over the years, evolved into a triangle of discord, tension and indifference; whose most damaging impact has been a stasis in national security affairs.

Elsewhere in the world, the pursuit of war has demanded equal attention from soldiers as well as statesmen, diplomats and bureaucrats. This has not been the case in India, because for two centuries preceding 1947 wars were fought by Indian armies, at home and abroad, on behalf of their British colonial masters; and Indians had no involvement in imperial planning or strategies. For the past six decades, however, India has been an independent nation-state, and this, coupled with the fact that we are heirs to a substantive cultural past, requires us to undertake some historical introspection.

Such an exercise calls for an examination of the socio-cultural roots that have fashioned Indian attitudes towards the use of force and shaped our strategic culture. But before that, we need to begin by seeking a brief insight into the nature of war.

The Compulsions of National Security

The Nature of War

Many political commentators mistakenly believe that French Premier George Clemenceau was disparaging soldiers when he said, "War is too important a matter to be left to the generals". In actual fact Clemenceau was merely emphasising the political character of war; a thesis highlighted by German strategist and theorist Carl von Clausewitz in his treatise 'On War'. Amidst his comprehensive treatment of numerous issues related to war, Clausewitz wrote with deep insight about the relationship between the statesman and the military commander. Elaborating on the repetitive theme that war is 'an instrument of policy', Clausewitz explains, "...war is only a branch of political activity; it is in no sense autonomous."

He advises that while the commander-in-chief must be in the war cabinet to keep the politicians informed, he is there to take orders, not give them. It is the responsibility of politicians to ensure that the military means they adopt are appropriate to their political ends. Speaking of the attributes of a good Minister of War, he says, "What is needed in the post is intellect and strength of character. The minister can always get the necessary military information and advice."[6] In the same breath he strongly urges upon the statesman and policy-maker that, "...a certain grasp of military affairs is vital for those in charge of policy."[7]

My main objective in referring to Clausewitz is to draw attention to his insistence on the need for the 'statesman' to maintain an open and continuous dialogue with the 'commander', especially when there is possibility of conflict. However, since the occurrence of military conflict is relatively rare, unless the statesman and soldier make a habit of engaging in dialogues of this nature during peacetime, it will not happen when required.

While transposing Clausewitzian dictums to the Indian milieu, we must make allowances for certain peculiarities. The Indian politician, in spite of his strident emphasis on the principle of civil control, keeps his distance from the military and delegates the responsibility for security related matters to civil servants or technocrats. Since the politician does not always involve himself in policy-making, 'civil authority', for the purposes of this discussion, may be represented by a duality or even trinity consisting of a combination of the politician, bureaucrat and scientist, who are said to form India's 'national security elite'.

Given the political origins and nature of war, it becomes obvious that any dividing lines between the civil and military components of national security are most undesirable. And yet that is exactly the bane of India's higher defence organisation. The politician employs a 100 per cent civilian Ministry of Defence (MoD) to exercise control over the armed forces headquarters which are external and subordinate to it. The current system has been not only been allowed to persist since independence, but is stoutly defended on the grounds that since it has worked for 66 years, there is no need to make changes.

Highlighting this delusional approach, an article in the April 2013 issue of *The Economist* magazine, identified the lack of a strategic culture as the prime impediment that stood in the way of "India's dreams of becoming a 21st century power". The article went on to say, "Since independence, India has got away with having a weak strategic culture. Instead of clear strategic thinking; India shuffles along, impeded by its caution and bureaucratic inertia."[8]

A closer look at our strategic culture may provide some pointers to the mindset of decision-makers.

Impact of Strategic Culture

Experience has shown that each nation has its own way of interpreting international events and reacting to them. Post WW-II a new discipline—strategic culture—emerged for prediction of a state's actions and rationalisation of its policies in the national security arena. In the Indian context, strategic culture has been an important factor in shaping the perceptions and in guiding the actions of our politico-military elite, and bears examination.

In 1992, George Tanham, a RAND researcher, stirred a hornets' nest with his monograph on *Indian Strategic Thought;* a study that analysed the historical, geographic, and cultural factors influencing Indian strategic thinking. Tanham remarks, "India is an extraordinarily complex society and Indian elites show little evidence of having systematically thought about national strategy.... Few writings offer coherent, articulated beliefs or a clear set of operational principles for Indian strategy" According to his interpretation, these lacunae arise from certain significant factors related to India's historical and cultural background:[9]

- Firstly, since India has lacked political unity throughout much of its history and has limited experience of being a nation-state, Indians have not developed the habit of devoting serious thought to national defence planning.
- Secondly, the Hindu concept of time, or rather the lack of a sense of time, tends to discourage long-term planning as a futile exercise.
- Finally, the Hindu considers life a mystery, largely unknowable and, not under man's control. Since he cannot, thus, forecast or plan with confidence, fate, intuition, tradition and emotions are allowed to play their part.

Tanham points to the role and status of the military in India as a manifestation of a skewed strategic thought process. Commenting on the "tight civilian control of the military", he adds that India has pursued this policy to a point, "where the military have almost no input at all in the formulation of higher defence policy and national strategy."

Exploring the genesis of this approach, he refers to Prime Minister Nehru's deep pacifism and "rather strong anti-military attitude" and attributes it, largely, to his perception "that the army did not take part in the nationalist movement" and was an instrument of the British Raj. Consequently, he says, Nehru, "...neglected the military, giving it few resources and downgrading its top leadership....while increasing the status and pay of both civil servants and the police."[10] Tanham draws attention to Nehru's disdain for military advice by citing an example where the C-in-C Army, Gen. Cariappa, was rebuked by him in the following words: "It is not the business of the C-in-C to tell the Prime Minister who is going to attack us where. In fact, the Chinese will defend our Eastern frontier. You mind only Kashmir and Pakistan"[11]

The roots of most current civil-military debates lie buried in legacy issues going as far back as 1947. At this juncture, it would be useful to trace the historic evolution of civil-military relations within the larger context of national defence.

The Historical Underpinning

Marginalising the Armed Forces

Tanham may be right in pointing out that the Indian army had served the British Sovereign in many wars, but it is unlikely that Indian politicians are ignorant of the Indian soldiers' contribution to the freedom struggle and its aftermath. The string of early British defeats in N Africa and SE Asia, in WW II, saw Indian Prisoners Of War (POWs) in Singapore, Germany and Italy eagerly answering the call of Subhash Chandra Bose to fight for India's freedom. Consequently, 3000 Indian POWs were formed into the Free Indian Legion as a unit of the German Army,[12] and in Singapore 40,000 out of 45,000 POWs joined the Indian National Army.[13]

The story of these expatriate Indian warriors is a forgotten chapter in India's freedom struggle, and not many are aware that a Provisional Government of Free India was established in Singapore by Bose in 1943, which formally, declared war on the British Empire.[14] Indian National Army (INA) units fought alongside the Japanese 15th Army in its invasion of India which ended in failure. Mention also needs to be made of the series of mutinies, in early 1946, by sailors of the Royal Indian Navy (RIN), with units of the Royal Indian Air Force (RIAF), the army's Signal Corps and Electrical and Mechanical Engineers (EME) joining their naval comrades in revolt against the British.[15]

These events, involving Indian military personnel, at home and abroad, not only inspired and galvanised the freedom movement in India, but also struck deep fear into British hearts, and certainly hastened their departure from India. The phase immediately post-Independence too, was extremely difficult for our fledgling republic. Apart from tenaciously holding on to Kashmir Valley and helping integrate recalcitrant princely states, the armed forces also played a sterling role during the violent upheaval of partition. Conventional history, as well as political folklore seems to have deliberately ignored this factor. Over the years, as our glaring strategic naiveté repeatedly led to adventurism by our neighbours in 1947, 1962, 1965, and 1999, it was invariably the gallantry and patriotism of the armed forces which saved the nation from disintegration and dishonour. The victory of Indian arms in the 1971 Bangladesh War will remain a glorious episode in the dismal history of sub-continental conflicts.

This recitation of past events is meant to convey three points in the context of strategic culture. One; that while ahimsa and non-violence are noble precepts; Indians must draw the right historical lessons regarding their role in a world governed by *realpolitik*. Two; that armed force is a necessary evil and its use must be guided by national interest rather than sentiment. And lastly, that the Indian armed forces made contributions of major significance to the freedom struggle as well as to the crucial post-independence stabilisation phase. These contributions cannot be either forgotten or belittled.

Tanham wonders, why civilians in India have remained apprehensive of a military coup since independence, notwithstanding the unblemished record of the armed forces in scrupulously steering clear of politics. Pointing out how this irrational fear has led to the military leadership being deprived of most discretionary powers and sidelined in policy-making, he comments, "The military resent the fact that these largely uninformed and inexperienced civilians make all the major decisions."[16]

Coming from a detached (foreign) observer, Tanham's summation of the situation is compelling in its accuracy and deserves to be quoted in full: "In effect the Services have been downgraded in status, taken out of the national security decision-making process, and kept ignorant of nuclear developments, while the MoD civilian staff has grown in prestige and power and controls almost all military activities and programmes...bureaucratic opposition has prevented the formation of much needed institutions for the coordination of the military services, as well as development of a national strategy. Civilians, bureaucrats and politicians alike, have opposed the creation of a Chief of Defence Staff (CDS) and an integrated staff...."[17]

There has been little substantive change in the 21 years since Tanham undertook this analytic assessment of India's strategic culture and status of the military *vis-a-vis* the politico-bureaucratic elite. To acquire a better understanding of this situation, it is necessary to trace the historical evolution of the civil-military relationship.

Evolution of Civil-Military Relations

Roots of Higher Defence Organisation

The genesis of our current higher defence organisation can be traced to the dawn of the 20th Century, when the British felt the need to reorganise and re-equip the Indian Army to fight a modern war in Europe. Field-Marshal Lord Kitchener had been sent to India as the Commander-in-Chief, where Lord Curzon was then the Viceroy.

One was a distinguished soldier and the other an able administrator, but both being strong personalities, a clash of views arose between Kitchener and Curzon. The Viceroy maintained that the civil being supreme, he should receive military advice from two sources, namely the C-in-C and the Military Member of his Council (a Major-General), so that he could better exercise his judgment and discretion. Kitchener on the other hand, urged that dual military advice was not only unnecessary but inappropriate since it would involve the C-in-C's recommendations being commented upon by the Military Member who was junior in rank.[18]

After an acrimonious debate, the British Government decided in favour of Kitchener and Curzon resigned. The Military Member was dropped from the Council and made a staff officer of the C-in-C, with the designation of Army Secretary. This appointment continued to be held by a Major General till 1920, when the Army Secretary was re-designated Defence Secretary. Thereafter, a civil servant was appointed to this post and continued to function as a staff officer of the C-in-C.

A year before independence, in September 1946, when an Interim Government came to power, with Pandit Nehru as the Vice President of the Viceroy's council, some radical changes were made in the in the defence organisation. C-in-C India was dropped from the Viceroy's Council and replaced by a civilian Defence Member. The Defence Department comprising the Defence Secretary and his staff were placed directly under the Defence Member. In August 1947 the Vice President of the Council became Prime Minister, the Defence Member became Defence Minister and the appointment of C-in-C India was abolished; each service now being headed by a separate C-in-C.[19]

Lord Ismay's Legacy

In 1947, it so happened that two of the most experienced Allied military leaders, Lord Mountbatten and his Chief of Staff, Lord Ismay were at hand in India. The Government of India asked them to evolve a system of higher defence management, which would meet the emerging needs of the newly independent nation.

Ismay was deeply conscious of the fact that no radical measures could be contemplated at that delicate juncture, when the sub-continent was about to be carved up into two nations, and the armed forces split asunder. He therefore came up with a solution which called for the least amount of turbulence and readjustment, and would serve in the interim till a proper system could be developed to suit Indian conditions.

Ismay's model was based on a C-in-C for the operational management and administration of each Service, and a Chiefs of Staff Committee (COSC) for central coordination between the three Services. The COSC was to be the highest body for rendering advice to the government and was to be supported by a series of other inter-Service committees to address details of coordination between the Services, and between the Services and the MoD, and to provide for quick decision making with a minimum of red tape. To facilitate quick transaction of business, one or more civil servants were positioned in each committee as members, and its decisions were not to be subject to further detailed scrutiny by the MoD.[20]

The Civil Service Intervention

The pragmatic system of higher defence management recommended by Lord Ismay had the potential to evolve, so that the Service Headquarters (SHQ) could have, with time and further experience, become separate Departments of the MoD. Alternatively, they could have integrated themselves completely with the Department of Defence (DoD) within the MoD. Even without any changes, the integrated civil-military committees had adequate decision-making clout to ensure streamlined functioning of the MoD/SHQ complex.

However, none of the above happened and within a short period of the new system being implemented, senior civil servants intervened to replace the concept of 'civilian supremacy' with a distorted version which actually established 'bureaucratic control' over the armed forces.[21] This was done by the simple expedient of designating the three SHQ as 'Attached Offices' of the Department of Defence, giving them a status exactly on par with organisations such as the Salt Commissioner, Commissioner for Handicrafts, Central Reserve Police Force (CRPF), and Central Industrial Security Force (CISF) etc.

The young and inexperienced military leadership of that era was probably well out of its depth when pitted against the veteran ICS officers in South Block, and it is difficult to blame them for not opposing this development resolutely. The SHQ, in keeping with their status of Attached Offices, found that they were reduced to adjuncts of MoD, and also placed completely outside the Ministry, which they could approach only through the medium of files.

The administrative effectiveness of the Service Chiefs steadily eroded, to the point where their recommendations to the RakshaMantri (RM) began to be routinely sent for scrutiny and comment down to the Director level, and would then slowly work their way upwards, open to comment (or even rejection) at every level of bureaucracy!

For 50 years the armed forces lived with this iniquitous and dysfunctional system, and it took the near disaster of Kargil to trigger some introspection. Regrettably, little has actually changed because the diverse forces in favour of *status quo* have always had the upper hand over those feebly clamouring for change or reform.

Latter Day Developments

Attempts at Reform of the System

The occupation of Kargil heights by Pakistan in 1999 represented the most dramatic threat to India's security in recent times. The degree of alarm created by this episode was enough for the Government of India (GoI) to constitute the Kargil Review Committee (KRC) headed by former civil servant and astute strategist K Subrahmanyam. Having probed the national security system deeply, the KRC observed that this crisis had arisen due to "grave deficiencies in India's security management system", and pointed out that, "India is perhaps the only major democracy where the Armed Forces HQs are outside the apex governmental structure."[22] The scathing indictments of the KRC prompted the government of the day to constitute a Group of Ministers (GoM) in 2000; tasked to undertake a review of national security.

This GoM, through the instrumentality of four dedicated Task Forces, undertook a comprehensive examination of shortcomings in national security. In February 2001 it rendered a report titled, *"Reforming the National Security System"* which contained, amidst much else, some critical recommendations relating to reforms in higher defence management. However, the government of the day, having lost its nerve, permitted the bureaucracy to undertake a cosmetic implementation of these well-considered recommendations. An historic opportunity to redress national security shortcomings was, thus, squandered.

12 years later, in mid-2011, another Task Force (TF) on National Security Reform was constituted under the chairmanship of a seasoned former bureaucrat Sh. Naresh Chandra. This *suo moto* initiative by the Cabinet Committee on Security (CCS), came as a surprise, and raised some hopes that the UPA government was perhaps earnest in seeking long overdue reform in national security.

I happened to be the only individual to have been a member of both the 2000 and 2011 Task Forces, and it was my observation that the issues, conundrums and lacunae confronting both the bodies remained substantially the same. Nor had the mindsets and attitudes undergone any change over the past decade. The retired bureaucrats nominated to the TF, as well as those serving in the MoD (who deposed before it), were insistent that all was well with the national security structures and no change or reform was either necessary, or possible.

As for political functionaries who interacted with the TF, apart from expressing anodyne sentiments, none of them had anything constructive to offer by way of guidance, direction or criticism of the current system. The strong plea for reform that came from the three Services would have remained a 'cry in the wilderness'; but for strong minority support from within the TF.

The report of this TF was submitted to the Prime Minister, with due ceremony, in May 2012; but at the date of writing (January 2014) nothing further has been heard on the subject. With the bureaucracy resolved to maintain *status quo ante*, and the politicians lacking the stomach to take a position on national security issues, the fate of this report was a foregone conclusion.

Fresh Controversies

It was in the year 1998 that first intimations of India's deep civil-military schism came dramatically into the public domain; a difference of opinion between a Service Chief and the Raksha Mantri (RM), snowballed rapidly into a confrontation, resulting in the unprecedented dismissal of the Navy Chief. The years 2011 and 2012, too, were notable for the huge predicaments faced by the MoD, and the trauma and damage inflicted; both on the armed forces and on the larger national security establishment.

The two controversies that erupted during 2011-12 demonstrated, yet again, not just the widening chasm between the military and politico-bureaucratic establishment, but also the sheer incapability of the latter to cope with crises of this nature. In the first instance, the serving Army Chief, obsessed with a personal grievance, and having failed to receive satisfaction from MoD, took the remarkable step of seeking redressal from the Supreme Court. To the deep embarrassment of the military, and a concerned public, many unsavoury details of the case were leaked to the media (allegedly from MoD sources) to be dissected in newspapers articles and TV studios.

While all this was going on, the armed forces were suddenly 'ambushed' by a prominent newspaper editor who splashed a report in banner headlines declaring that the government had been "spooked" by intelligence reports of troop movements towards Delhi. The barely disguised innuendo was that an incipient *coup d'état* by a disgruntled army Chief had been uncovered. While both the PM and RM issued belated denials, it was clear that a clumsy attempt had been made to plant suspicion about the loyalty of India's armed forces in people's minds.[23] The main source of concern arose from the suspicion that the media could not have dared to concoct a canard with such serious implications without a nod from the bureaucracy and/or intelligence agencies.

Reference has been made to these episodes because much of the farce enacted, would not have occurred if (a) an appropriate Higher Defence Management (HDM) system had been in place and (b) if the relationship between the military and the politico-bureaucratic elite had been less adversarial. Most disturbing was the fact that, well into their second terms in office, neither the PM nor RM were willing or able to intervene and defuse issues with potential for serious damage to national security.

The Price of Mistrust

An Environment of Suspicion

Two major factors have contributed to systemic flaws whose effects manifest themselves, periodically, in times of security crises. Mention has already been made of the politician's detachment from national security matters, because of his intuition that this is not a vote-catching issue; and his, near-exclusive, focus on political agendas. A second factor is the total reliance that the politician places, for advice, decision-making and problem resolution, on the non-specialist MoD bureaucracy; despite the Service Chiefs and the SHQ staffs, being available for professional advice on the full range of defence and security related issues.[24]

This stubborn adherence to a unique and archaic system extracts a heavy price, in many ways, and the nation certainly does not receive commensurate return from the annual defence expenditure of US$ 38 billion (and growing). The succeeding paragraphs cover some of the more glaring anomalies in the system and the severe penalties they impose in terms of national security shortcomings.

The 'Invisible' Service Chiefs

For all the pomp and ceremonial that attends the three Service Chiefs, their voice remains unheard in the corridors of power, because they have neither been accorded recognition, nor granted any powers in the edifice of the GoI. Proof of this is to be found in the 'Government of India Allocation of Business Rules' (AoB Rules), and the 'Government of India Transaction of Business Rules' (ToB Rules); the 'bibles' which guide the conduct of Government of India (available in the public domain at http://cabsec.nic.in/allocation_order.php).

According to the Business Rules, the MoD comprises four Departments viz. Department of Defence (DOD), Department of Defence Production (DDP), Department of Defence Research & Development (DDR&D) and Department of Ex-Servicemen Welfare (DESW), and the Finance Division. The designation of the three SHQs as 'Attached Offices of the Department of Defence', subordinate to the DoD, evoked this interesting comment in the 2001 Report of the GoM (headed by, then, Deputy PM LK Advani):

> "In the setup of the Government, besides ministries and departments, there are "Attached Offices" and "Subordinate Offices". For merely administrative reasons and not as a management device, the Service HQs are referred to as "Attached Offices". Consequently there is an erroneous perception that the Armed Forces do not participate in policy formulation and are outside the apex Governmental structure. In order to remove this impression, the Transaction of Business Rules and Standing Orders should be amended to re-designate Service HQs as "Integrated HQs" of the MoD."[25]

The GoM was being disingenuous when it attributed 'administrative reasons' to justify the designation of the SHQ as Attached Offices, and described the exclusion of SHQ from the governmental structure, as an 'erroneous perception'. Neither statement is correct, because this arrangement has been in place since independence, and its inception as well as continuance for over six decades has been a deliberate policy for management of the armed forces with full political approval. As a consequence of the GoM recommendations, the AoB Rules were, indeed, amended to re-designate the three Service HQs as 'Integrated HQs of MoD'. But this superficial change was mere eyewash since no integration had actually taken place and, the *inter se* equation between SHQ and MoD remains unchanged.

This is confirmed by the fact that, even after amendment of the Business Rules, the three Service Chiefs neither find mention, nor are allocated any responsibilities therein. The Manual of Office Procedure states that the Integrated HQs of the three Services will be"...associated in the formulation of policies in relation to matters concerning the defence of India and armed forces..."[26]

At the same time, the 2nd Schedule of the AoB Rules allocates responsibilities to the DoD, for: (a) defence of India, and every part thereof including preparation for its defence and all such acts as may be conducive in times of war to its prosecution (b) the Armed Forces of the Union, namely, Army, Navy and Air Force and (c) the Integrated Headquarters of the MoD comprising of AHQ, NHQ, Air HQ and Defence Staff Headquarters.

However, a serious dichotomy arises from the fact that the Service Chiefs, apart from being Chiefs of their respective staffs, are also the operational commanders of India's land, naval and air forces. As such they bear full responsibility for planning of war and for the deployment of the army, naval and air forces in wartime operations. In this context the current arrangement raises some intriguing questions.

- Since the Business Rules make no mention of the Service Chiefs, but allocate responsibility for the 'defence of India, and every part thereof....', to the Defence Secretary, what is the relationship between the two, and who should be held accountable for failures and shortcomings in military operations?

- What is the standing of the Chiefs in relation to Secretaries who head the other three Departments of the MoD and take decisions with a critical impact on the combat readiness of their forces?
- Is there an anomaly in the fact that the Service Chiefs are, notionally, on par with the Cabinet Secretary, and yet they remain the heads of organisations that have been designated as Attached Offices?
- Why can the armed forces staff not be subsumed within the edifice of the GoI as done in all other democracies?

While the Chiefs may 'propose' it is the civil-servant who has been empowered to 'dispose' of all important matters. It is this exclusion of the armed forces from the decision-making fora, which seems to have set the overall tone for civil-military relations in the government. With a few exceptions, successive Prime Ministers and Defence Ministers have taken their cue from the Rules of Business and kept the military leadership at arm's length. They have, thus, not just alienated the armed forces but also deprived themselves of professional counsel and advice. As a direct consequence of the civil-military divide we suffer from significant debilities which continue to have a serious impact on national security.

A Half-empty Arsenal

Foremost amongst these, is our failure to attain self-reliance in production of weapon systems and the heavy price that we pay for our abject dependence on external sources. Not only does the cost of imported systems, spare parts and ammunition keep escalating at exorbitant rates, but even their availability remains unreliable and unpredictable; thereby eroding combat readiness.

The root of this debility lies in the fact that the armed forces are neither adequately consulted, nor permitted a say in programmes of the DRDO—the agency responsible for indigenous development of military technology. The autonomy granted to this organisation enables it to decide its own priorities and to expend research effort and funds on technologies, which often do not have a bearing on the capabilities urgently needed by the armed forces. Since the user has no say and the bureaucracy does not know enough, the scientist does what he pleases.

Similarly, the vast public sector defence production complex, under the supervision of an uninformed but authoritarian bureaucracy, has succeeded in misleading the nation with spurious claims of 'indigenous production' and 'transfer-of-technology' whereas all they have really undertaken is assembly of kits and production under licence.

Had the armed forces been permitted close involvement with the functioning of DRDO as well as defence production units, far more could have been achieved in terms of efficiency, innovation and self-reliance over the past six decades.

Lagging Modernisation

The second damaging consequence of the isolation of the armed forces from the MoD is the interminable delays that bedevil the processing of cases; whether they relate to acquisition of hardware and ordnance or to infrastructure and manpower accretions. Each case emanating from the SHQ is required to be steered through multiple layers of bureaucracy, that exist in four departments of the MoD as well as its Finance Division and finally in the Ministry of Finance.

Queries are sequential, repetitive and often raised to prevaricate; and every file movement takes weeks, if not months. Adherence to these processes has not only thwarted force modernisation, inspite of recent reforms in procurement procedures, but also affected combat readiness.

Were the SHQ to be brought into the MoD and functionally integrated with it, all the expertise would be available under one roof; thus eliminating the need for queries on file. Moreover collegiate discussions could take place around a table and decisions then recorded on file.

An Un-informed MoD

Finally, with budgets likely to dwindle, in real terms, there is a dire need for prioritising the requirements of weapon systems and other hardware projected by the Services, so that funds can be channelised in the right direction at the right time.

This prioritisation has to be based on an objective evaluation of the need and relevance for a capability projected by a Service, against the prevailing threat scenario. The proposal for acquisition of a capability must not only be justified by the sponsoring Service, it must also stand in the face of competing claims from other Services. Military modernisation, especially in an era of financial stringency, must be viewed as a continuum in which hardware acquisition choices are exercised across the full spectrum of land, maritime and aerospace warfare capabilities, rather than as decisions taken to meet the aspirations or enhance the prestige of one Service or the other.

In the current set-up the generalist MoD civil-servant lacks both the inclination and the necessary experience/expertise regarding military force planning and architecture to critically examine the validity of many weapon systems demanded by the Services. Lacking a collegiate system of consultation with the armed forces, the preferred solution for the un-informed bureaucracy is to stall the case, and delays ranging from 5-15 years are not unknown. Should the SHQ persevere with its demand, approval is eventually accorded—at a huge cost; to the Service in terms of combat capability and to the exchequer in terms of price escalation.

Impediments to Civil-Military Integration

Major resistance to change comes from the civil services who have resolutely stalled every attempt at integration of the SHQ with MoD (and the creation of a Chief of Defence Staff (CDS)), since they apprehend erosion of their influence and authority. They are stubborn in their conviction that advice to the politician must come only from the bureaucracy, whose role in decision-making is the key to 'civilian control' of the armed forces. Notwithstanding their own lack of domain knowledge, the bureaucrats maintain that the SHQ are best retained as Attached Offices of the DoD, and since there is 'adequate consultation' between the MoD and SHQ, further integration is neither necessary nor desirable.

Cross-posting of officers between the MoD and SHQ does not find favour with the bureaucrats because, they argue that the Service officers deputed to MoD would either be of poor caliber or not serve their civilian superiors 'loyally'. At the same time, they are quite clear that it would be *infra dig* for an IAS officer to serve under a military superior. The creation of a specialist cadre of civil servants to serve in national security related billets is rejected because it would be an impediment to the career prospects of rising IAS stars. The consensus is firmly in favour of *status quo*.

The Indian politician is intuitively aware that there are serious flaws in the national security structure, but political survival remains his first priority. His comfort level with the bureaucrat being high, he is happy to leave the management of defence and security matters in his hands. At the same time, he is ill at ease with the soldier and, contrary to all empirical evidence, ready to believe murmurs—possibly originating from bureaucratic or intelligence sources—about the dangers of a praetorian military.

For these reasons politicians have, conveniently, used the contrarian arguments emerging from political circles, the bureaucracy and even from within the military to block reforms that seek to enhance the cohesion, jointness and combat efficiency of the armed forces—or indeed free them from bureaucratic strangleholds.

The Panacea

Resistance to change, both from within the armed forces as well as the bureaucracy is a known phenomenon world-wide, mainly because each community sees it as a zero-sum game. It is for this reason that defence reforms in all major democracies have, been pushed through by a visionary political leadership.

The best example of political activism on this count is the USA, where visionary lawmakers, deeply concerned about national security issues, have ensured that systemic reforms are periodically legislated as laws through Acts of Congress. As a consequence, the bedrock of US national security is formed by the historic

National Security Act of Congress 1947 and the Goldwater-Nichols Defence Reorganisation Act 1986.

Far more important than this is the fact that US lawmakers have unambiguously outlined, in Title 10 of, the US Code of Federal Laws, the functions of the armed forces and their combatant commanders. Title 10 provides the legal basis for the roles, missions and organisation of each of the services as well as the department of defence. By way of contrast, no military functionary, including the three Chiefs, finds mention in any context, in the GoI Rules of Business. At the same time, the Defence Secretary has been designated as the functionary responsible for the defence of India and for the armed forces and their HQs.

It is entirely up to India's lawmakers and politicians to find the time and capacity to take a call on the issue of national security reform. If their wisdom informs them that civil-military dissonance has, indeed, created an urgent need for reforms in India's national security structures, there are a number of options that they can exercise:

- Reports of the 1999 and 2011 TF on security reform can be resurrected and studied afresh to ascertain why certain recommendations were not implemented and whether they can be implemented now.
- A fresh committee/task force can be constituted exclusively for examination of civil-military relations as they pertain to national security, with the mandate to suggest amendments to the GoI Rules of Business that will eliminate ambiguities, streamline functioning of the MoD and sources of internal conflict.
- A Parliamentary Committee can be constituted for the drafting of an Armed Forces Act which specifies the roles, responsibilities and relationship between the MoD and its constituent departments with the Service HQs, and spells out details of the 'national security pyramid' and all its functionaries.

Given the current indifference of India's leadership to national security issues and their overwhelming pre-occupation with politics, the suggestions above may appear unrealistic and Utopian. However, there is nothing in the items mentioned above that a clear-headed and resolute Prime Minister or even Defence Minister cannot implement progressively on his own; through a series of executive fiats.

Conclusion

India's strategic environment is progressively becoming more fraught with hazards. Threats to the nation's security, both internal and external, are far more serious than in any time in the past. The reassurance that we derive from our large military establishment and nuclear arsenal may be quite illusory; because of the shortcomings of our national security structure—civil-military dissonance being a primary fault-line.

Former Prime Minister Manmohan Singh, in his address at the Combined Commanders' Conference (CCS) 2013, making a rare departure from the customary expression of proforma sentiments, focused on two of the most debilitating inadequacies of India's national security edifice. He called for "urgent and tangible progress" in establishment of "the right structures for higher defence management" and spoke of "the appropriate civil-military balance in decision making". He also struck an ironic note by making mention of "the different TF reports that our government has initiated."[27]

The right structure for higher defence management is obviously one in which the armed forces are totally integrated with the MoD, and the appropriate civil-military balance will be struck once they are allowed participation in national security decision-making. However, the fact that recommendations of successive committees, groups of ministers and task forces have been consigned into oblivion speaks, as much of the helplessness of a myopic and beleaguered polity as of an obdurate bureaucracy.

The PM's speech may have been a case of 'too little, too late', but the admission by the head of government, of serious national security voids, and the crying need for reform may act as a goad for the new government in 2014. The established world powers—democracies and autocracies alike—have defused civil-military tensions and retained firm 'civilian control' over their armed forces, by subsuming them within the central edifice of the government. The resultant synergy produces quick and sound decisions and any gaps in military/technical knowledge at the political level are remedied by the availability of integral expertise.

NOTES

1. Smith, Rupert. *The Utility of Force.* London: Penguin, 2005, p. 4.
2. Huntington, Samuel H. *The Soldier and the State.* Cambridge, Mass: The Belknap Press, 1957, p.2.
3. Ibid, p. 81.
4. Ibid, p. 83.
5. Ibid, p. 84.
6. Von Clausewitz, Carl, *On War,* New Jersey, Princeton University Press, 1984, p. 610.
7. Ibid, p. 608.
8. The Economist, *Can India Become a Great Power?* April 05, 2013.
9. Tanham, George K., *Indian Strategic Thought: an Interpretive Essay.* Santa Monica, RAND Corporation, 1992, p. 52.
10. Ibid, p. 66.
11. Ibid, p. 69.
12. Vas, Eric A Lt Gen. *Subhash Chandra Bose: The Man and his Times.* Lancer Publications: New Delhi, 2005, p. 115.

13. Ibid, p. 150.
14. Ibid, p. 159.
15. Singh, Satyindra, RAdm, *Blueprint to Bluewater*, New Delhi, Lancer International, 1992, pp. 30-31.
16. Tanham, p. 70.
17. Ibid. p. 71.
18. Hiranandani, GM, VAdm (Retd), *Transition to Guardianship: the Indian Navy 1991-2000.* Lancer International: New Delhi, 2009, p. 276.
19. Ibid, p. 278.
20. Ibid, p. 279.
21. Ibid, pp. 279-80.
22. Subrahmanyam, K, et al, *Kargil Review Committee Report*, Sage Publication: New Delhi 1999, p. 258.
23. In April 2012 the Indian Express carried a highly controversial story on allegedly unplanned troop movement and the resultant civil-military discord, see Shekhar Gupta, Ritu Sarin and Pranab Dhal Samanta, "The January night Raisina Hill was spooked: Two key Army units moved towards Delhi without notifying the Government," *Indian Express*, April 04, 2012.
24. Prakash, Arun, Adm. (Retd), *Defence Reforms: Contemporary Debates and Issues*, IDSA Monograph Series No.6, July 2012, p. 23.
25. *Reforming the National Security System*, Recommendations of the Group of Ministers, February 2001, p. 99.
26. *Central Secretariat Manual of Office Procedure*, 13th Edition, Ministry of Personnel, Dept of Administrative Reforms, New Delhi, September 2010, p. 12.
27. Excerpts of address by the PM at the Combined Commanders' Conference on November 22, 2013, accessed online at http://pmindia.nic.in/speech-details.php?nodeid=1396 on January 01, 2014.

4

India's Defence Organisation: A Re-Orientation and the Need for Change

Srinivasapuram Krishnaswamy

Indian Military: A Historical Perception

Role and objectives of the Military in any democracy is dictated by the government of the day and bound by constitutional provisos. The Armed Forces in India are primarily responsible for ensuring territorial integrity of the nation. The responsibility for national defence rests with the Cabinet. The Military is the State's instrument of war and represents the nation's coercive power. Considering the challenges posed, the Military has got to be a disciplined professional body highly trained, well organised, well managed and remain credible. The focus of the Military is 'war-fighting' and it fights to win—staking precious lives and resources. Battles would be fought against similarly equipped and trained Militaries. Winning calls for hard training, good strategy, vigilance and preparation among other essentials. Consequence of failure could be enormous that could affect a nation's morale besides suffering serious losses. Any changes/improvement/ proposals on structure or organisation or role of the Armed Forces must conform to these principles.

Indian Government and the military to a large extent were traditionally confined to a 'colonial mind-set', that defined how the 'Native Military Forces' in India should be structured, organised, trained and employed to serve the colonial interests. Traditionally, since the days of British Raj the Indian Military was equipped and trained to fight defensive operations. Entire combat inventory that the military had was the 'pass-on' from the Wars by the British. Soon after independence, the first call to the military came in 1948 to defend. Thus, the primary role of Indian Military got established—to ensure territorial integrity of Republic of India. The Government of India that rose out of peaceful independence movement felt use of military to be the last resort to save the nation and therefore an unavoidable necessity. At the other end of the spectrum of national strategy were those of Europe and America. These nations traditionally employed their military as 'Expeditionary Force' to expand their influence and trade (and riches). They became quite adept in employing military to their advantage. Significant effort and investments were made by these nations to develop military technology towards greater fire-power and speed. Strategies were continually evolved to out-smart their adversaries and achieve 'Domination' as the objective. There were no such compulsions for the Indian Republic which focussed on keeping the nation together and alleviate poverty. Therefore, it is no surprise that 'military strategic thinking' in Indian mind was never nurtured. Few flashes that appeared in this could not ignite action at policy levels. Military systems in the West were continually 'modernised' through Research and Development (R&D) driven by strategic necessity. India simply bought many of these 'off-the-shelf' and exploited their use in Indian environment. The first Maritime Squadron of the Indian Air Force (IAF) consisted of a few Liberator bombers that were salvaged and reconditioned by Hindustan Aeronautics Limited (HAL) from the junk left behind by the US Air Force (USAF) after the War. Cold war politics such as non-alignment prevented India's access to global military technologies. Subsequently, having no choice, Indian military hardware was mostly confined to those of Soviet origin supplied at 'political concessional' rate.

India's gradual ascendency as a 'Potential Power' called for a strong military to contribute to peace in the region. However, the political mind-set restricted our vision. The state of economy gave low priority to spending on the military. India hit upon non-alignment as the means to obtain collective peace and avoid expensive non-development expenditure. But all hell broke loose when China struck India in 1962. Chinese troops over-ran Indian positions and annexed a huge tract of land. Over the next decade, India had to fight two wars and prove its own mettle. Lack of adequate capabilities to design, develop and produce worthy operational systems indigenously had been a serious handicap to the Indian military. Regrettably, the old 'mind-set' rarely changed that affected developing a strong enough military Force that is balanced and well supported indigenously which is necessary for a Regional Power in the making.

Management Dysfunctions

It is therefore not the budgetary resources alone that are responsible for slow and erratic progress but the limited perception of military as being 'Defence (orientated) Forces' that was managed by a government body that is traditionally risk-averse and devoid of expertise on military matters. Over the last two decades, elsewhere in the world saw Revolution in Military Affairs (RMA) which to a large extent by-passed the Indian Military. Many Committees were formed to explore ways to improve organisational efficiency. Much of the recommendations were either not implemented or done half-heartedly. Political level lacked vision and the bureaucracy avoided accountability for long delays to obtain decisions. Organisationally some changes came about as the consequence of Kargil Committee report through which few financial powers were extended to the military along with improved authority. However, no change has taken place at the core-ethos or functioning of Ministry of Defence (MoD). The politico-military structure was weak and unsuited to nurture a professional military along the lines of Western democracies.

The Government of India gave importance to maintain credibility of its Defence Forces since its failure to defeat Chinese aggression in 1962. It took some 50 years after independence to emerge as a confident democracy with a voice of its own and to build a reasonable economic strength. However, achievements in the military field fell short of the resolve. Since 1962, on every occasion that a military operation was envisaged (1965, 1971, Kargil, "Op Parakram"), the military was found ill prepared mostly due to shortage and un-serviceability of operational systems. Connectivity between the government and military was disharmonious and poor that led to serious delays in acquiring urgently needed operational systems and spare parts.

War-Fighting Capability and Strategy

When pushed into an adverse situation, the Indian Armed Forces performed credibly against odds. If one may call it a 'strategy', India had been passive and consistently shown reluctance to pre-empt or to punish perpetrators irrespective of what the intimidation may be. India may have got branded as a 'Soft-State' but this should be acceptable if there was a hesitation to act, or incapability to defend. Adversaries took initiatives and often surprised Indian defences that India had to absorb and respond. India and its hostile neighbours possess nuclear weapons. Global powers and other neighbouring countries would intervene at any signs of serious armed conflict in the region. If such conflicts do arise, the military must achieve its objective quickly in weeks or a month at the most before being halted. Therefore, the essence of future wars/combat operations would be speed and mobility and long gone are the days of lumbering manoeuvres. Interestingly, military movement and deployment are and would be continually monitored by satellites and other intelligence networks and hence surprise would be near-impossible. To manage contingencies effectively calls for comprehensive ownership and capability package with each Service constituting all operational, support and maintenance systems besides combat Units. This is vital considering the sharp short battles that the Indian Military is expected to fight.

Operational Commands of the Indian Army are structured as 'geographical Armies' (their Commanders-in-Chiefs are addressed as 'Army Commanders') denoting that the 'Armies' are capable of planning and executing operations independently. Each of the three Services have their interface elements as an entity under two-star rank in the Command formations of other two Services to facilitate secure planning and effective execution. Once the Services HQs and MoD approve an operation, these could be launched speedily by the Commands concerned. Operations planned and executed in a delegated manner offer secure and speedy execution. Esprit-de-corps is vital to achieve the impossible. It is essential that these traditions are maintained.

CDS: 'Over-Kill'

From the experiences gained so far, one could conclude that the military organisational structure withstood the test of time. Untested concept of Chief of Defence Staff (CDS) in Indian context may not work a miracle since a single centralised structure (of all military operations) is expected to be slow at decision-making and impersonal. Such a centralised operational authority in a democracy could be better suited to manage operations to meet 'out-of-area contingencies' or for a military that has global responsibilities. India, as explained, is focused on territorial defence and not expeditions. Indian Government never articulated any opinion or wish for India to be a Regional Power or willingness to deploy military overseas in support of friendly governments. Once the Indian Prime Minister voiced from the Red-Fort of India's interest from Gulf of Aden to Sea of Japan but no clear strategy emerged other than articulation of 'look-East' policy to develop trade and other relations. India's arm-chair strategists professed endlessly how India must pursue its 'Power' and Influence regionally and globally. Indian Navy on its own has articulated a strategy to explore 'Blue Waters' and spear-head India's strategic influence but it had little government backing. They towed with the US Navy learning the art of protecting convoys against piracy in Indian Ocean. Japan has welcomed India's desire to promote peace in Indian Ocean Region (IOR). However, translation into action lacked government backing or initiative. It would need tremendous logistics and support infrastructure including appropriate ships, logistics chain and protection systems to be in place (and lots of resources). Today, the Navy lacks ability to recover a damaged submarine in 'Blue Waters' and has had serious problems recovering a Submarine even within a well-equipped harbour. Wherever Vikramaditya goes, it would be pursued by satellites and other means very closely by our adversaries. For a long time to come, India's directive for its military would remain that of protecting its national boundaries from trouble-makers.

India is not expected to fight long protracted battles. Therefore, it would be un-fructuous to make organisation lead-footed and heavy. The CDS for an operational role for India that aims only to defend its own territory is an 'over-kill'. CDS would be more meaningful if Indian military has a role to play in the region. In the interim, military officers of appropriate experience should be posted in Ministry of External Affairs (MEA) and interact with military attaches and Service HQs to effectively contribute to diplomacy. This would give a good exposure to military diplomacy, prepare better and to participate effectively if and when envisaged.

What India needs is a 'mean and light-footed' elite military that can perform at lightning speed before being halted by intervention. Yet, India's current military structure has the capability to mobilise its forces (as done during Op Parakram) if and when required. Indian military is already flooded with too many top ranks (related to any other military of its size in the world) after 'Ajay Vikram Singh Committee' and we should not make it more 'Brass-Heavy' like some South East Asian nations.

Kargil Review Committee (KRC) dwelt on the need to modernise the military, streamline procurement policies and establish an effective partnership between the Defence Research and Development Organisation (DRDO) and the Services. The Report also focused attention to streamline the interface between the Service Headquarters and the MoD. Among the recommendations made, an important one was creation of a single senior most military point of contact, the CDS to advise the government on defence matters as well as direct all operations undertaken by Indian military. An Integrated Defence Staff (IDS) under a three-star Commander-in-Chief post was to be created to manage the range of staff and operational management under the CDS. When the CDS is in place, the Chiefs of Staff would be reporting to the CDS but retain access to Minister of Defence. A Strategic Forces Command and Andaman and Nicobar (A&N) Command were to be created that would function directly under the CDS. The government implemented majority of the recommendations made by the Committee but for the post of CDS. The IDS were created so also Strategic Forces Command (SFC) and A&N Command. These three structures (created in 2001) reported to Chairman, Chiefs of Staff Committee (COSC). Creation of CDS has been an 'on-going' dialogue with the government and yet to conclude.

Since independence, it had been the practice for the government to discuss directly with the concerned Service Chiefs or at times with a Commander-in-Chief about a situation that they can absorb quickly and give direction. Matters concerning security within the national boundaries or at the borders are complex and require quick decisions as well as close monitoring unlike those that may happen at far off territories beyond the shores that do not directly affect the public. It is not practical that one senior most General would be the single point of contact with the government to brief and interact in all situations at least till India settles its borders. It would be more prudent to manage operations in a delegated manner which would be more secure.

Ideally, all war-fighting, training and operational logistics/maintenance should be left to the respective Chiefs of Staff as is managed today. India need not copy other countries blindly but develop its own model. Difficulties faced in effective functioning of the military are NOT due to weaknesses in managing operations. But these are about how the government manages the military. Practical difficulties have been about MoD-Military relations and getting decisions on resolving issues related to routine management and procurement. This had led to enormous differences and heart-burn. Military brass is allergic to bureaucracy wielding power over their institutions.

A Permanent Chairman, Chiefs of Staff Committee

The Chairman, Chief of Staff Committee(COSC) post as it stands today is headed by the senior most of the three Services Chiefs of Staff who has the responsibility to manage his own Service apart from overseeing SFC, A&N Command and oversee the work being done by Chief of Integrated Staff to the Chairman, Chiefs of Staff Committee (CISC). The CISC is given the responsibility to process the modernisation programme of the three Services, plan and report on budgetary matters, manage the work of Intelligence wings of the three Services and function as the interface between Service HQs and MoD on most of the management and organisational matters. While he is given adequate senior and functional staff, current Chairman COSC invariably finds it difficult to meet the functional needs of his post due to commitments towards his own Service. The government is consistently blamed for not providing adequate budgetary support for modernisation. This could only be partly true. Macro-management process of MoD indicates lack of continual monitoring of the health of the military such as status of inventory, manpower and training besides testing operational capabilities against war-plans. Unlike the US or other Western democracies, Indian Government does not conduct annual review of the status (including inventory) of the armed forces, their deficiencies and capabilities to undertake operations against defined threats. Also, no comprehensive document is made annually on threat to our nation and steps to be taken (from which the annual plan must emerge). The combined commanders' conference that takes place once a year with the Prime Minister is not really a 'conference' but more a ritual. MoD rarely conducts or directs studies on ways of improving existing structures and management methods (unless these are the outcome of an investigation). Suggestions that go from Services HQ lose their momentum once they enter the labyrinth of MoD offices. Reforms of MoD and the Military must take cognisance of historical background and the status of the 'Military-in-being' which should lead to taking most appropriate steps to improve in a time-bound manner. This calls for perseverance.

Ideally, the post of Chairman, Chiefs of Staff Committee should be made permanent and independent of Service HQs and given the responsibility for well-being of the military, ensuring that it is well equipped, well protected and its equipment and men in good order to take on operational commitments when required. Most of the woes of the military are in these areas. In the new configuration, he would also be responsible to ensure that the military modernisation is well planned and executed and that the budget is spent correctly and effectively. Cost of managing Defence would be another important concern. Cost of maintenance of operational systems including the cost of spares is going sky-high. Infrastructure costs such as maintenance of harbours, runways and ground support systems and civil infrastructure are moving up at a rate most unanticipated. Every pay-commission increases the burden on pay, allowances and pension since expectations run high.

It would be sooner than later that the compulsions would force the military to trim its man-power, tighten inventory control and apply modern management techniques. Even the Chinese have initiated serious exercise to reduce military manpower. Archaic methods need to be replaced by modern scientific management. The Services and MoD need specialists on financial control, contracting, operational logistics and supply chain. There has got to be a more systematic way to manage. Planning and financial and performance accountability need to improve. Organisationally, there is significant scope to integrate and optimise activities which would improve cost-effectiveness of the military. Working on all these would need experience and firm directions. A permanent Chairman COSC would be in the ideal position to handle these difficult areas. He would interact with Comptroller and Auditor General (C&AG) and various Committees on behalf of the military and also maintain harmonious relationship with the Service Chiefs. This would permit Chiefs of Staff to focus on quality training, sharpen capabilities, test out war-plans and evolve strategies.

Subsequently, the post of permanent Chairman, Chiefs of Staff Committee could well be called the 'CDS'. Chief of Joint Staff (CJS) could be more appropriate—but this post would not have any responsibilities towards conduct of operations. An efficient proposal could be to remove the CISC position after appointment of the Chairman COSC reducing one three-star post. Current CISC organisation has three or four three-stars who could effectively manage without a CISC as a flat organisation.

The post of CJS should be elevated to Minister of State and brought 'into the government' since the argument has gone on for too long for the military to be a department or an 'Attached Office'. The CJS would work directly under the

Minister of Defence and help him in understanding the issues. The elevation would relieve the difficulties of the Service HQs dealing with the bureaucracy. The CJS being a Minister of State (MoS) and having IDS as his secretariat with a complete range of staff could smoothen out difficulties without impinging on the work and responsibilities of the Defence Secretary. IDS would interact with the bureaucracy to resolve issues other than those concerning operations and hence would reduce the need for Service HQs to deal with MoD and its bureaucracy.

The Armed Forces Medical Services (AFMS) that function independently under the MoD should be brought under the CJS as is done in the UK. This would also help Medical Services to project their needs and issues more systematically and also gain from working with IDS.

Theatre Commands

A concept for India to have 'Theatre Commands' (military) had been in circulation for a long time. Theatres are generally interpreted as regions beyond national boundary that have military significance. Indian military does not envisage a 'Theatre' beyond national boundary. However, Indian Military is expected to support Diplomacy and maintain good understanding of the happenings that may impinge on our own national security. In recent times, this idea has re-emerged substantially modified referring to Theatres as permanent military organisational structures within national borders to improve military management and operational efficiency. It suggests demarcating the country into geographically separate 'Military Theatres and unify operational control of the three Services present in each Theatre under one 'Theatre-Commander'. Each Theatre is expected to have unified and comprehensive operational and support elements from the three Services 'Under Command' that would in turn would report to CDS. India currently has a unified command (A&N) initiated as an experiment. This Command operates with limited autonomy where all its operational resources are held and trained in the mainland with their current formations. Creation of Military Theatres would call for additional ranks, personnel and infrastructure. This would also lead to expanding the existing cantonments or create new ones. Such expansion could create a discomfort among the public who may feel a threat to be imminent. Theatre Commander would have no responsibility for training which would rest with the individual service. This could create a discontinuity which is not conducive to operational effectiveness. 'Theatre Command' and 'Operational Theatres' are jargons of the World War and certainly India should not have any military Theatre within its own geographic boundary. No democracy of regional influence in the world has Theatre Commands within its contiguous geographical bound.

A better alternative could be to merge geographical Command HQs of the three Services under one common roof in their respective areas under which the Commanders-in-Chief of the three Services and their staff shall function. This would enhance the opportunities to work together at all levels within Command HQs. The Command infrastructure and administration should then be pooled to have a common support system. This in effect would permit closure of two other Command HQs premises in each area and thus help reduce expenditure and manpower. This could effectively optimise resources and encourage joint planning and functioning. However, this may not prove practical or easily acceptable by the Services.

Colonial Remnants

Military cantonments and other titles such as "Garrison Engineer" are the remnants of colonial establishments and India has still not got rid of them! In fact, there is strong case for India to dismantle military cantonments and dispose surplus land held by Military Estates. We could follow the example of British Government which has decided in principle to sell off a large chunk of real estate assets other than the essentials. As part of the drive, last year UK Government decided to sell off their historic War Office at an estimated cost of 100m Pounds Sterling. Indian Government could follow the example and give a serious consideration to wind down the department of Military Estate and hand-over all surplus land to State governments. Shedding surplus real estate and closing superfluous offices would permit reduction of manpower deployed in non-military functions.

Organisation for Joint Operations

The KRC recommended radical changes in the apex decision making structure of MoD and integration of Service HQs with the MoD. The Group of Ministers called for greater "Jointness'" in the armed forces. To take an example, the British Government brought-in a major 'Defence Reform' during 2010 to the structure and top management of UK MoD and the Services. The objectives were to improve organisational efficiency, accountability and cost-efficiency that included reducing manpower to the minimum. One of the drivers was to create a 'Joint Forces Command' (JFC) that would enable joint warfare development and reduce infrastructural costs. 'Jointness' require some clarity. The British, after years of experience and experimentation have come to believe that an "...Effective MoD is one which builds on the strengths of the individual Services and the Civil Service and does so within a single Defence framework **that ensures the Whole is more than the Sum of its parts...**". It is therefore a time-tested theory that that the ethos and strengths of single Service must be preserved what-so-ever the frame work that they may come into being. The opinion of British MoD is "...focus on Service Chiefs on running their Service and empower them to perform their role effectively...". It is most sensible approach where the Services are given freedom to manage with financial authority and yet stay accountable to "**Financial Accountability and Control**".

Typically, efficient management demands that each Service operate in its core-domain. For example, detection, interception and destruction of enemy aerial assaults are integral responsibility of the Air Force and so also Interdiction, Air-Superiority and 'Air Offensive'. Navy is responsible totally for operations at sea and the Army holds the ground. However, certain military capabilities that are duplicated or triplicated could be brought under joint basis to manage and to operate more cost-effectively. For future Joint Operations, certain modalities are necessary which are developed as Standard Operating Procedure (SOP) based on well researched and tested 'Joint Doctrine'. British MoD believes that certain operations must be delivered on a 'lead-Service basis' and that 'Jointly' should not be pursued for its 'own sake'. Many capabilities such as Intelligence, Surveillance, Targeting, Acquisition, Reconnaissance, Command and Information Systems, Cyber and many more are not single-service orientated but each of these are being led by one designated Service. In the UK, these capabilities are developed in support of Expeditionary Forces and not just to defend their Island. Their battlefields could be anywhere in the globe! Similarly, the US Joint Forces and Special Forces are a part of Expeditionary package. Focus for Indian military as dictated extends only up to the national boundaries. Therefore, some aspects of Western military management structure will not work for India or these would be outside our scope or 'over-kills'. India may seriously run into 'expenditure trap' imitating Western military structure and technology-driven-sophistication. The West, with all its sophistication got beaten by turbaned horsemen with archaic weapons in Afghanistan and in Vietnam by rural militia with rudimentary weapons.

Modern technology such as 'Net-Centric Operations' facilitates an integrated, secure, flexible and parallel processing of demands and directions in the battle field seamlessly and not processed through traditional top-down approach. These systems work in a manner that decision-making is distributed down to the last soldier. The 'sensor-to-shooter' time in modern warfare is less than eight minutes while it could be hours or a day in Indian context. Such speed can be achieved only by directly linking a soldier in the field into the decision-making matrix. The modern 'package' of decision-making is a total package meshing decision makers with highly automated combat systems and real-time information centres. Such capabilities do not exist in India and may take a decade or more to get close enough. For India, It is nearly impossible to integrate such complex command and control systems with weapon systems that are sourced from different origin and vintages (Being L-1s after global bid). Indian method of procurement does not easily adapt to standardisation. Therefore, military management structure would continue to remain traditional for a long time to come. Europe and the US have effected major changes in Joint Operations only during the last decade or so. This was possible by advances in weapon systems that are closely integrated with sensors that are distributed. Today, it is possible to give a mid-way correction to a weapon launched from air, by a ship at sea or a soldier on ground. That is a true integration! What a soldier in battlefield observes is seen in real time by his commander sitting miles away or may be a thousand miles away and that would be a modern network!

For India, 'Joint Capability Assets' must be identified and brought under the Permanent Chairman of the Chiefs of Staff Committee that could be renamed as Chief of Joint Staff (CJS). These are essential support for conduct of operations but do not strictly confine to any one Service that include functions such as Intelligence, Space management, Industrial functions (4th line maintenance), procurement/modernisation, civil engineering and construction, Cyber, budget management, education, Ex-servicemen welfare and Internal Security support. Some elements of these could be deputed to function at operational commands based on the need. Integrating Intelligence assets have already been initiated under the Chairman, Chiefs of Staff and so also National Defence University (NDU) and all related higher-end military education. The importance of inter-operability is well understood and there is significant positive movement taking place in this sphere. Management of Space Assets and Cyber is also being centrally managed by the Chairman, Chiefs of Staff. We need a government and bureaucracy who would work closely with the military and understand complex issues related to operating and maintaining assets and managing personnel. This calls for integration of military top management with the government.

War fighting should be led by the Service that has the experience and is trained for the specific purpose. Accordingly, combat domains are differentiated between the three Services. Air Force for example would provide the required air support and afford air defence cover for all operations undertaken by the other two Services; besides these, they have other independent roles as well such as strike and air-defence. Every Service is used to integrating different skills and specialisation. The Army for example has specialised Arms such as Artillery and Armoured and Special Forces which are integrated to achieve a certain objective. There could be serious shortage in some of the elements; being so, they would be 'shared' depending on priority. Similarly, Services extend support to each other as required and prioritised. Much of these are planned and anticipated jointly. It is essential that the plans are well made and understood. Adequate means and communications should be available to monitor in real time and to make changes as required.

The difficulties of the past have been about poor interface communication and inadequate inter-operability. There has got to be greater joint training and joint exercise to achieve good understanding. The difficulties cannot be overcome by simply demanding all support forces to be 'Under-Command' which spells danger to flexibility and speed of operation. Certain resources, including heavy artillery or Air Force strike elements are shared between many adjacent combat formations that make it impossible for these forces to be brought 'under-command' but would be accountable for their output. These have to be learnt through the process once the 'framework' of structure starts operating.

A&N Command

The A&N Command has been in existence for a while. The C-in-C is rotated between the three Services every two years or so. It is exercised more as a 'right' and strict rotation between the Services is followed but continuity of Command has not been the criteria. The operational assets are maintained and trained in the main land. The tri-service staffs manage routine function and the three Services do not consider these positions to be very important because nothing much happens there! The structure as a joint command was more a 'show-case' and an experiment—now a stone tied to the leg. The government must review the requirement. There are good reasons to revert this Command to the custody of the Navy. SFC on the other hand is functioning very purposefully and the inter-services environment works efficiently.

Army Medical Corps

The Army Medical Corps, which functions directly under MoD for all practical purposes (though expected to be managed by Chairman, Chiefs of Staff Committee) should be brought under the CJS. This would remove existing anomalies.

Summary

India's military was built over the years through sacrifice and hard work and most importantly with immense support from the public at large. It is capable and respected. To manage effectively periodic upgrade is essential, not just the assets alone but also management and structure.

Cost-Effectiveness. Military expenditure might run into a wall without strong accountability and close monitoring. The government must monitor the status of inventory and combat status of personnel regularly which require a real-time 'Status-Board'. Upkeep of equipment must be assured as the first priority. Instead of budget driven, the military must be run expenditure driven. Currently there is no interest or incentive to save on expenditure. On the contrary, there is always a rush to spend the budget by March 31 of every year! This requires a major attitudinal change. Serious effort must be initiated to keep the military lean and mean. Teeth-to-tail ratio of our military is poor and higher ranks are inflated. Military must have full authority over revenue expenditure. The military must have specialists integrally to support financial management and control. Cost-accounting should be introduced of all activities and so also specialists in finance, contracting and logistics management inducted. We should be able to individually cost running of each Battalion, each Squadron of aircraft and each Ship and evaluate variations and reasons. We should be able to get realistic assessment of cost of man-power and analyse every heading of expenditure from shoe-lace to Vikramaditya. This requires a strong leadership at MoD; that would be CJS in the capacity of MOS.

Permanent Chairman Chiefs of Staff. The post of Chairman, Chiefs of Staff should be made permanent and renamed as CJS (Chief of Joint Staff). The CJS would head the current Integrated Defence Staff and would be responsible for 'the military in being' other than operations, operational training and combat support which would be managed by respective Chiefs of Staff. The Joint Assets discussed in Para 26 would be held under CJS and deployed in operational Commands as required. Formation of Joint Forces Command may become necessary if and when India becomes truly a Regional Power. The CJS would be a part of the government and given a 'Minister of State' status. He would advise the government on all matters of the military other than operations. Being 'in the government' there would be a better cohesion between the military and the Minister of Defence. The CJS as Minister's direct subordinate would monitor the 'Status Board' of the military on behalf of the Minister and prepare an annual document on threat perception, capability of military to handle these, priorities and oversee budget preparation and allocation. This would negate the yawning gap between the government and the military. Strategic Forces Command would be directly under CJS. A&N Command should be reviewed for reverting it back to Navy. The tenure of the CJS should be a minimum of three years.

Chiefs of Staff. The three Chiefs of Staff would continue to exercise operational and training responsibility of respective Services. Support infrastructure necessary for operations, routine maintenance including the Bases would be held and managed by the Chiefs of Staff.

Joint Operations. Chiefs of Staffs would organise and train their forces for joint operations. They should further explore enhancing cross-posting at field and staff level between the Services. Joint planning function should be systematised. The CJS should take active part in advising, guiding and supporting the Services towards cooperation and joint functioning.

Research on how to improve Defence organisation and infrastructure has no end. But it is important that the government of the day should spend time and effort to analyse and implement improvements. Importantly, there should be political consensus across all political parties, especially the opposition. The structure and decision-making are extremely complex and should not be played around to meet a limited objective.

5

Higher Defence Organisation and The Pursuit of Jointness

Deepak Kapoor

Higher defence organisation and jointness are two seemingly unrelated subjects, which, on initial examination may leave one with the perception that both of them should have been dealt with separately. However, if one studies them a bit deeper, one would realise that both are interlinked and work towards achieving the same objective, viz. 'a strong, efficient and responsive military'. While higher defence organisation seeks to provide a structure for the defence of the country which incorporates the current realities at the national, regional and global level and crystallises a timely and appropriate response to developing crisis situations, jointness is one of the important means, among others, to achieve it in the least time making optimum use of available resources. Thus, while the former suggests structural improvements in the organisation, the latter is a refined means of executing policy laid down by the organisation.

Having said that, it needs to be clarified that conceptually at another level, the two subjects are diversely different. While the objective of achieving timely and appropriate military response may be the same in both cases, methodology of how it is to be brought about differs. Higher defence organisation looks at the whole gamut of handling of defence of the country to include national security, national strategy, interaction with other organs of the government, financial support, modernisation, response to crisis situations both internal and external etc. Jointness, on the other hand, is intra military in character and is a means that any good higher defence organisation must seek to achieve. In its wake, it brings in synergy, optimum use, professionalism, economy of resource and focussed approach. Thus, it would only be appropriate to discuss them separately to begin with. Subsequently, the two would be synthesised to arrive at the common objective.

Higher Defence Organisation

Conceptually, the stake holders in higher defence organisation of any country would be the people, the political authority duly supported by the bureaucracy and the military. The people are the most important stake holders because the organisation is created to ensure national security. The political authority being the democratically elected government of the country is expected to ensure territorial integrity and defence of the country. The bureaucracy is expected to carry out directions of the political authority and give advice whenever it is sought. Finally, the military performs the dual function of rendering professional advice and undertaking execution of approved plans. Such an arrangement presupposes adequate knowledge of defence related matters by all the stake holders, especially since vital issues of national security are involved. Within this broad overall design, different nations have created their own higher defence frameworks, depending upon what suits their governance structures best. With passage of time, these frameworks have been further refined to suit their respective requirements.

History of Higher Defence Organisation in India

Our higher defence organisation was set up, based on the advice of Lord Ismay, by a cabinet resolution on September 24, 1947. It envisaged setting up of the Defence Committee of the Cabinet (DCC) to take all decisions related to military power which required cabinet approval. The armed forces chiefs were to be in attendance and hence, a deficit in terms of regular dialogue between military and political leaders was born with this proposal. In practice, the chiefs had direct access to the PM Shri Jawaharlal Nehru which reduced dramatically after the 'Thimayya Affair' in 1959. But the DCC had stopped functioning by 1957 when Krishna Menon took over as the Defence Minister.

Simultaneously with DCC, the most important committee that was set up based on Lord Ismay's recommendations, on the military side, was the Chiefs Of Staff Committee (COSC), on the lines of the British and US pattern, which was located in the Cabinet Secretariat. The COSC was to be supported by a series of other committees to address details of coordination between the services and the Ministry of Defence (MoD), to provide for quick decision making. The incorporation of civil servants as members of each of these committees was meant to eliminate the need for detailed scrutiny of their decisions by the MoD. It was also meant to sow the seeds of civil military integration. It was envisaged that with passage of time, the three Service Head Quarters (SHQ) will be fully integrated with the MoD.

Here, at the risk of digression, it must be clarified that the Indian military has never, since independence, ever questioned the concept of 'civilian supremacy' over the military. It implies control by the elected representatives of the people in a democracy, viz. the parliament and the political hierarchy. Unlike in some of our neighbouring countries, the Indian military has always remained apolitical. However, since independence, this concept of 'civilian supremacy' has gradually been sought to be converted to 'bureaucratic control' by a wily bureaucracy with a series of seemingly innocuous actions, thus delivering a body blow to national interest and national security in the long run. Lack of military knowledge of the political class, transitory nature of the political hierarchy, its excessive dependence on bureaucracy and its inherent fear of the military played upon by the bureaucrat has not helped matters.

The first of these actions was the promulgation of the Rules of Business of the Government of India in 1961. As per these rules of business, with one stroke, the COSC and SHQ were classified as 'attached' offices within the MoD (like CPWD) thus effectively excluding them from decision making loops of the government of India on all matters, including those pertaining to national security. The service chiefs find no mention in the 2nd schedule of the Allocation of Business Rules and the following responsibilities of the MoD are obviously, therefore, assigned to the Defence Secretary:

- Defence of India and every part thereof including preparation for defence and all such parts as may be conducive in times of war to its prosecution and after its termination to effective demobilisation.
- The Armed Forces of the Union, namely, Army, Navy and Air Force.
- Integrated headquarters of the MoD comprising of Army Headquarters, Naval headquarters, Air Headquarters and Defence Staff Headquarters.

Mr Krishna Menon took over as the Defence Minister in 1957 and under him the methodology of higher defence management which was envisaged by Lord Ismay became the first casualty. Institutionalised decision making gave way to a system of personal preferences where merit was given a back seat. Over time, DCC lost its relevance and ad hoc decision making based on political expediency became the norm. In 1962, the COSC was taken out of the cabinet secretariat and thus was no longer part of the government, giving effect to the aforesaid Rules of Business of the Government of India 1961. When the Chinese struck in October 1962, a total lack of higher defence management further compounded the disastrous consequences. Post 1962, the DCC was never revived and instead gave way to Cabinet Committee on Security (CCS) to which the service chiefs were invitees on request. This signalled further weakening of the link between the political hierarchy and military leadership on national security matters.

Here, we need to take note of the fact that whenever the political and military leadership have worked in harmony and understanding, the outcome of India's conflicts with its adversaries has been favourable. Thus during 1948, 1965, 1971 and 1999 conflicts, the political leadership of the day, recognising its limited knowledge of matters military, sought and obtained sound professional advice from the military leadership and the end results were excellent. In contrast, in 1962, when the political authority was not in touch with reality because of lack of synchronisation with military leadership, we suffered a major defeat. A second aspect which needs to be noted is that during all these conflicts, while there was informal interaction between the political and military leadership frequently, a formalised institutional framework for such interaction was never put in place. In the long run, this has harmed national security. The only change that occurred on the institutional side post 1971 and up to 1999 was the creation of Defence Planning Staff (DPS) under the COSC in 1986.

Kargil Review Committee

Precisely for these reasons, post the Kargil conflict of 1999, the Government of India realised the overwhelming need of defence reforms in the interest of national security and constituted the Kargil Review Committee (KRC) to come up with its recommendations. The KRC observed, "India is perhaps the only major democracy where the armed forces headquarters are outside the apex governmental structure. The status quo is often mistakenly defended as embodying civilian ascendancy over the armed forces, which is not the real issue. In fact locating the service headquarters in the government will further enhance civilian supremacy".

The KRC made a set of excellent recommendations which were approved by the government for implementation. The actual implementation of the KRC recommendations, however, is a different story. In brief, these could be divided into three categories. In the first category would fall those recommendations which were considered benign and whose implementation would fall within the services and their effect would be limited to the military alone, e.g. creation of the Integrated Defence Staff (IDS), Defence Intelligence Agency (DIA), Andaman and Nicobar Command (ANC), Strategic Forces Command (SFC) etc.

In the second category would fall those recommendations which had an effect on other organisations and which led to changes in the existing methodology and functioning, e.g. integration of service headquarters with the MoD, creation of civil military liaison mechanisms at various levels from Command HQ to operational formations, need to modernise the military, establish think tanks, invigorate universities and organise exchanges between them and the policy community etc. These were imperfectly implemented and tweaked in such a manner that even though the paper requirement of implementing was met, in reality the status quo was left untouched, thus effectively killing what was sought to be achieved.

The third category involved creation of structures which would result in taking away some powers from both the services as well as the bureaucracy and creation of new equations between the political authority, the military and the bureaucracy, e.g. creation of the post of Chief of Defence Staff (CDS), future pay commissions to have to have a senior retired 'defence advisor', publication of war history and declassification etc. To creation of the CDS, resistance stemmed from both the bureaucracy and some elements within the military, specifically the Air force. The bureaucracy worked overtime to highlight differences within the military while effectively concealing its own objections.

Resistance Over Creation of the CDS

Unlike other countries, Indian military is approximately 85 per cent army, 10 per cent air force and five per cent navy. While the army and the navy fight in the medium of land and ocean respectively, air force classically supports the conflicts to dominate these two mediums. This lack of separate identity coupled with its size compared to the army, has left the air force with misplaced apprehensions of being swamped by the army, thus not getting its due in the envisaged scheme of things. In reality, the air force has a distinct identity of its own within the Indian military and its recognition as one of the battle winning factors is never in doubt. It is, therefore, bound to retain its prominence in any scheme of things and apprehensions to the contrary do not appear to be justified.

The bureaucratic resistance stems from its efforts to retain the role of sole adviser, arbiter and executioner of the political authority. Its military knowledge being limited, the political authority is dependent on outside advice to even run day to day affairs, leave alone aspects of national security, strategy, objectives and operations. This is rendered to him by the bureaucrat, whose own knowledge of professional military matters is limited to the extent of exposure he may have had to the MoD in his earlier tenures. While the generalist nature of the bureaucracy may be acceptable in the other ministries dealing with the civil side, the MoD requires professional military advice to tackle vital issues of national security. Recognising this need, the KRC had recommended creation of the CDS. Resistance to change, continuation of the regime of authority without accountability and reluctance to share turf account for bureaucratic antipathy to this sound recommendation.

Finally, one might ask, why is the political authority not implementing recommendations approved by itself in the past, even while it has the authority both over the military as well as the bureaucracy to override their objections? After all, decisions cannot be unanimous always and anyone adversely affected by a decision is bound to differ. The overriding basis for such a decision being advancement of national interest, it must be implemented even in the face of opposition from entrenched quarters.

Unfortunately, this has not happened. Watered down version of these recommendations put forward by the Naresh Chandra Committee constituted in 2011, is reported to have suggested that there should be a Permanent Chairman Chiefs of Staff Committee (COSC) instead of a CDS to provide single point advice to the political authority and to head the Headquarters IDS. The Naresh Chandra Committee report was submitted to the government more than a year back. Not only has it not been made public till date, grapevine has it that the committee's recommendations have not found favour with the powers that be, and thus have been given a quiet burial. Even if a Permanent Chairman COSC is appointed at some later stage, it would be a half hearted measure which would not meet the requirements of the situation. With consensus being the guiding principle in the COSC and service chiefs retaining their control in all spheres including operational aspects, decision making on important issues may become contentious and delayed. The Chairman would be one among equals enjoying no authority over the others.

Reluctance to implement the KRC recommendations on appointing a CDS is also perhaps indicative of the unstated apprehensions of the political class, fuelled by the bureaucracy, to the danger of placing too much power in one person. Recently, a Chief of Army Staff taking the government to the Supreme Court over his date of birth issue appears to have reinforced these apprehensions. However, this antipathy to reforms is likely to prove harmful to the national interest in the long run. Moreover, the apolitical nature of the Indian military has been proved time and again since independence. Its loyalty to the constitution of the country and its efforts to preserve the unity and integrity of the nation even at the expense of supreme sacrifice of its soldiers finds no parallel in our neighbourhood or elsewhere. Nor is it possible for any such misadventure to succeed, keeping in mind the vastness of the country and a host of other factors.

Conceptual Framework of Higher Defence Organisation

The conceptual framework of a higher defence organisation demands that the political authority must first of all lay down national objectives which would form the basis of forming a National Security Strategy (NSS). Unfortunately, there is no single document wherein India's national security objectives have been specifically and clearly spelled out. What exists is a series of pronouncements made by the political authority from time to time in different contexts and circumstances depending on the prevailing mood in the country. Besides being ambiguous, these could even be contradictory leading to confusion. No wonder then that strategic analysts like George Tanham have remarked that India has no strategic culture.

Having spelled out the national objectives, the political authority needs to undertake a *Strategic Defence Review* which would then form the basis of a NSS. The formulation of a NSS should be in the realm of a wider public debate wherein all the stake holders also put forward their views. Once finalised after incorporating all suitable viewpoints, it must be approved by the parliament to give it the necessary sanctity and backing for implementation. The issue of the Defence Directive by the MoD to the service headquarters would be based on the guidelines laid down in the NSS. The responsibility for making specific operational plans in implementing the defence directive and executing them would rest with the service headquarters.

Structures for Higher Defence Organisation

This issue needs to be discussed at two levels, within the government and within the military. Within the government, while most of the structures are existing, our tendency to activate them only when crisis situations occur rather than on a regular basis, defeats the purpose of their existence. It also reduces the scope for interaction between the political authority and the service chiefs who are expected to implement the operational plans. Thus the CCS meets more to tackle crisis situations than on an ongoing basis to review national security. Service chiefs are expected to join its deliberations only by invitation, which happens rarely. The National Security Council (NSC) which is expected to function regularly to implement CCS directions, consequently, has also not met often, making it almost defunct. The National Security Advisory Board (NSAB) has minimal interaction with the service headquarters and any advice that it may be rendering to the government on security issues has not been a subject of discussion with service headquarters. There is limited structured interaction at the staff level between National Security Council Secretariat (NSCS) and the service headquarters. Finally, the weekly interaction between the Raksha Mantri (RM), the service chiefs and the defence secretary is not formalised, its deliberations are not recorded, and what is more, it may not take place for as long as a month at times. This casual approach to issues of national security is debilitating.

Within the military, the Chairman COSC wears two hats, that of the Chairman as well as the chief of his service. This has some serious flaws. Firstly, it is not possible for the same individual to take on the burden of two important offices simultaneously. Despite adequate staff, he is unable to devote sufficient time for both appointments, thus doing injustice to both. Secondly, as Chairman COSC, he may be constrained to take decisions which are not necessarily in the best interests of his service of which he is the Chief, thus placing him in a serious decision dilemma. Thirdly, the Chairman COSC has no authority to enforce a decision on the other two services. Besides this, his domain knowledge of the other two services being limited, there is reluctance in taking decisions without concurrence of the other two services. Fourthly, COSC decisions are expected to be unanimous which is rarely possible when each service is concerned about protecting its own turf. Thus, precious time is lost during crisis situations in nudging the dissenting service towards concurrence.

Moving a little lower, the service chiefs also wear two hats. Each chief is a commander in chief of his service, whereby he is expected to plan and prepare his force for any eventuality and execute operational plans if the need arises. Secondly, he is also the chief of staff in which capacity he is both the advisor to the government as well as planner for force development for the future. Recruiting, training, organising, equipping, logistics and welfare of his service are overseen by him. Interacting with other departments of the government and maintaining external relationships of his service also fall under his charter, thus keeping his plate full.

Keeping the above in mind, the KRC in its wisdom had recommended a reorganisation whereby the operations function would be removed from the charter of the service chiefs and placed under the CDS who would execute it through the integrated theatre commands, on the pattern of the US, UK and other advanced militaries of the world. The theatre commands were envisaged to be tri service commands with resources of the three services integrated under them, depending on their charter of responsibility. The CDS in turn was expected to report to the political authority. However, non implementation of the recommendation regarding creation of the CDS has effectively stalled the entire process, to the detriment of efficiency and synergy so important for conduct of operations in the present day environment.

Integration of Service Headquarters

The KRC had made a strong pitch for integrating the service headquarters with the MoD. This process would have ensured that service personnel got posted to the MoD and the civilian bureaucracy held appointments within the service headquarters. There are major advantages in organisational functioning that would have accrued if it had been implemented. Firstly, it ensures better understanding of service requirements by the bureaucracy and thus a greater commitment on their part to see it fructify. Secondly, longer tenures on the civil side provide a degree of continuity to processes which take long to fructify and thus make up for the disadvantage of short tenures by the service personnel whose career progression requires their moving out to command assignments. Thirdly, processing of the cases which currently takes much longer because of the existing divide with files moving back and forth, would be tremendously hastened if the two worked in unison rather than in separate water tight compartments. Fourthly and finally, presently, in a number of cases the best advice does not get conveyed to the RM, the final decision making authority in the MoD, because it primarily reflects the bureaucratic understanding and viewpoint. Integration would ensure that the political authority gets the best advice incorporating all views resulting in sound decisions.

However, this recommendation too has not been implemented. Instead, a cosmetic change has been carried out with service headquarters now being termed as integrated headquarters of the MoD. The functioning and inter se relationship between the two continues as hitherto. This has reinforced the feeling of a serious civil military divide and a 'we' and 'them' approach to issues, which hardly bodes well for our national security. The rationale of the bureaucracy in opposing integration of the service headquarters and changing their status from 'attached offices' to integral part of Government of India has not been explained anywhere. On the face of it, reluctance to share turf appears to be perhaps the only reason. Whether such a narrow and parochial approach should be allowed to persist with, is a call that the political authority needs to take. Suffice to say here that lack of integration is affecting decision making capability and improvements in the important sphere of national security.

Defence Planning Process

To remain relevant and contemporary, the military requires a planning process which is continuous, timely and responsive to its needs. Since defence planning deals with the future, it has to have a long term perspective. A clearer understanding of where we wish to be at a particular time in the future would enable identification of an appropriate course of action to get there. It would also give an indication of the resources required to achieve those goals.

Acquisition of military hardware for force modernisation is time consuming and therefore cannot be held hostage to yearly budgets. In fact, yearly budgets are one reason why some projects do not fructify for years on end. Some major weaknesses noted in the current system are as follows:

- Five year defence plans do not receive formal government approval resulting in their implementation being questioned. Both the 10th Defence Plan (2002-07) and 11th Defence Plan (2007-12) were never the beneficiaries of governmental approval.
- As opposed to a requirement of approximately three per cent of the GDP for defence, the average allocation for the last five years has hovered around two per cent of the GDP, which is woefully inadequate. Actual utilisation falls short of even this amount because the funds allocation

agency and the acquisition approving agency for major projects is the same, viz. Finance Ministry. Thus, whenever the finance ministry's funds planning goes awry or is constrained due to shortages, it is conveniently possible for it to delay approving some big ticket defence projects.

- Lack of a CDS limits ability to cut down duplication among the services and to allocate priorities for acquisition in view of limited fund availability as each service, with the backing of its chief, tries to bulldoze its way through.

Night blindness, obsolete artillery and air defence artillery equipment are major areas of concern of the army which have yet to be addressed. Augmentation of fighter squadrons by the air force is an issue which needs immediate attention. Finally, submarine fleet of the navy, both nuclear and conventional, needs to be urgently built up. Timeframes for achieving these goals are so long that currently in-service hardware would reach obsolescence by the time the new equipment comes in, leaving a feeling of insecurity on a continuing basis.

A major infusion of funding, immediate approval of Long Term Integrated Perspective Plan (LTIPP), increasing annual expenditure on military to at least three per cent of the GDP, hastening up of acquisition process by systemic reforms, adequate staffing of the MoD to follow through acquisition requirements of the services and installation of a CDS need to be undertaken on priority to improve the defence planning and acquisition process.

Intelligence

Failure of intelligence was a major reason for our debacle during 1962 and initial reverses during the Kargil conflict. In fact to retrieve the situation during Kargil conflict, we had to pay heavily in terms of large scale loss of precious lives and casualties. To go into battle without adequate intelligence about the adversary amounts to fighting the battle blindfolded, which is a sure recipe for reverses.

Any conceptual improvements in higher defence management must inevitably look at our intelligence acquisition, collection, collation and dissemination ability in real time. Our biggest problem stems from the fact that we have a plethora of intelligence agencies that are tasked for different aspects of information gathering but are invariably trying to outdo each other to the extent of even undercutting at the expense of national interest. They are more keen to be the first to report information to the political authority even though its authenticity may be doubtful or its accuracy requires immediate counter measures at the ground level. A related aspect is that of systematised collation of all information gathered by different agencies to convert it into actionable intelligence after due analysis. This intelligence needs to be cross checked and reconfirmed by advanced satellite, sea and ground based surveillance and reconnaissance systems before being used by the higher defence management.

The above process underlines the necessity of a national intelligence coordination mechanism under a designated head. While a large number of the recommendations of the NC Saxena task force on intelligence reform, set up post the Kargil conflict, have been implemented to bring coherence to the function of intelligence gathering and dissemination, the reform process would not be complete without a coordinating national mechanism. The attempts at one-upmanship and turf protection need to be curbed and overlap of functions and duplication avoided under the overall national coordination authority for intelligence.

Inter Ministerial Coordination

There are facets of defence which are linked very closely with other ministries of the government and a good higher defence organisation must have a systematised methodology of interaction with these ministries on an ongoing basis. Thus, Finance Ministry is expected to plan for and provide appropriate funding for defence. Resolution of complex boundary issues with neighbouring countries, defence cooperation and training with like minded nations, fulfilment of the country's commitments with the UN and honouring of bilateral mutual aid agreements requires close coordination between the defence and Ministry of External Affairs (MEA). Likewise, both internal and external security being closely linked, the military and the paramilitary are to be conceptually looked upon as a pool of trained manpower with one readily available to augment the efforts of the other in case of a crisis to national security. Thus, the defence and Ministry of Home Affairs (MHA), which controls the paramilitary forces, need to coordinate their functioning on an ongoing basis.

It is interesting to note that below the CCS, which comprises defence, finance, home and foreign ministers besides the Prime Minister, there is no structured methodology of regular interaction between these important ministries from a national security perspective. Instead, resort to ad-hocism, meetings on as required basis and attendance depending on availability is the norm with rarely a record of these meetings being minuted and kept. In the absence of regular meetings at the bureaucratic level, which should form the basis of ministerial level interaction, CCS meetings are few and far between since they are based on movement of files which is painstakingly slow. Additionally, CCS meetings tend to tackle crisis situations based on specific issues. Possibly crisis situations would not occur in the first place if the CCS was to hold regular meetings touching on issues of national security. Lastly, even service chiefs are rare invitees to the CCS meetings, resulting in the decision making being restricted to the politician and the bureaucrat, leaving scope for politically motivated rather than professionally sound decisions being taken at times.

The above once again underlines the need for integration of service headquarters with the MoD. Secondly, structured interaction on an ongoing basis at the bureaucratic level between the MoD, finance ministry and MEA is essential on national security issues to ensure sound decision making at the political level when CCS meetings take place. On aspects pertaining to higher defence management, coopting of service reps at each level of interaction should be the laid down norm in order to arrive at informed decision making.

Defence Research and Development Organisation (DRDO)

The DRDO has a distinct role to play in arriving at higher defence management decisions relating to equipping and modernising the country's military as well as paramilitary forces. Indigenous weapon systems, ammunition and equipment developed by the DRDO independently and in conjunction with public and private sector undertakings would assist in taking the country towards self sufficiency and reducing dependence on expensive imports which may dry up in times of a crisis. With the available funding for defence projects at a premium, any higher defence organisation must plan for and support building up of a strong indigenous DRDO for continuous modernisation of the military. The Chinese have followed this practice with great success for the past 30-35 years and today they boast of a predominantly self sufficient military.

Unfortunately, in our case, The DRDO efforts have at times been frittered away on non essential projects, leaving us dependent on expensive imports even 65 years after independence. There is a need for a focussed approach by the DRDO and encouragement of JVs including ToT for bolstering indigenous private sector.

Jointness

Conceptually, jointness implies synergised use of the resources of the three services in a seamless manner as to achieve the best results in the least possible time, thus avoiding duplication and making optimum use of the available resources. In absolute terms, the validity of jointness as a concept in modern day warfare is indisputable. However, the methodology of achieving this jointness has varied from country to country.

There is invariably a debate over how does one differentiate between integration and jointness in practice. It would be correct to say that both are two faces of the same coin. However, by its very nature, integration implies a higher degree of jointness.

For greater clarity, let us discuss jointness as practiced by us in operations, and integration in a little detail. Jointness, as currently implemented by us, implies that while the three services progress and develop in their respective spheres, maintaining their independent identity, they function together and so coordinate their operations in war as to achieve the best results. To achieve jointness, a set of coordinating mechanisms are constituted which plan for envisaged operations under various contingencies/scenarios. In case the war takes a different course than what was envisaged, these mechanisms are expected to come up with a coordinated response, whereby role of each service in an ongoing operation is defined in a time bound and sequential manner. Thus, while retaining individual service identity, it seeks to achieve a coordinated response to developing situations during operations.

Integration, on the other hand, seeks to merge individual service identities to achieve a composite and cohesive whole. It implies enmeshing the three services together at different levels and placing them under one commander for execution of operational plans. They are thus an already dedicated resource which is employed by the commander in the manner he deems appropriate to achieve the best results. Integration presupposes the ability of the commander to comprehensively understand the employment of all three services components functioning under him. It aims at cutting down the response time to developing situations during operations, thereby exploiting fleeting windows of opportunity contributing to success in war.

From the above, it should be fairly clear that integration is a step ahead of jointness in ensuring a synergised approach to operations. While in jointness, consent of the parent service for allocation of a resource is mandatory, in case of integration, resources from all three services already stand allocated to the appropriate commander. In jointness the employment of a resource is a subject of debate and discussion at a crucial time while in integration its employment is immediate based on the commander's appreciation of the operational situation. Thus, the Kargil war would have been a much shorter affair if the air force had provided support to the army's operations from the beginning rather than a few days later. While the air force may have had its own reasons for their actions, that is not under discussion here. What is relevant is that immediate air force support would have brought in synergy to win the war earlier. An integrated response ensures optimum utilisation of available resources while a joint response may sometimes not. Finally, in a joint response, the possibility of inter service friction is much greater since differences in employment are bound to keep cropping up continuously as opposed to integrated response where initial resistance to giving up one's turf having been taken care of during the reorganisational process, operations by the integrated force are likely to be more focussed and timely—a battle winning factor. It is for these reasons that most of the advanced countries of the world have adopted the integrated approach to conventional war fighting.

Proponents of jointness often make the point that the domain knowledge of the integrated force commander is likely to be limited in respect of the other two services components under his command, thereby limiting his ability to employ them in the most suitable manner and at the appropriate time. However, once integration is adopted as a policy, cross postings into other services and joint institutions would be the norm and it would only be a matter of time when officers adept at handling all three services with equal ease come up. No change can come about overnight. We need to work at it and since it is time consuming, ways and means to shorten that time frame have to be evolved. In fact we are already late in starting it.

Status of Integration in Leading Countries of the World

In the US, the process of integration was started in 1986 when the Goldwater-Nichols Act was passed by the congress in the face of strident opposition from embedded interests and today postings to joint institutions are rated higher than those to service specific institutions. The culture of integrated operations stands fully established and is functioning successfully with theatre commanders employing allocated resources of all three services and the Marine Corps as they deem appropriate.

In the UK, from where the Indian defence structure has been inherited, the system has so evolved over the last half a century that jointness has become the norm and integrated operations form the backbone of war fighting. In the *Strategic Defence Review (SDR)* promulgated in 1998, Chief of Defence Staff (CDS) has been designated as the professional head of the armed forces and the Principal Advisor to the government. He is responsible for all operations with resources allocated from the three services. Again in the UK, this integration had to be pushed through by the political hierarchy in the face of resistance from the three services and the bureaucracy.

In the Russian model too, by the process of evolution, practicality and experience, integration seems to have taken firm roots. By a decree in 2010, four strategic commands have been created (Central, Southern, Eastern, Western) with appropriate allocation of resources from the three services and independent arms directly under the Centre viz. Missile, Space and Airborne forces. Even though the communist party is the all powerful single authority in the Russian system, as opposed to democracies in the West, the importance of integration in operations is equally realised and appreciated by the Russians.

Similarly in the Chinese model, which is a derivative of the Russian system, it is the seven military regions, each under a Regional Commander, which control the allocated resources of the three services and Logistics and Armament Department, for operations.

Integrated Logistics

In the current system, each service plans and caters for its own logistics back up for the operations. This leads to tremendous amount of duplication, large inventories and colossal wastage of precious resources. When the logistic requirement of all the services is somewhat similar in operations, it does not stand to logic that each of them follows its own planning, provisioning, transportation and delivery model. With a little bit of forethought and coordination, it is possible to integrate the logistics organisations of the three services and create one integrated structure which caters to the requirements of all, thus optimising utilisation of resources. To support integrated operations, the need for integrated logistics can hardly be overemphasised.

Today, in all the leading militaries of the world, through a process of logical evolution, logistics already stand integrated. In the US, the Defence Logistics Agency (DLA) which is part of Joint Logistics Environment (JLE) provides the requisite logistic back up. In the UK, the Chief of Defence Material (CDM) performs the same function and is a four star rank officer. Likewise, the Russian and the Chinese militaries follow a somewhat similar integrated logistics system.

The Current Picture in India

Today, in case of war, each service chief is expected to control the operations of his service. To carry out his directions, he has functional commands headed by three star rank army commanders (or equivalent in navy and air force). Thus, the army has seven commands (Northern, Eastern, Southern, Western, Central, South Western and Army Training Command (ARTRAC)), the air force too has seven commands (Western, Eastern, Southern, South Western, Central, Training and Maintenance) and the navy has three commands (Western, Eastern and Southern). An interesting aspect to note is that none of these 17 commands are co-located at the same station! Each one is at a different station, giving a feeling as if a conscious effort has been made to stay away from each other and not to tread on each other's toes! Besides these, there are two tri service commands Strategic Forces Command (SFC) and Andaman and Nicobar Command (ANC), the command of which is rotated among the three services.

Coordination of operations in case of a war is expected to be carried out in various committees set up under the Chiefs of Staff Committee (COSC), which is headed by the senior most service chief who is designated as Chairman COSC. He, therefore, is expected to simultaneously perform both the roles of being Chief of his service as well as the Chairman COSC. The COSC generally functions on the principle of consensus. In practice, such a system suffers from serious flaws which have been discussed earlier. The delays in arriving at a consensus during an ongoing war may affect the very outcome of the war, which is detrimental to national interest. Jointness cannot be achieved and put in to practice when a war or a crisis is being faced by the country. It has to be planned for, practiced and put in to effect during peace time with various likely situations war gamed. While the current practice provides for carrying out joint training on as required basis, the level of jointness achieved would be much greater in case the integrated command system is instituted.

Integrated Theatre Command System

There is an overwhelming need to get away from a service specific approach to operations towards a system which avoids duplication, ensures optimum utilisation of available resources, brings in greater jointness, leads to timely and mature decisions to developing situations and ensures flawless execution of orders to achieve success in battle. This is where the integrated theatre command system fits in better in the scheme of things than the current system. It aims to put the resources of the three services at the disposal of the theatre commander, keeping in mind the tasks assigned to him and thereafter leaves him free to train his command to make it a cohesive fighting force capable of achieving its designated charter in the shortest possible time frame. The logistic resources required to support his operations are also placed at the disposal of the theatre commander so that he does not have to look over his shoulder for anything when the operations are ongoing.

The theatre commander would be expected to carry out his tasks in consonance with the overall national plan as approved by the political leadership and given to the Chief of Defence Staff (CDS) for implementation. Thus, he would be functioning under the directions of the CDS who would be responsible to the political leadership as well as be the coordinator of all operations at the national level. It, therefore, also emerges that the need for theatre commands cannot be viewed in isolation but has to be a part of the total restructuring of the higher defence management system of the country.

It is often argued that the US, Russia, China and the UK have global interests and hence the integrated theatre command system is perhaps best suited for their requirements. In case of India, it is argued that we have no territorial ambitions on anyone's territory and we are primarily concerned with ensuring our territorial integrity, therefore the existing system is good enough to meet our needs. Unfortunately, the proponents of this line of reasoning are missing out on the basic premise that integration ensures a more cohesive, timely and synergetic response in any scenario. It is inherently more suited as a concept than any other arrangement to accomplish national security goals. Therefore, we need to rise above the service specific loyalties and turf battles to move towards integrated structures in national interest.

It is also a fact that in the current environment, force multipliers will play a crucial role in determining the outcome of conflicts. Use of surveillance, cyber warfare, space and robotics can be better exploited to advantage in an integrated command structure than in any other organisation. It gives a commander a clear idea of his capabilities and limitations thus ensuring instantaneous employment to exploit fleeting opportunities in the noise and din of a battle, resulting in greater possibility of success. The government is also expected to move forward in creation of three additional joint commands, namely cyber, space and special operations, recognising the importance of force multipliers in the future battlefield environment.

Unlike in other major countries of the world, in India, the proportion of the three services as part of the overall military is heavily skewed in favour of the army. While the apprehensions of the smaller services that they may be swamped may not necessarily be correct and may be misplaced, they still need to be addressed specifically, if only to remove the feeling of mistrust. As long as national interest and merit remain the backbone of any restructuring, there cannot be any rational and legitimate reason for heart burning and unhappiness.

Charter of the Military

The likely tasks that that may form the charter of the Indian military could be one or more of the following:

(a) Protection of territorial integrity of the nation.
(b) Defence of the country against external aggression.
(c) Preserve the unity of the country.
(d) Provide aid to civil authority, whenever requested.
(e) Be prepared to provide resources for disaster relief in case of natural calamities.
(f) On directions from the government of India, be prepared to proceed overseas for operations or provision of humanitarian assistance.
(g) Provide troops for UN Peace keeping missions on orders.

Depending on the geographical location of the command, a prioritised list of some or most of the above tasks would be assigned to it. The resources required to carry out these tasks would also be made available to the command. It would thereafter be its charter to work out detailed plans under different contingencies and rehearse the troops allocated from different arms and services in executing these tasks in an integrated manner. Logistic support required by this force would be made available to the command who would decide upon its deployment and execution in the most optimum manner. The detailed planning, coordination and rehearsals required to knit all the components in to a cohesive whole and function like a well oiled machine is a gigantic task which requires months/years to prepare. This in itself is a forceful argument for shifting from the current system to one of integrated commands as quickly as possible.

Proposed Reorganisation

It is proposed that we move away from the current system and create integrated commands as follows:

(a) **Northern Command**. Incorporating the states of UP, Uttaranchal, Himachal and J&K.
(b) **Western Command**. To include Punjab, Haryana and part of Rajasthan.
(c) **South Western Command**. To include balance of Rajasthan and Gujarat.
(d) **Southern Command**. To include Maharashtra, Karnataka, Goa and Kerala.
(e) **South Eastern Command**. To include Tamil Nadu, Andhra Pradesh, Orissa and West Bengal.
(f) **Eastern Command**. To include Sikkim, Assam. Arunachal Pradesh, Meghalaya, Nagaland, Manipur and Tripura.
(g) **Central Command**. To include Bihar, MP, Jharkhand, Chhattisgarh and Puducherry.

The above is one suggested reorganisation. Inter command boundaries can be finalised after a detailed and in depth analysis. Other states not mentioned herein, could fall within the boundary of one or the other command depending on administrative convenience. In addition to the already existing ANC and SFC, there is a requirement of creating cyber, space and special operations functional commands whose resources could be allocated to the integrated commands on as required basis depending on the tasks they are expected to carry out.

The next question that would exercise a thinking mind would be as to which service should head these commands. It is my considered opinion that, irrespective of the colour of the uniform, two main considerations should dictate the answer to this question. Firstly, the tasks that a command is expected to carry out should become a determining criteria. Secondly, merit and professional competence and not the colour of the uniform should be an important factor in conjunction with the first consideration to decide as to who should be the force commander and which should be the lead service in a command. A dedicated and competent officer who can analyse the tasks assigned and has adequate knowledge of employment of all arms and services under his command would be able to produce and execute a successful plan. It is more important to select the right person than worry about which service he belongs to.

A related aspect that would need to be tackled would be the acquisition of domain knowledge of various arms and services and their integrated application. Not only the commanders but the staffs must get used to integrated functioning. This requires much greater emphasis on joint training as compared to service specific training, which has been the practice so far. As far as possible, all our training institutions should shift to joint training. Tenanting of appointments at the joint training institutions and joint staff headquarters should become a precondition for progressing to senior ranks. Officers from all three services should attend courses at service specific training institutions to gain knowledge and insight into services other than their own. The list is endless. In fact a study should be undertaken to enumerate steps required to integrate the three services and enhance jointness. Our efforts so far in this direction have been of a peripheral nature and touched the problem only at the fringes. The need is for a conceptual shift in our thinking towards integrated operations and ruthless implementation overcoming service prejudices. The whole process is a time consuming one and the sooner we get started on it, the earlier we would be able to achieve the ultimate goal.

Integrated theatre commanders should report directly to the CDS on all operational matters, who would be the single point advisor to the political authority and accountable to it. His charter should also include:

(a) Defining national security strategy in consonance with laid down national security objectives.
(b) Promotion of jointness in the three services.
(c) Formulation of Long Term Integrated Perspective Plans (LTIPP) of the services.
(d) Prioritising defence acquisitions based on availability of funding.
(e) Coordinating intelligence both within the services and with the national intelligence grid.
(f) Coordinating and refining the defence planning process.
(g) Undertake inter ministerial coordination where necessary.
(h) Develop joint training institutions and doctrines.
(i) Suggest projects to be undertaken by the DRDO.
(j) Exercise control over tri service functional commands.
(k) Manage the nation's nuclear resources.

The above list is by no means exhaustive and is more indicative in character. In fact any aspects requiring tri service approach, coordination and implementation should conceptually fall under his purview.

Moving upwards, the RM's weekly meetings comprising the CDS, the three service chiefs, the defence secretary and the joint secretary (G) should be regular and their proceedings recorded for appropriate follow up action. Likewise, for inter ministerial coordination at bureaucratic level, structures need to be created for regular interaction between the ministries of defence, home, external affairs and finance to discuss, debate and finalise issues relating to national security, infrastructure development, force modernisation, overseas deployment/training, funding and defence five year plans before they are put up to CCS for its approval and post CCS approval, to implement them. Debating these issues on files is an excruciatingly slow process which does not reach its logical culmination a number of times. No wonder the 10th and 11th defence FYPs never got cleared during their currency.

The inputs given by the NSAB, a body constituted by the government with a number of able experts and specialists, need to be shared with the MoD and the service headquarters for a meaningful discussion and debate before being incorporated as part of government policy. Service headquarters and MoD could also use the NSAB as a sounding board for some of their proposed changes. Here again, there is a requirement of laying down structured interaction between the two for improved inputs to national security related decision making.

The National Security Council (NSC) too has hardly been meeting on a regular basis. It must be appreciated that national security has to be kept in focus at all times of a nation's existence. There is a requirement of continuous planning and direction on existing and emerging security issues to ensure good higher defence management. The NSC secretariat inputs need to be regularly discussed before being adopted. Likewise, the CCS must move away from issue based meetings to regular interaction with all stakeholders to arrive at sound security related decisions.

The aspect of civilian control over the military is not in doubt and has been scrupulously followed since independence. However, to exercise this control, there is a requirement of adequate knowledge of defence affairs by the political class. Unfortunately, whether in the government or in the parliament, there is hardly anybody who has had worthwhile exposure to national security issues leave alone higher defence management. The parliament, which is expected to approve defence budgets as part of the national budget, has seldom debated it in more than a perfunctory manner with the shroud of secrecy thrown around it. The Standing Committee for Defence of the parliament, which is expected to be the parliamentary watchdog over the MoD, has members who have had little or no experience of defence matters. Their occasional visits to defence establishments have ended up being ceremonial rather than learning trips. The annual recommendations of this august committee are not being followed up in right earnest or ignored, as a result its contribution to higher defence management has been negligible. It is important to constitute this committee with members who have an aptitude for security and defence related issues and institute a training capsule for them to familiarise them with their charter and responsibilities.

On the government side too, we have rarely had a RM or a minister of state since independence who is well versed in security and defence affairs. As a result, his on the job training happens at the expense of higher defence management and the duration of this training may stretch depending on his interest and competence. National interest and not political considerations should dictate the choice for such a responsibility. Additionally, he should have staff which is knowledgeable on defence and security related issues so that right advice is rendered to him to take an appropriate decision. In this context, the suggestion by KRC of cross posting service officers to the MoD and vice versa is relevant. Another suggestion which has been mooted in some quarters is to have a specialised cadre of officers to deal with security and defence related issues. This may be worth examining.

Finally, the channel of communication between the CDS, or the service chiefs till CDS comes into existence, and the Prime Minister should invariably remain open on an ongoing basis. This channel is crucial to ensure intervention by the highest authority without delay should a crisis develop or things start going wrong. It also builds confidence between the political authority and the military chain of command.

Conclusion

Modern warfare is continuously evolving. Doctrines, concepts, methodology and weapon systems of war fighting are constantly getting refined to achieve success in the shortest possible time. We have been witness to the massive differences in all these spheres during World War 1 and World War 2. Post World War 2, a revolution in military affairs has taken place in almost all militaries of the world. Driven by technology, these changes are likely to have much more profound influence on war fighting than ever seen hitherto. Real time intelligence, transparency of the battlefield, cyber warfare, information warfare, space based weapon systems etc. are some the oft spoken and discussed terms among military strategists in the present day environment. A relevant and vibrant military needs to move with changing times if it has to deliver.

In India, on becoming independent, we inherited a system of higher defence management instituted by the British as it suited their interests best. In the last 66 years we have made changes to it which were driven more by crisis like the 1962 war against the Chinese or the Kargil war, than a genuine desire to improve higher defence management and jointness. Most of the countries around the globe, including Britain, have moved away from the system they followed during the Second World War to a more responsive and better suited system which meets the requirements in the current day environment. Our attempts to change our system have been half hearted and jettisoned at the first signs of internal resistance or apprehensions. Experience of other countries clearly shows that reforms have to be top driven and at times forced down in national interest.

Direct collusion between China and Pakistan, which has been in existence since the fiftees, has gradually been strengthening. In the words of Hu Jintao the Chinese Pakistan relationship is "higher than the mountains and deeper than the oceans". We have unsettled boundary issues with both these neighbours. National interest demands that we should be prepared to defend ourselves in case of a two front war. While we have a conventional edge over Pakistan, China is militarily superior to us and this gap is gradually increasing with passage of time. In case of a war, collusion between our two neighbours will put us at a major relative disadvantage. We have to fully prepare ourselves to face such a situation and plan for it.

Improving our higher defence management and enhancing jointness between the three services to achieve total synergy are important steps towards building and managing a force capable of meeting any challenges to national security and territorial integrity. Reforms suggested are only indicative in nature. A lot more can be achieved once we start moving on the right path. In fact we are already late in starting the reform process, thanks to entrenched interests and opposition to change. Since reforms will take time to be absorbed, the sooner we get them going the better.

6

Defence Planning in India at Crossroads

Amiya Kumar Ghosh

When on April 02, 2012 it was officially announced by the Ministry of Defence (MoD) that the Long Term Integrated Perspective Plan (LTIPP) 2012-27 and the 12th Defence Plan (2012-17) have been approved by Defence Acquisition Council (DAC), it did not evoke much enthusiasm amongst defence analysts, as is evidenced by the lack of discussion on it in media and elsewhere. It looked like an event of no consequence.

That the MoD gave lot of importance to this announcement, is brought out by the fact that Standing Committee of Parliament on Defence which was deliberating on the Demands for Grants for 2012-13, and had shown anxiety earlier about the fate of the 12th Plan, was also apprised that both the Long Term Integrated Perspective Plan (LTIPP) 2012-27 and the 12th Plan have been approved by DAC.[1] Apart from the lack of transparency as to what these plans contained, one reason for the general lack of enthusiasm about the approval of the plans was, that it was an 'in principle' clearance. This probably means that the major step of getting the approvals of the Ministry of Finance (MoF) and Cabinet Committee on Security (CCS), were still awaited.

Secondly, DAC which has a mandate to give policy guidance to acquisitions as also to clear all major acquisitions, would not normally be regarded as a forum for clearance of Defence Plan, which involves expenditure on both Revenue and Capital account. Expenditure on revenue account constitute 60 per cent of defence budget and has to receive major attention in any defence plan concerned with force planning as also readiness. This also brought out that till today there is no forum in the MoD, like for example a Defence Planning Committee (DPC), to consider and approve defence plans.

Thirdly, defence planning in India is not viewed as strategic document and has not played much role in influencing allocation of resources for meeting strategic objectives and even for annual budgetary allocations. There has been complete disconnect between strategic planning and budgeting.

Approval of a defence plan is no more treated as a significant event by defence analysts. Over decades there has not been any consistent attempt to formulate and approve defence plans which have in general been hamstrung internally by overall resource problem. An approved defence five year plan has become a rare event. The following brief account will show that:

The experience of the Chinese aggression in 1962 brought home the need for systematic planning to ensure defence preparedness. A Five Year Defence Plan was for the first time formulated in 1964 for the period 1964-69. "This plan, however, was not based on long term requirements nor did it have the assurance of resources to support it."[2]

This was followed by 1969-74 Plan which was supposed to have taken into account the changes in strategic needs as well as ten year forecast of requirements. "The Plan was also resource based in that an assurance was given that the financial resources and foreign exchange would be made available as laid down in the Plan."[3]

That, optimistic assumptions were made about availability of resources were clear from the critical comments made subsequently. As D.S. Nakra wrote: "For all practical purposes, the Plan was based on the then current level of expenditure of about Rs 1,030 crore and an escalation of Rs 50 crores per annum was built into it. It was really no Plan at all. The needs of the three Services were not spelt out in terms of definite programmes; they were not coordinated and integrated and adjusted—it was only a statistical projection of current level of expenditure escalated marginally. A need based and programme oriented Plan was not attempted."[4]

The general criticism about how the plans were formulated remained valid for subsequent plans also. The result was the constraint of limited resources could not be applied rationally for determining inter-services and intra-service priorities to develop the capabilities. The concept of Five Year Plan was negated in 1970 by adopting the concept of Roll-on Plan, primarily because of inability to assure resources for a longer time frame. The Roll-on Plan was upset by events of 1971 Bangladesh war.

Owing to the inflationary pressures in 1971 and 1972 the entire situation was reviewed in 1973 and the next Defence Plan for the period 1974-79 was drawn up. It was indicated in the Annual Report of the MoD that in the light of lessons of West Asia war in October 1973, large scale acquisition of hardware by our neighbours, the phenomenal increase in the international price levels, the hike in oil prices the totality of Defence efforts was again reviewed. Based on this review, the Defence Plan 1974-79 was modified in 1975. In April 1976, the situation was again reviewed by MoD and it was decided to prepare a Roll-on Plan for 1976-81. Before this plan could be finalised it became necessary to consider certain new schemes due to change in geopolitical situation and certain other reasons.[5]

The Five Year Defence Plan for the period 1979-84 was approved by Cabinet Committee of Political Affairs (CCPA). Change in the security environment in the neighbourhood led to the review of the Plan and a revised Defence Plan was drawn up for the period 1980-85. This was the Sixth Defence Plan. The Annual Report of the Ministry 1979-80 for the first time indicated that the Services Hqrs have started drawing up Perspective Plans for 15 year period and more coordinated approach has been taken for drawing up the Five Year Plan. To quote, "A number of steps have been taken during the year to qualitatively upgrade the planning process from a purely fiscal approach to physical systems plan. *In this context, action has been initiated by the Service Hqrs to draw up perspective plans.*"[6] The perspective plans, however, continued to remain independent plans of three services, without any attempt to integrate them or get the approval of the government. We had to wait till 2002 for preparing a LTIPP by newly constituted Integrated Defence Staff (IDS) and wait till 2012 for its approval by the DAC.

It was also indicated in the Report that steps had been taken to ensure coordination between needs of the three Services on the one hand and the production plans and research programmes of the Department of Defence Production (DDP) and the Defence Research and Development Organisation (DRDO) on the other.

The Sixth Defence Plan attempted this coordinated approach in planning. But that this remained more in the realm of theory than in practice, is evident from the fact that problem regarding coordinated approach remains even today. The IDS which is assigned the task of Defence planning, only puts together the individual five-year plans prepared by the services, has no jurisdiction over the DDP and DRDO. As an eminent analyst comments "In effect, therefore, there is no single organisation at present in the ministry that deals with defence planning in its entirety and monitors its implementation."[7]

But is defence planning just putting together plans drawn up by the three Services? What about the strategic aspects of it? Attention to this aspect was drawn in the Annual Report of the MoD 1983-84 in distinguishing defence planning from planning in other sectors. To quote, *"Planning in defence stands on a different footing because it has in it elements of strategy, and operation, Intelligence appreciation and, the most important, evaluation of the schemes and intention of other agencies and states with whom the country has to live in continuous state of interaction and on whose programmes the planner has no or little control. Defence plan is not isolated from the operational world. Strategic management is an integral process of defence planning.*"[8] (italics mine) In this context, importance of Intelligence input in defence planning was stressed. It is doubtful however, how much this paragraph, important though it is, has been kept in view in the formulation of defence plans. The strategic aspects of defence planning could not have been given the due weightage is evident from the fact that plans remained unapproved or approved late, which cannot be done to a strategic document.

Probably it was assumed that Perspective planning would take care of it. But it is to be noted until now the LTIPP was not approved at the level of the government. It remained Perspective Plan of each service reflecting their strategy and perspective. If the LTIPP is nothing more than putting together the perspective plans of three Services with minor adjustment, the strategy underlying it would lack coherence.

As regards the implementation of the Sixth Plan (1980-85) in spite of stressing the importance of strategic aspects of planning all it said about the plan was, "The emphasis is on modernisation and replacement of equipment, securing greater fire power, mobility and more modern means of communication, and on self-reliance and import substitution"[9] There was no clarification as to how and in what way the modernisation efforts would meet the strategic objectives. Even if it is a defensive strategy, it need to be spelt out and linked to specific programmes by resource allocation decisions, instead of formulating a plan following a bottom-up process.

Regarding the aims of Seventh Plan (1985-90) it was stated, "The Plan aims at providing the defence services with weapon systems of increased mobility, fire power, accuracies, improved surveillance techniques, increased night observation and fighting capability and improved communications."[10] Again, one is not clear about strategic objectives apart from the fact that modernisation is necessary for better preparedness. As it was, the Seventh Plan was approved in the fourth year of the plan, which indicated in a way, that strategic aspects in resource planning and modernisation was not important and it has become a ritual. The budgetary allocations made during the five year period of the Seventh Plan was much less than the amount approved in the Plan as the fiscal deficits had already started worrying the government.

A view that emerged and continued to prevail was that, modernisation 'was an on-going process', meaning by this oft-repeated phrase, that what can not be done now because of lack of resources, can be done later when the resource permits. Therefore, approval of the Plan or its timing did not really matter. This indicated there was no prioritisation in modernisation schemes nor were there strategic goals.

Owing to economic crisis in the beginning of nineties, there was no clarity about the resources that could be made available for defence and the Eighth Defence Plan 1992-97 did not get the approval. Gradual revival of the economy allowed the 1994-95 defence budget to be raised to Rs 23,000 crore, the first real increase in defence spending in 1990s. The growth in the economy had picked up. The aggregate fiscal deficit as a ratio of GDP, declined from 9.4 per cent in 1990-91 to 6.4 per cent in 1996-97. The net fiscal deficit of the central government declined steadily to 3.1 per cent in 1996-97.[11] This trend also allowed a steadily increasing defence budget which in 1996-97 was Rs.29,505 crore.

In this propitious circumstance the Ninth Defence Plan (1997-2002) received the approval of the CCS. With the economy looking up, the Ninth Defence Plan (1997-2002) not only got approval in time, the budgetary allocations made available during the five year period closely corresponded to the approved amount in the plan. The experience of Ninth Plan was thus different from the other plans. There was close interaction with the MoF in arriving at an agreement in 1998 about the overall size of the Plan and the Prime Minister's Office (PMO's) played an important role in getting it through.

But, from 1999-2000 to 2003-04, substantial funds amounting to Rs. 32,740.26 crore for capital expenditure lapsed due to non-fructification of modernisation schemes. Clearly, there was disconnect between planning and its implementation. There were basic bureaucratic hurdles. An attempt to create a Defence Modernisation Fund did not succeed.

It was rather fortunate that the Ninth Plan did get its approval in 1997. From next year onward the impact of pay and pension revision came to be felt. The full effect of pay revision was seen in 1998-99. Much of the increased expenditure had to be financed by borrowing which led to increasing interest payments. There was a sharp increase in expenditures from 25 per cent of GDP in 1996-97 to 28.5 per cent in 2000-01 and further to 30.6 per cent in 2003-04. The net fiscal deficit which declined to 3.1 per cent in 1996-97 increased to 5.3 per cent in 2001-02.[12]

Therefore, it is not surprising that the 10th Defence Plan did not receive the clearance from MoF for the amount projected by the MoD. There was enactment of Fiscal Responsibility and Budget Management Act (FRBMA) in 2004. It set the target for revenue deficit-GDP ratio to be reduced to zero and fiscal deficits to be brought down to three per cent by 2007-08 which was subsequently shifted to 2008-09. The Twelfth Finance Committee (TFC) reiterated the core strategy indicated in FRBMA.

In this background it is not surprising that clearance of the 10th Defence Plan was not easy, and the issue dragged on at discussion stage between the MoD and MoF regarding the figures to be approved.

The projections of the MoD for the 10th plan were reviewed thrice between March 2003 and July 2004. The MoF finally agreed in principle to the projections made by the MoD of Rs 4,18,101 crore for the Tenth Defence Plan 2002-07.[13] However, total budgetary allocations for the Tenth Plan period on the basis of annual budgets came to Rs.3,64,000 crore, a shortfall of Rs.54,101 crore from the agreed amount.

The concept of LTIPP was introduced in 2001. The IDS, which among other things, was to prepare LTIPP also came into existence. The LTIPP 2002-17 did not get approved as there was delay even in getting 'in principle' approval of the Tenth Plan. A revised LTIPP 2007-22 was drawn up covering, 11th, 12th and 13th Five Year Plans. This also did not get approved as the 11th Five year Plan was not cleared because of lack of clarity on the resource issue. Approval of the LTIPP which is supposed to cover strategic and force structure issue which calls for long-term planning, should stand on a different footing than approval of the five year plan which is in the nature of the action plan.

As mentioned above, the LTIPP 2012-27 have been drawn up along with 12th Five year Plan (2012-17), to both of which the DAC has given its approval. However, the apprehension that, without approval of MoF it would be difficult to implement the plan got justified as the budget for 2012-13 was cut by 7.7 per cent (Rs.14, 903.8 crore) at the revised estimate stage. Of this cut, Rs.10,000 crore pertained to capital account and rest on revenue account. The budget allocation for 2013-14 increased only by 5.3 per cent (to Rs 2,03, 672 crore). Thus, whatever assumptions were made about the likely budget allocations during the 12th Plan period while DAC approved the Plan, must have been belied.

As per a report in January 2014, despite the 'in principle' clearance from the DAC in April 2012, the Defence Ministry was still awaiting the approvals of the Ministry of Finance and CCS to its 12th Five Year Plan.[14]

It is also learnt that though the 10 per cent austerity cut on non-plan expenditure has not been imposed by MoF on the budget of MoD for 2013-14, it has also not agreed to any hike in the budget, though efforts were made in this direction. Rather, as per a recent report, a sum of Rs.6500 crore is required to be transferred from the funds earmarked for modernisation to expenditure on revenue account because of shortfall there (due to increased expenditure on fuel and other expenses).[15]

The LTIPP 2012-27 and the 12th Plan is likely to meet the same fate as the 10th and 11th plan as the implementation of the FRBM Act has been reemphasised by the Finance Minister. As per the revised targets the fiscal deficit is to be brought down to three per cent of GDP by 2017-18.

This brief narrative is to indicate how the overall fiscal health affects the approval of the defence plans. Defence expenditure in the fiscal parlance is regarded as 'consumption' expenditure. While committing expenditure for five years it is not forgotten by the MoF that this expenditure is of 'discretionary' nature and can be approved if the overall fiscal and macro-economic trends are not uncomfortable. Can a way be found, in the overall context of low growth in the economy and determination of the government to rein in fiscal and revenue deficits, so that defence plans do not become a casualty year after year?

II

What is the relationship of the long term plan LTIPP 2012-27 with the Defence Five Year Plan 2012-2017? To be specific, is the LTIPP a strategic document, in the sense that it deals with likely cases of aggression, their duration and likely impact and required strategy and force structure to meet them? Deciding on likely cases of *aggression* is the most important means available with the government to direct long-term planning within the defence organisation. Force structure planning has to be based on it. That is why a perspective plan needs to be approved at the highest policy making level.

Perspective planning is expected to describe those activities which are designed to lay down the aims of the long-term policy of national defence and its alternative structures including force structure to meet strategic needs. In doing so, it has to make long-term assessment of political, strategic, military-technical and economic developments and their future evaluations.

Perspective planning has also to pay attention to considerable uncertainty that is always connected with long term assessments. Uncertainty has to be met by demanding increased flexibility for our national defence. The cases of aggression accepted by the government as relevant for perspective planning impose demands on national defence which are dependent on factors in the international milieu. But this planning must also be based on internal Indian conditions. These may be termed as internal restrictions on planning. These restrictions are of two kinds. The first type concerns financial restrictions on planning. The second concerns restrictions of political and cultural importance.

Cases of aggression relevant to long term planning, additional requirements and general restrictions define the problem of resource allocation in defence planning. The allocation of resources must produce the most balanced deterrent effect possible in all likely cases of aggression over a certain period of time. *The final choice of economic frame, relevant cases of aggression and the level of balanced effect is a political decision and has to be taken at highest decision making level.* The problem is that our LTIPP has never been approved at this level. Taking inputs from various sources is only part of the process; no less important is to get the 'output' of the process from the appropriate level.

In this context, what was stated by MoD to the Standing Committee in regard to preparation of LTIPP 2007-22 is worth noting: "The revised LTIPP (2007-22) is being prepared following a deliberate and integrated "Top Down" approach by articulating National Security Strategy (NSS), National Military Strategy (NMS), National Military objectives and so on. *Such an exercise has been undertaken for the first time and an extremely involved process with inputs from three Services, MoD, National Security Agency (NSA) and various other agencies.* This document is expected to be ready by December 2009"[16] (emphasis added).

From this it would be clear that LTIPP which is to be prepared by following a 'Top-Down' process is a strategic document of great importance and should therefore be approved at the highest political level. Getting it approved at the DAC level is not good enough.

Secondly, being a strategic document laying the basis for force planning, formulation of LTIPP had to precede the formulation of the Eleventh Five Year Plan. But the Plan had already been prepared on usual basis and projected to MoF to MoF in July 2006.[17] In preparation of the Plan as in the case of past five year plans, account had been taken of "committed liabilities, prioritised modernisation schemes, obligatory charges and maintenance requirements of the defence services and departments".[18] In other words, it followed a Bottom-Up process, the same as in case of annual budgeting. Prima facie, from this deposition Eleventh Plan did not appear to be a strategic document at all, and could not, therefore, be treated as subset of LTIPP.

Is that the position as regards the relation between LTIPP 2012-27 which have been prepared by following a deliberate 'Top Down' process, and the 12th Plan which most probably followed a bottom-up process? The Five year Plan should be treated as a programme plan for the development of the defence forces for five year period, which should be worked out with regard to the strength and weaknesses of existing forces as also to maintain a sufficiently strong operational capability throughout the period. In fact, both the LTIPP and the Five Year Plan which have to have a strategic orientation need to be approved by the National Security Council (NSC) and CCS.

While announcing the clearance of the LTIPP by DAC, it was also indicated that consequent to its clearance which covers the *vision* for 12th, 13th and 14th Defence Plans, the unclassified version of the LTIPP will be cleared in the form of Technology Perspective Capability Roadmap (TPCR) to enable DRDO, DPSUs and the Indian industry to plan their R&D roadmaps. It was also stated that while LTIPP was a broad vision document, the 12th Defence Plan dealt with details with specific requirements and modernisation plans for the armed forces.

TPCR states that LTIPP "identifies the shape and size of the Forces over the designated time period based on foreseeable strategic trends. From this document flow the 5 year plans which translate the LTIPP into an action plan with committed funding."[19] What is not clear; however, whether the nature of threats, likely cases of aggression have been analysed in detail to identify the shape and size of the forces, as 'strategic trends' do not convey the same meaning.

To say the obvious, 'shape and size of the Forces' can not be decided upon without deciding on the resource dimension and 'strategic trend 'is a weak substitute for 'likely cases of aggression'. Without these two elements a perspective plan loses much of its meaning. From above statement, it also appears that five year plan which is an action plan, cannot be drawn automatically from it; there is an element of 'translation' involved in it.

In this regard it is a departure from past thinking on the subject. To quote from two eminent analysts in this field, "A Defence Plan has to be prepared on the basis of a 15-year long perspective planning system, such that first five years are of the plan are very firm (Definitive Plan), the second five years less firm (Indicative Plan) and the third five-year term tentative (Vision Plan). There has to be reasonably firm allocation of financial resources for the first five years and the indicative allocation for the subsequent period."[20]

The conception here is clearly of a fixed 15 year plan consisting of three plans from which first five year plan can straightaway be derived. The vision element is only for last five years. Compared to this, the entire LTIPP 2012-27 stated to be a vision document from which the Five Year Plan cannot be automatically derived. LTIPP is subject to revision from time to time depending on the change in vision about the future based on global events. To quote from TPCR, "The unpredictability of global events in a increasingly 'Flat' world necessitates a periodic review of the LTIPP, *which is a continuous exercise. It facilitates mid-course corrections based on discernible emerging trends and the need to adapt to newer technologies.*" (emphasis added).[21]

For a long time, the approach prevalent among defence analysts was to conceive of the Perspective Plan as a capital acquisition plan "covering the next three Five-Year Plans".[20] Lt. Gen V.K. Singh (retd), "Budgeting for Defence: a Rational Approach" *Indian Defence Review*, July-September 1996.

On this basis, if one has to derive a five year plan from the Perspective Plan, it can only cover the capital acquisition plan for the five years, leaving the revenue expenditure out of it. A capital acquisition plan is not good enough for force structure planning which has a large element of revenue expenditure and as such cannot serve the purpose of a strategic plan. One can only hope that LTIPP 2012-27 is not a capital acquisition plan for 15 years, which it should not be as it is a vision document.

III

As mentioned above, with a lot of effort LTIPP 2007-22 was prepared following a 'Top Down' approach While deposing before the Standing Committee it was also stated that this long term plan will be different from earlier plans in that there will be a shift from *equipment based approach* to capability based approach.[22]

Let us look into this so called 'Top Down' approach. Perspective planning for defence in India has always been conceived as a 'top down' process starting from national vital interests then going by stages to military strategy, forces necessary to carry out the strategy, then the budgetary allocation to sustain the forces.

> "But the major pitfall in this approach is that it considers budgeting constraints late in the planning process. When the budgeting constraints are applied, the gap between desires and constraints may be so great that major adjustments between ends and means might become necessary."[23]

This problem is not peculiar to Indian defence planning but afflicts planning in other countries also. We can, for example, refer to critical comments of defence analysts in the context of the Congressionally mandated U.S. Quadrennial Defence Review (QDR) 1997.[24]

The defence planners of QDR, 1997 followed following top-down and step-by-step approach:

1. Identify national goal and threats to these goals.
2. Determine the strategy to counter the threats.
3. Determine the forces needed to execute the strategy.
4. Determine the budget needed to build and maintain these forces.

To quote Franklin C. Spinney, "In theory, each step of the procedure depends on the preceding step but it is independent of the subsequent step. Strategy is the key link in the chain; it ties our relations to the outside world (goals and threats) to our internal conditions (forces and budgets). But it is wrong to think that strategy depends only on external factors, like goals and threats." He added, "the simplistic assumption that strategy uniquely determines forces and budgets in effect presumes resources (money) are unlimited...By far the most important internal constraint shaping the evolution of our military capabilities is the perpetual budget squeeze."[25]

Let us also look at a key tool available to implement a top-down process in decision making in resource management, namely Defence Planning Guidance (DPG). It is to enable US Secretary of Defence in giving guidance to the services on priorities to be reflected in their programmes through their Programme Objective Memoranda (POM). "Ideally, the service programmers should be able to find in the DPG a planning framework to guide them as they build their POM. *It has seldom worked.* The DPG is usually too late and mostly too broad to provide a framework for service programmers or a metric against which service POM can be evaluated."[26]

As per the US experience, it was found necessary for the defence department to draw *budget scenarios* based on long term pressure to balance the budget while financing increasing burden of Medicare and Social Security. Military planners would construct their most effective force package under each scenario. The crucial decision however was selecting a realistic range of budget scenario. In the next phase it would be the responsibility of the Joint Chiefs of Staff (JCS) and Office of the Secretary of Defence (OSD) to synthesise the priorities of each service into a coherent system of *national* defence priorities. But if the budget scenario is not properly drawn national defence priorities will lack coherence and it will not be resource constrained defence planning.

While theoretically it is alright to aim resource constrained defence planning, it is not easy to achieve it because of the process involved where the crucial role would be played by services projecting their requirements. If the projections are not resource constrained, then objective of resource constrained planning cannot be achieved. In this context, at what really happened under PPBS process during the Cold War period as far as the role of JCS is concerned is worth noting. To quote an analyst, who had served in the U.S. DoD, "Each February, just one month after receiving the Defence Guidance, the JCS respond with a statement of long term military forces and support requirements called the Joint Strategic Planning Document (JSPD). This document, throughout my years in government, was virtually identical. Each time the chiefs ignored resource constraint and called for large force increase for each military service above the level of Defence Guidance. The reports contained no analysis, no dollar estimates and no list of ranked priorities; and JSPD did little to respond to the concerns enunciated by the Secretary. Thus, they were (and continue to be) essentially useless documents."[27] Each individual (other than the chairman) heads a different military service and the dual responsibility makes objectivity in military advice almost impossible. "Over the years the members of JCS, recognising mutual need to promote, have tacitly agreed not to criticise programmes of other services. Thus, the advice that comes out of the JCS—in documents like the JSPD—is likely to be uncritical of existing programmes and dedicated to increasing each service's forces and budget."[28] The established force levels of each service are difficult to change except in an incremental way.

Non-linear nature of strategy has to be kept uppermost in mind. In the real world, actions to neutralise threats and the resource constraints limiting those actions continuously interact. Therefore, a "Top-Down" process of strategy making would be flawed. One should not make too much about the 'scientific' nature of defence planning. Much of it is guesswork. As noted defence analyst Colin S. Gray in the context of strategic review of U.S. defence called "Bottom-Up Review" (BUR) (1993) which was Clinton Administration's first defence planning document (done before the QDR 1997 mentioned above), drew attention to absence of foreign policy guidance in making the strategic review. He also makes the important point, "The fundamental dilemma of the defence planner is that he or she has to make choices on the basis of too little information. The defence planner is in the business of deciding how to provide military capabilities to meet the requirements of strategic effectiveness when these requirements are unknown (indeed often unknowable).... No amount of analytical modelling, computer print-outs, fancy graphics and coloured slides can hide completely the fact that for the most part, defence planning is guesswork.... That so much of defence planning is not itself a problem. It is rather that, mesmerised by our analytical methodology, we forget that it is guesswork."[29]

If much of defence planning is guesswork, it may be more prudent to go by fiscal reality and goals in setting strategic objectives. This is what apparently the decision makers of BUR did, instead of going by the 'top-down' process proceeding from political guidance about US interests and its role in the world. "Thus, there are grounds for suspecting that the force structure selected for the late 1990s is geared more nearly to fiscal goals than strategic ones This suspicion is reinforced by the apparent mismatch between the BUR force structure and the strategic requirement: many analysts believe that the BUR force is incapable of meeting two Major Regional Conflict (MRC) war-fighting standard even in the absence of other demands on those forces."[30]

The same can be said about the force structure that emerged out of QDR 1997. For purposes of fiscal planning, the QDR projected a stable annual defence budget of $250 billion per year in constant terms. It noted that the funding for modernisation had been inadequate in the past. Path decided to be followed was to reduce active military personnel, reserve component personnel by significant numbers. These force reductions were expected to allow increases in investment for modernisation.

The strategy followed in QDR 1997 was clearly resource constrained. One is reminded of the defence planners in US in 1960s who talked of waging two-and-a-half wars simultaneously which was later reduced to one-and-a-half war by President Nixon in view of resource constraint in the 1970s.

Because of avoiding mismatch between strategy and resources and having cost-effective force structure, periodic in depth defence reviews are required. US Defence has instituted QDRs which is mandated by the Congress, which have regularly taken place since 1997. Defence spending started rising in US since 1999. The Global War On Terror (GWOT) undertaken after 9/11 led to enormous increase in defence spending. Compared to 1999, in 2010, when the war spending peaked, defence spending outlays grew 77 per cent in real terms. The non-war portion grew 46 per cent. It was recognised that this was an untenable position and Budget Control Act (BCA) was passed in 2011. The current plan is to grow Pentagon budget slightly slower than the inflation rate for the rest of the decade resulting in an eight per cent real cut by 2020.[31] The Pentagon may face deeper cuts. The BCA—the deficit deal passed in summer 2011—requires cuts of roughly

$1.2 trillion in federal spending by 2021. It created a joint Congressional Committee to identify the savings. Half of those savings are to come from Pentagon which after adjustments may amount to about $500 billion over nine years. "Under sequestration, non-war defence spending would fall by about 17 per cent in real terms from 2010-20."[32] Realities of budget will call for adopting more modest defence strategy which would no doubt be reflected in the next QDR.

Britain had the Strategic Defence and Security Review (SDSR) which was presented to Parliament in October, 2010. It was a hardheaded reappraisal of Britain's foreign policy and security objectives, and the resources necessary to meet them. The SDSR noted with concern that there was an unfunded liability of around 38 billion pound over next 10 years. That was more than the entire Defence budget for one year. "We must start to tackle this legacy before we can begin to put Defence on a sound and sustainable footing for the future. Defence must, like other parts of the government contribute to reducing the deficit in order to restore the economy."[33]

An important review was about the future of aircraft carriers. The previous Administration had ordered two new carriers three times the size of their existing ones with a combat fleet of 150 aircrafts. It was found that this 20 billion pound programme was crowding out other important investment in the Armed Forces. The NSC of UK had a hard look at the strategic and financial aspects of the programme. The result of the review was that Britain would need to operate only one aircraft carrier. The review report said, "We cannot now foresee the circumstances in which the UK would require the scale of strike capability previously planned. We are unlikely to face adversaries in large scale air combat. We are more likely to engage in precision operations which may need to overcome sophisticated defence capabilities. The single aircraft carrier will therefore routinely have 12 fast jets embarked for operation while retaining the capacity to deploy upto 36 previously planned.... It will be able to carry a wide range of helicopters..."[34]

A major focus of the review was how to eliminate over-commitment of resources in programmes and generate savings wherever possible. It was estimated that the legacy of over-commitment in Defence programme amounted to around 38 billion pound of which some 20 billion pound related to unaffordable plans for new equipment and support. It was also recognised that there are systemic pressures in two blocks of Defence expenditure—equipment and personnel. It observed "On the average military pay is increasing at between 1 and two per cent above the rate of inflation. This is not unique to Defence—the increases are in line with average UK earnings—but it needs to be properly recognised in our plans…The legacy of unaffordability, and these systemic pressures, mean that a major focus of work in the Strategic Defence and Security Review (SDSR) *has been to eliminate over-commitment, to the greatest extent possible by reducing running costs to allow resources to be focused on the front line. This has identified new non-front line savings of at least 4.3 billion pound over the Spending Review period.*"[35] (emphasis added)

Non-front line savings included among other items (i) reduction in civilian work force and non-front line service personnel, (ii) rationalisation of defence estate including sale of surplus land and building, (iii) efficiencies and improvements in military training, (iv) savings from contract renegotiations etc. Overall it represented a 25 per cent reduction in non-frontline organisations such as headquarters, support roles and organisations such as Defence Equipment and Support (DE&S), saving at least two billion pound per year by 2014/15. A total reduction of around 17,000 personnel was planned by 2015 when the current strategic review period would end. It was assumed that further reduction in force structure would be possible in the next review period.

As per reports in 2013, because of overall cuts in public spending, UK MoD might have to 'revisit' the SDSR and curtail their plans. Earlier assumptions were that budget for equipment will rise in real terms in 2015/16 and the following years. As the position emerged in 2013, it looked that this might not happen and plans have to be revaluated.

Strategic review of the force structure has been undertaken by Russia also. Anatolie Serdyukov appointed in 2007 was the first true civilian Defence Minister. He made personnel reforms his first priority. In October 2008, Serdyukov announced several radical reforms. He began the process of drastically altering the size and composition of Russian Armed forces. First announcements involved massive personnel cuts by 2012. Serdyukov's end-state envisioned one million uniformed personnel, down from1.2 million, with the vast majority of reductions coming from the officer rank.[36]

Then there was transition to brigade system which was under discussion for some time. The importance to Serdyukov for promoting the brigade transition was not only a more streamlined command and control system, but also to significantly reduce the number of mid-level and senior level billets and provide justification for a large scale reduction of the officer corps. The transition was aimed at abolishing almost all division/regimental structure and replaces them with 85 modular brigades. Each brigade will have approximately 4,500-5,000 personnel and its own organic support providing capability for independent action. Force reductions would not only affect the skeleton cadres in the field but also the personnel at the MoD and General Staff. The MoD is scheduled to be reduced from 11,920 to 5000 personnel The reductions of the General Staff was from 10,523 to 3,500 personnel.

Another reform of major significance was introduction of 'joint regional command' system in 2010 by a presidential order. Now the regional commander will directly control most armed forces units in his territory of responsibility vis-à-vis a diffused situation in the military district system. The transition changes the role of branches of service from operational command, to training and long term development. The adoption of this reform could be thought of, as Bartles comments, as Russian version of Goldwater-Nichols Defence Reorganisation Act of 1986.[37]

Concluding his survey of reforms undertaken in Russian Military since 2008 at the initiative of the Defence Minister, Bartles says, "Serdyukov has approached the MoD from the perspective of a businessman, not a general. No clearer illustration of this could be given than Serdyukov's style of managing resources. Serdyukov has taken a hard look at the threats Russia will likely face and has discovered the Armed Forces are too top heavy and bloated to meet these threats. Like the CEO of any large corporation in trouble he is downsising, restructuring, and ridding the organisation of toxic assets. If such restructuring occurs as planned, the Russian military will likely emerge much leaner, and capable of existing on a budget which the Russian Federation can afford, instead of a budget the Armed Forces wants. These reforms, if successful, could substantially increase salaries and free capital for needed modernisation programmes."[38] Serdyukov's actions must have been approved or even directed by Russia's civilian leadership; otherwise such far reaching reforms could not be pushed through.

There is an important lesson for us. It is absolutely necessary to rationalise the force structure if we have to bring in resource constrained defence planning. All the three services are incrementally adding to the forces without looking into future in terms of limited budget. The strength of three services is now 1.3 million. As an informed analyst points out, in the year 2000 the then Army Chief V.P. Malik announced that around 50,000 soldiers would be reduced over two years by not filling vacancies in non-combat jobs. This is not talked about anymore. In 2007, the Comptroller and Auditor General (CAG) reported that 33,000 soldiers had been recruited above the authorised strength by the army which claimed that it had wrongly estimated the 'wastages'.[39] Now more than 89,000 men and 400 officers are to be recruited by the army for the new Mountain Strike Corps, along with two mountain divisions that are being raised during the 12th plan period.[40] This will have very significant impact on pay and allowances apart from other expenditure which has not been properly assessed. As an eminent analyst states, "The unimaginative defence planning and budgeting has tranquilised the system into overlooking a clear and present danger in the context of revenue budget—the rising expenditure on Pay and Allowances (P&A)"[41] Just before the implementation of the sixth Pay Commission (in 2008-09), P&A accounted for 46.16 per cent of revenue budget and 25.18 per cent of the total budget. In BE 2013-14, P&A accounted for 61.75 per cent of the revenue budget and 36.61 per cent of the total defence budget. With the setting up of the seventh

Pay Commission and subsequent implementation of its recommendation, revenue P&A expenditure may witness a similar spurt. "If the spurt is similar to what happened in the past, P&A could possibly account for more than 75 per cent of the revenue budget and around 50 per cent of the total defence budget, unless, of course, the outlays go up significantly."[42]

This scenario is going to adversely affect pursuing an 'output oriented' and capability based planning. The trend is ominous. The share of stores and equipment which in 2008-09 was 34.62 per cent in the revenue budget has come down to 18.94 per cent in 2013-14. In the present fiscal scenario and dismal growth in GDP, it is difficult to conceive of double digit increase in percentage terms of defence budget in next few years. The cost of personnel is increasing at a rate which would be difficult to accommodate, without a double digit increase in defence budget the increase, in replacement cost of defence equipments. Going by the experience of the implementation of last pay commission report, we will be facing a totally untenable position if immediate steps are not taken to reduce the force levels by instituting a strategic and spending reviews as other countries mentioned have done to counter the growth in pay and allowances. Defence planning in India will be perpetually in a crisis situation, if we do not undertake such comprehensive reviews to streamline the forces and reduce the manpower significantly on the basis of likely availability of funds in the medium and long term, so that modernisation does not suffer.

IV

Defence planning should not only be fiscally constrained, as argued above, it should also be 'output oriented'. To bring output orientation we have to bring in programme budgeting to aim at capability-based planning. The Defence Procurement Procedure (DPP) brought out in 2006 (DPP 2006) indicated that policy decisions relating to acquisition of weapons and systems are being taken on the basis of capability based planning in the context of operational requirements. It talked in terms of existing 'capability gaps' and examination of alternative means of overcoming them while processing a case for procurement. This was also stated before the Standing Committee of parliament in the context of preparation of LTIPP 2007-2022. Capability based planning has various implications from resource allocation point of view, which are yet to be addressed by us in a systematic manner. There should be close link between defence strategy and defence budgeting. In a sense, defence budgeting for capability is defence strategy. This is because defence capability building is not done for its own sake. Capabilities are developed to achieve military objectives. To determine the objectives and to select a proper course of action for achieving the objectives we have to introduce the concept of 'Planning' as is understood in the context of

Planning, Programming and Budgeting System (PPBS) which was introduced in US Defence in the 1960s. PPBS or programme budgeting was introduced because they wanted capability based planning in defence. What is this Planning in the context of PPBS? As David Novick puts it, "Planning is the production of the range of meaningful potentials for selection of a course of action through systematic consideration of alternatives."[43] Cost effectiveness was chosen as a key measure of merit in choosing among alternatives in the defence programme. Along with planning goes programming. "Programming is specific determination of the manpower, material, and facilities necessary for accomplishing a program."[44]

By adopting programme budgeting concept, budgeting for desired defence capability becomes possible. Some need was felt for introducing this concept for resource management in defence in India but was not given a concrete shape. The Group of Ministers (GoM) in their report, Reforming the National Security System 2001 stated, "A need has been felt for a review of the form and content of Defence Services Estimate and the expansion of budgetary classification to promote programme-based budgeting, while ensuring compliance with security requirements.[45]

Unfortunately, the GoM did not go into the basic implications of programme-based budgeting which involved linking budgeting with strategic planning. In this context it is important to remember what programme budgeting is not. The important point to keep in view is that: "Program budgeting is not a new accounting system nor does it necessarily require changes in the existing accounting and statistical reporting system to fit the programme structure."[46]

The emphasis on programme in PPBS is on output, or end-product measurement, rather than on the inputs as they are emphasised in traditional budget-making. "In short, programme budgeting is characterised by an emphasis on objectives, programmes, and programme elements, all stated in output terms. Cost, or the line items of the traditional budget, is treated at appropriate level of aggregation which ensures that plans and programs are developed with adequate recognition of resource implication."[47]

There is another important point which relates to time dimension and brings the concept of multi-year planning and budgeting. It is in this background the Five Year Plans become important but the meaning of the plans is not five year acquisition plans as we tend to think when talking of our Five Year Defence Plans. To find out implications in budgetary terms of decisions already made is very important because whether plans are approved or not, commitments in terms of acquisitions continue to be made having very significant implications for future years' budgets. That is why we often find that more than ninety per cent of current budgets are already committed, leaving very limited scope for new commitments.

In UK, under the Public Expenditure Survey Committee (PESC) system, five year forward estimates of revenue and expenditure were published by late 1960s. Although, development of these estimates were not within a programme budgeting system, development of these estimates were compatible with programme budgeting.

Based on this experience and that of USA and Canada, the Australian DoD introduced both programme budgeting and 'Five-Year Rolling Programme' in 1970. It aimed at the production of a programme which identified major objectives of Defence Forces like antisubmarine warfare, air defence, and so on and assigned all the costs, R&D, capital expenditure, operating costs associated with each activity far enough into the future to show the full resource needs.[48]

After the Cabinet decision the cycle would begin again. Thus, it is a continuous process of review and analysis taking into account latest information on costs, delivery schedule etc as also change in strategic guidance. In-depth studies would be made throughout the year. The Five-Year Rolling Programme system is different from our system of Five Year Plans which is for a fixed period of five years. We thereby ignore the developments occurring in in-between years, until the next plan is formulated. Under PPBS, large number of programme change proposals were made by the services and many approved, and the changes were incorporated in the updated Five Year Plan. Thus, each year there is an updated Five Year Plan.

Through a 'rolling plan, we can also get over the problem of commitment of resources for a five year period. As the author stated in a similar context, "A solution can be found through the concept of rolling Five Year Defence plan and a rolling five-year defence budget, as we have advocated. This practice has been adopted in defence budgeting and planning in many countries. Planning in defence is a continuous activity. The assumptions and assessments have to be updated every year. It should not be done only at five yearly intervals."[49] The problem is about the rolling budget. From what level should it roll and at what annual rate? This is the crucial question.

Taking into account the experience of the 12th Plan, we have now three successive plans when there has been no agreement on the overall size of the plans and the plans are getting executed in ad hoc manner depending upon budgetary allocations made from year to year. Apparently, planning has ceased to have any operational meaning. Five Year Rolling plan where there need not be agreement on the overall size of the plan for a five year period, could be one of the answers.

The Estimates Committee (1992-93) noted that the MoD seemed almost reconciled to the situation of not having an approved Five Year Plan. The Committee was apprised by the MoD about various legal and technical difficulties for getting assurance about budgetary allocation for a period of five years. The

Committee, however, concluded that "on practical consideration, a five year budget allocation should be feasible, legal and technical difficulties notwithstanding."[50]

Is there any solution in sight which enables us to get over this perpetual problem of planning in face of uncertainty about the availability of resources? One can, in this context, take note of an important suggestion made by MoF while examining financial implication of the 11th plan as reported by the report of the Standing Committee of parliament: "The proposals of the MoD were examined and the views of the MoF were conveyed...indicating therein that it would be realistic to assume year-on-year increase in defence allocations in the range of 8-10 per cent for the purpose of planning exercise for the 11th Plan as against the annual average growth rate of 12.35 per cent per year indicated by the MoD."[51]

Defence planning in India has to take note of the fiscal framework as instituted by the government to be of any practical utility. In this context, attention is drawn to definition of defence plan as given by Major General Len Le Roux of South Africa, "The defence plan is essentially the document that specifies the measurable outputs that defence will produce in pursuit of Government objectives against the identified financial allocation within the Medium Term Expenditure Framework (MTEF) of three (to five) years."[52]

In our case, MTEF has to be provided within the parameters of FRBM Act. A MTEF is the first necessary step towards an MTEF which should contain fiscal policy objectives and a set of integrated medium-term macro-economic and fiscal targets. A MTEF builds on this by developing medium-term budget estimates for individual spending agencies. This gives certain amount of budget predictability to spending agencies enable them to plan their expenditure within the overall fiscal objectives. "But despite their theoretical popularity, there are few established medium term frameworks in a developing country. They are still evolving."[53]

There is another problem in our planning. We tend to ignore the consequences of current decisions on future budgets. In this context, it is worthwhile to note how the tool of Five Year Defence Plan (FYDP) was used in US Defence under PPBS. A basic idea behind introduction of PPBS was to have a plan which combines both forces and costs and project them into the future to see the foreseeable implications of current decisions. To implement this idea the tool of Five Year Defence Plan was used. It was not a future expenditure plan but a tool to help current expenditure decisions by bringing out its implications in terms of future commitments. As Enthoven and Smith put it, "A decision by the Secretary to Defence to develop, procure, or operate a weapon system affects not only the current defence budget but future budgets as well, the latter far more than the former as a rule... He needs not only a record of current costs and manpower but also projections of this information far enough ahead to enable him to estimate the main consequences of today's decisions. The FYDP, was developed to provide this record.

Physically, the FYDP was a series of force tables giving an eight year projection of forces and a five-year projection of costs and manpower, displayed in mission-oriented programmes."[54] The question arises what was the role of FYDP conceived in this way, in other words, what did the FYDP do? The answer was given succinctly by above two authors. "Most importantly, it tied together force and financial planning. As we have argued, sound decisions on forces cannot be made without carefully reviewing their total cost and manpower implications. For example, when deciding how many tactical aircraft to buy and operate, defence planners should consider not only the costs of aircraft but the costs of the personnel to operate and maintain them, cost of training the pilots, and the costs of housing, runways, depot stocks, hospitals, equipment, and other resources needed to support the force. With the aid of such tools as the FYDP, for example, defence planners found that every dollar spent directly to buy and operate a tactical aircraft leads to at least another dollar in support costs."[55]

This is the most important lesson that emerges from the FYDP tool as used in the PPBS: every dollar spent in buying and operating a system another dollar is required in support costs. This is, however, valid for any medium term resource planning in defence, but often ignored.

We have often, in planning for acquisitions, ignored to plan for required manpower to operate them and also provide for all the elements of various other support costs. That means a capability cannot be properly exploited. All the elements of costs to make optimum use of a capability have to be included in a Five year Plan. That is why programme budgeting (PPBS) concept is so very important to bring in capability based planning. Our input oriented budgeting only provides for a resource allocation which leads to ignoring the output aspects of defence budgeting in terms of capabilities. That is why an eminent Indian analyst of defence budgeting and planning recorded more than three decades back, "The introduction of P.P.B.S. is the only answer to the need for allocation of adequate resources for maintaining defence capability at the acceptable optimum level. Neither progressive increases of defence allocation or even allocation on the basis of G.N.P. as advocated by some, will ensure effective planning and programming."[56]

There is another important aspect of viewing FYDP in this way as a tool of decision making by enabling the top management to look at consequences of today's decisions on future budgets and as an internal control mechanism to control future commitments. Today we have no such mechanism. It has been brought out that in 2012-13 of the total capital acquisition budget the committed liabilities accounted for 91.64 per cent and during the current fiscal it is expected to go up to 95.98 per cent. This would leave very little for new schemes.[57]

If we can do proper costing of existing commitments in terms of programmes of force planning, including expenditure on both revenue and capital account and project them for next five years then we can have an FYDP as in PPBS. This would call for introducing the concept of programme in defence planning and budgeting. This is absolutely necessary. There is no point in looking separately at the revenue budget and capital budget. This would not help in force planning nor in bringing together force and financial planning. In other words we can not do capability based planning in the real sense, without introducing the concept of programming.

Let us look more closely at the Capability Based Planning (CBP) as to what it entails, which is stated to be the basis of LTIPP. "Over the past decade, the CBP has become something of a 'gold standard' in defence planning throughout the NATO alliance."[58]

Capability is the ability to achieve desired operational effects under specified standards and conditions through a combination of means and ways to perform a set of tasks. Without defining missions and tasks to be accomplished and allocating resources for carrying those tasks capability planning cannot be attempted. The concept of capability based planning was first formally articulated in Quadrennial Defence Review (QDR) Report 2001 of USA. "The new defence strategy is built around the concept of shifting to a 'capability-based' approach to defence. That concept reflects the fact that the US cannot know with confidence what nations, combination of nations or non-state actors are threat to vital U.S. interests." It is however possible "to anticipate the capabilities that an adversary might employ."[59] This thought led to capability-based approach in QDR 2001, which was continued in QDR 2006.

CBP for U.S. defence meant broadening of the strategic perspective compared to threat based planning, in focusing on emerging threats from adversaries relying on asymmetric warfare to attain their objectives. It also meant exploiting opportunities provided by the information-led technological revolution. It is to be remembered that CBP is more of an approach towards long term planning for capability building, than a total system incorporating costing and resource management aspect. Therefore in U.S. defence, PPBS (renamed PPBES) is still operating as the core of the planning and resource management system. The basic idea of CBP is best brought out by Paul Davis of RAND Corporation, "planning, under uncertainty, to provide capabilities suitable for modern day challenges and circumstances while working within an economic framework necessitating choice."[60] While discussing CBP the key point in the above definition 'working within an economic framework that necessitates choice', should not be lost sight of.

The key intuition behind CBP is to start by defining *what needs to be done and then derive an affordable force that can do that.* This is fundamentally different approach from starting with the current force and then working out how to improve it. Scenarios play a key role in the defence capability-planning process though it is being realised that it may not be enough. Until about a decade ago, defence capabilities were mostly identified in terms of material and to a smaller extent, in terms of personnel. After that the trend was towards more 'joint' material and personnel capabilities. "Most countries are now also taking a step further by recognising that true defence capabilities consist of more than just material and personnel solutions. They have broadened the definition to include important capability elements such as doctrine, training, leadership and so on—leading to new acronyms such as Doctrine, Organisation, Training, Material, Leadership, Personnel and Facilities (DOTMLPF) in the US, TEPID OIL (Training, Equipment, Personnel, Information, Doctrine, Organisation, Infrastructure and Logistics) in the UK and PRICIE in Canada."[61] (This trend, for example became most visible in concrete terms in new capability areas such as counter-Improvised Explosive Devices (IED). To meet the challenge, most graduated to 'broader' analysis of capability requirement "such as increasing emphasis on training or tactics, techniques and procedures in order to provide better value for money than instinctive material-only solution.... The key trend here is that the very term 'capability' is moving away from being equated with military hardware to instead a much broader conception of capability as the 'ability to...'If this trend is consolidated, it may lead to profound consequences for both the ways we do forward defence planning and the actual outcome of such processes. "[62] To combat IED and better protect U.S. forces in Afghanistan and Iraq a new organisation named Joint IED Defeat Organisation (JIEDDO) was established in USA in 2006. Apart from the solutions like sensors to detect the IEDs in the ground and electronic jammers that prevent their detonation, "The organisation has also covered cost of critical counter-IED training for service members and, what is most valuable, funded the analysis of the enemy networks responsible for IED attacks..."[63] But material solution like development and fielding of Mine-Resistant Ambush Protected (MRAPS) vehicles played an important role to counter the IED threat. But this required a Task Force approach.[64]

For identifying capability needs (and capability gaps) under the Capability Based Planning (CBP) approach, as per QDR 2001, the requirements of *joint force* was to be the basis. We still have a *single service* approach to establish capability needs and capability gaps. What is important to remember is that there are several options in CBP *to solve* the capability gaps. The crucial word here is 'solve'. For example, one can develop concepts to determine potential options to solve the gap. Then one can identify a material or non-material solution. Let us remember that CBP is mainly a methodology for identifying capability needs and capability gaps rather than a resource management system.

Selecting the best option would be largely dependent on how much information we have about the 'gap'. Information required would include the operational needs, *the ability to solve the gap with the current capabilities*, cost involved, the technological advancements, and the impact joint interdependence has on the gap.[65]

Cost is a very important factor in determining which solution is chosen to solve a capability gap. "CBP is fiscally constrained...in most cases, divestures pay for new capabilities...The bottom line is that with a zero-sum resource environment, new capabilities can only be funded by divestures."[66] The point to note is that CBP may have to work and can work in a zero resource environment. Additional resources are not required to bring in CBP as new capabilities can be funded by divestures of existing capabilities or by adopting innovative approach.

CBP, however, did not have much impact on force structure planning. This is true for NATO countries as also USA. As Spiegeleire put it "If the CBP was revolutionary in its content, its actual impact on force structure have been *underwhelming*" (emphasis added).[67] As regards USA where in QDR 2001 the CBP was introduced following is what the US General Accounting Office (GAO) who reviewed the QDR 2001 had to say, "The QDR legislation asks DOD to define the size and composition of the force that it needs to successfully execute the full range of missions called for in the national defence strategy...However, the force analysis had a near-term focus that provided few insights into how future threats and technological advances in U.S. capabilities may affect future force structure requirements."[68]

The main determinant of defence capability is the force structure. So force planning should become the key element in capability planning. Force planning has to be accompanied by defining the missions and tasks to be accomplished and resource allocation for those purposes. Does our LTIPP which is supposed to follow capability based planning fulfill the requirements? In India, we are yet to attempt force structure planning through our FYP. Absence of approved plans for such a long time corroborates that. We are carrying on with existing force structure without any strategic guidance, incrementally adding to it when we can. Main drivers of costs in defence are the strength and composition of the forces. "If we want to use budgeting for building up desired defence capabilities, then an affordable force structure should be its main focus for all the three Services."[69] Nothing is more important than having a comprehensive *Defence Review* to address the issue of affordable force structure within likely budgetary resources for next 10 years. Without it, defence capability building will take an ad hoc character. The most important thing in budgeting for defence capability would be to examine what the options available within a budgetary allocation are which, in real terms, may not grow by more than two to three per cent per annum. "The options would be to acquire new capabilities such as advanced aircrafts, tactical missile defence, UAVs, and C4ISR which would come under the option of modernisation. The cost of these elements of modernisation have to be balanced against reduction of air force squadrons, reduction of army divisions by x numbers as against modernisation options, for more firepower, greater mobility, more attack helicopters, UAVs, C4ISR, for the navy, reduction in number of surface ships as against increase in submarine strength or vice versa. These options are to be examined on the basis of criteria of costs and effectiveness."[70] If options are exercised intelligently then it will lead to augmentation of capability within given resources.

These are hard decisions which can no more be postponed because of budgetary realities. That is why periodic defence review from now on should be the order of the day. In fact, one of the best ways to generate funds would be to foreclose those schemes which have lost their utility. The Joint Services approach in necessary for CBP, not only for more effectiveness to meet capability needs but also to avoid duplication and overlap between capabilities being acquired by each Service.

While following the CBP methodology for defence planning, the current budgetary realities are to be kept in view. Making a review of progress of CBP a decade after it was introduced, Spiegeleire observes, "A number of factors are now likely to push CBP in new directions. These include the *budgetary tsunami* hitting most of the NATO defence organisations..."[71]

To avoid being hit by budgetary tsunami in following capability based planning we need to have a long term financial plan for defence. Since our budget is prepared on the cash-outgo basis it permits entering into contracts with large commitments of expenditure in future years. With several such contractual obligations bunching together, it will create an untenable position for defence planning making it difficult to undertake new modernisation schemes. To control the future commitments for developing capabilities within reasonable limits as also to provide adequate amounts for operation, maintenance and support costs, it is necessary to have a 10-year budget and capability plan. It is feasible to do so by following the approach indicated by the Thirteenth Finance Commission in their report emphasising the need for fiscal consolidation and returning to the goals laid down by the FRBM Act though with an altered time-frame.[72] They made projections for defence budget upto 2014-15. To quote from the report, "For defence expenditure, MoF has projected a growth rate of seven per cent per annum for defence expenditure. Capital expenditure is projected to grow at 10 per cent per annum. The MoD has emphasised the need to provide adequately for enhanced force multipliers. We also recognise the need for some real growth in defence revenue expenditure, to allow for adequate depreciation and maintenance. We are of the view that the MoF's projections address these needs and have, therefore, adopted them. The resultant projection for overall annual growth rate of defence expenditure works out to 8.33 per cent."[73]

The projected defence budget as per the Thirteenth Finance Commission for the period 2010-15 and actual allocation of defence budget indicates that, projected figures for 2012-13 and 2013-14 are much less than actual allocations and that projected for 2014-15 is less than what was allocated for 2013-14. This is a healthy trend and may not continue for long considering the fact that the Fourteenth Finance Commission is due to submit its report towards the end of 2014 and government has renewed its commitment to FRBM Act. Government has to consider the possibility of a 10-year defence budget plan to finance its capability-based plan. A White Paper indicating such a plan providing for yearly rate of growth of defence budget for example, of 8.5 per cent (keeping in view earlier recommendation) and its main thrust of capability building plan should be brought out.

Along with it we should introduce the concept of FYDP as in PPBES to tie together force and financial planning and control of future commitments. Decisions on forces have to be made keeping in view their total costs and manpower implications. FYDP has also to provide a vehicle to control future commitments by providing necessary data.

As mentioned above, unless the existing force levels are given a hard look it will not be possible to contain the defence expenditure and make available funds for modernisation. Therefore, immediately a *Defence Strategy Review* should be conducted with a clear mandate to rationalise the force structure to make it affordable. That is why periodic strategic reviews have been conducted in other countries as brought out above. It cannot be done under the normal process of planning and budgeting. Reduction of manpower from present 1.3 million to 1.2 million forces during next five years must be attempted through strategic reviews. Reduction should be as in the case of *UK Strategic Review* in 'non-frontline' forces.

The rate in the growth of budget allowed for planning purposes should be uniform for all the three Services, taking the present share of their budget allocations as the basis. The force structure and force level reviews has to be done by each Service keeping in view the budget plan. Without such in-depth reviews of force structure, defence planning and budgeting will continue to follow diverse paths with defence strategy being the casualty. If defence planning has to move forward then *Strategic Defence Review* is a must. Otherwise, defence planning would continue to be at a cross roads and we may soon have to write its epitaph.

NOTES

1. Para 1.43 of the Report of the Standing Committee on the Demands for Grants 2012-13.
2. Annual Report of the Ministry of Defence (MoD), 1977-78, chapter II, para 1.
3. Ibid.
4. D.S. Nakra, Formerly Financial Adviser Defence, 'Defence Budgeting in India' United Service Institution of India Paper no. 5, 1979, p. 26.

5. Annual Report of the Ministry of Defence, 1977-78, p. 5.
6. The Annual Report of the Ministry 1979-80, para 10 of the Report.(emphasis added).
7. Amit Cowshish, 'A Perspective on Defence Planning in India', Strategic Analysis IDSA July-August 2012.
8. Annual Report of the MoD 1983-84, para 11.2.
9. Annual Report 1982-83, Ch II, para 12.
10. Annual Report 1986-87, para 8.4.2.
11. M. Govinda Rao, 'Mid-Year Review of the Indian Economy 2005-2006', Shipra, India International Centre (IIC), New Delhi, 2006, p. 132.
12. Ibid.
13. 11th report of the Standing Committee on the Demands for Grants (2006-07).
14. *The Financial Express*, January 21, 2014.
15. *The Indian Express*, January 12, 2014.
16. Op.cit para 3.4, Standing Committee on Defence Report on Demands for Grants 2006-07.
17. Op.cit para 3.5.
18. Op.cit. 3.12 and 3.16).
19. Ministry of Defence, Government of India, Technology Perspective Capability Roadmap (TPCR) , April 2013, Introduction, para 3.
20. General (retd) V.P. Malik and Brigadier (retd) Gurmeet Kanwal, 'Defence Planning in India', p 8.
21. TPCR.
22. 21 Report of the Standing Committee on Demands for Grants 2007-08, para 3.5.
23. Amiya Kumar Ghosh, 'Defence Budgeting and Planning in India, The Way Forward' USI and Knowledge World, p. 294.
24. Franklin C. Spinney, 'Porkbarrels and Budgeteers: What went wrong with the Quadrennial Defence Review?' *Strategic Review*, Fall 1997.
25. Ibid.
26. Stuart E. Johnson, 'A New PPBS Process to Advance Transformation', Defence Horizons, National Defence University, September, 2003.
27. Richard A. Stubbing with Richard A. Mendel 'The Defence Game', Harper and Row, 1985, p.71.
28. Ibid.
29. Colin S. Gray, 'Off the Map: Defence Planning After the Soviet Threat" *Strategic Review*, Spring 1994.
30. Ibid.
31. Benjamin H. Friedman and Justin Logan, 'Why the Military Budget is "Foolish and Sustainable' Orbis, Spring 2012.
32. Ibid.
33. Spending Review 2010, HM Treasury, Cm 7942 October 2010.
34. Securing Britain in an Age of Uncertainty, http://www.official— documents gov.uk, October 2010.
35. Ibid.
36. Charles K. Bartles, 'Defence Reforms of Russian Defence Minister Anatolii Serdyukov', *Journal of Slavic Military Studies* 24, pp.55-80, 2011, Routledge.
37. Ibid, p. 75, Bartles.
38. Ibid, p. 80.
39. *The Hindu*, May 26, 2007.

40. Gautam Navlakha, "Giant with Feet of Clay", *The Economic and Political Weekly,* June 15, 2013.
41. Amit Cowshish, 'What is Choking Defence Budget?', 38 IDSA Comment, February14, 2014.
42. Ibid.
43. David Novick, "Programme Budgeting, RAND, 1965, p. 91.
44. Ibid.
45. Reforming the National Security System 2001, Para 6.52.
46. David Novick, 'What Programme Budgeting Is and Is Not' "Programme Budgeting" ed by David Novick, RAND, 1973, p.14.
47. Ibid, p. 16.
48. S.G. Herring, Asstt. Secretary, Treasury Australia, Programme Budgeting ed by David Novick, RAND, 1973, p. 58.
49. Amiya Kumar Ghosh, 'Defence Budgeting and Planning in India: the Way Forward', USI and Knowledge World, 2006, p. 379.
50. Estimates Committee Report, 1992-93, on Ministry of Defence, Force Levels etc para 1.75.
51. Report of the Standing on Demands for Grants, 2007-08, para 3.2, p. 30.
52. Len Le Roux, Major General (retired), South Africa, "The Military Budgeting Process: An Overview", prepd for SIPRI workshop, Accra, Ghana February 2002.
53. Amiya Kumar Ghosh, 'Defence Budgeting and Planning in India: the Way Forward', USI and Knowledge World, 2006, p. 380.
54. Alain C. Enthoven and K. Wayne Smith, 'How Much is Enough?' Harper and RoW, 1971 p. 48.
55. Ibid, p. 49.
56. D.S. Nakra, Formerly Financial Adviser Defence, USI Papers, Number five, United Service Institution (USI) of India, 1979, p. 27.
57. Cowshish, Feb. 2014, op cit.
58. Stephan De Spiegeleire, 'Ten Trends in Capability Planning for Defence and Security', *The RUSI Journal October/November 2011.*
59. QDR 2001 Report, p. 14.
60. Paul Davis, 'New Challenges for Defence Planning' RAND, 1994.
61. Stephan De Spiegeleire, op.cit.
62. Ibid.
63. Ashton B. Carter, 'Running the Pentagon Right' *Foreign Affairs,* January/February, 2014.
64. Ibid.
65. Boyd Bankston and Todd Key, 'Draft White Paper on capabilities Based Planning', March 30, 2006. www.mors.org/userFiles/file/ meeting/06cbpIL,www.gao.gov/docdblite/accno= A05465
66. Ibid.
67. Op.cit.
68. GAO report on Quadrennial Defense Review 2001, http:/www. gao.gov/docdblite/ Accno=Ao5465, November 2002, p. 18.
69. Amiya Kumar Ghosh, 'Resource Allocation and Management in Defence: Need for a Framework', KW Publishers and Centre for Air Power Studies (CAPS), 2013, p. 276.
70. Ibid, p. 285.
71. Spiegeleire, op cit.
72. Amiya Kumar Ghosh, 'Resource Allocation and Management in Defence: Need for a Framework, p. 401.
73. 13th Finance Commission Report, p. 83 (para6.27 read with Annex 6.3).

7

DEFENCE PLANNING, PROGRAMMING AND BUDGETING: AN AGENDA FOR REFORM

Narendra Singh Sisodia and Amit Cowshish

Defence planning and budgeting in India suffer from several infirmities. As a consequence, planning and budgeting remain inefficient tools for effective management of India's defence. This essay is an attempt to discuss their weaknesses and suggest some measures for improving the planning and budgeting processes.

At the outset, it must be pointed out that hardly any objective, in-depth research has been carried out on the subject and literature on defence planning and budgeting is meagre. This could be attributed partly to Ministry of Defence's (MoD's) obsessive focus on maintaining secrecy. Defence plans are classified documents and no public version is available for review even by parliament. While budget documents are presented annually to parliament, the data provided by them offer limited opportunity for in-depth research. Annual reports of MoD are sanitised documents, often containing less information than provided by newspapers. Available materials on planning and budgeting are individual recollections of authors based on their subjective interpretations or judgements. As would be pointed out later in this article, developed democracies of the world provide voluminous material relating to their defence plans and budgets, without disclosing any sensitive information. This is an example India needs to emulate in its own interest.

We begin this article by a brief discussion of the concept of Planning, Programming and Budgeting System (PPBS). This is followed by a discussion on the evolution of defence planning in India, preparatory steps needed for planning; practices followed in some other democracies; methods of resource allocation; and issues concerning long-term financial commitments for planning. The article also touches upon the need for coordination with other sectors of national plan and capabilities-based planning. In conclusion, it offers some suggestions about possible measures for reform.

The PPBS developed by Charles J. Hitch was first introduced in the US by Robert McNamara, Secretary of Defence in 1961.[1] The PPBS was founded on the following key principles:

1. Decisions should be based on explicit criteria of national interest, not compromises among institutional forces.
2. Needs and costs should be considered simultaneously.
3. Major decisions should be made by choices among explicit, balanced, feasible alternatives.
4. Secretary of defence should have an active analytic staff to provide him relevant data and unbiased perspectives.
5. A multiyear force and financial plan should project the consequences of present decisions into the future.
6. Open and explicit analysis, available to all parties, should form the basis of major decisions."

The system was implemented through Draft Presidential Memorandums (DPMs). In all, 93 of such DPMs were issued. They emphasised full definition of the objectives and consideration of the entire range of alternative ways of achieving the objectives. They focused on the most effective means of achieving the objective.

During his term as Secretary of Defence, McNamara enforced hard decisions on contentious and complex issues, frequently at the cost of weapon systems, fiercely protected by military services. McNamara's assertive leadership and decision-making deeply offended some in the senior military leadership. PPBS thus proved unsettling to many in the services and came under severe criticism. In 1968, Secretary of Defence Melvin R. Laird restored to the military departments the responsibility to identify future needs. However, the broad principles enunciated under McNamara's leadership have been internalised in US Department of Defence's (DoD) decision-making processes. They continue to be used for defining and resolving issues. Although much controversy and debate surrounds PPBS, "every Secretary since Robert McNamara has relied on PPBS, adapting it to suit his circumstances and management style."

The PPB system offers a sound basis for decision-making in any sphere of public policy. It is even more relevant for defence planning and budgeting, as they face particularly complex challenges, given the many uncertainties defence has to deal with. Despite its merits it has not been attempted by MoD in India. This can be attributed to three reasons. Firstly, there has been more discussion on some negative aspects of PPBS rather than its many virtues. In any case, MoD has been essentially status-quoist, ignoring many of its own reports for reform and slow to change. Secondly, there is a strong belief that Armed Forces are the experts, they know best what is needed for national security and any questioning of their judgements would be an avoidable encroachment of their functional autonomy. Thirdly, MoD simply does not have the expertise which was available in the office of US Secretary of Defence to analyse and evaluate the Armed Forces' programmes. Most unfortunately, even the Armed Forces do not have the skills at present to introduce PPBS in their planning and budgeting process.

We now proceed to consider defence planning in detail and begin by tracing its evolution in India.[2] Prior to independence, India faced no major outside threat, except during World War II. Defence outlays were fixed at Rs.55 crore per annum, constituting more than half of the Central Government Revenue. While defence expenditure rose sharply after independence, there was no systematic effort at planning. Funds were utilised essentially for acquisitions from abroad, financed mostly by India's sterling reserves. After India's defeat in the Sino-Indian Conflict of 1962, the need for according high priority to defence was acutely felt. The First Five Year Defence Plan was formulated for 1964-69. The plan focussed on modernisation and expansion. It also sought to reduce the country's dependence on foreign sources by paying attention to indigenous production and strengthening of Defence Research and Development Organisation (DRDO). A planning cell was set-up in the MoD in 1965, to coordinate the national and defence plans. By this time, insufficient availability of foreign exchange had become a major impediment to planning. In this context, the Second Five Year Defence Plan (FYDP) was developed on a "roll-on" basis. After conclusion of each year, another year was added so that the plan could be revised and adapted to intervening developments. The India-Pakistan War of 1971, compelled the government to focus on meeting immediate requirements and it was found difficult to continue with the "roll-on" planning process. MoD's planning cell was not taken seriously in the economic planning process. It was recommended by an Apex group under the Union Minister for Planning that "steady long-term defence programmes would be more cost-effective and economical." It was also decided that the defence and national plans should be co-terminus so that the two could be co-ordinated.

Another experiment to improve exercises for defence plans was undertaken in1977 through a Defence Planning Committee (DPC) under Cabinet Secretary, but this also failed to achieve its objectives. Within the MoD, Planning units were established in the Department of Defence Production (DDP) and DRDO. A planning and coordination cell in the MoD was assigned the overall task of coordinating and compiling the plans of various agencies and to prepare a coherent whole for cabinet approval. However, this cell lacked the required professional expertise and staff support to perform its mandate effectively.

In 1986, a new organisation named Directorate-General of Defence Planning Staff was established, under the Chiefs of Staff Committee. Unfortunately, like all its predecessors, this mechanism also failed to achieve its objectives. One major reason for its failure was the lack of continuity at the leadership level. As observed by the Parliamentary Standing Committee on Defence in 1996, in the first decade of its existence, the agency saw six Directors General. The Group of Ministers (GoM) on 'Reforming the National Security System' in chapter VI of its report noted other deficiencies in defence planning like the absence of a national security doctrine and commitment of funds beyond the financial year. The key recommendation of the GoM on National Security was to create the institution of the Chief of Defence Staff (CDS) with the objective, inter alia, of ensuring integrated defence planning, which was till then service wise and thus disjointed.[3] This proposal for creation of CDS was referred by the government for broad-based consultation to political parties. In the interim, a Chief of Integrated Defence Staff (CIDS) under the Chiefs of Staff Committee was created. Despite the establishment of CIDS as the co-ordinating Secretariat, the improvements envisaged are not yet visible. Firstly, the five year plans are still not formulated in time nor are they approved at the appropriate level i.e. the Cabinet Committee on Security (CCS). Secondly, there is little evidence of interservice prioritisation and integration in the planning process. Thirdly, the plans do not necessarily have a linkage with annual budgets and one can proceed without the other.

From the foregoing account it would be evident that the history of India's Defence Planning structures is a story of adhocism and experimentation. Successive governments have experimented with different mechanisms for planning. None of these have proved effective or been sustained. In contrast, the Planning Commission, created through an executive order, has been a more successful organisation. It has regularly prepared perspective and five year plans; got them approved timely; produced a host of studies and data both for better planning and evaluation; and during the years that India's economy had a greater degree of centralised direction functioned as an effective instrument for economic planning. Despite limited formal authority over a host of central ministries and state governments it acted as an effective instrument of coordination. Its relative success is attributable to the importance assigned to it by the political leadership on a sustained basis and its expertise in planning. Its authority has also been reinforced by the debate generated by its exercises in the parliament, the media and the public. It needs to be considered whether some of these aspects also have relevance for defence planning.

One of the recurrent criticisms of India's defence planning process has been that the government has failed to bring out any formal documents systematically articulating national security objectives, national security strategy and defence policy. This position has been acknowledged by the government in parliament and its Standing Committee on Defence.[4] Long and medium-term defence plans should follow from a consensus-based and coherent articulation of national security objectives and strategy. These would be based on an assessment of India's security environment, technological developments, and the country's overall interests and ethos.

It may be pertinent in this context to consider some examples from other democracies. The American National Intelligence Council (NIC) carried out a security environment forecast titled 'Mapping the Global Future'. Thereafter, another assessment was brought out in the document titled 'Global Trends 2025: A Transformed world'. The formulation of these long-term assessments is an outcome of an intensive collaborative effort among strategic experts, intelligence professionals in government, think tanks and universities. The U.S. government announced a National Security Strategy in May 2010. In January 2012 another document called 'Sustaining U.S. Global Leadership: Priorities for 21st Century Defence' was brought out. The U.S. DoD regularly brings out a Quadrennial Defence Review (QDR) which is a legislatively-mandated review of DoD strategy and priorities.

In France, a system of publishing white papers is followed. The last white paper on Defence and National Security was presented on April 24, 2013. This was followed by presentation of Military Estimates for 2014-19. This bill puts into practice France's defence policy guidelines for the next six years.

Likewise, Australia also brings out a defence white paper.[5] The last one, released on May 03, 2013, addresses a range of significant international and domestic developments affecting Australia's National Security and defence. Australia's MoD also prepared an elaborate set of documents, including National Security Strategy, Defence Planning Guidance (DPG) (Classified), Intelligence Assessments and Defence Capability Plan (DCP) Review. Australia also publishes a public version of its Defence Corporate Plan, which sets out in a clear and concrete fashion its goals, strategic targets, key strategies and benefits. Classified information concerning the plan is retained in an Annex. The Australian Parliament thus has a clear idea about how would their government go about meeting the security challenges and what outcomes might be expected.

In the U.K. too, a number of documents on National Security and related issues are published which inform the defence planning process. In February 2010, a *Defence Green Paper* titled "Adaptability and Partnership: Issues for Strategic Defence Review" was presented to the parliament.[6] The *Green Paper* opened discussion, set out the emerging thinking on issues of national security and defence and commenced the process of building consensus.

A *Strategic Defence Review* titled "Securing Britain in an Age of Uncertainty: The Strategic Defence and Security Review" was presented to the Parliament in October 2010.[7] Quite significantly, it acknowledged that UK's "Armed Forces ... have been overstretched, deployed too often without appropriate planning, with the wrong equipment, in the wrong numbers and without clear strategy". It also outlined the specific remedial measures to be undertaken. Another important document published for the first time in2008 under the aegis of the British National Security Council (NSC) was the National Security Strategy which set out how the government would address and manage a diverse range of threats. It lays down a whole-of-government, integrated approach, in which MoD's role is also defined.

From the above account, it would be evident that other democracies like France, Australia, USA and UK undertake a series of exercises towards defence planning and the findings of these are shared with their legislatures and citizens. These documents inform the public about threats and challenges the nation faces and how they are proposed to be met. They lay down clear goals and objectives and performance measures on the basis of which the performance of the, National Security establishments and the government as a whole can be measured.

In India, often an argument advanced is that no such information can be shared with the public or the parliament because unlike UK and France. India faces real and live threats. This argument has hardly any validity because even in the cases of countries discussed above, sensitive information is classified and only public versions are shared. The perusal of relevant documents clearly shows that they do not in any manner compromise national security, while they do enrich the policy making process through debate and enable law makers to ensure parliamentary accountability. By not undertaking such exercises or sharing them with the parliament, India's national security establishment only suffers a disadvantage.

We now turn to the issue of resource allocation for defence plans, which invariably poses a difficult choice for political leadership in democratic countries. Every rupee spent on defence cannot be spent elsewhere for other priorities like health, education, infrastructure etc. Neglect of such vital needs in a developing nation creates internal fault-lines which are prone to exploitation by hostile actors outside. Recent history provides an example of cases where military strength alone has failed to guarantee security. The collapse of the Soviet Union is an oft-cited example. A nation's security, in the ultimate analysis, depends on its comprehensive national strength and not military prowess alone.

In the past, alternative criteria have been applied to determine defence outlays. American political scientists, Glenn Snyder and Samuel Huntington in their work on defence policy making under Presidents Harry Truman and Eisenhower have pointed out that in arriving at defence outlays, they followed the 'remainder method', which estimated tax revenues, "substracted domestic spending and gave whatever was left over to defence."[8] The method adopted by President Kennedy was to impose budget ceilings on defence. This approach compelled civilian decision-makers "to substitute their judgements for those of the military professionals and turned budget discussions into a test of Civil-Military Relations."[9]

It has sometimes been suggested that defence outlays should be fixed as a percentage of GDP over an extended period of time to ensure a steady and adequate flow of resources for defence. The Parliament's Standing Committee on Defence (1995-96) in its sixth report had proposed a long-term commitment of four per cent of GDP.[10] Fixing a percentage of GDP may also not be rational as it does not take into account the growth rate and size of the economy. While useful as a guide and as a measure of comparison, this standard is "just as disconnected from a net assessment of enemy threats as was the remainder method."[11]

In India's own case, in recent years, it has been possible for governments to provide adequate resources for modernisation due to rapid economic growth. A higher share of GDP is not helpful, if the economy itself is doing poorly. At around one percent of its GDP, Japan's defence expenditure is nearly twice that of India's. While a share of GDP is a good way to make comparisons, a country's defence outlay should be determined in the light of realistic assessment of the threats it faces and the capabilities it may actually need. However, finally a political judgement would be needed to balance the needs of defence with those of other key sectors.

Government's failure to commit itself to long-term modernisation plans for the Armed Forces and the uncertainty about long-term availability of funds for such plans has been cited as a major handicap for defence planners. Given the long gestation of defence modernisation plans and the risks attached to under funding and delays, the expectation of services about long-term commitments is justified. However, the problem arises when indications given by Ministry of Finance about available funds for future periods are unacceptable to MoD/Armed Forces and the process for negotiating higher outlays continues indefinitely. If defence plans take into account the possibility of alternatives and the costs and risks attached to them, resource allocation can become more rational and the process of negotiation can reach a successful closure.

Given the fact that resources for defence would always remain limited, there is need to focus on increasing the efficiency of defence expenditure. Planning for defence therefore needs to become integral to planning for national security on a holistic basis. Since defence plans are a part of the Union government's non-plan expenditure, there is at present no satisfactory mechanism to ensure inter-sectoral coordination. Past efforts in this direction did not yield much success. Currently, such efforts are mostly piecemeal and ad hoc. The NSC which could have taken up the task of coordination has not done so. A more systematic attempt to coordinate defence plans with other related sectors, like external affairs, surface transport, ports and shipping, civil aviation, information and broadcasting, telecommunications, industry, science and technology will ensure more robust defence and optimise the value of money spent on defence.

In the past, defence planning, both in India and elsewhere, has tended to be input oriented and equipment and platform-centric rather than capability based. Paul K. Davis defines Capabilities-Based Planning (CPB) as "planning, under uncertainty, to provide capabilities suitable for a wide-range of modern day challenges and circumstances while working within an economic framework that necessitates choice. It contrasts with developing forces based on a specific threat or scenario." CPB places stress on flexibility, adaptiveness and robustness of capability. In involves "a modular, building-block approach to force design and operations."[12]

Capabilities-based planning adopts an integrated approach, looking at complete capabilities rather than discrete equipment or complement of manpower. It makes choices among alternative capabilities. It focuses on outputs and outcomes rather than inputs. It considers costs and benefits of each alternative and selects, what in the judgement of planners, would be the most cost effective option for meeting the same objective. While doing so, it should look at the total cost of owning and maintaining the capability through its life-cycle. Capabilities-based planning would also involve abandoning overtime capabilities no longer required. The process calls for a certain degree of ruthlessness and entails rigorous intra-service and inter-services prioritisation.

Given the fact that in the future, military forces may be needed less for conventional inter-state wars of the classical type and more for entirely anticipated surprises and shocks, there is a need to focus increasingly on flexible and broad-based capabilities. These will have to be increasingly inter-services and inter agency structures. For effective capabilities based planning in India, two conditions need to be met. Firstly, there is need for greater integration among the defences forces. Secondly, much greater expertise is needed in the defence establishment in the spheres of Operations Research (OR), Systems Analysis (SA), Cost-Benefit Analyses (CBA) and capabilities-based planning techniques.

The case of 11th Defence Plan highlights the principal roadblock to timely finalisation of defence plans. The Parliament's Standing Committee on Defence had attributed the delay to lack of agreement regarding the financial outlay for the plan. The Ministry of Finance had proposed a defence plan outlay based on year-on-year increase in the range of eight-10 per cent whereas the MoD had asked for an annual average growth rate of 12.35 per cent. This tussle continued. This difficulty is not unique to the 11th Plan; earlier plans had also met a similar fate. Commenting on the problem, a former Secretary (Defence Finance) A.K. Ghosh observes that a discussion about defence plans basically boils down to "the extent of financial commitment the Finance Ministry was prepared to make and whether it was acceptable to the Ministry of Defence."[13]

The inability or reluctance of MoD/Defence Services to finalise the plans within the indicated financial outlays appears to be a perennial problem. As the chairman, Chiefs of Staff Committee (COSC) does not find it possible to effect inter-services prioritisation which involve cuts in service outlays, the difficult task of making trade-offs is passed on to the MoD. Any significant changes in services plans evoke strong resistance from the services as civil servants in the Ministry are perceived to lack the operational or professional expertise. Thus, decision-making in regard to defence plans often becomes a test of civil-military relationship between the Armed Forces and the civilian bureaucracy in the ministries of defence and finance. In this context, it is argued that a Chief of Defence Staff (CDS) or permanent chairman, COSC with freedom from day-to-day operational pressures, necessary authority and with the advantage of being able to view defence needs holistically from a relative distance would be much better placed to guide integrated defence planning exercises than is possible now at the level of COSC or MoD.

In the absence of a CDS or permanent Chairman, COSC, the suggestion to set up a Defence Planning Board under the chairmanship of Defence Minister with a strong staff of professional experts merits serious consideration. The Board could comprise National Security Advisor (NSA), Cabinet Secretary, Secretaries of Planning Commission and Ministry of Finance, Defence Secretary, Chairman COSC and two or three whole-time experts. The Board can be serviced by the Chief of Integrated Defence Staff (IDS), supported by a strong but lean team of professional experts, able to analyse and evaluate services plans with relevant analytical tools. The Board's tasks would be to oversee planning on a regular basis in close collaboration with the services, other relevant ministries and agencies, the Planning Commission and the Ministry of Finance. Such a Defence Planning Board would be more effective than the existing structures for the following reasons: (1) It will have the requisite authority of Defence Minister; (2) Supported by two-three whole-time expert members and a professionally qualified Secretariat, it will be able to provide regular and qualitative attention to defence planning exercises; (3) The Defence Minister will have access to the regular counsel of member, Planning Commission, NSA, Cabinet Secretary and Finance Secretary, in addition to the Chairman, COSC. These members would be in a better position to take a holistic, integrated view, free from any service bias; (4) With the support of expert staff, proficient in relevant disciplines like OR and SA, the Planning Board will have strong analytic support for sound decision-making; and (5) Given its membership the Planning Board will be in a better position to ensure coordination between defence and other relevant sectors on the one hand and the NSC on the other. The modest cost likely to be incurred on such a Board would be more than offset by the cost efficiencies it will bring about in defence planning and management.

A nation's security is the key to its survival. The resources needed for its defence must be invested wisely as the attendant risks in terms of time, costs and national security, would be unacceptable. Defence planning, therefore, deserves as much attention as national planning. In summing up, therefore, it would be worthwhile to consider some measures to reform the defence planning and budgeting processes. Based on the foregoing discussions, the following measures are suggested:

1. The NSC should lay down National Security objectives and National Security Strategy. Absence of Coherent National Security Objectives and Strategy handicaps defence planners in India and they have to often resort to their subjective interpretations of a variety of statements and speeches, lacking the sanction of formally approved policy statements. A former chairman, Chiefs of Staff Committee has identified the "total absence of a central focus and direction, as far as the articulation/formulation of national interests and national strategy are concerned".[14] The process of formulating and promulgating National Security Strategy and related exercises will help consensus-building, facilitate a coordinated approach to national security across government and offer a sound basis for defence planning.
2. Urgent steps need to be taken to formulate integrated defence plans which are based on inter-services prioritisation. Currently, defence planning tends to be an aggregation of service-wise plans which fall woefully short of contemporary warfare requirements. They are also highly cost-inefficient. The need for jointness in planning and operations is very well appreciated in the defense establishment, however, its implementation is lacking.
3. The quality of defence planning needs to be improved by introducing the principles of planning, programming and budgeting to the extent they are relevant in the Indian context. In essence, the system would involve clear definition of objectives to be achieved, consideration of range of alternatives to achieve the objectives, evaluation of costs and benefits and choice of the most cost effective alternative. The process should also move rapidly towards capability-based planning, which focuses more on capacities to achieve outcomes rather than discrete inputs like equipment, operations and personnel etc.
4. The chronic problem of a gap between MoD's financial projection of perceived needs and MoF's indicated financial outlays should be resolved, so that defence plans can be made more meaningful and relevant through timely approvals. The Ministry of Finance needs to convey timely indication of resources likely to be available to MoD and the latter should

have the willingness to accept realistic outlays. Once MoD/Services begin to work out alternatives of plan programmes to match different levels of financial outlays, such statements can be avoided.

5. The MoD/services should begin to grapple with the problem of escalating manpower costs. The total wage bill of defence is growing rapidly. This increasing burden is likely to crowd out resources for modernisation. As a former Chairman, Chiefs of Staff Committee, Admiral Arun Prakash (Retd.) observes, "There is an urgent need to substitute man-power with technology (air-mobility, night-fighting capability, precision-guided weapons, surveillance and reconnaissance, network-centric warfare) and become lean."
6. For a consideration at a whole-of-government level and to acquire necessary sanctity, FYDP must be approved at the level of CCS. It is reported that Defence Plans have in recent years, been approved by the DAC, headed by Defence Minister. This creates the impression that Defence Plans essentially focus on acquisition. Also, in the absence of consideration at the level of Ministry of Finance and the CCS, Defence Plans remain an in house exercise without the benefit of any independent, external advice.
7. To achieve qualitative improvement in defence planning process, the concerned military and civilian personnel must be imparted necessary expertise in the relevant analytic techniques. No significant improvement can be expected unless the analytic expertise is enhanced.
8. In order to bring about the much needed 'jointness' in the planning process, government should take an urgent view regarding the creation of the institution of a permanent Chairman, Chiefs of Staff Committee or Chief of Defence Staff.
9. In any case, whether or not a CDS is created, the government may set up a Defence Planning Board, supported by a professionally qualified but lean, secretariat under the Chief of Integrated Defence Staff to provide continuing and high quality attention to defence plans.

Reforms in defence planning processes and structures would facilitate the task of financial allocations for defence plans and budget making, which would be based on carefully assessed needs rather than any ad hoc criteria. Sound defence plans, formally approved well in time would ensure more efficient budget making, timely utilisation of funds, value for money and speedy development of capabilities needed to safeguard national security.

II. BUDGETING FOR PROGRAMME-BASED PLANNING

It has been argued in the first part of this chapter that it is necessary to pay greater attention to defence planning with a view to ensuring optimum utilisation of the financial outlays which invariably fall short of the projected requirement. One of the essential steps for improving the process of planning would be to adopt PPBS which has planning and budgeting as its main planks with programming being a common link between them.

In this scheme of things, budgeting is as important as the process of planning itself for two reasons. One, even if the long term and medium term plans are based on a realistic assessment of the funds likely to be made available during the entire plan period, the actual availability of funds during a given year would continue to be determined by MoF based on a number of factors, such as the state of economy, the precise requirement during the year, the prospects of the projected requirement being utilised and the demand from other sectors. This requires a paradigm shift in the way defence budget is prepared at present.

The second reason is the utility of the budgeting process as an extremely useful tool to keep a close watch on whether the allocated funds are being spent to achieve the plan objectives. This too requires a paradigm shift from the way the defence budget is presently structured to a format which is outcome-oriented.

What process-related and structural changes need to be made would depend on the requirement arising out of the new system of planning as suggested earlier in this paper. But there are some fundamental issues that will need to be addressed in any case. These are discussed in this part of the chapter.

The Budgeting Process

The process of budget formulation is kicked off by MoF every year sometime in the month of September by issuing a detailed Budget Circular to all ministries and departments. The circular contains detailed guidelines on preparation of estimates of receipts and expenditure, apart from a number of related instructions, due date for submission of estimates to MoF and the calendar for pre-budget discussion between MoF and other ministries/departments. This ensures commonality of approach to formulation of budget.

By contrast, MoD, in turn, issues no such detailed circular to the services and other departments, responsible for preparing the estimates in respect of their respective organisations. It does, however, issue some rudimentary instructions on whatever is considered relevant by MoD (Finance) for preparation of the estimates. For the most part, these instructions relate to the due date for submission of the estimates and such broad guidelines as the need to make sure that all committed liabilities are taken into account while assessing the requirement.

This tokenism causes aberrations in the process of budget formulation and has far reaching consequences. First, the DoD loses the opportunity to fix the targets in terms of outcomes to be achieved during the year because of its non-involvement at this stage. The services and other departments are left to themselves to set their own targets, which may not always be in harmony with one another.

This, incidentally, is one of the reasons why it is virtually impossible to prepare a consolidated outcome budget for MoD as a whole as there are no common targets for MoD as a single entity against which the outcomes could be benchmarked. At best, every service and department could be expected to prepare its own outcome budget with reference to whatever annual targets they had fixed for themselves. Though for several other reasons even this is not happening, such an array of outcome budgets, even if prepared, would be of no help in providing a clue to the state of defence preparedness.

Secondly, it could result in estimates being prepared by the services and other departments on different assumptions. For example, while preparing the estimate for pay and allowances, one department may assume a certain rate at which the dearness allowance would become payable during the year, another department may either assume a different rate or not make any provision at all in the estimates for increase on this account.

Thirdly, it has serious implications for costing of goods and services proposed to be procured during the year. While one department may prepare the estimate of current cost based on the Last Purchase Price (LPP) of some equipment by applying a certain rate of escalation, another department may assume a different rate of escalation or not factor in any escalation at all. This problem is also related to the absence of common databases and lack of expertise in the costing techniques.

Fourthly, by not mandating that the budget estimates should be prepared keeping in view the pre-determined likely rate of growth in the annual allocation, MoD allows a situation to arise where the sum total of the projections made by services and other departments far exceeds the allocation which could reasonably be expected to be made by MoF.

This gives rise to a rather bizarre situation every year as would be apparent from the observations made with monotonous regularity by the Standing Committee on Defence without much effect. This is what the committee had to say in the context of the defence budget for 2013-14:

> "…. Therefore, the Committee desire that the Ministry should impress upon the Ministry of Finance to allocate entire amount as per the requirement of the Services otherwise the services shall have to reprioritise their activities, which may lead to cutting of expenditure on essential items."[15]

A year earlier, the Standing Committee had said:

> "..... As such, the Committee strongly recommends that the requisite allocations should be made available to the MoD for their different programmes."[16]

There are similar observations in the earlier reports of the Standing Committee which, however, only serve the purpose of creating the impression that (a) the requirement projected by MoD is accurate, and (b) MoF is in a position to, but does not, meet the projected requirement in full either because of its indifference to the security concerns or because of MoD's inability to convince MoF of the genuineness of the projection or, worse still, because of both these reasons. Needless to say, this impression is misplaced.

To demand far in excess of what one knows will in all probability be allotted could perhaps be called a good tactic as long as the services and departments are also ready with a plan to make do with inevitable lesser allocation. But there is no such Plan B in place. Therefore, there is a lot of *ad-hocism* in 'reprioritisation' of activities to cope with inadequacy of allocations, with MoD again playing no role in the process.

The most disturbing implication of the existing process of budget formulation is the inability of MoD to ensure availability of funds for some areas which are critical from the point of view of defence preparedness. The following observation of the Standing Committee on Defence confirms this:

> "1.23 When asked to state where the compromises have been made or likely to be made due to the reduced budgetary allocation against the projections made by the three services and other organisations/heads, the MoD in their written reply stated:
>
> > "Under the revenue segment, after providing for salary and other obligatory expenses the balance allocation is distributed to meet the requirement of stores (including ordnance), transportation (of personnel and stores), revenue works and maintenance, etc. These areas are likely to be impacted by the reduced allocation.
> >
> > "In so far as the capital segment is concerned, the acquisition of land and progress of capital works may get affected. The procurement plan for capital modernisation schemes may also have to be reviewed and reprioritised." "[17]

Lastly, in this scheme of things, the fact that the allocation made to the DRDO and the Ordnance Factories (OFs) is also invariably less than their projections, possibly adversely affecting their plans, gets completely overlooked.

These issues related to the process of budgeting need to be addressed even if MoD does not adopt programme-based planning, or the PPB model, as discussed in the first part of this chapter. Adoption of the PPB model might throw up a different set of procedural challenges. It will not be possible to achieve the results expected from migration to the PPB model of budgeting if the procedural issues discussed here, which basically arise from lack of direction and professionalism in budgeting, are not addressed along with any other issue that may arise in the course of migration to the new model.

Structural Issues

The defence budget is presented by MoD in the form of a document, called the Defence Services Estimates, which comprises six Demands for Grant (DDGs). Five of these six demands cater for the revenue expenditure of the three services, OFs and the DRDO, while the sixth demand contains the capital outlay for all of them.

MoD presents another two DDGs—one related to the civil estimates of the ministry and the other to defence pensions—but the provision made in these DDGs does not form part of what is popularly known as the defence budget.[18]

The existing structure of the DDGs is not conducive to efficient budgeting, monitoring and control. The most significant drawback is the lack of outcome orientation of the DDGs. This distorts both the internal assessment and the public discourse on the impact of defence budget on defence preparedness. For example, the fact that between 2002-03 and 2013-14, a total sum of INR 42,084 crore was underutilised on capital acquisitions gets more attention that the fact that during the same period a total sum of INR 4,25,580 crore was got spent.

The focus, therefore, shifts to MoD's failings, which is unexceptionable. The problem, however, is that in this process the need to assess the outcome of the actual expenditure in terms of the capabilities acquired gets overlooked. The capital acquisition budget is meant primarily for modernisation of the armed forces but the existing structure of the defence budget does not facilitate a transparent assessment of the impact of spending on modernisation of the armed forces, and consequently, on defence preparedness.

The existing system also facilitates obfuscation of the fact that not all expenditure out of the capital acquisition budget goes towards modernisation of the armed forces or acquisition of military capabilities. A sizeable proportion of the budget is spent on replacement of the existing capital assets, which neither adds to the existing capabilities nor to modernisation of any kind.

There is no alternative to providing some kind of outcome-orientation to the defence budget if the impact of the expenditure on defence preparedness is to be monitored. This is not going to be easy, primarily because of the problem relating to identification of outcomes in measurable terms. What is, however, quite evident is that outcome orientation of the budget is not possible unless the existing structure is also modified to facilitate assessment of outcomes, which is what PPBS is all about.

While some lessons could be learnt from the outcome-oriented defence budget structures of countries like the US, UK and Australia, we will have to evolve our own unique model, keeping in view the constitutional requirements, the specific objectives of defence planning and the objectives we want to achieve through outcome-budgeting making it a three-dimensional issue.

First Dimension of Restructuring

The first dimension concerns the broader structure of the budget. The Constitution of India requires the capital expenditure to be shown separately from the other expenditure and the 'charged' expenditure to be indicated separately from the 'voted' expenditure. This rules out the possibility of doing away with these classifications—as suggested by many—in the defence budget, whichever way it is structured.

The Constitution also requires budgetary projections to be presented to the parliament every year by way of DDGs. This rules out the possibility of multi-year budgeting, unless the constitution is amended to provide for it.

However, these constraints do not rule out the possibility of restructuring the DDGs, which is the first pre-requisite step for adoption of PPBS.

Broadly, there are two options. The first option is to remove the drawbacks in the existing structure and continue with the system of organisation-related DDGs. This would imply the following:

(a) Taking out Military Farms, National Cadet Corps (NCC), Inspection Organisation, Ex-servicemen Health Scheme and Rashtriya Rifles (RRs) from the DDG for Army but bringing into its fold JAKLI from the civil estimates of MoD.
(b) Taking out IDS from the DDG for Navy.
(c) Creating another DDG to include auxiliary organisations, including the Military Farms, Coast Guard (to be taken out from the civil estimates of MoD), Border Roads Organisation (BRO) (to be taken out of the DDG for the Ministry of Road Transport & Highways), Armed Forces Medical Services (to be take out from DDGs of all the three services) and IDS. The newly created DDG could also include Inspection Organisation as it presently functions under the administrative control of the Department of Defence Production, unlike the Directorate General of Aeronautical Quality Assurance (DGAQA) or DGNI which function under the respective services.
(d) Clubbing Ex-servicemen Health Scheme with defence pensions under a separate demand, which could be called DDG for Ex-servicemen Welfare.
(e) Since RRsis engaged in internal security/counter-insurgency operations, it should ideally be a part of the DDG for Home Affairs. However, if it

is not considered appropriate for reasons of command and control, it should be transferred to the DDG for auxiliary organisations.

This is only a tentative suggestion. Rationalisation of the structure of DDGs would require a very careful consideration. It would help the process of budget formulation and monitoring if every DDG pertains to an organisation under the administrative control of a single authority, with the exception of the DDG for auxiliary organisations. This could also be a precursor to investing DDGs with an outcome-orientation in future.

The other option as regards restructuring of the DDGs would be to make them function-specific. For example, there could be a DDG for Armed Forces/ Defence Services, covering the operational complement of the services. There could be separate DDGs for Logistic Services, Maintenance Services, Support Services and Auxiliary Services, apart from the Ex-servicemen Welfare. This too is a tentative suggestion, intended to indicate that challenges associated with introduction of PPBS can be met.

Second Dimension of Restructuring

The second dimension concerns the classification of expenditure under each DDG. Here again, there are two options. One, expenditure could continue to be classified in terms of objects of expenditure, such as pay & allowances, stores, etc. These budget heads could even be refined, modified or new ones added, if required, to ensure that dissimilar objects do not remain clubbed under the same category. For example, the expenditure incurred on free issue of rations could be separated from other expenditure on dry and fresh rations procured for the troops.

The second option could be to break down the budgetary outlays into programmes with every programme accounted for under a separate budget head. This arrangement would probably synchronise better with PPBS but it may be difficult to break down the entire defence budget into programmes. For example, if there is a DDG for Armed Forces/Defence Services, as suggested earlier, what programmes could the outlay under the DDG be broken down into? But this option need not be ruled out without a careful consideration.

This approach to classification of expenditure would also require greater flexibility to be given to MoD to discontinue budget heads related to completed programmes and create new ones for the new programmes. Since, however, all defence expenditure has to be factored into the standard classification of central government expenditure, a system would need to be evolved to ensure that discontinuation of old budget heads or creation of new budget heads does not hinder migration of data from defence accounts to civil accounts.

Third Dimension of Restructuring

The third dimension of the issue concerns integration of the process of outcome budgeting with whatever changes are made in the structure of the DDGs. This is also not going to be easy for two reasons. One, it is difficult to identify the outcome of all activities in terms of measurable outcomes. For example, what measurable outcomes could be fixed in respect of the outlay on Armed Forces/ Defence Services, assuming that there is a separate DDG for them, as suggested earlier?

Two, working out the methodology for linking the outcome with various levels of funding could, in itself, prove to be a difficult task, especially in view of the fact that non-financial factors also have a bearing on the outcomes.

An associated challenge would be to devise the system of reporting the outcomes. To begin with, progress made towards achieving the pre-determined outcomes will have to be reported periodically during the year. This is required for the purpose of monitoring utilisation of budgetary allocation and also to make any mid-course corrections that might become necessary. This reporting system will have to be carefully evolved, keeping in view the quantum of work involved in aggregation and analysis of data at various levels of decision-making.

At the second stage, the outcome budget will need to be presented to the parliament. Under the existing system, the budget document, when presented to the parliament, contains the projections for the year to which the budget pertains, the revised estimates for the year coming to a close when the budget is presented and the actual expenditure for the year preceding the one in which the budget is presented.

The question is whether the outcome budget could be made a part of the DDG, or could be submitted simultaneously with the DDG, and if so, how. Making it a part of the DDG would bring tremendous pressure on the Finance Division. On the other hand, if it is not to be a part of the DDG, it will have to be decided by MoD as to who will be responsible for submitting the outcome budget(s) to the parliament. In either case, unprecedented level of coordination among services and various departments of MoD would be necessary to discharge this responsibility.

This is an important issue. The Finance Division of MoD is responsible for presenting the DDGs to the parliament. Since outcome budgets are more in the nature of a performance report, and, in all probability, more than one outcome budget will have to be presented to the parliament, it will be impractical to entrust the responsibility for presentation of the outcome budget(s) to the Finance Division.

What emerges from the foregoing analysis is that despite all the difficulties it is possible to adopt a customised system of outcome budgeting for defence. A beginning has already been made by MoD in 2013 by preparing outcome budgets at a rudimentary level for the NCC and the Married Accommodation Project (MAP). Taking a cue from this, the possibility of carving out even formations, such as commands, divisions, and squadrons, as distinct units for the purpose of outcome budgeting and expressing their outcome in terms of their capabilities requires serious consideration. If such outcomes cannot be made public, these could remain as classified documents as even that will serve the purpose of internal monitoring and review.

What is important is not only to keep making the efforts but to invest the exercise with a sense of urgency, shutting the door for taking an easy way out by preparing outcome budgets for organisations which do not constitute the core of India's defence preparedness. If MoD thinks hard, or seeks professional help for doing so, the modalities for introducing outcome budgeting on a large scale can be worked out, with outcomes being indicated in a broad way.

Outcome budgeting is more in the nature of performance appraisal than an exercise in number crunching, which is what budgeting is perceived to be all about. If rechristening outcome budget as outcome appraisal helps in breaching the psychological barrier that militates against its acceptability, it will be worth the while to do so.

Summing Up

There is no question that the resources allocated for defence must be spent wisely, especially keeping in view the overall scarcity of resources. This calls for paying greater attention to various aspects of defence planning as brought out in the first part of this chapter. Whether the process of planning is predicated on the concept of programming or any other model, it would remain incomplete without a robust system of outcome appraisal.

The issues related to programme-based budgeting have been examined in this part of the chapter. Essentially, there are two aspects to it. The first aspect relates to the process of budgeting. As analysed earlier, the existing system lacks the kind of reliability which is necessary for smart planning. Whether it is non-involvement of MoD in the process of budgeting right from its initial stage, absence of guidelines for preparation of estimates, or lack of expertise for preparing the estimates using standard techniques and common databases, the existing system needs to be refined, irrespective of whether or not programme-based budgeting is adopted by MoD.

The second aspect relates to structural issues that would need to be addressed to facilitate migration to programme-based planning. This includes restructuring of the DDGs, classification of expenditure and outcome appraisal. The issues raised in this context cannot be wished away. The suggestions made in this context are intended more to generate a discussion on the nitty-gritties than to offer final answers to seemingly intractable problems.

NOTES

1. For an excellent account of the salient features of PPBS, see the foreword to the New Edition by David S.C. Chu and Kenneth J. Craig in 'How Much is Enough: Shaping the Defence Programme 1961-1969' by Alain C. Enthoren and K. Wayne Smith, available at www.rand.org
2. For a brief history of defence planning organisations, see ids.nic.in/history.htm (Accessed 13.12.2013). See also "Defence Planning in India" by General V.P. Malik and Brigadier Gurmeet Kanwal, p. 3.
3. See Laxman K. Behera, "Defence Planning in India", *Journal of Defence Studies*, 4(3) July 2010.
4. Report of the Standing Committee on Defence, 1995-96, Tenth Lok Sabha, Defence Policy, Planning and Management, Lok Sabha Secretariat, New Delhi, April 1996.
5. www.defence.gov.au/whitepaper2013 (Accessed on November 16 2013).
6. www.gov.uk/government/uploads/system/uploads/attachment/data/file/35927/ defence_green_paper_cm7794.pdf, (Accessed 18.12.2013).
7. See the document at www.direct.gov.uk.
8. For an analysis of different methods followed by US Presidents, see Richard K. Betts, "A Disciplined Defence: How to Regain Strategic Solvency." *Foreign Affairs*, 86(6), November December 2007, p.70.
9. Ibid.
10. Standing Committee on Defence "Defence Policy, Planning and Management", Sixth Report, Lok Sabha Secretariat, New Delhi, 1995-96, p.37.
11. Richard K. Betts, "A Disciplined Defence: How to Regain Strategic Solvency." *Foreign Affairs*, 86(6), November December 2007, pp.79-80.
12. Paul K. Davis, Analytic Architecture for Capabilities Based Planning, Mission-System Analysis and Transformation RAND, National Defence Research Institute, p. 11.
13. Ghosh, Amiya Kumar, "Defence Budgeting and Planning in India: The Way Forward", Knowledge World: New Delhi, 2006, p. 224.
14. Admiral Arun Prakash (Retd.), in response to author's questionnaire.
15. Paragraph 5 of the chapter on Recommendations/Observations in the 20th Report of the Standing Committee on Defence (2012-13) on the Demands for Grant of the MoD for 2013-14, Lok Sabha Secretariat, April 2014.
16. Paragraph 5 of the chapter on Recommendations/Observations in the 15th Report of the Standing Committee on Defence (2011-12) on the Demands for Grant of the MoD for 2012-13, Lok Sabha Secretariat, April 2014.
17. Paragraph 1.23 Chapter 1 of the 15th Report of the Standing Committee on Defence (2011-12) on MOD's Demands for Grant for 2012-13, Lok Sabha Secretariat, April 2012.
18. For a detailed analysis of the existing structure of defence budget, see the chapter on Financial Management in Defence in this volume.

8

DEFENCE R&D

A Sivathanu Pillai

Introduction

Government of India setup Defence Research and Development Organisation (DRDO) on January 01, 1958 by merging the units of Defence Science Organisations with technical development establishments of the three Services and appointed Professor DS Kothari as the head of DRDO and the Scientific Advisor to the Defence Minister. DRDO was initially a small organisation with only 10 laboratories. Today it is a vast network of 50 laboratories and establishments, spread across the country with a strong scientific force of 7,000 scientists, 12,000 technical personnel and 10,000 support staff. It has a vision to empower the Armed Forces of India with cutting-edge technologies and competitive war fighting products and systems. Driven by the focus of Self-Reliance, DRDO contributed immensely to develop and provide advanced strategic systems such as Long Range Agni-5, Medium Range Prithvi and Submarine Launched Ballistic Missile B-05; and a variety of critical technologies combating the control regime, sanctions and technology denials imposed by the industrially developed nations. Also DRDO developed and led to production of equipment and weapons for the Indian Armed Forces in the areas of aeronautics, armaments, combat vehicles, electronic warfare systems, radars, ground vehicles including bridging systems, sonars and other naval systems, materials and life-sciences. These continued efforts of DRDO's scientific community with the network of multiple academic institutions and industries, resulted in a production value of Rs.160,090 crores worth of systems for the Armed Forces, steadily increasing the Self-Reliance content. DRDO, by virtue of its high competence in state-of-the-art technologies, has matured enough today for international collaborations and Joint Ventures (JV) for futuristic systems and equipment, thus making it a vital organisation in the country.

Defence Technology Competence

During 60s, DRDO was involved in the basic research towards defence R&D in support of the Indian Armed Forces. During this era, India was involved in license production of military systems to cater for the immediate needs of the defence forces. Later, as the years progressed on, DRDO transformed into development of specific military systems like first generation Anti-Tank Missiles (ATM) and a surface to air missile system. When the technology demonstrator phase for these projects was reached, these systems were out rightly rejected in terms of technology obsolescence. During 80s, aided with the success of space and nuclear programmes, major mission mode programmes in Defence technology development were launched. Notable is the Integrated Guided Missile Development Programme (IGMDP). In this programme, Academia and Industries were closely involved and they proved their capability. Industries were graduated from licence production capability to build to design capability. Boost given to the economy of the nation during the early 90s enhanced more participation of the private players (facilitated the emergence of many companies), which resulted in the industries attaining build to specification capability. Ultimately, the Indian industries attained maturity in design, development and production capabilities of certain defence systems/subsystems (Fig.1).

Fig. 1: Defence R&D Capabilities

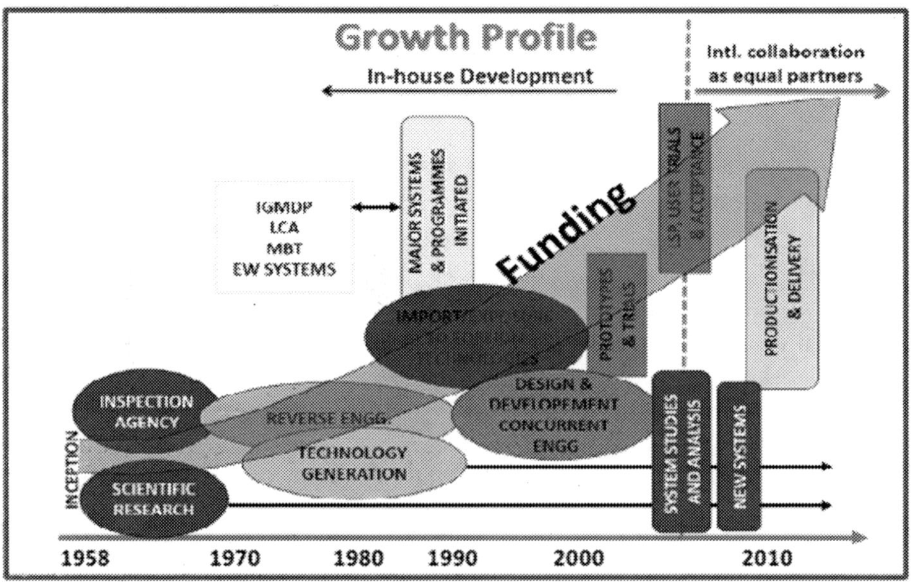

Today, DRDO has established core competence in systems design and integration of complex sensors, weapon systems and platforms, development of complex high-end software packages, their encryptions and information security, development of functional materials, Test and Evaluation procedures, and Technology Transfer & Absorption. These core competencies are in the areas of Aircraft systems, Unmanned Aerial Vehicles (UAVs), Guided Missiles, Radars with multi-target detection & tracking capabilities and Electronic Warfare (EW) systems, Autonomous underwater technologies, torpedoes and mines, stealth technology, super computers, advanced software packages, combat vehicles, bridges and certain life support systems (Fig. 2).

Fig. 2: Defence R&D Production (Value addition Rs in Crs)

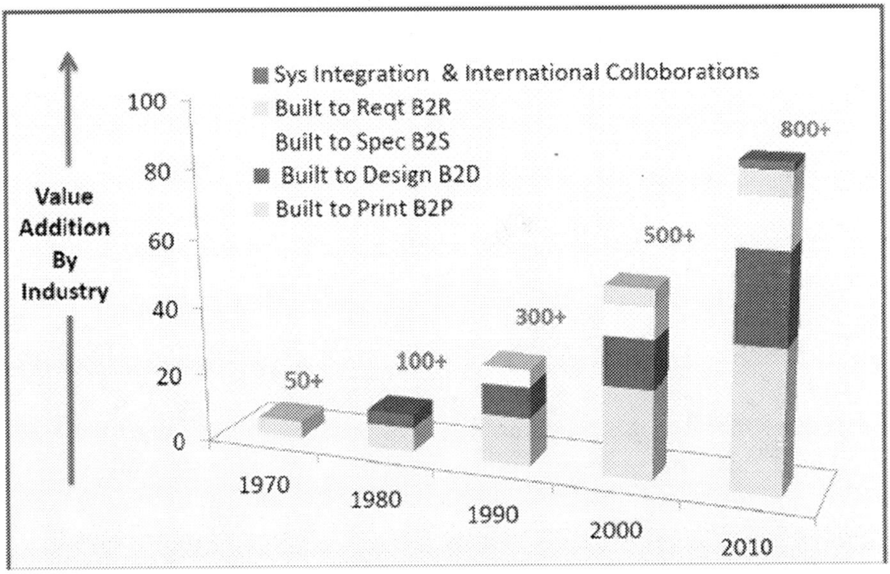

DRDO also achieved breakthrough in many technologies, which come under denial regime which have been realised using indigenous effort. Some of such state-of-the-art technologies are re-entry module, inertial guidance system, sensors including phase-shifters, super components for electronic warfare, super computer and integrated chips etc. The overall production value for the DRDO developed sub-systems amount to Rs.1,60,090 crore as shown in Fig.3 (system wise), considerably improving the Self-Reliance index.

Fig. 3: Production Value of Systems (Inducted & Under Induction) Developed by DRDO

Systems	*Cost (Rs. in Crores)*		
	Inducted	*Under Induction*	*Total*
Missile Systems	4668	60606	65273
Electronics and Radar Systems	7605	21514	29120
Advanced Materials & Composites	3505	139	3644
Armament Systems	8304	4340	12644
Aeronautical Systems	3049	23700	26750
Combat Vehicles & Engg Systems	12686	8237	20923
Life Sciences Systems	247	286	533
Naval Systems	873	330	1203
Total	**40940**	**119150**	**160090**

Technology Denial Regimes and Combating MTCR

The present level of technological competence was not easy to accrue. It was not only the usual hurdles that are faced in any technological development programme but also technology denial regimes and embargoes imposed by the developed countries. In the mid 70s, geopolitical scenario was not in favour of India. This situation forced India to embark on the initiation of new programmes for the development of strategic systems. In continuation of this, the IGMDP was started in the year 1983. But this programme had to be taken forward against all odds.

During that time, one such odd was Missile Technology Control Regime (MTCR), which was formed in 1983 by the G-7 Countries (Canada, France, Germany, Italy, Japan, the UK and US). The principle behind the formation of this regime is to prevent the developing nations from acquiring advanced missile technologies. The MTCR aims to curb proliferation by denying missile, UAVs, and related technologies for those systems capable of carrying a 500 kilogramme payload for a distance of 300 kilometres and beyond, as well as systems intended for delivery of Weapons of Mass Destruction (WMD). It is essentially a trade ban seeking to impair the military capability of the nations. It also bans the supply of economic goods that may strengthen an opponent's military machine and arms, and place arms embargoes on adversaries or nations engaged in war. The MTCR was originally concerned only with the nuclear capable delivery systems. In January 1993, the partners extended the guidelines to cover delivery system capable of delivery of all forms of WMD (nuclear, chemical, and biological).

Due to the introduction of technology denial regimes and embargoes, many critical technologies were denied by the developed countries to India. One of the examples of mastering the critical technology is the indigenous development of supercomputer when the CRAY Supercomputer was denied by the US.

Development of Agni (the Intermediate Range Ballistic Missile (IRBM) of India), re-entry configuration was complex due to severe environmental conditions that would prevail at the time of re-entry of the vehicle from space to atmosphere. At the time of re-entry, the speed of the vehicle is of the order of 14 Mach and experiences a temperature increase of the order of 3000°C due to air friction. Such conditions, demand special materials and special aerodynamic structure to protect the payload against such conditions. Optimal aerodynamic structure has to be arrived only through hypersonic wind tunnels or through Computational Fluid Dynamics (CFD). In the absence of a hypersonic wind tunnel facility in India, the other option was CFD. But CFD of this order required a supercomputer and new software codes to arrive at an optimum shape and dimensions.

In the absence of this, manual calculations would have taken years to arrive at the required configuration for one particular point in the entire structure. There were hundred thousand such points to arrive at. This necessitated the immediate requirement of a supercomputer. India had a CRAY XMP super computer for weather prediction at Indian Meteorological Department (IMD), New Delhi. Restrictions had been imposed by the US Government not to use this computer for any other purpose. Hence, India could not use it though it was available and our request for a new purchase was turned down by USA. Because of this, DRDO created Advanced Numerical Research and Analysis Group (ANURAG), to develop within the shortest possible time—but not exceeding 30 months—a parallel processing computing system which could meet the requirements of Agni and similar projects. Also, an advanced group was formed for the development of new software codes for CFD. Initially, the work started using conventional Euler Codes and conventional PC's were used. Each iteration took nearly eight to nine days. With the use of advanced indigenously developed software codes like BHEEMA, KAREESHMA led to PACE++ 128 node super computer and consequently each of these iterations now take less than eight minutes. Our CFD codes are claimed to be one of the best in the world.

Another example is the realisation of Control Law for Light Combat Aircraft (LCA) overcoming technology embargo. Control Law was developed by adopting a novel idea of formation of National Team, based on the concept of integrating knowledge spread in multiple institutions. The LCA management wanted to develop control law for LCA indigenously as no country was parting with the technology. The status of existing competencies in various work centres in the country to undertake the design, the availability of software and hardware engineers and the views of experts were considered. They realised that the capabilities were spread out in various institutions, R&D laboratories and industry. It was decided to form a national team, integrating the expertise and adding young scientists to the team and for defining the missions for the development of control law on a fast track. The team took up the challenge and successfully completed the development of the control law and validated it through simulation.

Strategy for Technology Development

The Overall strategy should be based on the identification of the current level of technology availability in all the required areas and adapting appropriate strategies to bridge the gaps. The different strategies followed (Fig. 4) were technology substitution, development through partnership, consortium approach, technology empowerment etc.

Fig. 4: Different Strategies for Critical Technology Development

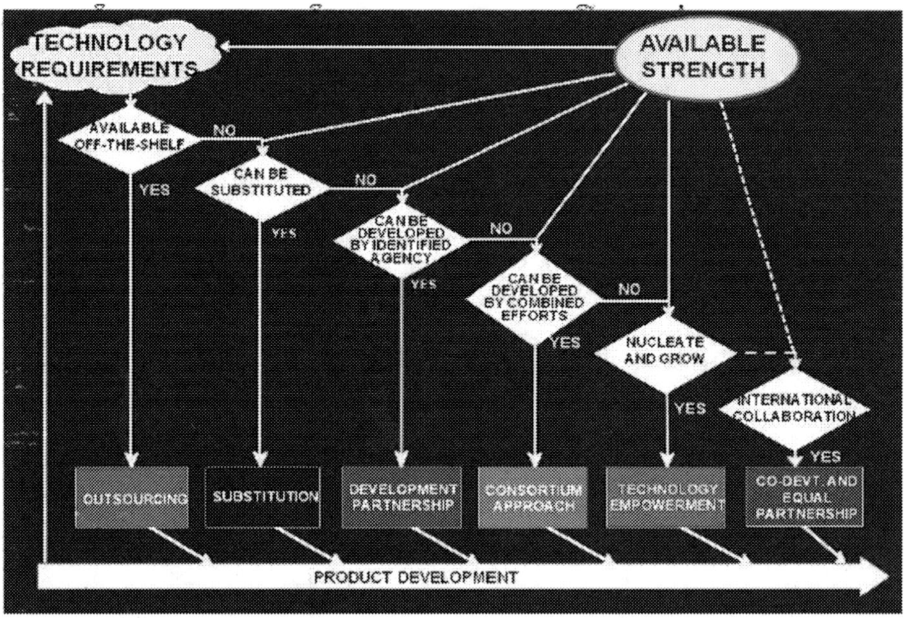

Emerging Defence Technologies

In order to keep pace with the technology progress in the world, it is essential to forecast the type of technological challenges based on the threat perceptions. A strong defence force is realisable only if the technology power is infused at the right interval. It is expected that future conflict will be a mix of conventional, irregular and asymmetric engagements spreading over land, sea, air, space and cyber space.

Cyber threat is already engulfing the nations worldwide as a new game changer. Therefore, the Armed Forces have evolved a Long Term Integrated Prospective Plan (LTIPP) which enumerates 15 years' profile of technology requirements and systems. The technologies include Nano-Bio-Info convergent technology, Robotics and Artificial Intelligence, Photonics—Laser MEMS based Sensors, Stealth materials, High energetic (Explosives, Thorium) Fusion, Space Technology and Hypersonics. Such technological innovations is revolutionising the warfare in numerous ways and significantly impacting the future defence and security scenario.

The systems include Beyond the Visual Range, Supersonic & Hypersonic weapons, Active Aperture Radars, UAVs and Underwater Vehicles, Robotic Systems, C4I2SR Network, Nuclear, Biological, Chemical (NBC) defence, homeland security and cyber security. High technology systems will be the decisive factors in future battles and self-reliance drives the nation towards having an independent techno-military strategy for defence. Therefore, the role of R&D in Defence is of utmost importance in developing and providing critical technologies to maintain the systems up-to-date.

Graduation of Industries

Realisation of any advanced technology product involves stages like Research, Development, Technology Transfer absorption and production of systems with performance, quality and cost effectiveness. There are three routes i.e. Route A, Route B and Route C to realise technology (Fig. 5).

Fig. 5: Technology Knowledge in Product Realisation

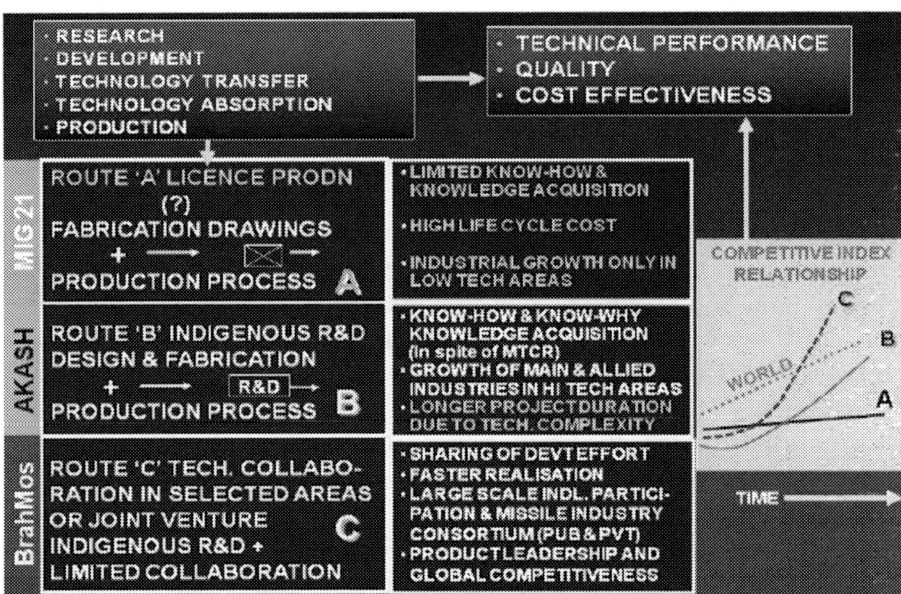

Route A (Know-How) is obtaining the licensed technology with fabrication drawings and the production process supplied by the foreign manufacturer. The industry concerned will realise the product but in this process, industries achieve only limited know-how knowledge acquisition with high life cycle cost. Industrial growth happens only in low technology areas. In India, what we have achieved is the creation of large infrastructure, manpower and focussing on the weapon delivery to the user. But we lost the indigenous design capability. Moreover, we have to depend forever on the foreign manufacturers for the spare parts. This approach will not result in acquiring the desired technology from all angles and would simply widen the technology gap.

Route B (Know-Why) begins with the design and development being done indigenously and the production process done within the country. Industries acquire not only 'Know-How' but also 'Know-Why' with low life cycle cost. Here, critical technologies have been realised and many main and allied industries in high technology areas grew. In this process, we had achieved the indigenous design capabilities for combat aircraft, warships and design and development of Advanced Light Helicopters (ALH) and Light Combat Helicopters (LCH) having export thrust. The main hurdle was the time and cost overrun. Though, there may be initial struggles in this route, the realisation of indigenous technologies can take us closer to the international level but won't be sufficient to overtake them.

Route C entails indigenous research and development with limited collaboration in the realisation of critical technologies. Indigenous R&D dominates this option. In this process, the development effort and cost is shared between the collaborators enabling fastest realisation of the product with the state-of-the-art technology resulting in global competitiveness.

Examples of Industries Development

Initially, after independence, through Five Year Plans (FYPs), thrust was given to Irrigation and Agriculture. Government of India invested money and formed 'Public Sector Undertaking (PSU)' involving heavy industries. The rationale behind this was that the government only had money to invest in industries in various sectors. There were only a few private players to maintain the competition by maintaining the quality and timely delivery of the product.

Around 60s, through technology transfer, industries got process for fabrication, equipment and training for the manufacture of the system. Through the DRDO initiated programmes, like sonar, EW and IGMDP, the industries slowly graduated to the level of evolving process and manufacturing. During 90s, industries attained the stage of build to design i.e. the design by the DRDO; Indian industries were able to make the systems like light combat aircraft. In another decade, industries grew to a stage wherein they achieved the capability to build and design according to the listed specification. Thus, a matured defence industry base with the conjoined efforts from public and private players was formed which became strategic partner to R&D.

One good example is building technology capability for sonar. Sonar development encompasses development of various technologies such as oceanography, transducers, and electronics. DRDO Laboratory, Naval Physical and Oceanographic Laboratory (NPOL) initially started the study of ocean environment and development of transducers and within a decade, started electronics development of small equipment. After achieving enough expertise in these areas, development of full sonar system started in late seventies and first indigenously developed sonar "APSOH" was delivered to the user in early eighties. The approach of Sonar design to production was realised by involving the Navy as user and Bharat Electronics (BEL) as the production industry right from the beginning.

The laboratory adopted the system development approach such as "Laboratory Prototype—Designed and Engineered (D&E) Model—Production Model" when sufficient expertise was not available. Prototype was made by the laboratory which was subjected to various technical trials. On successful completion of technical trials, the D&E model was produced by the production agency and the model was subjected to user's trials. After which, the production model was produced by the production agency. Having attained sufficient amount of expertise and success, D&E model was produced directly, which was subjected to user trials and on successful completion, trials production model were supplied by the production agency to Indian Navy. In the later stage, sonar systems were produced directly by the production agencies. After attaining maturity in these technologies, the laboratory developed multiple types of sonar which are being produced by the Indian Industry. Active and continuous involvement of Navy and joint effort of NPOL & BEL from development to production and induction, enabled achieving indigenous capability for Sonar Systems.

When we embark on the development of high technologies, the uncertainty element also plays a part contributing to delays in the realisation of products as required by the Armed Forces. Therefore, DRDO is often criticised for slippages in schedule. With the constraints of technology denial regimes and to build every system from scratch using our own limited resources, some of the systems like Main Battle Tank (MBT) Arjun, LCA Tejas had been delayed with time and cost overrun. This should not deter us because the technology build up started in India nearly after thirty years as compared to the industrially developed nations. These nations also took considerable time for development of first generation systems with very high cost. Also, some projects like Trishul Missile was fore-closed as Technology Demonstrator Project (TDP) drawing the technologies developed through this project to the futuristic projects. However, this trend is getting changed due to the growth of laboratories in multiple disciplines, expertise built over the years and more so through international cooperation. BRAHMOS Supersonic Cruise Missile is one such example where the deliveries could be accomplished ahead of schedule. With new concepts, technology forecasts, management methods and concerted efforts with strong focussed leadership, it will be possible to overtake the developed nations in providing advanced systems.

With the strong base of indigenous technology and software capability, many breakthroughs have been made in areas such as super computer, micro electronics, sensors, high energetic & advanced materials and stealth, software solutions. These helped to realise advanced technology products including strategic systems. In parallel, industry capability has also been built-up by careful selection of industries for the production of systems by involving them right from the very beginning. This resulted in the maturity of industries from "Build to Design" as fabricators to achieve "Build to Specification" as Knowledge Houses.

Self-Reliance Mission

Dr. V Siddhartha, a Former Senior Scientist of DRDO once said, "In the global defence market, no country parts with the best product to buyer country. The second graded defence product is sold under license in the name of technology transfer, recovering the cost spent on development. The seller country then controls the production at Buyer country through spares and critical inputs". This means that the buyer country cannot reach the level of technology achieved by the seller country. Hence, to keep up the technological edge in the high technology defence product, the only way is to indigenously develop it.

In view of this, DRDO has envisaged a Self-Reliance Mission (Fig. 6) to give thrust for increasing self reliance in Defence systems so that the indigenous content would be enhanced from 30 to 70 per cent or more. Clearly, this cannot be achieved by DRDO alone without matching commitment of User Services, Production Units and adequate availability of funds. It must be an integrated effort with strong commitment by all stakeholders including the policy makers in the Government.

The main thrust of the Self-Reliance Plan is development of strategic systems which includes long range missile, nuclear warheads, Electronic Warfare Systems (EWS), Directed Energy weapon systems and Military satellites; Critical Technologies in the area of Super Computing, micro electronics, sensors, high energetic, advanced materials, stealth and Information Technology (IT). These two developments will be carried out exclusively by DRDO. Development of 'Platform Systems and subsystems' (Tactical Systems) will be carried out by DRDO in partnership with the Industries.

Fig. 6: Self-Reliance Mission in Defence

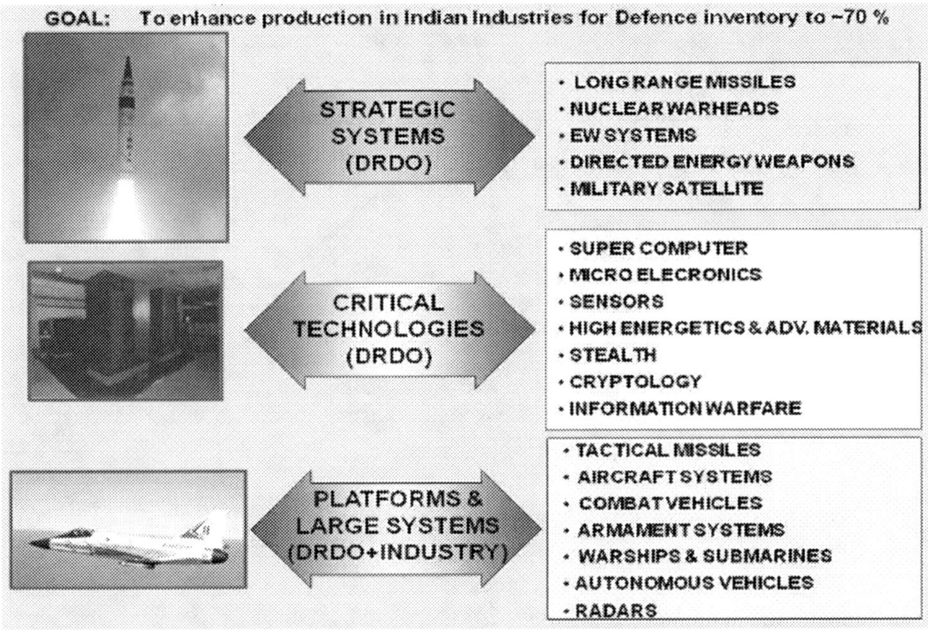

The real long term goal of the Self Reliance Plan is to ensure that the country should not be dependent on import of high technology systems due to lack of indigenous capability. Hence indigenous capabilities in critical technologies, high-tech production infrastructure and professional management for competitive productivity are essential ingredients of the Self Reliance Plan.

For any country, indigenous technological development in critical technologies and strategic industries will bring faster economic growth and needed inputs for national security. The indigenous technology development efforts will establish a strong R&D base and production capabilities which will give time, cost and quality leverage and make the nation globally competitive. This will generate international collaborations for joint development of new technologies and joint ventures and export potential. The large requirement for products to meet the global demand will make the R&D and production economically viable and profitable.

India needs strong vision for self-reliance and develop technologies to become competitive in the world (Fig. 7). We have today, "Technology Vision 2020" and "Self-Reliance in Defence" documents giving a road map for economic growth. Mission mode programmes launched in 1970s and 80s in the form of Green Revolution, ICT, Nuclear, Space and Missile Programme have yielded spectacular results.

Fig. 7: Self-Reliance in Defence through Synergy

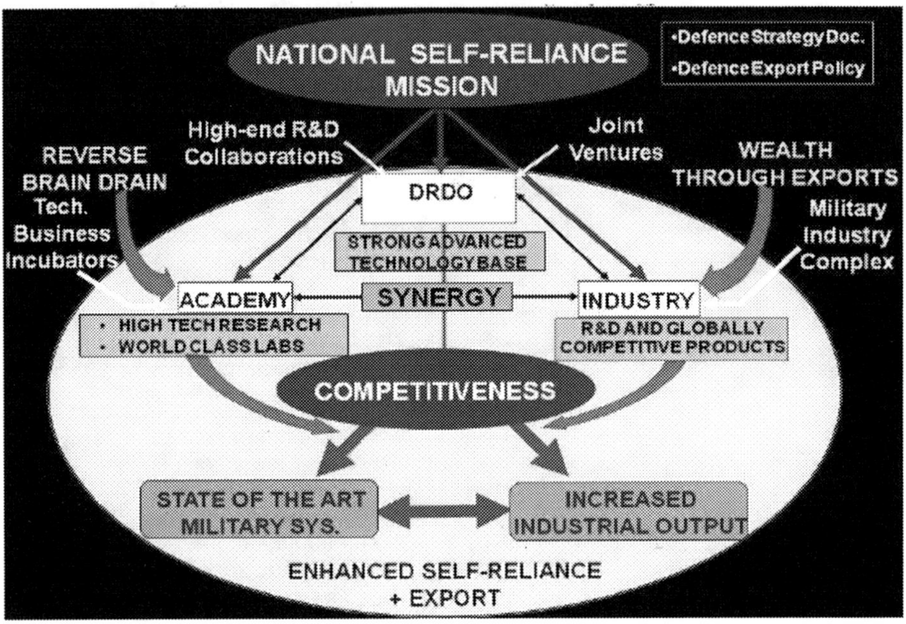

For building critical technologies and strategic industries, a vision for technology development is a necessity which has to focus on the core competencies prevailing in the country. Core competencies relate to certain areas where inherent strengths are there and a much better output and results can be expected in a short time.

Defence Budget and R&D Funding

India's Defence budget for the financial year 2013-14 stood at Rs.2036 billion which is approximately 1.79 per cent of the GDP. The budget has an increase of 5.31 per cent over that of the previous financial year 2012-13. The share of DRDO is only five per cent of the Defence budget (Fig. 8). Out of the allocation, majority of the funds goes only towards salary payments and capital purchases. In spite of the present technology capability, India still remains as top arms importer with 70 per cent of the armament needs being met with the imports. The reason for this condition is due to the pre-existing technology gap and failure to address this condition properly. Though efforts have been made to address this through the thrust for Self-reliance in Defence and push for indigenous defence R&D, we could flourish only in a few areas of defence like strategic systems and EW systems. As compared to the spending of 20 per cent and 16 per cent of China and US Defence budgets on R&D respectively, India's percentage share of R&D on defence budget is very low. Hence, an increase in the share for Defence R&D is absolutely necessary.

Fig. 8: Defence Budget (% Share)

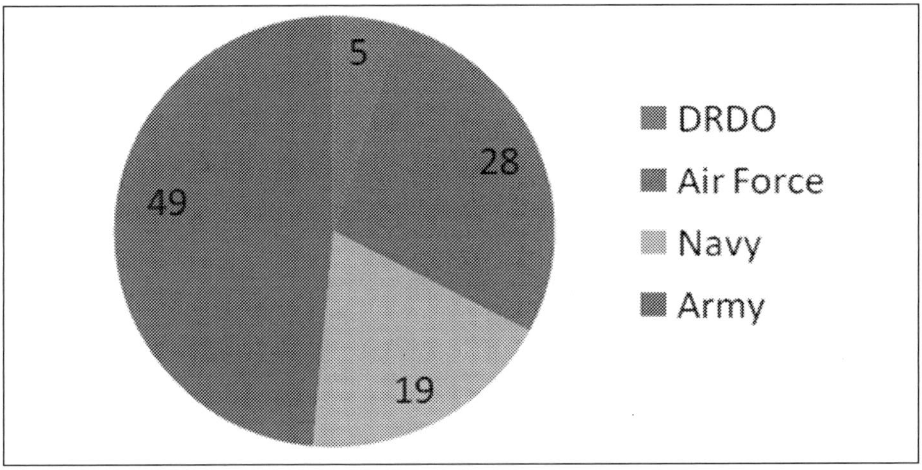

Military System Requirement

India's defence market saw robust growth over the past decade. In the next five to seven years, the defence requirement for India is around $150 billion putting together the requirements of all the three services (Fig. 9).

For example, the Indian Air Force (IAF) which has an authorised strength of 42 combat squadrons is presently operating only 34 squadrons. Among these aircraft, many of the aircraft are overdue to be replaced with new generation aircraft. Another portion of the present aircraft is to be phased out in the near future. In conservative estimate, to reach the authorised combat squadron strength, it may take another decade. In view of the present threat scenario, there are opinions both informed and uninformed that there could be a possibility of a two front war with China and Pakistan. In view of this, the IAF may need more combat squadrons to meet the requirement. Along with this combat squadron strength, the supporting elements like rotary wing, transport and trainer aircraft numbers must also increase proportionally.

Similarly, the Indian Navy needs aircraft, diesel electric submarines (SSK), nuclear attack submarines (SSN), Nuclear Ballistic Submarines (SSBN), aircraft carriers, combat surface vessels in large numbers. This is because the area of responsibility of the Indian Navy extends from Madagascar to Malacca straits. Also, Indian Navy has the responsibility to provide maritime security and guard the vast coastlines of India. Indian Army has a vast requirement in terms of tanks, armoured personnel carriers, infantry combat vehicles and artillery guns (fixed, towed, light weight and tracked) etc. All the forces will require Missiles, arms and ammunitions for all the platforms that they will be purchasing. The above estimates do not include the requirement of homeland security forces which cater the internal security duties and fighting insurgencies and terrorism.

Fig. 9: Defence System Requirement for Next 5-7 years ($150 Billion Business)

Plat form		*Spending ($bn)*	*Main orders expected*
AIR	Combat/ trainer	26.3	Medium multirole combat aircraft and other fifth generation aircraft, Mirage upgrade, MiG 29 upgrade. Jaguar engine upgrade, basic trainer
	Support	15.8	Transport aircraft, aerial tankers, long-range maritime patrol aircraft, midrange maritime reconnaissance aircraft, Phalcon AWACS, mini AWACS
	Rotary	9.1	Light utility helicopters replacing Chetaks for Navy, multirole helicopters for Navy, attack, heavy lift, light utility, light combat
LAND	Fighting Veh.	15.8	Arjun main battle tank (MBT), T-90 MBT, light tank, futuristic ICV
	Artillery	4.2	155 mm towed guns, 155 ultra light guns, 155 mm self-prop. tracked guns, 155 mm self-prop. whelled guns
	Missiles	3.4	Antitank missiles, CBU-105 sensor-fuzed weapon, short- to medium-range SAM, Agni-V, MICA
	Infantry Sys	1.1	Futuristic Infantry Soldier as a System (e.g. weapons, helmat, visor, clothing)
SEA		20.8	A/c carrier, P-71; Destroyer, P-15B; Frigates; P-17A & 17B; corvette; P-28A
		46.7	Nuclear, Arihant follow-on, Scorpene, P-751 spl midget
		4.1	Landing platform dock, landing ship tank, landing craft utility
C4I2SR		0.3	Navy 3-D radar, radar-jamming integrated electronic warfare systems

Source: Literature search, McKensey analysis.

"BrahMos": A CASE STUDY

The realisation of BRAHMOS Supersonic Cruise Missile is a shining example of networking and harnessing the core strengths of the R&D organisation and the Industrial capabilities of India and Russia.

India and Russia jointly established "BrahMos" to design, develop, produce and market a world class supersonic cruise missile system. The BRAHMOS missile is the fastest operational cruise missile existing in the world today and can be launched from any type of platform—land, sea, and air and precisely reach the targets either on land or at sea with high lethal effect (Fig. 10). The missile has undergone several successive successful flight trials with highest reliability index and has been inducted by the Indian Navy and by the Indian Army. In addition, the product being internationally competitive, it is able to cater to a large market with availability in time and state of the art performance. The product has been developed and led to production and induction, in a relatively shorter time frame. Early entry of the product into the world market, well before any competitor could emerge, has been made possible due to the superior performance of the system, cost effectiveness, high reliability and availability.

Fig. 10: BRAHMOS Universal Missile System

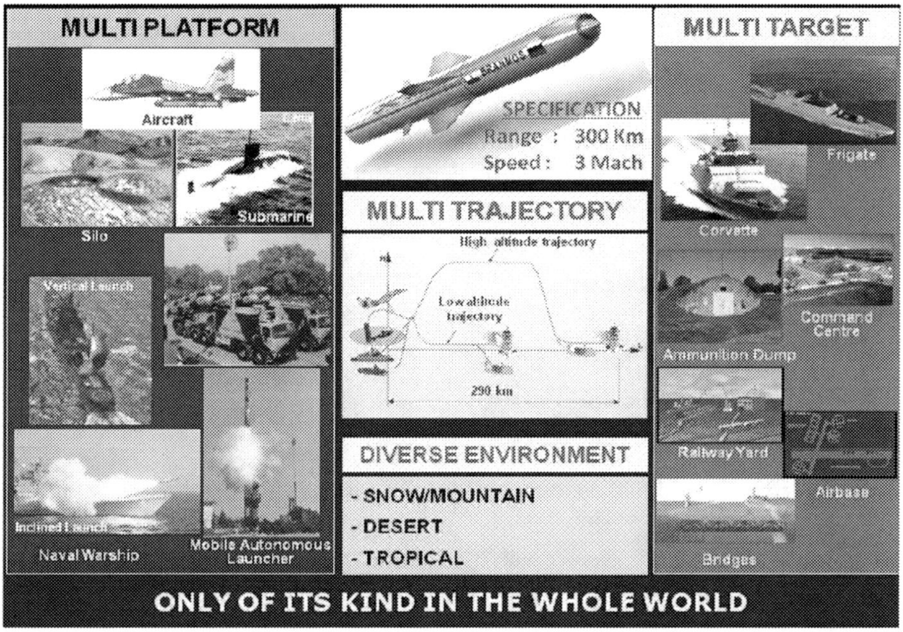

The foundation of the JV BrahMos is an example of integration and promotion of jointly developed high technology military products in the world market. The success of BrahMos has emerged due to the shared visions of both countries creating common culture and strategic relationship. The industry consortium established with active participation from both Public and Private Industries from India and Russia has also played a pivotal role in the success of this venture. It definitely would set an ideal example for collaborative ventures amongst partners from other countries with India.

BRAHMOS Public-Private Industrial Consortium

The concept of implementing role of public-private industry partnership in the production of BrahMos missile is unique. Criteria for the identification of Industry partners had been laid out and was carefully reviewed and verified. The criteria for industries selection was based on (a) their willingness to invest own funds to support or sustain the capacity and also to increase quantity on requirement basis, necessitating a modular approach; (b) experience in aerospace technology products; (c) the ability to absorb the state of the art technology with high level of knowledge competence; and (d) high governance indicators. The joint specialists' team from both the countries assessed the manufacturing and production capabilities of various industries, and short listed specific industries who could be the partners to BrahMos.

Based on the finalisation of the list of major industries by the Board, Government approval was obtained for the consortium of public and private industry partnership. The best part was that the industries came forward, enhanced their infrastructure by funding from their own source and manufactured subsystems for an advanced supersonic cruise missile. The industries expanded their infrastructure and made exclusive production set-up for the missile subsystems. There are many other small private industries who could either provide support to BrahMos directly or who could become subcontractors to major industries. 20 major industries and more than 200 small and medium scale industries became partners to BrahMos. All these tasks were carried out in record time in a concurrent manner, without knowing the number of units to be produced as there was no production order with us at that point of time. It was amazing to see the response of the industries expressing full confidence in the leadership that this missile will be produced in large quantities and they will not be treated like other defence products during production stage. In many other cases, the industries participated in development, product acceptance by the user took many years; by the time, the technology became obsolete; and when the production order came, PSUs only were given the orders. The industries lost interest in participation in the development of defence equipment. This trend was reversed by BrahMos.

Thus, the 'BrahMos Missile Industry Consortium', the first of its kind in India was established. Human Resources of more than 20,000 specialists, technicians and engineers are contributing for the manufacture of BRAHMOS subsystems at different industries. The major industries and the systems/sub systems produced by them are shown in Fig. 11. The list is not exhaustive.

BrahMos team evolved a policy to retain system design, system engineering, system integration and system management with the Company and go for partnership MoUs with leading industries for production of subsystems, components and materials. The contractual obligations are fulfilled and industries produce and deliver the products well in time which ensure smooth functioning of the missile integration and its timely delivery to the user.

BrahMos Success Formula

- Robust Design with unique world class capabilities (Best in the World)
- Systematic validation of systems, Simulation, Checkout procedures and reviews establishing reliability at every stage of development
- Incorporating the lessons learnt through earlier experiences of Prithvi and Agni, and thinking a step better in the product performance

Fig. 11: BrahMos Industry Complex—A Blend of Public-Private Enterprises

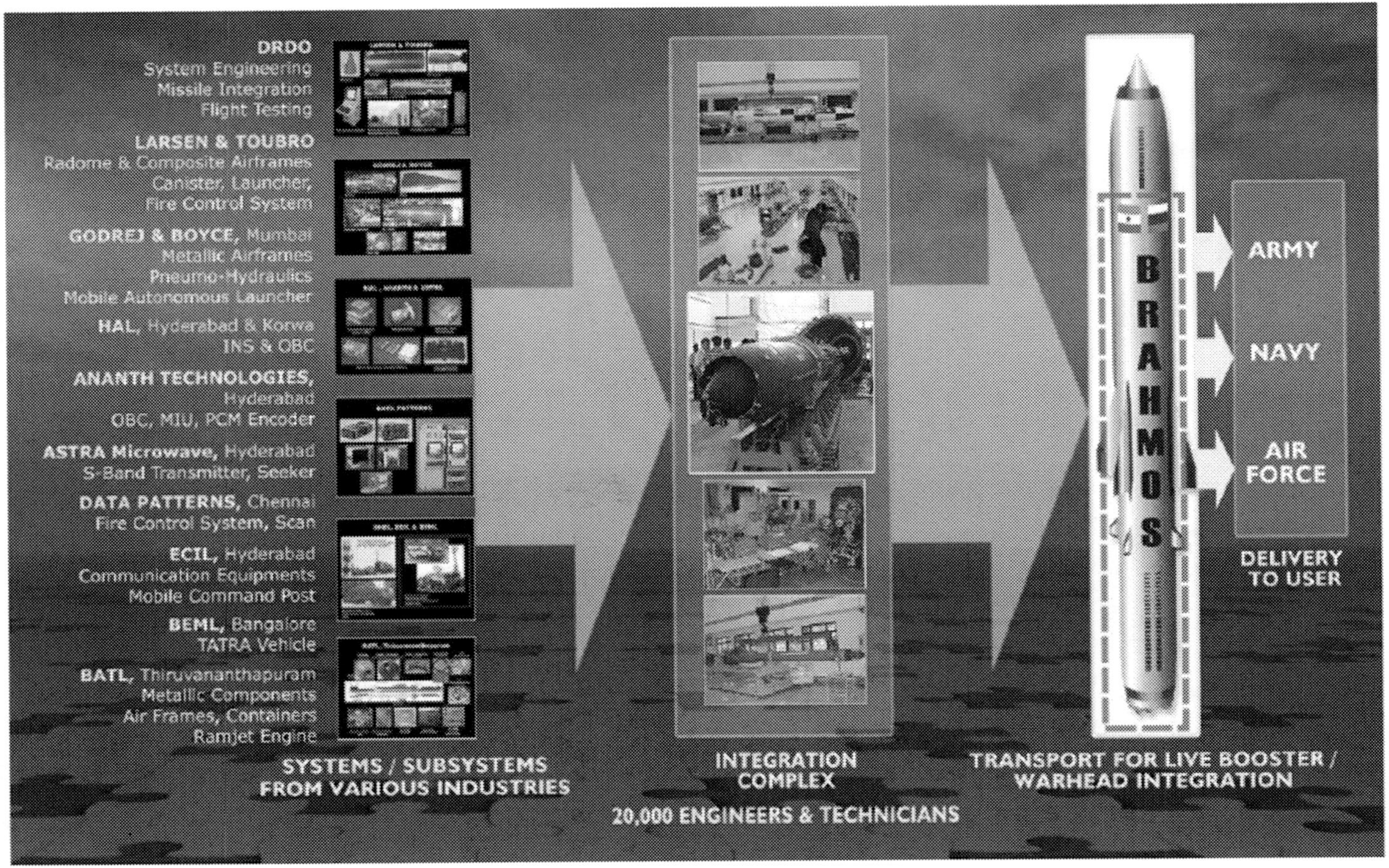

- Continuous performance improvements, upgrades and new versions for Customer delight, utilising the experts from India & Russia
- Strong customer loyalty towards the Brand
- Consortium of industry partners keeping design, integration and management with JV. All stakeholders networked with integrated management system and transparency in operation
- Faster execution of the tasks due to autonomous operation of JV & empowerment
- Utilisation of young energetic talent force with Pride in working for world-class missile for the nation

Achieving Self-Reliance

Present Ambience

An important factor prevailing in India in the present context is the absence of coherence and discrete relationship between the stakeholders viz. Government; Armed Forces; R&D Organisations and the Industries. This resulted in the large import of weapons and equipment due to which there is continuous dependence on other countries for spares/equipment; there is no effective coordination between R&D organisation and Industry as a single entity; and absence of "Mind to Market" thinking.

There are both advantages and disadvantages in all these four sectors of stakeholders. Identifying the bottleneck areas and resolving them and by unifying the strengths of the stakeholders will bring synergy in developing products in the niche areas of technology. Let me narrate the strengths and weaknesses of the stakeholders in the succeeding paragraphs:

Government has got progressively improved Defence Procurement Policy (DPP) to boost the indigenous production of systems and equipment. Moreover, the offset policy guidelines outlined will induce active participation of industries in the development of systems. What Government can do further is that the thrust should be given on the Long term Defence Strategy and Vision for Defence Industry growth, involving large number of Private Industries as production partners. Government should open up the access for renowned global Companies for having partnership with Indian industries to result in the flow of new manufacturing techniques and state-of-the-art technologies to share with our industries. This will in turn result in the realisation of high quality technology products. Allocation of more funding by Government for R&D & infrastructure for establishment and nurturing of advanced research labs and Foundries will strengthen our indigenous R&D capability to help the industries. As in many countries, Legal provision for "Use only Indigenous Weapons" will definitely necessitate the indigenous industry growth and their investment in R&D and go for JVs in high technology products. Defence PSUs, OFs and major identified private industries should become a single entity.

Our highly committed Armed Forces need contemporary, state-of-the-art weapon system to fight against the enemy in the process of protecting the nation. No country gives the best of the weapon and equipment to other countries. When it comes to the development of system indigenously using home grown technologies, there must be level playing acceptance procedures for these systems. At the time of formulation of Qualitative Requirement (QR), user takes the requirements from the existing best systems and adds tough specification to that. The QR once formulated should be the final and there should not be any change in the midway. This will definitely affect the schedule since change in QR affects the entire chain right from the design to process to production to validation. The change in the trained manpower affects the usage of system by the Armed Forces personnel. In the case of BrahMos, the Armed Forces have raised a separate regiment for the BRAHMOS. Training is imparted to the crew at different levels to familiarise them with the system and ease of operation. Frequent change of personnel will result in the delay in operation and extended man efforts in providing training to them.

DRDO has got the best brains who put in all-out efforts to succeed in various missions and development of defence systems. In these five decades, starting with the basic research, today, DRDO is capable of building bigger systems and has attained the technological maturity. DRDO has got an excellent track record with success in focused mission mode projects. As the technologies become obsolescent, fast and proactive adaptations are required to sustain in the rapidly changing technology environment. Technology denial regimes added to the problem of restricting in-flow of technologies, component, materials and equipment. With limited resources and manpower and many projects on hand caused non completion of projects in time. Long drawn procedures become hindrance to the completion of the projects within time though steps have been taken to devise multilayer boards etc. Judicious allocation of resources to multiple projects will resolve the problem. Giving thrust on quality of technology transfer documentation and productionisation aspects will accelerate the smooth Transfer of Technology (ToT) to the industries.

Large industrial infrastructure is available with Indian Defence PSUs for specific product lines to support Armed Forces (SU-30MKI, T-90S, Radars, Missiles and Ships). At the time of establishment, the main motive was to produce defence systems to cater to the immediate requirement, looking for technology inflow from outside. This has resulted in technology know-how and not the technology knows-why due to low absorption of technologies. Low R&D effort in the industries has further worsened the situation. Technological obsolescence and the non-up gradation of machineries suiting to the modern manufacturing techniques led to low productivity and quantity production which has resulted in the high cost for products. Moreover, dire requirement of equipment and systems for Armed Forces forced them to go for import due to the exorbitant delay in delivering the products by the industries. What is required is the fast absorption of Technologies and increased level of R&D effort. Participation of more Private Players through attractive policies ensures competitiveness.

Way Forward

Presently, the responsibility of the defence R&D solely rests with the DRDO. Right from the design of small arms and ammunition to the design and development of complex missile systems, aircraft etc., DRDO takes the responsibility of the entire spectrum of defence research including farming and animal husbandry. Due to such extended area of responsibilities, DRDO is very much over stretched and this results in time and cost overrun in the realisation of the systems. As suggested by the Rama Rao Committee, DRDO has been decentralised and domain based laboratory clusters have been established.

Further, the programmes that are being undertaken by the DRDO have all three dimensions—tactical systems, strategic systems and futuristic systems. Tactical systems include all battlefield weapon systems, and weapon platforms. Strategic systems include all nuclear ballistic and cruise missiles, nuclear submarines, Anti Satellite Weapons (ASAT) and missile defence.

It can be thought of that DRDO can concentrate on the research in futuristic technologies that will lead to futuristic weapon systems, and enhancement of the present strategic systems, whereas development of subsystems for the tactical system can be entrusted to the identified industries. As a progressive step, in the near future, an industry can be identified and given total responsibility for the final integration of the tactical systems. In that stage DRDO can help the lead industry which develops the entire system by providing technical support, laboratory facilities and consultancy services.

Presently, Indian industries are majorly concentrating on the production of systems required for the Indian Armed Forces through R&D Organisations. Main component missing in majority of the Indian Defence Industries is the in-house R&D facility. This will further delay in the realisation of the system. The new policy can be formulated that facilitates the compulsory establishment of R&D within the industry. Suitable incentive mechanisms for having in-house R&D can be employed to attract the industries to venture into research in their respective areas.

Indian Academic Institutions have got their specialisation and conduct basic researches which are purely of academic in nature. But it is these technologies which form the building blocks of a complex technology behind Defence systems and equipment. The strengths of these institutions have to be identified and these institutions have to be supported to widen their research that can converge into a product. Also, the national needs and requirement which are to be realised by the Academia are to be properly channelised by the R&D Organisations. Through this, the academia will be aware of the potential of their researches and the new areas that they have to venture. The critical aspect of self-reliance is the availability of the knowledgeable work force. It is the academia which can create innovative workforce that can further contribute in the realisation of higher end defence technology.

Synergy between R&D establishments, academy and industry will ensure development of critical technologies with unified effort. Development of high end technologies with collaborations and joint ventures based on the self-reliance mission will further result in competitiveness in the global arena. What is required is the Military Industry Complex (MIC) that connects all these stakeholders to take the best out of all.

MIC—The Roadmap to Future

At the international level, the developed nations have fielded weapon systems and platforms only through their military industry complex. Whether it is USA or erstwhile USSR/Russian Federation, it is the strength of their respective military industry complex that resulted in their enormous military capability. Such a military capability when used properly will be the deterrent factor for the enemy against any misadventures.

In India, with the present geo-political scenario, it is such a deterrent factor that is required for the defence of the nation. Presently, the elements of our military industrial complex which generally consists of Armed Forces, R&D Organisations, Public and Private Industries and Academia are discrete. It is utmost essential to integrate all these elements by forming a MIC with members from each element. Procedures are to be formulated which will enable participation of cluster of industries to respond to *Request For Proposal* (RFP) to design, develop and produce the systems (Irrespective of Private or Public). More thrust needs to be given for Government funding for R&D even to Private companies to strengthen the indigenous R&D capability. Regulations and control procedures like in the USA should be implemented in managing the private industries for manufacturing of defence systems. As in many countries, legal provision for "use only indigenous weapons" to be made compulsory that will accelerate the indigenous industrial growth. The authority can encourage and facilitate high technology tie-ups/JVs between Indian and other global defence industries that will achieve not only competitiveness but also envisage the product for export. MIC can also encourage industry partnership with renowned global Companies that will enable flow of new manufacturing techniques to our industries resulting in quality production of high technology products. This Networking concept is not new to India. We have employed this methodology and fully exploited its potential in realising the critical technologies and systems during IGMDP days even under different technology denial regimes.

We have proved to the world that India is a technologically capable nation by way of indigenously developing every denied critical technology. Hence, Technology denied is Technology gained. Successful development and deployment of various versions of Agni Strategic missile has given the nation enormous deterrence against all adversaries. Aided by these achievements, formation of the joint venture BrahMos has resulted in the realisation of advanced supersonic cruise missile in the shortest possible time with minimum investment and maximum quality. The BRAHMOS cruise missile so far has not seen any competitor nor a defensive system thus making it a world leader in the cruise missile family. Indian Armed Forces have the tremendous advantage of having the force multiplier BRAHMOS. Continuous quality sustenance has been possible due to BrahMos industry consortium which was created by the joint venture for the first time in the country. To attain self-sufficiency in military systems, the only possible way for India is to form a very strong MIC. Realisation of the Proposed MIC following the BrahMos model will lead India into building strong defence capabilities. This will not only cater to our domestic defence needs but also will make India an exporting giant from a gigantic importer.

NOTES

1. India's Defence Budget 2013-14: A Bumpy Road Ahead, Laxman K Behera, IDSA, March 4, 2013
2. A Brief Report on Defence Sector in India, Corporate Catalyst India, October 2013
3. 2013 Global R&D Funding Forecast, Battelle and R&D Magazine,
4. Ajaishukla.blogspot.in/2013/04/drdo-chief-wants-7-of-defence-budget.html
5. India remains top arms importer while China becomes fifth largest exporter, Sruthijith KK, ET Bureau Mar 18, 2013; (http://articles.economictimes.indiatimes.com/2013-03-18/news/37815093_1_top-arms-importer-largest-importer-weapons-importer)
6. Revolution in Leadership, Sivathanu Pillai, Pentagon Press, 2011

9

Acquisition in Defence

Vinod Misra

Acquisition in Indian defence is, by far, one of the most critical activities towards attainment of comprehensive national power rooted in a carefully balanced basket of full spectrum capabilities. This task has to be necessarily imbued, at all times, with a compelling sense of urgency against the backdrop of a not unlikely two-front war and the consequent imperative for an effective and strong dissuasive and containment capability against our northern neighbour and clearly superior punitive strength vis-a-vis our Western neighbour. Our credible deterrence needs have, accordingly, been established in relation to force level comparisons with potential adversaries, a sufficiently short mobilisation period bordering on a 'cold start', the state of the art in weapon technologies and weapon systems and high readiness level at all times. This apart, India has had to factor in some inevitable 'out of area' contingencies and certain key obligations and concerns as a regional economic and military power. All this forms the basis for the Long Term Integrated Perspective Plans (LTIPP) spanning capability build up needs over a 15-year time horizon.

An all-pervasive sense of urgency, quality, economy and efficiency must, thus, guide the complex and elaborate acquisition process. Unfortunately, however, individual programmes have tended to suffer from a host of inefficiencies ranging from laying down of essential quality parameters, which, unwittingly or otherwise, contributed to a normally unacceptable single source situation, protracted trial evaluation, inability to professionally benchmark prices for an efficient price discovery, life-cycle weapon system maintenance challenges contributing to low serviceability levels, post-contract management concerns leading to time and cost overruns, mismatched induction of resources such as infrastructure, utilities and manpower affecting timely induction of weapon systems and our inability to nurture a vibrant domestic defence industrial base with a persistent and dominant import orientation in defence acquisitions.

By far the most crucial determinant of the acquisition programme is the process of laying down Qualitative Requirements (QRs) for the weapon system (comprising the platform, sensors and armaments) in the context of our terrains, environmental and climatic conditions, the current state of relevant defence technology, mission objectives, worldwide availability of such systems and life cycle management issues. In the event adequate professionalism and due diligence is not imparted to this activity, we run the risk, as on innumerable occasions in the past, of ending up in an unacceptable single-source situation or specifying a capability and a weapon system which does not exist worldwide in actual operational deployment. It is in this context that a stage of Request for Information (RFI) has been prescribed mandatorily in the Defence Procurement Procedure (DPP) which would contribute to firming up of more realistic and critical and minimum need-based QRs and also culminate in a competitive setting. The other important aspect of qualitative requirements is the fact of extremely high cost of incremental quality features and specifications beyond a reasonable quality threshold. It is in this background that acquisitions in defence target vital and essential quality parameters as a single benchmark and there are no extra weightages for 'desirable' parameters. It would also be useful to clarify at this stage why the Indian system does not seek to grade different technical proposals for a weapon system based on an enunciation of distinct quality elements and weightages to be assigned to each of them whereby a ranking of technical proposals for the same system would be possible and the final decision to award a contract could be taken based on a weighted sum of technical and commercial offers from the various bidders. It is clear that the balance of advantage would lie in specifying a reasonably high minimum quality criteria whereby non-compliant offers do not figure further in the evaluation process and competition is confined among only such of the bidders who clear the well deliberated and pre-decided quality benchmark. It should be noted in this context that it is virtually impossible to assign a price tag to perceived quality advantages beyond a professionally well laid down threshold.

In the context of quality, it has also become imperative for decision-makers to take a conscious call on the need, in every case of parts, components and sub-systems, to go in for the highly ruggedised military specifications rather than the significantly cheaper Commercial Off-The-Shelf (COTS) items which are readily available in the global supply chain.

Long drawn user trials of weapon systems on offer from different Original Equipment Manufacturers (OEMs) whose offers were found meeting the technical benchmarks during the technical evaluation of technical bids has been the most conspicuous feature of defence acquisitions. This is, of course, far more pronounced in respect of the Army with the Air Force and Navy being able to guide this vital activity in a more focused way. There are inevitable scheduling challenges in the process of user evaluation of weapon systems in deserts, plains and mountains during summer, winter and rainy seasons. This gets compounded by controllable factors such as lack of continuity of the project team/team leader, delays in availability of firing ranges, non-availability of ammunition, time allowed to vendors for removal of glitches and minor and remediable deficiencies encountered during the user evaluation phase and delays in finalisation of the user evaluation reports. All in all, compression of this vital stage of the acquisition process to an internationally well-accepted norm of 12-18 months at most would go a long way in more time-bound capability acquisition in Indian Defence. In the event the weapon system on offer is already in use else where, the sharing by vendors of exploitation data in respect of other prime customers could also be potentially of great value in the evaluation phase.

Commercial evaluation of bids has, over time, stabilised into a well-honed and transparent process. The essential challenge here has been to lay down, in each specific acquisition case, a comprehensive format for the Best And Final Offers (BAFO) required to be submitted by the bidders to whom Requests For Proposal (RFPs) were sent. The structuring of the BAFO format in an all-encompassing manner related to each distinct cost element requires full understanding of the operational and maintenance facets of the weapon system planned to be acquired. This is possible only through rigorous application at the earlier stages of RFI and a pre-bid conference with the short-listed OEMs. The underlying idea is to spell out, in precise details, all the elements of supply of weapon systems and services, which would take care of life cycle operation and maintenance of the system in a cost-efficient manner. No ambiguities and uncertainties can thus be allowed to exist in the matter of commercial and financial safeguards on the one hand and technical parameters on the other. In order to avoid a non-level playing field, the draft contract is also appended to the RFPs issued to the intended OEMs.

A fresh challenge has been added to the evaluation process in recent years by way of seeking to establish the lowest commercial offer based on potential Life Cycle Costs (LCC) over the likely calendar life/total technical life of the system being acquired. The LCC evaluation system, per se, is quite unexceptionable linked as it is to user defined criteria of unit-wise deployment, proposed monthly usage rate and a specified maintenance philosophy while the OEM is required to specify the total technical life/calendar life, Mean Time between Failures (MTBF) for all major systems/sub-systems/assemblies/sub-assemblies/parts/components, Mean Time to Repair (MTTR), Turn Around Time (TAT) and an Itemised Spares Parts Price List (ISPPL) together with the pricing basis for spares supply over the system's life. However, since the objective of this exercise is apparent to all the bidders, there could be a natural propensity to inflate the relevant numbers based, may be, on the design objectives rather than actually realisable or achieved pattern of life cycle product support. There are inherent difficulties in enforcing financial guarantees in the event of significant shortfalls in performance below the contractually obligated benchmarks. The process is rendered even more difficult as the OEMs do not share with the Indian MoD/ concerned service HQ, information they would have about the exploitation and maintenance experience in respect of other major buyers worldwide of the same system. Consequently, the LCC based evaluation process has to be undertaken extremely carefully and tempered with reasonable realism. Hopefully, with passage of time, the Indian MoD would acquire adequate experience to fully streamline and refine the LCC methodology and avoid some of the pitfalls that potentially exist in the system.

A formidable challenge in defence acquisitions is the aspect of price discovery. In the event a strong competitive state is achieved, even among two or three OEMs with proven track records, the objective of cost efficient acquisition is found to be adequately served. However, in effectively single source situations, which have tended to become the norm rather than exceptions, securing a reasonable price has remained a recurring theme. The prevalent procedure mandates that negotiations would be carried out only in the event the lowest offered price is higher than the price benchmark determined in advance. Instructions also provide for a 'Professional Officers' Valuation (POV)' which could form such a basis. Actual experience has, however, shown that, by and large, the POV is totally out of line with the eventually offered/contracted prices. The reasons for this are not difficult to seek. One, of course, is our non-familiarity with the complex manufacturing processes based on design, engineering and manufacturing excellence worldwide with the added challenge of deciphering material composition for many of the defence goods. Then there is the fact that commercial offers for weapon systems are not based on a simple aggregation of manufacturing, integration and quality assurance costs but contain varying elements of the initial design, development and certification costs depending upon the amortisation of such costs which might have already taken place through sale to other customers. Indeed, the timing of the acquisition becomes a key element in determining the acquisition costs with the first and early customers potentially meeting much larger elements of development costs. On the other hand, however, delaying acquisition, from the point of securing lower costs, could lead to earlier obsolescence with the inexorable march of defence technology and an out-dated system in our inventory.

It should be noted that in the decades till the 90s, most of the capability build up in the Indian Defence Services was through acquisition from erstwhile Soviet Union/Russia. Till the 80s, such arms supplies came under extremely concessional credit terms with an initial moratorium on principal repayment, low interest rates and 10/15 year repayment periods not to mention the very reasonable basic price of these weapon systems which, in any event, were difficult to source from elsewhere in a reliable, dependable and price efficient manner. However, with the subsequent economic compulsion for the Russians to increasingly demand near price parity with Western prices for similar systems and our own serious and sustained problems with life cycle product support from Russia not to mention significantly lower (than Western systems) reliability and maintainability parameters, a conscious effort has been underway to target acquisitions more holistically based on LCC principles and provide a fair and equal opportunity to the best in class OEMs worldwide. Nonetheless, India has had an extremely strong and vibrant strategic relationship with Russia which has clearly stood the test of time.

During the last 8/9 years, USA too has been able to steadily forge a reasonable relationship with India in the realm of defence acquisitions. Though most of the high value defence contracts have been entered into through the Foreign Military Sales (FMS) route, there is a sharp increase in the participation by all the major defence suppliers in the US in the Indian capability build up programmes. However, these are early days though the clear expectation is that it would be mutually rewarding for both India and the US to nurture a long term relationship rooted in sound principles of reliability, high readiness levels for weapon systems sourced from the US, sustainability and cost effectiveness of life cycle product support and leading eventually up to transfer of technology, co-development and co-production, and setting up of joint ventures and integrating Indian companies into the global supply chain. Conscious efforts towards increasing such reciprocities would alone lay a strong foundation for a potentially strategic partnership between the two countries on a lasting basis. It should be noted that the DPP envisages single-source acquisitions on strategic considerations and depending upon our progress in acquiring key defence technologies, critical system integration capabilities and collaborating with the best in class US entities in design, development, engineering and manufacturing, there would be great merit in nurturing strategic defence ties with both the US and Russia.

Indeed, in the interest of collaborating with the best in class worldwide, it might be advantageous overall to seek to acquire major weapon systems invoking the strategic consideration clause in the DPP which would help nurture long term strategic ties with the identified foreign OEM/country. It is for this consideration that India has insisted in the past on an inter-Governmental agreement for strategic acquisition even while the foreign OEMs were separate corporate entities. The only challenge in such single source situations, devoid of a competitive setting, is the aspect of rational and professional price discovery particularly when reliable commercial intelligence with regard to prices and commercial terms is conspicuously missing. Nonetheless, this route can be selectively adopted even with countries other than Russia and USA where the strategic purpose is abundantly served and worthwhile preliminary work towards benchmarking prices can be done through the RFI stage and otherwise. In the preceding context, two more points need to be made. Defence acquisitions have consistently recognised the resource affordability issue by giving primacy to the option of upgrade rather than replacement of all existing platforms (tanks, guns, aircraft, helicopters, ships, submarines and the like) and focusing on cost efficient replacement of weapons and sensors with state of the art products. Thus, with appropriate life extensions or based on adequate balance useful technical/calendar life, fleet modernisation and upgradation has generally been in respect of force multiplier elements of sensors and weapons. Given our experience with the slow pace of acquisition even while significant capability gaps continue to exist, it would also appear clearly necessary to mandate acquisition through the significantly shorter Fast Track Procedure (FTP), to the extent of at least 25/30 per cent of the yearly modernisation/capital acquisition outlays.

One of the most critical aspects of the acquisition process is to be able to put in place a comprehensive lifetime product support package intended to achieve the highest possible level of serviceability/readiness once the system has been deployed and through the entire life cycle. Aspects such as total calendar life, time between overhaul, guaranteed Mean Time Between Failures (MTBF), Mean Time To Repair (MTTR), Turn Around Time (TAT) and an itemised spares part price list with an agreed long term spare parts pricing basis have all to be generally structured into the acquisition contract. In actual fact, however, there have been recurring problems in assuring high serviceability levels with unreliable product support, primarily in respect of the Russian systems, by way of long delivery lead times, non supply of critical components, unjustifiable escalation in spares prices, premature failures and absence of domestic capabilities of repair/maintenance/overhaul of key components/sub-systems/systems. Notwithstanding comprehensive facilities available in-house with the Defence Services/Defence PSUs for carrying out first to fourth echelon maintenance, repairs and overhaul for most of the weapon systems, the fact of the matter is that serviceability levels continue to be a matter of serious and constant concern. The problem also stems from the fact of an extremely large number of sub-suppliers for each weapon system and the challenges of channelising, as in the Russian context, product support from the principal OEM as well as all his numerous vendors in a stable, reliable and focused manner. The problem of uneconomic annual order quantity has been addressed through consolidation of requirement over a longer term giving the manufacturer the flexibility to plan economic production runs with physical deliveries suitably staggered. Life cycle support costs are seriously distorted with irrational and sharp escalation in prices of critical spares. Efforts to persuade the foreign OEMs to set up a product support centre in India well stocked with the requisite range and depth of spares whereby needs of user services could be swiftly met as per the agreed pricing basis have also not been successful. Product support has been generally unreliable and inefficient even in respect of systems manufactured and supplied domestically by Defence PSUs/Ordnance Factories with their principal focus on fresh manufacture and meeting contractual deadlines.

Against this backdrop, the concept of Performance Based Logistics (PBL) is also sought to be tried out. A PBL arrangement is intended to entrust logistics responsibilities to the OEM (foreign or DPSU) or their nominated company whereby the desired level of serviceability at all times would be guaranteed by the OEM. There would be penalties to be imposed for failures to do so while an incentive scheme could also be in place to reward consistently high performance levels beyond the mandated threshold. While prime facie this could be potentially a far more efficient arrangement ensuring judicious allocation of maintenance funds in consonance with desired readiness levels for various weapon systems, the jury is still out on whether this would indeed have greater efficacy and reliability in the Indian milieu.

Weapon systems required in large numbers were generally acquired through the Buy and Make route based on limited imports initially of complete systems and the manufacture of the rest under a phased domestic manufacture programme linked to a Transfer of Technology (ToT) arrangement. The phases covered initial manufacture from Semi Knocked Down (SKD)/Completely Knocked Down (CKD) supplies and full scale manufacture of major assemblies/sub-systems/systems in the second phase while raw material based manufacturing was sought to be undertaken in the final phase. In actual fact, however, the transfer of know-how left a lot to be desired while there was very little gained by way of know-why. As a consequence, capabilities for critical value addition in the manufacturing process and know-how for key manufacturing technologies/systems could not be satisfactorily acquired. This was partly attributable to the inadequacies in contractual commitments built into the formal agreements as well as to the lack of vigour in making the fullest use of intended training, technical documentation and technical assistance obligations set out for the OEMs. It was also unfortunate that, largely owing to the urgency displayed by the concerned user service and inadequate absorption of technologies and the elongated learning curve, the numbers made through the raw material route in the third phase indigenisation programme were generally very low. It is disturbing that even in the matter of meeting the needs of repairs, maintenance, modifications, improvements and overhaul, the domestic manufacturing capability linked to ToT proved grossly inadequate. Close association of the DRDO with these ToT arrangements would have been rewarding for both the Defence R&D organisation on the one hand and the Defence Services on the other. Unfortunately, DRDO remained preoccupied with its own research, development, design and prototype manufacture programmes.

Vibrant domestic R&D capabilities are a sine qua non for cost efficient acquisition in defence. True self-reliance by way of ownership of core defence technologies and critical final system integration knowledge. skills and capabilities is the most vital element in our evolution as a significant regional power unaffected by potential embargoes, sanctions. denials and control regimes. It also eventually makes for a far more cost efficient basket of critical capabilities. This would also permit factoring in of low life cycle costs as a necessary design objective. While the DRDO has done the country proud in the strategic realm of missiles and nuclear weapons technology, serious time and cost overruns and quality inadequacies have beset most of its other forays. Since capability acquisition by the Services, in the context of the existing capability gaps, brooks no delay, DRDO has to perforce meet more reasonable design, development and manufacturing timelines. DRDO's determined pursuit, in recent years, of collaborative design, development and manufacture programmes with some leading entities worldwide is clearly the way forward. Increasingly, DRDO should develop capabilities for 'build to specifications' rather than 'build to print 'in respect of systems falling in the collaborator's share of design and development. DRDO would also have to display far greater courage in short-closing projects which are facing interminable delays and unacceptable cost excesses. At the same time, there is a compelling need for independent peer reviews of its on-going projects at pre-defined milestones. Finally, DRDO also has to be a strong catalytic force in encouraging specific defence related project research, innovation and entrepreneurship in premier academic institutions such as the IITs and the Indian Institute of Science as well as the private sector.

Affordable defence in the long term is critically dependant on a strong and vibrant domestic industrial base. Life cycle sustainment costs by way of operations, maintenance, modifications/upgrades, overhaul and the like could aggregate to three to five times the high initial acquisition cost. Consequently, there is considerable business even by way of MRO and upgrades of the already inducted systems or acquisitions on the anvil. The business case becomes truly substantial in the Indian context if the potential for self-reliant defence industrialisation is fully tapped. Domestic defence manufacture has largely remained confined to the nine defence PSUs and the thirty-nine ordnance factories. Considering the large order books for ships, submarines, aircraft, helicopters, missiles and other platforms, sensors and armaments which would take several decades to fulfil with current levels of turnover, there is space enough for creation of greenfield capacities in the private sector in many areas apart from tier2 and tier3 capabilities needed for manufacture of major systems, sub-systems and components by a carefully created and nurtured set of Medium, Small and Micro Enterprises (MSMEs) as well as larger private sector entities. The focus should indeed be on critical value addition and final systems integration by the DPSUs/OrdFys with substantial outsourcing of the rest to the private sector players. The key determinant for this is clarity concerning the business case for meeting the potential long term order book and whether the Government is willing to build long term, stable and reliable relationships based on professionally well established benchmark price, quality and performance yardsticks and a rational and transparent price escalation basis whether in a single source situation or a limited competitive basis with the competition confined to two or three carefully shortlisted players depending upon economies of scale. A rigorous short-listing criteria could be adopted for identifying well-endowed private sector entities for this long term partnership with the Indian MoD/Defence Services. Given the likely outlays for defence modernisation and acquisition over the ensuing 15-20 year time horizon, it is eminently possible to attract the biggest and most accomplished industrial entities in the country on considerations of past turnover, accumulated reserves, managerial and technological strengths, infrastructure, pan-India presence, project and supply-chain management efficiencies, potential investments and the like to be enthusiastic partners in rapid defence industrialisation.

It would also be useful in this context to consider elements of a Public Private Partnership (PPP) in this defence industrialisation programme. This could manifest in a reasonable fee to be charged from intending private sector users of substantial spare capacities available in DPSUs/Ordnance Factories/DRDO/Defence Services by way of infrastructure (land/plant and machinery), training, testing, evaluation, quality assurance, certification and the like which require heavy initial capital investment and would be a strong deterrent particularly for the MSMEs for entering the defence space.

A significant stumbling block in the path of creation of a sound defence industrial base is the near absence of a cogent export policy governing exports of defence goods and services. We have instead a case-by-case approach which cannot be an acceptable basis for creation and optimal utilisation of domestic capacities. It would have to be recognised that potential exports have to be factored into creation of economies of scale in the domestic defence economy. The meeting of export demand could also potentially result in lower prices for domestic supplies to the defence services through more economic production runs and a larger base for amortisation of the significant design, development, engineering costs and substantial fixed overheads. Exports will also engender managerial, technical and project management efficiencies. This apart, exports, if carefully nurtured, could serve a major role in the consolidation of strategic relationships with several countries of interest to us in Asia, Africa and Latin America. Notwithstanding these obvious ramifications, India has been extremely reluctant to accept the compelling logic for defence exports both from the point of view of the Indian economy as well as the even more important aspect of cementing strategic relationships with countries of interest. Once basic decisions concerning the imperatives for defence exports have been taken, other policy initiatives concerning an appropriate fiscal and financial incentives package including the possibility of setting up exclusive defence SEZs could follow.

While the subject of offsets is comprehensively covered in two separate chapters in this book including the aspect of international best practices, it is considered necessary to highlight how offsets, as an integral element of all major acquisitions (Rs 300 Crore and above), were expected to transform the domestic defence industrial landscape through leveraging of India's enormous buying strength in respect of defence goods. With defence capital acquisitions from abroad in the magnitude of around 70 per cent of the defence modernisation capital outlays (around 74,000 Crore allocated for modernisation during 2014-15) and an offset obligation at the minimum level of 30 per cent of the main acquisition contract, potential offset inflows would be significant in the foreseeable future. It would remain so over the next 15-20 years even if the pace of indigenisation and self-reliance gathers the much needed momentum in the coming decade. Offset contracts worth around US$ 5.0 billion have been concluded since the offset obligation became mandatory in 2005/2006. The expectation was that carefully nurtured offsets would offer a reasonable and competitive return on investments by the foreign OEMs rather than proving to be an unavoidable cost element for them. With a wide range of choices, offsets were expected to contribute significantly to setting up of joint ventures with Indian entities for design, development, engineering and manufacture of weapon systems, sub-systems, major parts and components and eventually contribute to their integration with the global defence supply chain and thereby provide a fillip to defence exports. Investment inflows were also likely to occur in infrastructure creation, MRO capabilities, training and simulation facilities, civil aviation and homeland security and filling in key frontline technology gaps and critical system integration strengths. Offsets were also expected to act as a catalytic influence on domestic R&D and manufacturing excellence through collaborative ventures with the best in class foreign OEMs. However, these expectations have been largely belied thus far due to a variety of reasons. These include a FDI limit of 26 per cent (resulting in an FDI inflow of just around US$ 5 million in defence since 2001), the continuation of a licencing regime when it has been dismantled in nearly all other sectors of the economy, non prioritisation of our most critical technology inflow needs, inability to mandate the principles on which a reliable long term relationship will be pursued with both foreign OEMs and domestic defence industry based on clarity concerning the business case in the medium and long terms and absence of a professionally well endowed structure and organisation to provide focused guidance to foreign OEMs for tie ups with competent Indian partners across the full defence technology spectrum as also for subsequent monitoring of the pace and adequacy of fulfilment of the offset contractual commitments. In the light of our experience with defence offsets so far, there is great urgency for developing RFP specific (i.e. each acquisition specific) offset choices based on our own priorities rather than leaving it to the foreign OEM, as at present, to offer the barely compliant low-hanging fruits in the offset basket. Carefully channelled offsets would not only substantially augment the defence resource base but help create and consolidate a capable defence industrial complex in the country so crucial to affordable defence.

Oversight in the context of defence acquisitions is mainly provided by the CVC, C&AG, CBI and the Parliamentary Standing Committee on Defence. In recent years, CVC has put in place a system of Independent Monitors (retired senior civil servants with domain knowledge) who look into specific complaints relating to purported violations of the Pre-Integrity Pact signed by all the bidders as well as issues concerning any of the stages of the acquisition process. All in all, any matter arising out of the abiding concerns for utmost probity, transparency and accountability and stemming from verifiable and focused representations/ complaints lodged by an affected individual/company is required to be addressed in an urgent time frame by the monitors. The statutory audit by the C&AG's organisation is intended to assess adequacy of the internal control systems and continuing compliance with systems and procedures formally in vogue and whether the objectives of economy, efficiency and effectiveness are continually being met. Since the C&AG's audit is in the nature of post-audit, often long after the event, there is an inevitable element of being wiser with hindsight. Nonetheless, the underlying focus of all the oversight institutions is to ensure that capability acquisition takes place in as urgent a time frame as possible consistent with long range plans, plan/annual outlays, contractual safeguards and commitments embedded in the contract and in full compliance with the letter and spirit of the acquisition procedures, guidelines and practices. It would be patently unfair to attribute acquisition delays and inefficiencies to a 'fear psychosis' among decision-makers at different hierarchical levels in the Government and the Services HQ. The civil and military bureaucracy cannot expect a carte blanche in the matter of defence acquisitions when the C&AG/CVC/CBI have been able to provide umpteen instances of short-circuiting/non compliance with established norms and procedures and a whole range of other violations, inadequacies and inefficiencies which have tarnished an otherwise reliable, well documented and unimpeachable process. Exemplary handling of cases of individual errors of omission and commission and continuing reforms based on inputs from the oversight organisations is thus clearly warranted. Given the complex challenges of the acquisition process and the imperative for rapid capability attainment, the stage seems appropriate for creating a Defence Ombudsman as a single point authority to handle complaints, representations, suggestions and inputs with regard to acquisitions, offsets and the domestic defence industrial base.

There is often uniformed criticism in the public realm of the interminable delays in the acquisition process. While the fact of unacceptable drift in many of the major acquisitions cannot be disputed, attention needs to bestowed upon each of the distinct facets of the procurement procedure. Specific capability acquisition programmes need to figure in the LTIPP and its component Five Year/Annual Plan based on clear acceptance of the basic necessity by all the stakeholders/decision-makers. This is followed by the QR formulation stage which would determine whether a competitive setting would indeed be achieved when bids are invited. Formulation of a comprehensive draft RFP is next required which is preceded by a RFI stage in order to fully comprehend the complexities of the specific weapon system on offer and thereby leave nothing out for a post-contract stage. With the participation of all stakeholders including the three Defence Services, DRDO, Dept of Defence Production (DDP), Defence Finance, Department of Defence and HQ IDS (Integrated Defence Staff (IDS)), decisions are then taken about the modality of the proposed acquisition viz. Buy (Indian), Buy and Make (Indian), Make (Indian), Buy and Make (Global) and Buy (Global). This is then ratified by the Defence Procurement Board and the Defence Acquisition Council (DAC) presided over by the Raksha Mantri. The RFP is then issued and commercial and technical bids invited. Wherever offsets are mandated, technical and commercial offset proposals are also invited separately. Technical bids are then technically evaluated and in the event only a single source situation emerges, the entire process is abandoned and QRs tweaked in order to achieve a competitive situation. User trial evaluation of the qualified technical bidders' weapon systems is thereafter carried out which too has often led to a 'resultant single vendor' situation.

In these early days of Life Cycle cost computation for determining the lowest bidder, LCC assessments have also posed their own challenges against the backdrop of a spate of assumptions, conditionalities, riders, footnotes and provisos inserted by the bidders in their commercial offers or later submissions. Given these complexities and the fact that acquisition takes place based on priorities envisioned by the concerned Service as well as the empirical evidence concerning protracted user trial evaluation, it would be improper to lay the blame for delayed acquisitions on the doors of the MoD alone. This is particularly so as annual fund outlays for modernisation are, in any event, being fully utilised (with a few aberrations in the past). At the same time, there is need to encourage and enforce more collegiate vetting and processing of acquisition proposals as there is a tendency on the part of some of the functionaries to record in writing, perhaps for posterity, objections and observations without a sound professional basis-a situation which could have been readily remedied through timely and comprehensive presentations and dialogue collectively among the stakeholders.

The ICT potential is also required to be fully tapped in the acquisition context.

Apart from monitoring time bound processing of acquisition cases by all the concerned functionaries in Services HQ/MoD, ICT capabilities are required to be made use of for creating a comprehensive pricing data base in respect of past contracts as well as for monitoring life cycle costs by way of operations and maintenance. ICT would also be a prerequisite for tracking MTBF warranties, premature failures, mean time to repair and turnaround time for efficient life cycle management including supply chain management efficiencies.

The setting up of a dedicated Defence Acquisition Management Institute (DAMI) under the aegies of the Acquisition Wing of the MoD is a crying need of the hour. Professional competence, in the present setting, is inculcated only through on the job experience and skill development with most key functionaries having little or no past background in this domain. While the tenures in MoD are longer (four to five years), the Defence Services face the far more daunting challenge of rotating officers, particularly at senior levels, in much shorter time frames to meet their career progression needs in terms of training and different job profiles. Defence acquisitions demand a skill and knowledge set spanning defence technology, manufacturing, logistics, contractual and legal aspects, offsets, economy trends in India/world, armament export controls, cost audit, financial management, IPR, project management and the like. Consequently, a blend of suitable on-line and in-class courses need to be developed in these distinct disciplines for meeting the acutely felt needs of acquisition functionaries in MoD/ Services. Defence think tanks too need to be actively encouraged to address the host of acquisition concerns in their round table conferences, seminars, debates and publications.

Finally, a word concerning blacklisting of firms by the Indian MoD in cases where specific violations of the Pre-integrity pact and/or the supply contract have occurred. It is noteworthy that in this process a very large number of foreign OEMs currently stand debarred from transacting any business with India. While the action to en-cash all the penal and financial guarantees is clearly unexceptionable, decisions concerning blacklisting of many of the best in class foreign OEMs could prove counter-productive and seriously undermine our capability acquisition plans. It has to be recognised that most of the blacklisted entities are global defence majors with a wealth of technology and manufacturing excellence with significant global armament supply market share. The companies are thus far bigger than the chief executive or other high functionaries at whose levels such criminal acts of commission occurred. From our point of view, it should suffice if such individuals cease to be associated with the OEM concerned and are proceeded against appropriately in their country's criminal court of justice. A similar fate should be ordained for individuals at the Indian end. Subject to this, we should remain steadfast in our pursuit of capability acquisition in the shortest feasible time frame.

10

Strengthening the Defence Industrial Base in India

Ravindra Gupta

After nearly a millennium of foreign domination, India became independent in 1947. Its enterprise, industry and academic excellence had suffered irreparably and naturally, the young India was suspicious of foreign domination and exploitation and wanted to develop an egalitarian society without foreign interference. The entry of foreign goods was restricted and the commanding heights of the economy were reserved for the public sector. Self-reliance was the avowed objective of the nation. However, it intended to achieve self-reliance with respect to domestic demand only. Naturally, it meant uneconomic capacities. Unfortunately, two other laudable objectives of 'Prevention of Monopoly' and 'Balanced Regional Development' affected Indian economy adversely. The first meant splitting the uneconomic capacities further into several licenses and the other meant location in remote areas of the country devoid of any infrastructure support. Despite these handicaps, 'Letters of Intent' and 'Industrial Licenses' were much sought after. Owing to high tariff walls and tough import controls, local products enjoyed a premium in the market, despite poor quality and obsolete technology. There were long queues for goods and services and a permit-quota raj prevailed.

There was a demand supply mismatch and industry made a play for premiums. The domestic industry was not encouraged to look for offshore markets to overcome scale problems. The approach remained inward looking. This adversely affected manufacturing, Research and Development (R&D) and product up-gradation. It brought inefficiencies in the system and killed innovation and the pursuit of quality. There is sufficient global evidence to show that protective environment promotes inefficiency while a competitive environment brings out the best.

The defence industry was reserved for the public sector. India's first industrial-policy resolution in 1948 made it clear that a major portion of industrial capacity was to be reserved for the public sector including all arms production. When this document was revised in 1956, it placed the munitions, aircraft and shipbuilding industries in the public sector under central government control, preventing private sector production.

The output from Defence Public Sector Undertakings (DPSUs) and Ordnance Factories has been insufficient to meet the requirements of Armed Forces. India spends about 30 per cent of its total military budget on equipment purchase. In 2011, the total budget for equipment purchase was US$ 10-12 billion out of the total of US$ 31 billion (Current exchange rate) of budgeted defence expenditure. The value of domestic output amounted to approximately US$ 7 billion in 2011; a substantial portion of this production, however, was low-end manufacturing and assembly with high value components and systems typically being imported. The actual value added by domestic industry accounted for only about 30 per cent or around US$ 4 billion, with the remaining being directly or indirectly imported.

India does have a very extensive defence manufacturing set-up within the country. Nine PSUs focus on production of defence related equipment along with 39 Ordnance Factories under the Department of Defence Production (DDP). In FY 2011, they accounted for a total annual sale of INR 37190 crore, primarily to the armed forces. The DPSUs produce combat aircraft, helicopters, warships, missiles, defence electronics, heavy earth moving equipment and special alloys. The total investment (equity) made by Government in the share capital of the Defence PSUs is of the order of INR 1,219 crore and their total net worth in the year 2009-10 was INR 17,554 crore. The DPSUs have also been the recipients of significant support from the Government in terms of research and development assistance (particularly through Defence Research and Development Organisation (DRDO)), investments in production capacity, tax breaks and prioritisation for tenders. However, the production activities of the DPSUs in relation to complex systems have typically been by way of licensed production based on technology developed abroad.

In aggregate, the DPSUs and Ordnance Factories employ approximately 1.8 lakh people. This is comparable to industry employment figures for several other countries like UK and France. Total employment in UK based defence industries was estimated at ~310,000. Similar figures for France indicate approximate domestic employment of ~200,000 people. However, when compared to the much higher output levels of these countries, the productivity of the Indian defence sector appears extremely low.

An analysis of the employee productivity reveals that the defence sector does not measure up to benchmarks from even the domestic private sector. The annual survey of industries reveals an output of INR 20 to 40 lakh per employee per year for a range of manufacturing sectors. Most of these sectors in India have a healthy mix of government owned and other enterprises. In contrast, the estimated output per employee for DPSUs and Ordnance Factories comes to INR 15 lakh per year. Defence production in India can be assumed to be in the mid-tech range of manufacturing and output figures should ideally be around INR 30 lakh per employee. This implies a doubling of efficiency from the current level.

In 1998, the Government set up six task forces to assess and consider the involvement of the private sector in defence production. Based on the recommendations of these task forces, the government accepted the principle of private sector participation in defence production to complement the efforts of the public sector. The government also clarified that the entry of private sector should not be considered as a threat to defence PSUs and Ordnance Factories, which have several inherent advantages.

However, it was only in 2002 that the guidelines for licensing of manufacturing of arms and ammunition were issued by the Ministry of Industry and Commerce. Therefore, until very recently, the private sector in India has been limited to the production of intermediate products, components and spare parts for defence equipment. Lack of a local supply and high dependence on foreign supply base has created several problems in the procurement of defence equipment. Some of these issues are:

(a) The over-reliance on foreign sources has led to complete lack of indigenous Intellectual Property (IP) development in critical defence areas posing a potential national security threat. In 2005, the Standing Committee on Defence reviewed the defence forces' procurement policy and procedures. This report noted that although India had been independent for 55 years, cutting edge military technologies had not been locally developed and the procurement of capital equipment remained reliant on imports.

(b) Due to the politico-strategic nature of defence contracts and security concerns, procurement from global vendors is extremely slow. At the supplier end, global suppliers typically need to customise weapon systems to Indian requirements resulting in both time and cost over-runs. Budget grants to the level of 20 per cent of the total have been surrendered on several occasions in the past owing to the procurement processes remaining incomplete.

(c) Different political and administrative systems and language barriers have created fertile playing ground for the middlemen. In the case of any illegality, it becomes difficult for the government to take strong punitive action, as foreign governments are involved in the process. Both middlemen and Ministry of Defence (MoD) officials have been placed under the scanner several times in the past decade.

Building India's defence equipment manufacturing capability is of the highest strategic importance. Nations invest heavily in building this capability in order to ensure independence of supply during times of crisis. India has already begun on a path of reform of its vast defence production and procurement establishment. It now aspires to move away from the historical pattern of foreign procurement and licensed production or assembly.

The DPSUs and Ordnance Factories have served the nation well. However, like state sector anywhere, they suffer from inherent handicaps. It is a well-documented fact that despite every proactive effort, at all levels, and in all related departments in government, critical decision making remains far from swift. A protective environment breeds inefficiency, a cost plus approach, and kills quality and innovation. With the current level of defence acquisition, DPSUs and OFs are unable to cope with the Services requirements. The Services are uniformly unhappy with the quality, costs, maintenance support and inordinate supply delays of DPSUs. The defence procurement may more than quadruple in 2025 from the current US$ 16 Billion to US$ 80 Billion annually. This would require a huge increase in capacities and capabilities. It would be imprudent to look for additional budgetary resources and augment capacities in the public sector when capacities in the private sector can be leveraged without straining meagre state resources.

If India is to achieve its strategic objective of 70-80 per cent domestic supply in defence, then it needs to rapidly grow its existing industrial base. Indigenous production would need to expand by an average of 30 per cent a year. Even with a doubling of current levels of efficiency to about INR 30 lakh per employee per year, this will still result in the creation of ~1.2 lakh new jobs. Additionally, several jobs will be created in-directly through sub-contractors, vendors and other allied agencies. NASSCOM estimates that indirect job multiplier for IT is three-five for every direct job created. Even using the lower limit multiple of three, would result in 3.5 lakh indirect jobs in defence manufacturing. Thus, a total of half a million jobs can be created over the next five years alone. With a smaller increase in efficiency, the workforce required to meet the targets would be even higher. For a 25 per cent efficiency gain, the industry would need an overall one million additional people. Thus, there is a potential for increasing the defence related workforce by half to one million people within five years.

In addition to the growth in 'job quantity', increased defence sector exposure is likely to have a larger overall impact on 'job quality' as well. The level of technical sophistication and precision in defence is definitely very high, as the margins for error available to manufacturers are very small. Moreover, defence now makes extensive use of sunrise sectors like robotics, biochemical, carbon, nanotechnology etc. Exposure at an employee level will bring benefits to the industry as a whole. It is obvious that leveraging private sector capabilities would not affect the state sector units adversely. We are looking at an exponential jump and there would be enough business for all. As a matter of fact, with the opening of the defence business and competition, the DPSUs will themselves become more efficient, competitive and innovative. This is what happened in the banking and telecom sectors.

Despite frequent averments regarding private sector involvement, nothing much has happened. The Industry is disheartened and feels that there is no will behind such policy pronouncements and the bias against the private sector continues. The Kelkar Committee had also interacted with workers unions in DPSUs and OFs. They were uniformly opposed to any meaningful role for the private sector because of unfounded fears about their own interests. However, they can be given assurance about job security to the existing incumbents to assuage their fears. Indeed, maintaining status quo is a greater threat to their future as it will render them uncompetitive. By extending to them an assurance regarding protection of their legitimate interests, both the workmen and officers cadre can be persuaded to see the overall benefits of a well calibrated change that will make even the public sector stronger and more vibrant. **Given the hollowness in our armed forces, obsolescence of their equipment and the poor self-reliance index, the answer is clear that the country must move in a mission mode and leave no stone unturned in reversing the self-reliance index. A wide spectrum of decisions and policies are required to bring this paradigm shift.**

Initially, the private sector in India was not competent to shoulder heavy responsibilities and the public sector had a role to play. Real transformation in Indian industry commenced in the mid 1980s when three things happened. The first chink in the industrial licensing regime appeared when 'broad banding' was permitted. The second thing to happen was the computer mission and the last and the best to happen was 'MARUTI'. The latter brought a paradigm shift in Indian manufacturing. The Japanese shop floor practices coming through the Maruti-Suzuki joint venture and other Joint Ventures (JVs) with Japanese auto component manufacturers revolutionised Indian manufacturing. The development of auto industry is a phenomenon that has received global acclaim. India is well on its way to becoming a small car and auto components manufacturing hub.

Two other important events that helped the revival of Indian industry were the economic liberalisation that started in 1991 when licensing was abolished and the signing of the WTO agreement by India in Marrakesh in 1994. There was great gloom in the country and it was feared that foreign multinationals would dominate Indian industry and markets. All these fears have not only been dispelled but the reverse has happened, in that, Indian multinationals have emerged with big-ticket acquisitions abroad. It would not be wrong to say that starting with IT, Indian industry has shored up Indian pride lost under a millennium of foreign domination. Many notable NRIs have also contributed to this resurgence. Our success in strategic programmes in atomic energy, space and missiles has also contributed to this process.

Define Defence Product

Existing rules and regulations do not adequately define a 'defence product'. Unlike some other countries and international arms control organisations, which define defence and dual use items through a comprehensive list (e.g., the Munitions List & List of Dual-Use Goods and Technologies of the Wassenaar Arrangement), in India there is no such list to give clarity to what constitute a defence and dual-use product. The lack of clarity becomes an issue when industry is required to provide the 'item code' and 'item description' while filling up the application form for industrial license. As per the current practice, the industry is required to provide the 'item code' from the National Industrial Classification (NIC) Code list of 1987, which has only one code (359.4: 'manufacture of arms and armaments') for entire defence manufacturing. The NIC code does not clearly indicate what constitutes arms and armaments and if dual-use items are also covered by it. It also does not clarify that if parts and components that go into arms and ammunition, but may or may not have dual-use, would fall under this head.

The issue with 'item description' is more nuanced. There is no unified specific list on which the Industry can rely to describe the nature of its product. Rather, they have to refer to at least three different lists, depending on which list best describes their production. Apart from NIC list (which is the most generic among the three), two others are: Indian Trade Classification (ITC) (Harmonised System) ITC (HS) Code, as maintained by the Director General of Foreign Trade (DGFT) of Ministry of Commerce for the purpose of India's external trade; and the 'Product List' as given in the DPP, for discharge of offset obligations by foreign vendors. The DGFT list, gives some broad sub-details of the items that can be covered under the defence industry. For instance, under the broad HS Code 93 (arms and ammunition; parts and accessories thereof), there are 16 sub-categories. The DPP has only made a feeble attempt in this regard.

Although, the lists of DGFT and MoD are more elaborate in comparison to the NIC list, they are still not defence specific. They cater to items of defence, dual-use and even to those commercially off-the-shelf in nature. For instance, under HS Code 88 (aircraft, spacecraft, and parts thereof) there are sub-categories such as 'gliders', 'balloons', and 'under carriages and parts thereof', which are commercially available products or at best dual-use items. But a company producing any of the above items is free to apply for a defence license and it becomes a part of the defence industry, even though the item in question may not be specifically a defence product.

Even this loosely defined industry list is problematic for companies in the Services sector. It is noteworthy that as per the DIPP guidelines, defence falls under the 'Manufacturing' sector. Consequently, companies in manufacturing business can apply for license and get it (subject to approval) and be formally part of the defence industry. However, this is not the case for companies in the services sector (such as engineering, design and software) that do not come under the purview of 'Manufacturing', and hence do not require a license for their product. Consequently, they are not formally a part of the defence industry, even though their services have direct application in defence products and with increasing use of ICT technologies, this problem is likely to be compounded in future.

Wassenaar Arrangement: Mexico has become the 41st State to join the Wassenaar Arrangement in January 2012. It is understood that we have also initiated the process to become a member. Given the present favourable environment, we should leave no stone unturned to clinch it. As a member of Wassenaar Arrangement, India would be free from the denial regime in respect of 'dual use items'. It would also help us in exports to member countries. Once, India becomes a member, it would have to adopt the Wassenaar List of Munitions and Dual Use items for export control. In the interim, a list harmonised with Wassenaar could be in category six of SCOMET. It may be mentioned that we have already adopted lists harmonised with the Nuclear Suppliers Group (NSG) and *Missile Technology Control Regime* (MTCR). The ITC (HS) codes should be accordingly generated. This will take care of the problem mentioned in the preceding paragraphs.

Infrastructure Industry Status

Governments have acknowledged the inherently risky nature of defence production. The industry is highly regulated in nature making it difficult for companies to freely expand customer base or use technologies in more than one product lines. This lack of markets is compounded by high volatility in demand. Production capacities need to be able to cater to critical demand spikes, as would occur in times of strife. Moreover, defence agencies must keep pace with global developments, and thus need to rapidly upgrade weapon systems. This requires huge investments in cutting edge technologies on continuing basis. Thus, industry needs the wherewithal to invest simultaneously on two fronts: high quality product innovation on the one hand, and on the other hand, in flexible product lines that can be rapidly up scaled or downscaled in response to the needs of its primary customer.

Globally, top defence industries receive significant levels of support from their nations' Governments. Incentives are provided in the form of risk-sharing contract structures, tax breaks on defence related production and R&D, research grants, access to Government research for licensed production, and a host of other possible incentives that help producers in ensuring their business remains viable and growing. Government will endeavour to build up a robust indigenous defence industrial base by, proactively encouraging larger involvement of the Indian private sector in design, development and manufacture of defence equipment. Several sectors of importance in nation building have been accorded 'infrastructure industry' status. This has not been done for defence industry probably because it just was not there. It is high time that it is done now.

Need for Defence Exports

During the first 10 years of post-Cold War era, world military spending fell by more than one-third in real terms. Defence spending as a percentage of global Gross National Product (GNP) fell by nearly half, from 4.7 per cent to 2.4 per cent, while worldwide per capita spending on defence dropped from US$ 254 to $142. In addition, the size of the world's armed forces declined from 28.6 million in 1989 to 21.3 million in 1999. In the United States, defence expenditures fell 28 per cent in real terms during the 1990s. Hundreds of thousands of defence workers were made redundant as armament factories cut back production or even closed down. To cope with the new reality, the arms industry went through a massive reorganisation.

Owing to consolidation in the past two decades, only about a dozen large industrial conglomerates dominate the global defence industry. DIB is an expensive attribute to sustain and most governments simply could not afford to have an appropriate national capability in every area of defence. They have tried to resolve their dilemma by reducing cost of maintaining a domestic industry, generally by privatisation, actively engaging in international trade in defence equipment, forming alliances and pooling resources with like minded nations. Offset, or reciprocal trade, is now a significant element of the international trade in defence equipment. Another important development has been increasing commercialisation of defence industry through use of Commercial-Of-The-Shelf (COTS) items that helped to reduce costs.

While dramatic reduction in defence spending prompted US companies to consolidate and rationalise, it also stimulated a major US defence export drive. With government leading the way, US defence industry targeted major export markets in East Asia and Middle East. President Clinton explicitly made defence exports a vital component of US defence policy. Indeed, all countries having meaningful DIB, export major portion of their defence production. In India, there is hardly any focus on exports. If the country is serious about enlarging its DIB and related R&D, it must bring a paradigm shift in its thinking.

A country's own requirement would hardly ever offer a viable economic size. **In order to run a sustainable defence unit and to effectively contribute to the national self-reliance effort, the country must enable domestic defence industry to augment its sales effort beyond our shores. All major armament producers have adopted aggressive export programmes.** Exports are backed by diplomatic effort, sometimes even by the Heads of State as well. There are defence aid programmes along with financing solutions. If the country is really serious about self-reliance, it should adopt a proactive export policy.

Sectoral export promotion councils have done a good job. There are export promotion bodies in several countries that have done a creditable job. It is, therefore, suggested that a Defence Export Promotion Council (DEPCO) be also set up.

R&D

With regard to promotion of R&D, the Government should adopt innovative methods of encouraging private industry to invest in R&D. These may include:

- Providing tax exemption;
- Providing infrastructural and technical support, hiring of renowned experts from around the world;
- Duty free Import of all test and laboratory equipment for conduct of R&D, tests, verification and validation;
- Intellectual Property Rights (IPR) and patents should be tradable;
- Facilitation of defence exports to achieve economies of scale;
- Industry should also be able to buy technology from DRDO on competitive basis;
- Industry should be allowed to outsource to DRDO specific projects against payments. This would allow DRDO to develop a corpus for its future growth. SMEs ability to manage innovation should be leveraged for Defence Research.

Raksha Udyog Ratna (RUR)

The Kelkar Committee had observed:

> It was felt by the Committee that effective participation by the Industry, both public and private, at various points of interaction and subsequent **long-term association in product development and productionisation,**

> **can be done through only those firms of proven excellence and which are capable of contributing, depending on their technical, managerial and financial strength. The Committee keeping in mind the "Korean" model of development has termed these firms as "Raksha Udyog Ratna" (RUR)/"Champions".** Such an approach was successful in Korea and given stage of development we would recommend this approach. This will enable us to proceed on a faster pace and in a cost effective manner. These firms are essentially platform producers and system integrators and the ones which we described as "first level" of Defence Industry.

The RURs, identified on their managerial and technical capabilities, were expected to be the key drivers for raising indigenous defence technological base and world-class manufacturing capabilities in India. Once a private firm is accredited and given the status of 'RUR'/'Champion' it would become entitled to circulation of RFPs under "Make" and "Buy and Make (Indian)" categories.

To identify these private sector RURs/Champions, an 'Accreditation' process was designed and the MoD had constituted a Selection Committee under the Chairmanship of Shri Probir Sengupta, Former Director, Indian Institute of Foreign Trade (IIFT), and Secretary, Defence Production and Commerce. The Committee had recommended the following 13 Indian companies to the government for according RUR status:

> Larsen & Toubro, Tata Power, BHEL, Tata Motors, Mahindra & Mahindra, Kirloskar Oil Engines, Bharat Forge, Godrej & Boyce, Tata Consultancy Services, Wipro, HCL Technologies, Satyam Computers and Infosys.

After considering the recommendation of the Sengupta Committee, the DDP felt that giving preferential treatment to a select few private companies would be unfair to the industry at large and thus dropped the idea.

It is necessary to revisit the concept of RUR recommended by the Kelkar Committee. There are three different levels for participation of private sector in Defence Production—major systems, assemblies and spare parts & components. While effective participation by the industry is required in all the three levels, but product development and production of specially major systems can only be achieved through firms of proven excellence that are capable of making contribution on the basis of their superior technical, managerial and financial strength.

It is difficult to support the contention that RURs would be given some special treatment at par with DPSUs since it would only perpetuate the practice of nomination. They would have to compete in an open and transparent process under 'Make' and 'Buy and Make (Indian)' categories. The country needs serious players having high level of technological and manufacturing capability with financial strength and risk taking capacity to get into defence industry. Their contribution is required now for the country to play its rightful role in global polity.

It is high time that the recommendations of the Kelkar Committee and the Sengupta Committee are accepted without further delay. This will be a great morale booster to private sector and give the much-needed fillip to indigenisation. This would not be a closed group. The Department of Defence production had notified the following criteria for RURs:

- Public Limited companies registered for a minimum of ten years;
- Companies with capital assets in India not less than Rs. 100 crore and turnover not less than Rs. 1000 crore for each of the past three years. (For this purpose, the group of companies engaged in manufacture will be treated as one company);
- A minimum credit rating equivalent to Credit Rating Information Services of India Limited (CRISIL)/ICRA (formerly Investment Information and Credit Rating Agency of India Limited)–'A';
- Company with consistent profitable financial record showing profits in at least three years of the last five years and with no accumulated losses;
- Companies with established track records in engineering (including software) and manufacturing for real value addition—not a trading company/agency;
- Companies with established R&D base or willing to invest in R&D as decided by the regulatory authority;
- Companies with units/divisions with established quality control systems meeting various quality certifications and standards as laid down from to time. Current standards should include ISO 9001 and ISO 14001 and preferably ISO 18001 also. The system should enable self-certification;
- Companies with security infrastructure meeting relevant requirements authorised by government agencies.

These criteria are rational and very reasonable and companies that meet them can always apply to the Government for being given such status.

It is important to sound a warning note here. The suggested measures would certainly create the required eco system for private sector participation but it would take some time to bring up their capabilities to handle major platforms. It is suggested that a beginning should be made by offering smaller systems like, Coast Guard vessels, APC, guns, UAVs etc.

In order to make its intent clear, the Government would do well to redesignate the DDP as "Department of Defence Industry and Trade" with an Additional Secretary looking after Defence Production and another to look after Defence

Industry and Trade. The Government should simultaneously promote a 'National Association of Defence Industries' (NADI).

Categorisation

In the acquisition of major defence systems, the MoD has generally opted for the 'Buy and Make (Global)' category where RFPs are sent only to foreign vendors. This results in licensed production with no enhancement in indigenous capability and no coproduction or freedom to export to third countries. In such cases, as yet, only DPSUs are nominated. The private sector has been expected to acquire the capability and wait for a suitable opportunity to participate in a tender. In 'Make' cases, there has been no assurance of orders after the development of a particular equipment or weapon system. As a result, the private sector has been reluctant to invest in R&D, design and related infrastructure for want of any assurance of return. The defence products are highly capital and technology intensive with a fluctuating market. It should also be noted that corporate entities are accountable to their shareholders. Lack of past experience has also prevented the entry of private sector.

In the DPP 2013, there is a welcome shift. The DPP 2013 has laid much needed emphasis on indigenisation. Various categories have been better defined and prioritised with 'Make' and 'Buy and Make (Indian)' having been accorded the highest priority. The anomalies in the determination of indigenous content have also been removed. However, there are no guidelines for this prioritisation to succeed. **As a matter of fact, the 'Buy and Make (Global)' category with the nomination rider should be completely eliminated. Government should only use 'Make' or 'Buy and Make (Indian)' categorisation for all flagship defence contracts.** Such categorisation is critical to provide Indian vendors with the scale and exposure that is required for the industry to move forward towards country's self-reliance. This approach would also ensure future order support. In the latter category, the government should liberally permit the local entities to enter into JVs with the relevant *Original Equipment Manufacturer* (OEMs). The desired capability transfers and provision for exports would also have to be ensured.

The participation of private sector would raise two other important issues. The first one is of testing facilities and proof ranges. It is not possible today to create such facilities anywhere and far less in the private sector. **The Armed Forces and DRDO would have to provide facilities to private sector for testing their products. Needless to say that Test Ranges are a national asset and must be available to domestic defence industry.** The other issue is that of trial of products. The Armed Forces today take up products for trial only when these come through RFI/SQR/RFP route. The armed forces must be proactive in promoting domestic innovation efforts.

Licensing

Under the Industries (Development and Regulation) Act, 1951 (the Act), an INDUSTRIAL LICENSE is required to manufacture arms and ammunition and allied items of defence equipment, parts and accessories. The license is granted under Rule 15(2) of the Registration and Licensing of Industrial Undertaking Rules, 1952. These rules have been issued under section 30 of the Act. This is also a mandatory requirement under the FDI policy for the defence sector. The license applications are considered by the Department of Industrial Policy and Promotion, Ministry of Commerce & Industry, in consultation with the MoD.

Ideally, there should be no licensing for defence industry also. Today, the private sector already faces many barriers to entry in the defence sector. Subjecting it to a licensing requirement does not serve any useful purpose. It is also pertinent to note that it is a 'monopsony' with Government as the sole buyer. This is reported to be the case in most other countries that have a highly developed DIB. In the US, for instance, no license is required to manufacture any item in their 'Munitions List'. If at all, licensing should be confined to major platforms and products covered by the Nuclear Suppliers Group (NSG) and Missile Technology Control Regime (MTCR) but none at all for components/sub-assemblies/systems that go into them. Since the entry of private sector into development of major platforms would only be through 'Make' or 'Buy and Make (Indian)' through the DG Acquisition, in keeping with the single window philosophy, the DG Acquisition could be empowered under the IDR Act to automatically give the license to the successful parties.

Deemed Export Status

The tax and duty structure on key inputs/goods forms a significant factor for growth of any sector. Overall tax/duties incidence on the cost is known to make or mar the performance and growth of any sector, and defence cannot be an exception. Notwithstanding the MoD's sincere efforts to ensure the progressive evolution of DPP and the repetitive plea from Indian industry, the Indian (private sector) industry has been facing regressive and differential treatment in terms of taxes and duties it has to pay vis-à-vis DPSUs and foreign OEMs. Indian industry players feel that this differential tax/duty treatment places the private players at a disadvantage, thereby restricting their contribution and effort to strengthening the national defence industrial base and in the national endeavour to largely indigenise the sector and reverse the import—indigenous ratio in favour of the Indian Industry through significant 'import substitution'. The relevant duty/tax issues are being highlighted along with possible solutions.

The present status of indigenous supplies is as follows:

- No exemption from Customs Duty on import of inputs/goods required for Manufacture/development of equipment;

- No exemption from Excise Duty on inputs/goods required for manufacture/development of equipment;
- Supply to DPSUs or defence organisations are exempt from levy of Excise Duty, hence, credit of input duties (such as specified components of Customs Duty and Excise Duty) cannot be claimed;
- Supplies to defence sector are not considered 'deemed export' and extended benefits of tax/duty on procurement of inputs used in manufacture and supplies;
- Supply of manufactured goods to defence organisations are exempt from levy of Excise Duty e.g. supply of Pistol of 9 mm, hence, credit of inputs duties (such as specified components of Customs Duty and Excise Duty) cannot be claimed;
- Contractors to DPSUs get no exemption from Excise Duty on inputs/goods required for manufacture/development of equipment.

In the event of 'Make' and 'Buy and Make (Indian)' categories being used for procurement in the country a lot of these inconsistencies would disappear. **Any way, it is important that 'deemed export' status be accorded to all supplies made to the armed forces or by sub-contractors to integrators of systems. Further, payment terms, as applicable to foreign vendors and DPSUs/OFs, must be extended to India's private sector companies also.**

Leveraging SMEs

Given the nature of defence industry, it will take time and considerable effort for Indian companies to be able to handle full systems or major platforms. Secondly, there is a big opportunity as well as tactical advantage in getting into the global supply chain for components/sub-assemblies etc. We must take a leaf out of automobile industry, where India is well on its way to becoming a global hub for auto components manufacture. Strategic acquisitions abroad have also propelled Indian auto companies into the Tier 1 league. We should promote Indian SMEs to use this opportunity in defence industry as well. Most businesses around the world are SMEs and contribute close to half of global GDP. Apart from component manufacture, SMEs benefit defence giants with targeted research, innovation, development and production of individual systems and parts. The US extracts their potential fully by actively supporting them.

The SME supply chain consists of three major players, Global players, sub primes and systems partners, and lower tier suppliers. Sub-primes and lower tier suppliers usually perform 60-75 per cent of the work content. The Confederation of Indian Industry (CII) estimates that over 6000 SMEs operate in the Indian defence sector supplying 20-25 per cent of components and sub assemblies to the DPSUs, ordnance factories and DRDO.

In India, we have yet to exploit their potential. There is no explicit programme to harness SMEs' significant capabilities in our self-reliance effort. Complicated procedures for entry of private sector discourage SMEs from entering the defence sector; especially, as few have the necessary capital or influence to venture out. The 'No Cost No Commitment' (NCNC) method for selection makes it even tougher. **To facilitate SMEs entry in the Indian defence Industry, a friendly and proactive policy framework is required.** The Kelkar Committee had recommended:

> "(i) MoD should create a Fund called the "Defence Technology Development Fund" with the Department of Defence Production (DDP) which is to be used for providing fund to SMEs to carry out design and development work either directly or through industry champions/Defence PSUs/OFs.
>
> (iv) Encourage the prime contractor/RUR or Champion maximize the participation of SMEs in defence contracts, through introduction of appropriate clause in contracts. This would essentially be confined to "Make" and "Buy & Make" categories. Wherever the prime contractor/ RUR or Champion faithfully follows the Code of Practice prescribed for sub vendors of the Champion, the SMEs associated in the backward linkage should get access to the "Defence Technology Development Fund" on priority."

It is, however, necessary to keep development of SMEs as an integral part of our self-reliance strategy. It would facilitate the entry of Indian SMEs in the global supply chain if offsets could be leveraged for Transfer of Technology (ToT) to them. To make it attractive, we could also provide a suitable multiplier for ToT to SMEs in the offset policy.

Being lean and less lethargic than the bigger enterprises, SMEs have the capability of higher innovation in niche manufacturing, ability to absorb technology, lower labour costs and offer more job opportunities. The offset requirements have pushed the global OEMs to work in close coordination with SMEs. This coupled with the fact that these enterprises have high manufacturing expertise and a non-proliferation record, makes SMEs a catalyst in augmenting the role of India as an outsourcing destination. SMEs have the potential of becoming the backbone of not only India's Aerospace and Defence sector but also making India a global outsourcing hub for small manufacturing needs. These SMEs have the potential to serve multiple industries such as automotive and heavy equipment that helps them navigate market fluctuations in individual market segments.

MRO Opportunity

An effective support system for emerging Aerospace and Defence industries in developing markets, the need to develop new MRO facilities across the globe is now more compelling than ever. Maintenance, Repair and Overhaul (MRO) costs far exceed those on manufacturing and procurement. Global experiences suggest that MROs are not just critical for expanding capacity for new fleet inductions but far more in facilitating life cycle extensions for existing fleet and keeping operational costs in check.

The MRO sector goes hand-in-hand with aerospace and defence sector. India, with its geographical advantage of being strategically located between Europe and the rest of Asia-Pacific region, has the potential of becoming an international hub for MRO needs. This allows India to avail a faster turnaround time, which can make the sector a lot more efficient and cost effective. Another factor, which adds to the effectiveness of India, as an MRO hub, is the low cost of manpower in the country, which is almost 60 per cent cheaper than that in the US and slightly lower than the manpower costs in other Asian countries. This, clubbed with an abundance of skilled workforce, is the biggest strength of the Indian MRO sector.

The opportunities and scales for MRO activities depend on the demand for defence and civil aircrafts in a particular area. Since the fleet size in India of civil and military aircrafts is expected to double in the next five years, there are tremendous growth opportunities in this sector. Moreover, the Indian MRO sector has the ability to absorb technology transfer at depot level for aircrafts as well as components given the large resource base and the technical abilities of the skilled workforce. Post 2009, India has one of the fastest growing air transports MRO market.

One of the major problems with the Indian MRO sector today is the shortage of land near airports. Since the MRO facility needs to be located near an airport, currently available locations cause supply chain location problems. This leads to inefficiency, wastage of resources and delays in execution. Another problem with the sector is the complex and multi-structured tax scheme. The tax structure in India hinders the growth of the sector when compared to the world. This makes the sector uncompetitive.

Moreover, there is a lack of recognised bodies to provide internationally accepted quality certifications. This also hinders global competition since it lowers the confidence other countries have in Indian products and services. **The government should increasingly plan to allocate land (near major airports) at fair lease rentals to encourage the creation of MRO hubs in the country.**

11

DEFENCE BUDGET: CONSTRAINTS AND CAPABILITY BUILDING

Vinay Kaushal

The Union Budget, referred to as the Annual Financial Statement in Article 112 of the Constitution, is the annual budget, presented each year on the last working day of February by the Finance Minister in Parliament. The budget, which is presented by means of the Finance Bill and the Appropriation bill, has to be passed by the House before it can come into effect on April 1, the start of the financial year. The estimates of expenditure embodied in the budget are to show separately:

(a) The sums required to meet expenditure described by the Condition as expenditure charged upon the Consolidated Fund of India; and
(b) The sums required to meet other expenditure proposed to be made from the Consolidated Fund of India, and shall **distinguish expenditure on revenue account from other expenditure.**

General Financial Rules, 2005 prescribe that the Ministry of Finance, Budget Division, shall issue guidelines for preparation of budget estimates from time to time and all the Ministries/Departments shall comply in full with these guidelines. As per these rules, the budget shall contain the following:

(a) Estimates of all Revenue expected to be raised during the financial year to which the budget relates.
(b) Estimates of all Expenditure for each programme and project in that financial year.
(c) Estimates of all interest and debt servicing charges and any repayments on loans in that financial year.
(d) Any other information as may be prescribed.

Guidelines for Preparation of Estimates (Non-Plan)

Receipts

The rules also prescribe that the estimating authorities will prepare the detailed estimates of receipts separately for each Major Head of Account in the prescribed form, along with actual of the past three years. **Any major variation in estimates with reference to past actuals or/and Budget Estimates will be supported by cogent reasons.**

Establishment Expenditure

The estimate of establishment charges should be framed **taking into account the trends over preceding three years and other relevant factors like changes in rates of pay, allowances, number of posts and their filling** and the economy instructions issued by the Ministry of Finance from time to time.

Other Expenditure

To facilitate appreciation and scrutiny of the estimates, any major variations between the Budget and Revised Estimates for the current year and also between the Revised Estimates for the current year and Budget Estimates **for the ensuing year should be explained cogently.**

Estimates are required to include suitable provision for liabilities of the previous years left unpaid during the relevant year.

Incremental Budgeting

Although the guidelines for preparation of estimates put no constraints, the approach to the Union Budget is incremental. Incremental budgeting is based on slight changes from the preceding period's budgeted results or actual results. This is also a common approach in organisations where management does not intend to spend a great deal of time formulating budgets, or where it does not perceive any great need to conduct a thorough evaluation of the activities. The current year's budget becomes the basis for the next year's spending plan, and the majority of the Govt's analytical and political attention focuses on how to modify this year's spending plan based on revenues anticipated in the next year.

An incremental approach is workable, although always suboptimal, in periods of reasonably stable expenditure and revenue growth because the current level of expenditures can be funded with relatively little controversy. However, the incremental approach to budgeting is not up to the financial challenges posed by the crying need for more funds in a developing nation with modest incremental revenues and pressing need for funds by all sectors.

The advantages of incremental budgeting are:

(a) **Simplicity.** The primary advantage is the simplicity of incremental budgeting, being based on recent budget that can be readily verified.
(b) **Funding stability.** If a program requires funding for multiple years in order to achieve a certain outcome, incremental budgeting is structured to ensure that funds will keep flowing to the program.
(c) **Operational stability.** This approach ensures that departments are operated in a consistent and stable manner for long periods of time.

There are several disadvantages of incremental budgeting that make it a less than ideal choice. The issues are:

(a) **Incremental in nature.** It assumes only minor changes from the preceding period, when in fact there may be major structural changes, level of activity or its environment that call for much more significant budget changes.
(b) **Fosters overspending.** It fosters an attitude of "use it or lose it" in regard to budgeted expenditures, since a drop in expenditures in one period will be reflected in future periods, too.
(c) **Budgetary slacks.** There is a tendency to be conservative on revenue growth and project excessive expenses into incremental budgets, so that they will always have favourable variances.
(d) **Budget review.** When the budget is drawn with minor changes, there tends to be little incentive to conduct a comprehensive review of the budget, so that inefficiencies and budgetary slack are automatically rolled into new budgets.
(e) **Variance from actual.** When the incremental budget is based on a prior budget, there tends to be a growing disconnect between the budget and the actual needs.
(f) **Perpetuates resource allocations.** If a certain amount of funds were allocated to a specific area in a prior budget, then the incremental budget assures that funding will be allocated there in the future, too—even if it no longer needs as much funding, or if other areas require more funding.
(g) **Risk taking.** Since an incremental budget allocates most funds to the same uses every year, it is difficult to obtain a large funding allocation to direct at a new activity. Thus, incremental budgeting tends to foster a conservative maintenance of the status quo, and does not encourage risk taking.

Outcome Budget

"Outcome Budget" began as an effort of the Government to be accountable and transparent to the people. The "Outcome Budget" was presented to the Parliament for the first time in 2005-06, covering only Plan outlays. In 2006-07, Non-Plan schemes with quantifiable and deliverable outputs were also covered. The achievements on the "Outcome Budget 2005-06" were also presented separately to the Parliament in the form of a "Performance Budget". Since 2007-08, the "Outcome Budget" and the "Performance Budget" have been merged and is presented to the Parliament as a combined document mandatorily by each Ministry. This is in addition to the demand for each ministry included in the Union Budget, which continues to follow 'incremental approach'. In addition to the other details, the outcome budget gives in a tabular format of the financial outlays, projected physical outputs and projected/budgeted outcomes for the major schemes of the Department during the financial year. Ministry of Defence's Budget demands are listed in the non-mandatory category. Parliament Standing Committee on Defence has consistently been recommending to the MoD preparation of Outcome Budget and lay the same in Parliament alongwith the Demands for Grants. The committee, in its report presented in April 2013 has once again like in the previous years pursued this recommendation year after year; but the MoD has not been able to prepare the Outcome Budget document. The committee has expressed that "it is disturbing fact that the Ministry is not keeping the assurance given during each year in this regard." It has also been constrained to conclude, "This clearly depicts the unwillingness on the part of the Ministry to prepare Outcome Budget".

Defence Budget: The Budgetary allocations of the Ministry of Defence are contained under Eight Demands for Grants. Six budgetary demands (Army, Navy, Air Force, Ordnance Factories, DRDO (all 5 Revenue) and Capital Budget (for the 5 demands included in the revenue) **are commonly known as Defence Budget**. Civil expenditure of the MoD (comprising of MoD Secretariat, Defence Accounts Department, Canteen Stores Department, Defence Estates Organisation, Coast Guard Organisation and Jammu and Kashmir Light Infantry etc.) and Defence Pensions are the other two demands and **are not included in the Defence Budget.**

Defence Budget is a line budget of the Union Budget and hence follows the same incremental approach. In its simplest form the definition of **Defence Budget is "A plan for the accomplishment of programs related to objectives and goals within a financial year"**. The incremental approach and predominantly centralised nature of expenditure results in very limited involvement of a few officers at Service HQs and MoD. This results in a conservative mind-set that may not address the changing and dynamic needs. Instead budget making each year should engage in a thorough strategic re-assessment when preparing budget estimates, as well as a detailed investigation of expenditures. The result should be significant changes in the allocation of funds from period to period, as well as targeted changes that are intended to improve the efficiencies. However, as is analysed in the succeeding paras these fears are confirmed.

The size of the defence budget is, in principle, the measure of the resources provided for a country's defence by its political executive. The size of the defence budget also serves to identify the relative importance of the Defence Services in comparison to other organs of state. Since each country is at a given time at a unique stage of its long term developmental process, the resources allocated for defence would vary at various times and also vary with the prevalent economic conditions. Toward that end, data revealing the size of the defence budget as a percentage of the GDP is an indicator. A graphic representation of India's defence budget and its relationship in percentage to the GDP, since 1951-52 is given below (a detailed table giving the absolute figures are given in the statistics appended to this book)

Figure 1: Defence Expenditure as per cent Share of GDP

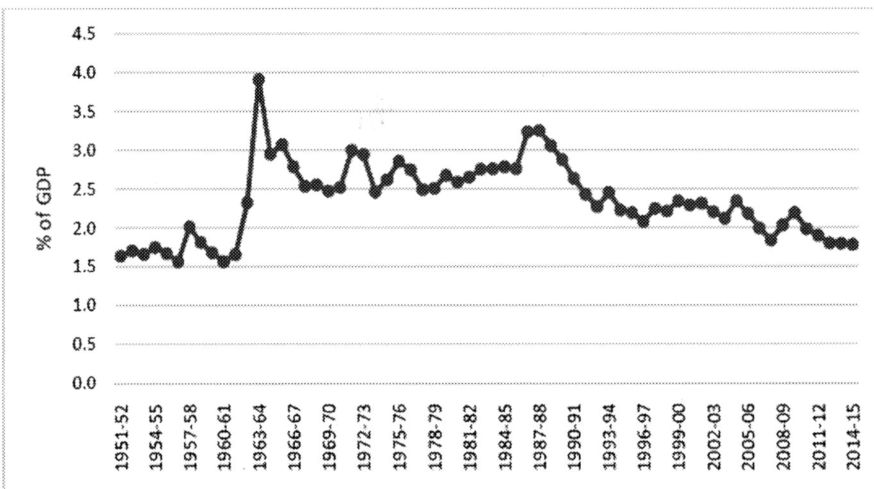

Perception Created by Incremental Budgets

A major problem is that the incremental budgets create a misperception in the mind of the environment about the extent of resources allocated. One can appreciate this more when one comes across how the perception of the knowledgeable gets impacted. The then Governor of Arunachal Pradesh, General JJ Singh (Retd), visited IDSA to give a lecture on—"Sino-Indian Relations in the 21st Century: An approach" on March 18, 2013. To a question on resources allocated for Defence, he said that today you are lucky; this year's budget is more than double of what was the allocation in my last year as the Chief of Army Staff. Factually he was right (he retired on 30 September 2007). If we compare the BE for 2007-08 (the year in which he retired) to the BE for 2013-14, when he was addressing IDSA, the budget has more than doubled (The increase is over 112 per cent) as may be seen in the tabulation below.

Figure 2

	2007-08 (BE)	*2007-08 (Exp)*	*2013-14 (BE)*
Defence Budget	96000	91680	203672

We need to examine whether the perception conveyed in the former Army Chief's answer is correct. We take the example of Fuel, which is a major component of the Air Force budget. The actual expenditure and its relationship to the IAF store Budget and the total Revenue expenditure is tabulated below.

Figure 3: Fuel Expenditure of the Air Force over the Years and its Relationship to the Stores and Revenue Budget (All Rs in Crs)

	Fuel	*Stores*	*Total actual revenue expenditure*	*Fuel expenditure as % of stores expenditure*	*Fuel expenditure as % of total IAF Revenue expenditure*
2012-13	**3768**	**7038**	**17529**	**53.53**	**21.86**
2011-12	3376	6931	17322	48.71	19.49
2010-11	2749	5774	15179	47.61	18.11
2009-10	2240	5640	14708	39.71	15.23
2008-09	2946	6820	13243	43.20	22.25
2007-08	2369	6191	10559	38.26	22.44
2006-07	2320	6250	10064	37.12	23.05

Each column of the above table gives us a different picture, the fuel expenditure increased marginally in 2007-08, the increase was substantial in 2008-09, the expenditure in comparison fell in 2009-10 and 2010-11 to substantially rise again in 2011-12 and 2012-13. Fuel which is a part of the Stores budget increased from Rs 2320 to Rs 3768 Crs, while the Stores expenditure increased only to Rs 7038 from Rs 6250 Crs. Fuel as a percentage share of the stores budget rose from 37.12 per cent to 53.53 per cent, whereas as a share of the IAF revenue budget it dropped to 21.86 per cent from 23.05 per cent in 2006-07. The relationship of Fuel to the Stores budget and the total revenue budget shows a different trend and it appears as if the fuel consumption substantially came down in 2009-10 and 10-11 in comparison to 2008-09.

Real Picture

Budget is a resource for getting the goods and services needed. Now, let us see how does this allocation help the Defence services to be better off. For the purpose of this analysis, a major component such as Fuel is selected. Within this category the major consumption for the Army, Navy and the Air Force are tabulated over the years. Since these items have unique indices available on the website of the Office of the Economic Adviser, Ministry of Commerce and Industry, we index the requirement based on actual expenditure of the base year and escalate it based on index for each of the subsequent years and compare it with the actual expenditure to quantify what the increased allocation in absolute figures translates into.

Figure 4: IAF—POL Items

(Figures of Actual Exp & As per indexed inflation are Rs in Crs)

FY	*2012-2013*	*2011-2012*	*2010-2011*	*2009-2010*	*2008-2009*	*2007-2008*	*Actual Exp 06-07*	*Total 07-08 to 12-13*
ATF Index	*257.89*	*229.44*	*164.92*	*137.03*	*194.54*	*157.38*	*151.59*	
Index based change	12.40	39.12	20.35	-29.56	23.61	3.82		
Actual Exp	3568	3218	2596	2084	2783	2225	2167	16474
As per indexed inflation	3687	3281	2358	1959	2782	2250		**16317**
Diesel Index	*183.56*	*164.54*	*151.72*	*132.97*	*135.82*	*125.57*	*130.19*	
Index based change	11.56	8.45	14.10	-2.10	8.16	-3.55		
Actual Exp	200	158	153	156	163	144	153	975
As per indexed inflation	216	194	179	157	160	148		**1054**

The fuel for IAF's weapons platforms is Aviation Turbine Fuel (ATF). IAF pays for the quantity of fuel lifted by it from the Oil companies monthly in arrears. The oil companies maintain the reserve stocks of fuel. Hence the expenditure above brings out the actual consumption and what the table tells us is that the average quantity of fuel consumption between 2007-08 to 2012-13, has maintained the consumption level of 2006-07. (The amount of actual expenditure is Rs 16474 Crs and the amount needed as per indexed escalation gives us Rs 16317 Crs), however there has been a marginal reduction in the levels of consumption of diesel (This head also accounts for Petrol and lubricants). However, when we see each year's consumption we find that in 2009-10 and 2010-11, the consumption increased and the annual consumption was more than the 2006-07 consumption. The consumption has come down in 2011-12 and 2012-13, which would mean that the number of hours flown by IAF in these two years is lesser than the achieved utilisation of the earlier years. This may be due to budgetary constraints or serviceability issues.

What we see from Figure 5 below for the Army is that the expenditure incurred on Petrol (primarily used for light passenger vehicles) would have enabled the Army to maintain its level of consumption at the quantity consumed at 2006-07 consumption levels. However in the case of Diesel (used for heavy and medium vehicles including weapons platforms [tanks, APC and prime movers] etc.), the expenditure is less by about Rs 931 Crs than what was needed to maintain the consumption at the same level as 2006-07. This could mean that either the physical consumption has come down i.e. the level of mobilisation for training and the number of exercises has come down or the reserve stock maintained has been used for consumption i.e. the War Wastage Reserves (WWR) of Diesel has been depleted by consumption and not replenished to the desired level or some bills of Oil PSU's have been carried forward i.e. due to budgetary constraints or a combination of all the three. The implication of each category is serious. This represents about 20 per cent of the actual consumption over the period.

Aviation Turbine Fuel (ATF or Superior Kerosene) expenditure vis-a-vis the funds needed to sustain the level of physical consumption at 2006-07 level reveals a pattern similar to diesel. The expenditure is less by about Rs 568 Crs than what was needed to maintain the consumption at the same level as 2006-07. This represents about 20 per cent of the actual consumption over the period, an indication that the number of hours being annually flown by the Army Aviation fleet is lesser than the hours flown in 2006-07 or the other two reasons as for diesel given above or a combination of all the three.

Figure 5: Army—Petrol, Diesel and Superior Kerosene (ATF)
(Figures of Actual Exp & as per indexed inflation are Rs in Crs)

FY	*2012-2013*	*2011-2012*	*2010-2011*	*2009-2010*	*2008-2009*	*2007-2008*	*Actual Exp 06-07*	*Total 07-08 to 12-13*
Petrol Index	*186.26*	*174.41*	*143.02*	*119.33*	*128.32*	*119.12*	*125.31*	
Index based change	6.79	21.95	19.85	-7.01	7.72	-4.94		
Actual Exp	193	220	201	154	152	154	155	1074
As per indexed inflation	230	215	177	147	159	147		**1075**
Diesel Index	*183.56*	*164.54*	*151.72*	*132.97*	*135.82*	*125.57*	*130.19*	
Index based change	11.56	8.45	14.10	-2.10	8.16	-3.55		
Actual Exp	745	830	786	675	697	710	782	4443
As per indexed inflation	1103	989	912	799	816	755		**5374**
ATF Index	*257.89*	*229.44*	*164.92*	*137.03*	*194.54*	*157.38*	*151.59*	
Index based change	12.40	39.12	20.35	-29.56	23.61	3.82		
Actual Exp	499	583	451	368	503	454	455	2858
As per indexed inflation	774	689	495	411	584	473		**3426**

Figure 6: Navy—Petrol, Diesel and ATF

(Figures of Actual Exp & as per indexed inflation are Rs in Crs)

FY	*2012-2013*	*2011-2012*	*2010-2011*	*2009-2010*	*2008-2009*	*2007-2008*	*Total 07-08 to 12-13*
Petrol Index	*186.26*	*174.41*	*143.02*	*119.33*	*128.32*	*119.12*	
Index based change	6.79	21.95	19.85	-7.01	7.72		
Actual Exp	48	42	32	37	43	43	245
As per indexed inflation	68	64	52	43	47	43	**317**
Diesel Index	*183.56*	*164.54*	*151.72*	*132.97*	*135.82*	*125.57*	
Index based change	11.56	8.45	14.10	-2.10	8.16		
Actual Exp	1008	1229	806	676	776	843	5337
As per indexed inflation	1233	1105	1019	893	912	843	**6006**
ATF Index	*257.89*	*229.44*	*164.92*	*137.03*	*194.54*	*157.38*	
Index based change	12.40	39.12	20.35	-29.56	23.61		
Actual Exp	178	175	100	106	124	114	798
As per indexed inflation	187	166	120	99	141	114	**827**

The trend in the case of the Navy (Figure 6) is similar to that of the Army, the only point of amplification is the Diesel is primarily the fuel for surface and sub surface vessels; the only consolation is that the diesel consumption is down by only about 12.5 per cent

The use of indices in the above case does bring out a picture of the budget that may not be conveyed by the absolute figures. A review of the total defence budget can also be done by apportioning it into some major heads of expenditure and using appropriate indices and assigning weightage based on the expenditure percentage. The picture of Indian Defence specific inflation impact and the actual budget increases that emerges is tabulated in Figure 7 below:

Indices Used

- For Modernisation expenditure, we use the Wholesale Price Index (WPI) and for 70 per cent of the expenditure we also use the change in the annual average of the US Dollar, which represents the import content.
- For Pay and Allowances, we use the actual change as seen, the period includes period prior to and post 6th pay commission as well as the two years when arrears were paid.
- For Stores budget we use the WPI and for the ATF and diesel elements we use the specific indices.
- Consumer Price index (CPI) is used for the expenditure related to Works services and other expenditure.

Figure 7: Inflationary Pressures on the Budget
(all figures in %age)

	2007-08	*2008-09*	*2009-10*	*2010-11*	*2011-12*	*2012-13*	*Inflation applicable*	*Weightage (Budget Break Down %)*	
WPI	4.7	8.1	3.8	9.6	8.9	7.6	*WPI + US $*	*33*	*Modernisation*
CPI	6.2	9.1	12.4	10.4	8.4	10	*P and A budget*	*37*	*P and A*
US $	11.1	14.2	3.2	-4.0	5.2	13.7	*WPI (11) ATF (3) Diesel (1)*	*15*	*Stores*
ATF	3.82	23.61	-29.56	20.35	39.12	12.40	*CPI*	*12*	*Works*
Diesel	3.55	8.16	-2.10	14.10	8.45	11.56	*CPI*	*3*	*Others*
Increase in P&A Budget	7.78	61.04	48.16	-3.69	12.81	13.62		*The weightage assigned above is almost the share of these heads as given in DSE Vol. I for 2013-14*	
Indian Defence Budget specific inflation impact	**2.30**	**33.00**	**21.49**	**3.86**	**12.88**	**14.88**			
Budget Increase over previous year	7.24	24.59	24.13	8.70	10.90	6.35			

If we apply the above-arrived annual rates of Indian Defence Budget specific inflation to the actual expenditure of the year 2006-07 we get the following figures tabulated in Figure 8 below:

Figure 8: Budget Comparison
(All Budget As per Indian Defence Specific Inflation & Actual Expenditure figure Rs in Crs)

	2006-07	*2007-08*	*2008-09*	*2009-10*	*2010-11*	*2011-12*	*2012-13*	*Total*
Budget as per Indian defence specific inflation	85495	87460	116321	141312	146772	165680	190338	847883
Actual expenditure	85495	91685	114230	141794	154130	170930	181776	854545
Difference								6662

The above table establishes that although the actual absolute expenditure has more than doubled in 6 years from Rs 85495 Crs in 2006-07 to Rs 181776 Crs in 2012-13, in purchasing power terms it has just about kept pace with the Indian Defence specific inflation to remain almost flat. (The difference between the total of indexed figures and the actual expenditure over the period 2007-08 to 2012-13 is Rs 6662 Crs over six years and is only 0.78 per cent of the total expenditure over the period)

Defence Budget and the State of the Economy

A fact that Defence Services have to bear in mind is that the resources to be made available are dependent on the state of the economy. The then Finance Minister, speaking on February 06, 2013 at IDSA while delivering the K Subrahmanyam Memorial Lecture had shared his predicament. He said that Defending and promoting national security stands on three important pillars: human resources; science and technology; and money. Money is also the pillar that supports the first two pillars. Money he said comes out of growth. He explained that revenues of Government are tax revenue and non-tax revenue. Non-tax revenue constitutes a small proportion of total revenue and is more uncertain. Tax revenue consists, mainly, of five taxes: excise, customs, service tax, income tax and corporation tax. Excise revenue is a function of growth in the manufacturing sector; customs revenue is a function of higher imports; service taxes are a function of more activity and more transactions in the services sector; income tax and corporation tax are a function of more incomes for individuals, families and corporations. Increase in tax revenue is, in a very large measure, the outcome of higher growth. As the anticipated growth in tax revenue declines, expenditure cannot be compressed in the short term; the gap between revenue and expenditure rises rapidly. The short-term response is to borrow more, leading to a ballooning of the fiscal deficit. The medium term response will be to contain expenditure, but that has its own consequences. A cut back on public expenditure further slows down the economy. It also curtails the number of jobs that are created. A cut back on social welfare hurts the poor: less money for education or health care denies, to many more people, access to basic education or basic health facilities. And, finally, a cut back on expenditure on defence or on the police forces severely compromise our defence and security preparedness and diminishes our capacity to meet the challenges to national security. The effect of what he stated is visible in the Figure 8 above. The increase in Defence Budget (Actual expenditure) was higher than the 'defence specific inflation index' in the years 2007-08 to 2010-11, but the increase has been lower than the defence specific inflation index' in the years 2011-12 and 12-13. The data for 2013-14, the current financial year is not available, the increase in the budget (Actual 12-13 to RE 13-14 has been only 12.04 per cent against a much higher impact due to the factors impacting defence specific inflation.

Detailed Analysis

In addition to the Defence expenditure as a percentage of the GDP, this macro-analysis should be refined by an analysis of the internal heads of account. As brought out in Kevin Lewis, "The Discipline Gap and Other Reasons for Humility and Realism in Defence Planning," and in Paul K. Davis (ed.), *New Challenges for Defence Planning* (Santa Monica, CA: RAND, 1994, pp. 101-132), "Specifically, understanding the distribution of resources among the various services provides a preliminary view of how a country understands the salience of relative threats, its desired structure of combat proficiency, as well as the relative power of various military bureaucracies. Similarly, understanding the patterns of disbursement in functional terms, that is, with respect to pay and allowances, operations and maintenance, acquisitions, and research and development, also provides critical information about a country's military power. When such data are aggregated in the form of a time series, they identify important trends as far as changes in national military effectiveness are concerned. The defence budget of a country can be analysed in multiple ways, but an analysis that focuses on understanding the character of national military capabilities must assess budgetary allocations and movements in terms of the disbursement of resources among combat forces, support and maintenance, operational and physical infrastructure, and defence management". The statistical data annexed to this book presents this detailed analysis over 9th to 11th plan periods and three years of the current 12th plan. While it is best left to the reader to draw their inferences some of bullet points that emerge are:

- Defence Expenditure as a percentage of Govt. expenditure and GDP has been steadily coming down.
- The actual expenditure up to the 10th Plan used to be less than the Budget Estimates (BE) i.e. the budget allocated for the financial year could not be fully utilised.
- Post 11th Plan the actual expenditure has been higher than BE.
- The ratio of capital to revenue expenditure has from 10th Plan onwards shows a bias towards capital expenditure.
- Expenditure on Modernisation is about 83 per cent of the capital expenditure.
- The share of Pay and Allowances as a component in the revenue expenditure has been increasing and substantial increase is seen post the 6th pay commission. Pension though not part of the Defence budget is 2/3rd of the P&A Budget.
- The impact of the shrinking share of the revenue budget coupled with the increased share of Pay and allowances has had to be absorbed by the stores budget (maintenance and operations expenditure).

FRBM Act and its impact on Defence Budget

The Fiscal Responsibility and Budget Management Act (FRBM Act) enacted in 2003 and originally required the elimination of revenue deficit and reduction of fiscal deficit to three per cent of GDP by 31 Mar 2008. The Union Cabinet approved the bill in Feb 2003, after due process in Parliament received the Presidential approval in Aug 2003 and became effective from 05 July 2004. The Act aims to ensure inter-generational equity in fiscal management and long-term macro-economic stability by achieving sufficient revenue surplus. The Act defines Revenue Deficit as "The difference between revenue expenditure and revenue receipts which indicates increase in liabilities of the Central Government without corresponding increase in assets of that Government". The financial crisis and the subsequent slowdown had forced the government to abandon the path of fiscal consolidation for a while. In 2012-13 BE, the fiscal deficit was 5.1 per cent of GDP and, of this, the revenue deficit accounted for 3.4 per cent of GDP, leaving no more than 1.7 per cent of GDP (plus some other modest capital receipts) for capital expenditure. The only way the govt. can create the fiscal space is to bring the revenue deficit to zero and limit the fiscal deficit to three per cent of GDP, as provided for in the FRBM Act, so that the amount that is borrowed—is available for capital expenditure. The 2013-14 budget had targeted a fiscal deficit of 4.8 per cent of GDP for 2013-14 (the target has been achieved and brought down to 4.6 per cent as per the budget speech in Parliament on 17 Feb 2014) and through a correction of 0.6 percentage point each year thereafter, a fiscal deficit of 3.0 per cent of GDP in 2016-17 is targeted. The Act has been amended for FRBM compliance to shift from the conventional Revenue Deficit to 'Adjusted Revenue Deficit' (revenue deficit adjusted to the extent of grants for capital assets). This should, however, be subject to rigid compliance to the definitional requirements of capital assets as well as maintenance of asset records/ registers available in public domain. Since the Defence Capital expenditure although part of the Govt revenue expenditure is not included for 'Adjusted Revenue Deficit' the Capital Budget has and will not get impacted by the FRBM Act but the Defence Revenue expenditure has and will continue to come under pressure on this account.

Planning Commission and the 12th Plan

The FRBM Act provisions were guiding the Planning Commission in its approach while formulating the 12th plan. The planning commission approach paper to the 12th plan has with reference to Defence expenditure stated that the Capital allocation is expected to grow at 15 per cent and the revenue allocation by 7.5 per cent. Defence expenditure is projected to fall from 1.83 per cent of GDP in the base year to 1.56 per cent of GDP in the final year.

The above-mentioned approach paper has been in Public domain since October 2011. Whether Service HQs/MoD had taken up the issue post the issue of the approach paper is not available in the Public domain. The allocation of resources has thus far been in line with the assumption in this approach paper

(Tabulated in figure 9) the only change has been the ratio of Capital and Revenue budget ratio. This precisely is the challenge facing those responsible for management of the defence post the FRBM Act. The Medium Term Fiscal Policy Statement presented along with the Union Budget on 10 July 2014 at para 38 states that the total defence expenditure as ratio of GDP is projected to remain at 1.7 per cent in FY 2015-16 and 2016-17 and that Defence services Revenue expenditure is projected to grow at 7.2 per cent.

MoD's Actions to Meet the FRBM Challenge

As may be seen in the table 'Capital and Revenue Budget Over The Years and the Share of Capital Budget as a percentage of the Budget and Expenditure' in the statistical data that Capital expenditure till 2003-04 used to be between 25-30 per cent of the defence expenditure and this shot up to 42 per cent in 2004-05 (the year in which FRBM Act became effective). It has been around 40 per cent and only got moderated in the years in which pay commission arrears were paid (2008-09 and 2009-10). The capital share at BE stage was even higher. This was a clear indication that it was a challenge, which would be difficult to sustain. This bias created in favour of capital expenditure and against revenue expenditure because of the FRBM Act would have led to a situation in which essential revenue expenditure like maintenance of assets would get neglected as the two major items of revenue expenditure. Pay and Allowances (P&A) (entitlement based) and Maintenance expenditure (prescribed preventive maintenance) (classified under the budget head stores) are not amenable to reduction.

In 2007, MoD issued instructions to classify some of the erstwhile procurements done through revenue budget (The instruction lists out the items of Capital nature for which DPM procedure will be followed for procurement) to be carried out using the 'Capital Budget' but following the revenue route and financial powers. The extent of expenditure incurred on such procurements/repair/overhaul post this instruction is difficult to be quantified for analysis as it gets booked in the Capital Budget. (In the case of IAF such expenditure post this instruction gets booked to the 'Aircraft and Aero Engines' code head under capital.) That it is substantial can be discerned from the table in the statistical digest e.g. 'Air Force Stores Budget Sub-Head Wise' and the 'Navy Revenue Budget' the expenditure under the following subheads extracted from this table is given in Table 10 below. However in the Army budget, usage of these provisions is not apparent as in the case of the IAF and Navy.

Figure 9: Defence Budget Forecast for XIIth Plan Period Based on Assumptions in the XIIth Plan Approach Paper

Financial Year	*Based on targeted reduction of defence Expenditure as a %age of GDP as per approach paper of the 12th Plan*				*As per approach paper of XIIth Plan Growth Figures of annual growth rate of 15% Capital and 7.5% Revenue*			*Actual expenditure for 12-13 RE for 13-14 and BE for 14-15*	*% age Share as per Planning commission estimates and as per actual expenditure (in brackets)) (RE for 2013-14 and BE for 2014-15)*	
	Actual Expenditure for 2011-12 and Expected Budget based on XIIth plan approach Paper	*GDP Projection for XIIth Plan*	*Defence Budget as % of GDP*	*Defence Budget Growth over Previous year BE*	*Capital*	*Revenue*	*Total Expected Defence Budget*			
2011-12	170913	89,80,860	1.9	11.6	67902	103011	170913		CAP	REV
2012-13	**188180**	1,02,83,085	1.83	10.10	78088	110737	**188824**	**181776** (70499+111217)	41.35 (38.80)	58.65 (61.20)
2013-14	**207225**	1,17,74,132	1.76	10.12	89801	119042	**208843**	**203672** (78872 +116931)	43 (40.28)	57 (59.72)
2014-15	**227835**	1,34,81,381	1.69	9.95	103271	127970	**231241**	**229000** (94588+134412)	44.66 (41.30)	55.34 (58.70)
2015-16	250066	1,54,36,181	1.62	9.76	118762	137568	256330		46.33	53.67
2016-17	275721 **1149028**	1,76,74,428 **68649207**	1.63 **1.67**	10.26	136576 **526497**	147885 **643202**	284461 **1169699**		48.01	51.99

Figure 10: Expenditure
(Rs in Crore)

	AIR FORCE (Head 741 & 742)		*NAVY*
	Air Frame and Aero Engines	*Aviation Stores*	*Repair and Refits*
2012-13	991	1066	654
2005-06	2011	1118	1206

The effect of the implementation of the above instructions is that the database of expenditure pre 2005-06 and post this period is not consistent. It would pose a challenge to any study of defence expenditure and its trends and to arrive at an optimal ratio between Capital and Revenue expenditure so as to address the asymmetrical constraint brought in because of implication of FRBM Act.

A much needed change to 'Cost of ownership' or 'Life cycle cost' being the basis to determine L1 for acquisition was brought about beginning with the MMRCA RFP issued in August 2007. It is understood that this has also been followed in the later competitive bidding cases of other platforms like the Basic Trainer and the Flight Refuelling aircraft etc. When decisions are based on these concepts, it becomes essential to monitor the actual 'Cost of ownership' or 'Life cycle cost' post induction. From a broad division of two broad subheads under revenue stores budget in the earlier days, unique sub heads were being created for budget allocation and capturing expenditure for each new platform e.g. there is a unique subhead under code head Major head 2078, Minor head 110 for repair, maintenance of Jaguar Aircraft, Mirage aircraft and all later acquisitions. The contract price of acquisition as per the contract and the expenditure booked under these detailed code heads over the years would help us determine the life cycle costs (excluding Fuel and manpower). However the practice of booking this expenditure under 'Capital Budget' as per the above instructions has resulted in negating the purpose of creating the unique code heads for each platform. This practice would not enable in collating the 'Life cycle cost'. MoD will not be able to validate the 'Life cycle cost' quoted in the bid and adopted for the L1 decision nor generate data to refine the model of arriving at 'Life cycle cost' based on the experience.

Parliament—Defence Budget

Parliamentary involvement in allocating, managing and overseeing the resources dedicated to the defence and security sectors is a crucial ingredient in the emergence of accountable governments, defence institutions and armed forces. This is exercised through departmentally related Standing Committee. With reference to the Parliament's Standing Committee on Defence, the functions of this committee (as with all other departmental standing committees) are:

(a) Consideration of Demands for Grants.
(b) Examination of Bills referred to by the Chairman, Rajya Sabha or the Speaker, Lok Sabha as the case may be.
(c) Consideration of Annual Reports.
(d) Consideration of national basic long-term policy documents presented to the House and referred to the Committee.

These Committees do not consider matters of day-to-day administration of the concerned Ministries/Departments.

With the emphasis of their functioning to concentrate on long-term plans, policies and the philosophies guiding the working of the Executive, these Committees are in a very privileged position to provide necessary direction, guidance and inputs for broad policy formulations and in achievement of the long-term national perspective by the Executive. **However, the recommendations of this committee are not binding on the govt.**

The committee renders two reports annually on the Defence Budget. One is on the 'Demands For Grants' and the second one is on 'Action Taken by the Government on the Recommendations/Observations' on Demands for Grants. A review of these reports of the standing committee over the years has a 'Template' presenting statistical tables giving comparative figures over the years and its percentage relationships including a table of projected vs. allotted. A refreshing change has been consistently seen since the first report of the 15th Lok Sabha to the 20th report wherein the committee enquired about the impact of reduced budgetary allocations; the question and the reply have nearly been the same,

> **"Where compromises have been made or likely to be made due to the reduced budgetary allocation against the projections made by the three Services and other organisation/heads".** The reply whether oral or in writing has been, *"Under the revenue segment, after providing for salary and other obligatory expenses the balance allocation is distributed to meet the requirement of stores (including ordnance), transportation (of personnel and stores), revenue works and maintenance, etc. These areas are likely to be impacted by the reduced allocation. In so far as the capital segment is concerned, the acquisition of land and progress of capital works may get affected. The procurement plan for capital modernisation schemes may also have to be reviewed and reprioritized."*

Normally the officers representing the Service HQs let the MoD officers answer questions raised by the committee unless they are specifically directed at them. Their response is measured and conservative. However, the candid response to questions by the committee and the concern of the committee in the 20th report are reproduced below.

Air Force

During the course of deliberations, the Committee was informed that shortfall in Revenue Budget **would have adverse impact on training thereby resulting into compromise in operational preparedness.** Notwithstanding the fact that in the recent past there had been large number of instances of aircraft accidents due to human error, accounting for nearly 40 per cent accidents, the Committee opine that lack of appropriate training is a major cause of concern and qualifies immediate attention.

The representatives of Air Force submitted before the Committee that **the fleet serviceability in Air Force is 60 or 65 per cent** and **if the spares were available they would be able to push it to 77-80 per cent thereby implying larger availability.**

In addition to this, **budgetary constraint in this segment will limit the fuel expenditure hence impacting every activity ranging from transportation, training, load carrying, testing etc. Insufficiency of resources will cause inability to procure spares and fuel,** therefore, funding towards this end may be reconsidered and sufficient funds be provided.

Navy

The Committee found that this is the fifth successive year of less allocation under 'other than salary' segment. The officials of Navy ascertained that **there is demand to liquidate carry over liabilities of FY 2012-13 to meet in addition to this year's obligatory requirement.** The Committee understands that there are huge gaps in money required and what is actually allocated. Therefore, it is recommended that adequate funds be provided to Navy under 'other head' to cater to various needs which include training, stores, repairs etc. since **this would otherwise lead to many compromises in operational preparedness of Navy.**

The report of the Parliament standing committee on Defence for the current financial year's demands is placed in the Parliament before a discussion on the 'Demand for Grants' for Defence is taken up for discussion. These demands have always been passed with minimal or no discussion nor has there been an occasion where the recommendations of Standing committee have resulted in any changes from what was originally placed as part of the budget.

Defence Budget and Capability Building

Capability as per the Oxford dictionary is defined as "the power or ability to do something." In military context it is defined as, "forces or resources giving a country the ability to undertake a particular kind of military action".

The notion of military capability as the output level of national power is premised on the understanding that a country's military organisations receive national resources and transform them into specific war fighting capabilities. The war fighting capabilities thus generated are effective to the degree that they enable a country's leaders to impose their will on enemies, existing and potential. (Chapter 7, page 134, Measuring National Power in the Post-industrial Age by Ashley J. Tellis, Janice Bially, Christopher Layne, Meilissa McPherson, Rand Corporation) **Military effectiveness is the outcome of the resources provided to the military and its capability to transform these resources into effective war fighting capability.** A country may provide its military with generous budgets and large cadres of manpower, but if the military's doctrine is misguided, the training ineffective, the leadership unschooled, or the organisation inappropriate, military capability will suffer. (Chapter 7, page 134, Measuring National Power in the Post-industrial Age by Ashley J Tellis, Janice Bially, Christopher Layne, Meilissa McPherson, Rand Corporation)

Military capability involves being able to respond to an increasingly wide range of scenarios, often in extremely short time frames; for example, interstate wars, peacekeeping, disaster relief and the expanding requirements of security such as providing protection from piracy, cyber warfare, and biological weapons etc. In the Indian context in addition to the above, 'Defence Services', as an institution are perceived by the Political executive and the general public as a national instrument of the last resort for disaster relief, rescue and relief in floods, Tsunami, earthquakes to rescuing infants from a deep tube well, from quelling rioters in communal strife to the internal counter-insurgency operations. Former Cabinet Secretary, Mr TSR Subramnian while appearing in a TV discussion during the Uttrakhand relief operations expressed surprise that the army soldiers engaged in providing rescue and relief only had basic resources like ropes etc. and yet their effort and spirit had won all round acclaim. This demands that the level of capability is maintained at all times so as to respond to any call of the nation at any given time. **Former US Secretary of Defense Rumsfeld captured the scope of these difficulties in an address to the US Air Force in 2001 when he stated, "Your task is to defend your nation against the unknown, the uncertain, the unseen and the unexpected".**

Defence Capability is a sub set of the National Capability, which is all-inclusive. What all largely contributes to creating 'Defence Capability' by utilising the Defence Budget is depicted in the figure 11 below. A nation constantly studies geo political developments and evolves a 'threat perception'. A policy to meet the perceived threat is decided by the political executive. Parliament mandates the executive to create adequate capabilities and in the Indian context, 'Defence of India and every part thereof including preparation for defence and all such acts as may be conducive in times of war to its prosecution and after its termination to effective demobilisation' is the responsibility of Ministry of Defence.

The Figure below shows that you need all of the elements for generation and maintenance of capability and you cannot afford to neglect one for another. The capability achieved through acquisition of the platform is to be sustained through its long life (which could be 20, 30 or 40 years) through maintenance. The conventional thumb rule is that the through life cost of military platforms resembles an iceberg. Where visible afloat portion (25 to 30 per cent) resembles the acquisition cost and the submerged portion (70 to 75 per cent) represents the cost to sustain that capability over its entire useful life. In broad defence budget parlance, acquisition (including mid life upgrade) is funded through capital budget and the through life cost on maintenance and exploitation through the revenue budget.

The response of the Air Force and the Navy recorded in the 20th Parliament Standing Committee report highlights the importance of maintaining the level of peacetime training activities and maintenance of weapon platforms to sustain the capabilities attained.

All readers will understand most of the components of capability building included in Figure 11 below; two unique defence capability terms are briefly explained.

Figure 11: Capability

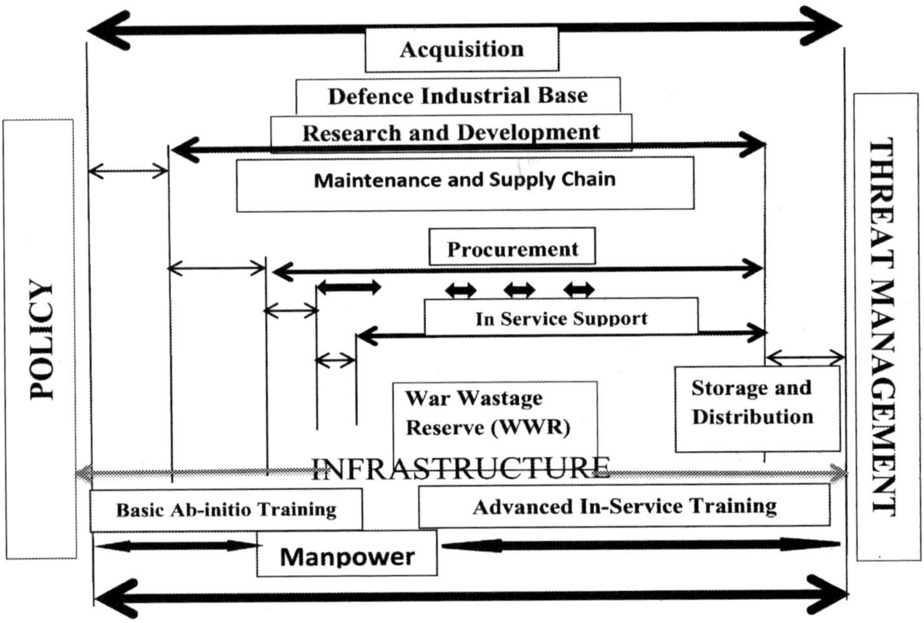

Training

Men and Women from amongst the eligible citizens of India (including subjects of Nepal) voluntarily apply for joining the Defence Services and post stringent selection process and subject to medical fitness and merit are asked to report for training. This training is termed as 'Basic Ab-initio' training. On successful completion of training they are posted to join Unit/Formation. An adage made popular by Gen George S. Patton "**The more you sweat in peace, the less you bleed in war** " dictates the daily life of a soldier, sailor and air warrior till the time he is in service. Physical Training (PT/Parade), classes, weapons training, exercises, sailing and flying are part of his daily training. The training encompasses all operational situations and it prepares him/her to smilingly make the supreme sacrifice in the service of the nation. Training is the nursery where future leadership is nurtured to be able to seamlessly take command of section/ unit/ship/squadron even while an operation is underway, should a contingency arise. This activity in equipment intensive services (platform-based arms of the Army, the Navy and Air Force) uses expensive resources and the platforms require regular preventive maintenance. In case of budget constraints the scaling down of this activity has an effect on all that is achieved through this.

War Wastage Reserve (WWR)

Everybody knows that the Armed Services need to have sufficient munitions to fight a war, such as bullets for the guns, rocket projectiles, bombs, air-to-air missiles, smart bombs, missiles of various ranges, torpedoes, precision guided munitions etc. All these are very expensive and have a life span. Life in the case of some is extendable. But they are needed if you want to utilize the very expensive weapons platforms (aircraft/Guns, tanks, launchers, ships etc.) to take full advantage of their design capabilities. The quantity of these items required to fight a war is referred to as War Wastage Reserves and to put in simply, it would take the following steps to work it out.

1. A policy decision commonly referred to as the RM's Op directive, which is to prepare for the kind of war, duration in number of days and its intensity etc.
2. Each service has to then draw out its 'War Plan' based on this directive.

In the case of the Air Force e.g. the subsequent steps would be:

(a) Take the number of aircraft, type wise and role wise available to it.
(b) Work out the availability of aircraft for operations, based on the expected serviceability of the fleets. The fleet serviceability is what has been referred to in an earlier paragraph. The higher the figure the better it is but this requires a herculean effort and an inventory and availability of spares and a facility to repair and recover the damaged aircraft that would be put in to get the maximum number of aircraft 'on line'.
(c) Identify the important targets that as per the war plan are planned to be neutralized.

(d) Work out the number of sorties each aircraft would be doing, taking into account the number of pilots available for the type and the maximum flying that they can do in a day (24 hours) and the capabilities of the ground crew to turn the aircraft around.
(e) Work out the requirement in numbers of the ammunition based on availability. For each munition you need to establish Single Shot Kill Probability (SSKP) based on the Circular Error Probability (CEP) and its integration with the weapon platform.
(f) Decide how many of each kind of missions that fleet would do per day. The missions could be against strategic targets, tactical targets etc.
(g) Total up the munitions required for each kind of mission per day for each fleet to undertake the assigned missions.
(h) Multiply this figure by the number of days you expect the war to last.
(i) But you would need to add to it the munitions that would be needed at the end of the War for any contingencies.
(j) Realistically assess the likely attritions in the number of weapon platform/ pilots.

Ammunition is a major component of the WWR. The defence services need to maintain a reserve of all resources used and consumed in war e.g. Ration, Fuel etc. e.g. Army had to purchase from US 500 caskets on an urgent basis during Kargil war in 1999.

A major casualty of the constraint in resources is that today's needs take precedence over the need to make up and maintain the WWR. Pressing needs result in dipping in to the WWR resulting in its further depletion. What should be the first charge on the resources gets pushed back and the consequences are lower capability to sustain operations.

Effects of Capability Shortfalls

Planning: Capability shortfalls can affect operations even before they are undertaken. They can translate into self-imposed limitations in the planning phase, with ensuing consequences on the operation's effectiveness on the ground.

Execution: Capability shortfalls do not only affect planning and force-size estimates. Their effect extends, more importantly, to the execution of an operation translating into reduced effectiveness on the ground and increased operational risk.

Political Awareness of Defence Capability

Selection and Maintenance of Political Aim is the most important principle of war. Political aim is to be selected by the Political executive and maintained and attained by the Defence Services. It is imperative that the Political executive has a clear idea of the Military capability so that the political aim selected is appropriate. They are the ones who have to provide resources for it. It is therefore the responsibility of the Defence services to educate the political establishment about the levels of existing capability vis-à-vis the requirement to meet the perceived threat and plan within the constraint of resources the best way to enhance the capability level to meet the threats.

For a better tomorrow, we as a country need a secure an environment so that all citizens can pursue their individual dreams and prosper contributing their might to a prosperous nation. Defence Capability provides that umbrella of security. 5-R's that are having impact on the capability building are:

> **Resources:** There sources allocated in purchasing power terms have not gone up. The share of Defence Expenditure as a percentage of both the Central Govt expenditure and the GDP has been gradually declining over the years. 12th Plan approach paper of the Planning commission had indicated this trend might continue.
> **Ratio:** The ratio of Capital and Revenue expenditure has got skewed in favour of capital expenditure. Capability is not built solely through acquisition of new weapon system but needs serviceable systems, which is achieved through efficient maintenance. All the other elements of capability listed in the figure need resources.
> **Restraint:** FRBM Act has imposed certain restraints on the Govt. through the fiscal deficit targets and the definition of effective fiscal deficit.
> **Resistance:** Defence services and MoD have been reluctant to submit outcome budget that the Parliament Standing committee on Defence has been asking for.
> **Review:** Defence Services have a long history and have strong roots in traditions. Review of legacy systems, procedures and practices is needed to adapt them to new weapon platforms.

Issues that Need Immediate Attention

Resources: There is always a temptation to compare with others. When it comes to 'Defence Budget' the two parameters used in the 'Parliament Standing Committee Report on Demand for Grants' are based on 'SIPRI Military Expenditure Database', the Defence expenditure figures in absolute terms and as a percentage of GDP. The reservations about this comparison are:

(a) Defence Budget's objective is creating capability to meet the threat that the nation perceives. Threat perception of each country is different.
(b) The category of expenditure that is included in each countries Defence budget is different. SIPRI for this reason does not adopt the figure published by each country but standardizes the expenditure by compiling

'what it defines as defence expenditure'. E.g. As per SIPRI, India's Defence expenditure for 2012 is US$ 46 Billion, whereas as per 2012-13 Defence budget (figures tabulated in the Stats Digest it is US$ 33.41 Billion. SIPRI adopts the following:

Where possible, SIPRI military expenditure include all current and capital expenditure on:

- The armed forces, including peace keeping forces
- Defence ministries and other government agencies engaged in defence projects
- Paramilitary forces when judged to be trained, equipped and available for military operations
- Military space activities

Such expenditures should include:

- Personnel
  - All expenditures on current personnel, military and civil
  - Retirement pensions of military personnel
  - Social services for personnel and their families
- Operations and maintenance
- Procurement
- Military research and development
- Military construction
- Military aid (in the military expenditures of the donor country)

Excluded military related expenditures:

- Civil defence
- Current expenditure for previous military activities
  1. Veteran's benefits
  2. Demobilisation
  3. Conversion of arms production facilities
  4. Destruction of weapons
- The key issues in the above which compromises the consistency because of subjectivity are, 'Where possible', 'Paramilitary forces when judged to be trained, equipped and available for military operations' and 'Military aid (in the military expenditures of the donor country).

(c) Transparency levels that Governments observe are not uniform (e.g. China's and Russia's expenditure is categorized as estimates) and Pakistan receives substantial Military aid, which is not included in its budget. Hence the budget estimates of these two countries of our immediate interest suffer from these infirmities.

(d) GDP is not a resource available with the Govt. The resource available to the govt. is revenue that it collects. The 'Revenue', which the Governments are able to generate, varies on the taxation policy and the income levels of its citizens.

(e) The constitution structure and the policy of each country determine the 'revenue' that the 'Central ' (Federal) and the 'State' (Provincial) governments may collect.

India has one of the lowest 'Tax to GDP Ratio' and comparative charts are given below:

Figure 12: Tax—GDP Ratio (%), 2010 (Central Govt.)

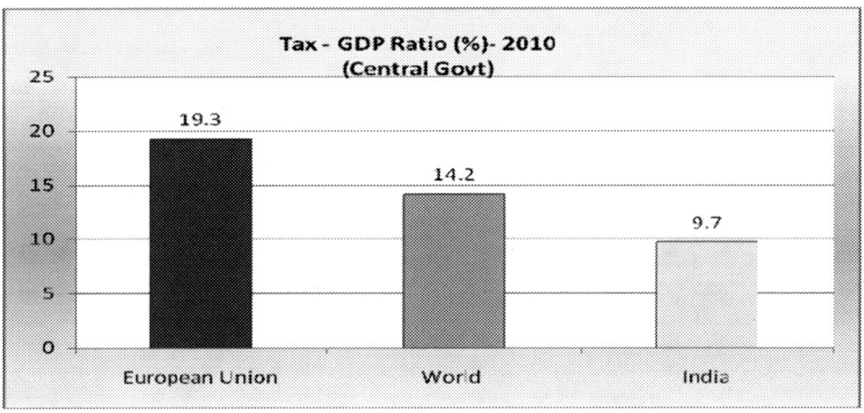

M. Govinda Rao and R Kavita Rao, *Trends and Issues in Tax Policy and Reforms in India*, National Institute of Public Finance and Policy.

Figure 13: Tax Revenue as per cent of GDP (India & World)

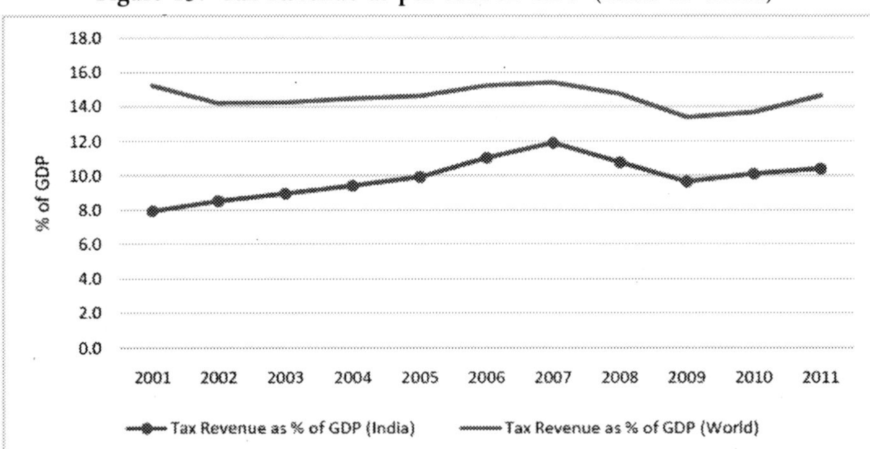

Source: Based on World Bank data.worldbank.org/indicator/GC.TAX.TOTL.GD.ZS.

Figure 14: Central Government Tax as per cent of GDP

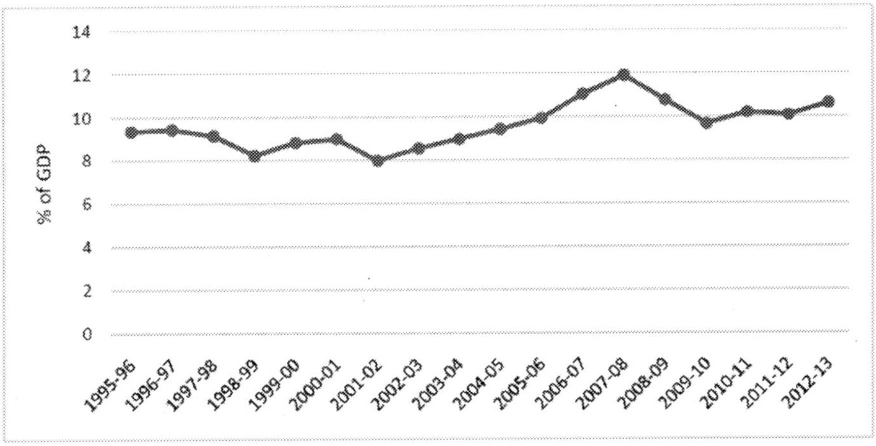

As defined earlier in the this chapter if the size of the defence budget is, in principle, the measure of the resources provided for a country's defence by its political executive, then a better indicator of this would be the Defence expenditure as a per cent of the central govt. expenditure. The graphical presentation of the **Defence Expenditure as a percentage of the Central Govt. expenditure** and **Central taxes (gross) as a percentage of GDP** in one chart below from 1955 below illustrates that while Central taxes as a percentage of GDP have slowly but steadily wormed up, the Defence expenditure as a percentage of central Govt expenditure has been steadily declining.

Figure 15: Defence Expenditure as per cent of CGE and Central Government Expenditure as per cent of GDP

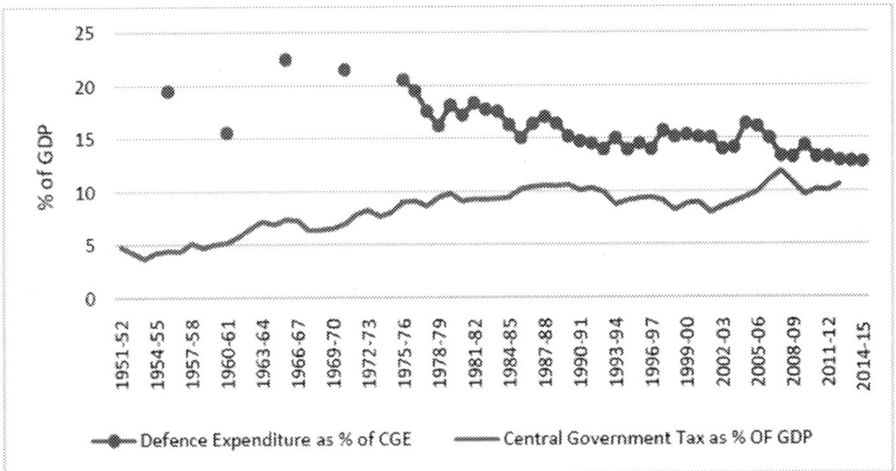

(*Table no 1.8; tax GDP Ratios, Indian Public Finance Statistics 2012-13 and Statistical Digest* annexed to this book)

Instead of comparison with others, our comparison needs to focus on ourselves i.e. is our capability better this year than it was in the previous year. This would require quantification/objective assessment. Capability can be enhanced both with additional inputs (resources), which the political establishment needs to provide, and with greater Military effectiveness through Doctrine, Training, Leadership and appropriate organisation structures. The defence establishment also needs to adopt the spirit, 'There is always a better way of doing things and the one best way is never achieved' so that the combined effort results in continuous capability build up.

Ratios: The pattern of expenditure in the defence budget is seen to have changed from what it was in the 9th Plan to the current plan. As they say 'the only constant thing is change', it should be a good sign provided it was reflective of the changing needs. The change appears to be induced by the constraints such as limitation of allocations, FRBM Act and 6th Pay Commission etc. and this has put strain on some key components of maintaining capability, namely operations and maintenance.

(a) ***Capital-Revenue Ratio.*** The ratio of expenditure between Capital and Revenue changed favourably for Capital expenditure. This change has come about post the implementation of the FRBM Act as may be seen in the share of Capital Expenditure to the Total Defence budget tabulated below.

Figure 16

9th Plan	*10th Plan*					*11th Plan*	*12th Plan For 3 yrs*
	2002-03	*2003-04*	*2004-05*	*2005-06*	*2006-07*		
26.35	26.86	28.07	42.18	40.15	39.56	38.57	40.03

There is a need for replacing aged weapon platforms/systems and make up for the shortfalls, however at the existing levels of resource allocation this higher share is not sustainable. Post 2004-05 the share of Capital allocation at BE stage has been higher than at the actual expenditure stage. E.g. at the RE stage in the 2013-14, Rs 7869 Crs has been withdrawn from the Capital and the Revenue allocation was increased by the same amount.

(b) ***Distribution of Capital Expenditure.*** The capital expenditure is broadly divided in to code heads representing various categories. The analyses of distribution of this expenditure shows that the largest share of expenditure is on Aircraft and Aero Engines and this has gone up from its share in the 9th plan of 35.37 per cent to a figure consistently above 41 per cent in the subsequent plans.

Figure 17: Per cent Distribution of Total Modernisation Expenditure

Plan Period	*Total Expenditure on Modernisation*	*Aircraft and Aero Engines*	*Heavy and Medium Vehicles*	*Other Equipment*	*Naval Fleet*	*Naval Dockyard/ Projects*	*Procurement of Rolling Stock*	*Joint Staff*	*Rashtria Rifles*
3 Years of 12th Plan	201572	42.91	2.85	34.97	16.22	1.45	0.18	1.18	0.25
11th Plan	211832	41.02	3.88	33.33	18.87	1.85	0.11	0.89	0.06
10th Plan	110912	47.41	1.82	28.96	18.85	2.13	0.10	0.61	0.10
9th Plan	51475	35.37	4.44	33.66	23.93	2.28	0.32	0.00	0.00
From 97-98 to 14-15	575791	42.41	3.17	33.09	18.39	1.80	0.15	0.86	0.13

(c) ***Air Power***, is the 'The ability to project power from the air and space to influence the behaviour of people or the course of events' and has, because of its three unique characteristics, Speed, Height and Reach ever since its advent been used decisively in dictating the final out come of operations. It is for these unique characteristics that it is no longer the sole preserve of the Indian Air Force but features in significantly and the share of 'Air craft and Aero Engines' in the Capital Expenditure of Army and Navy has doubled from the 9th Plan to the current Plan. (Table 18)

Another unique characteristic of 'Air Power' is that the 'Cost of Ownership' is very high. It is not just the initial investment but also the operations and maintenance cost. In our context, it becomes a bigger challenge since most of our 'Air Power' assets are imported and when manufactured in India are License produced thereby making us dependent for their entire service life on a foreign source. It may be seen in Figure 19 that the 'Stores Budget' of the Air Force during 9th and 10th plan was around 60 per cent of the Revenue Budget. The increased expenditure on acquisition of 'Aircraft and Aero Engines' would put an even greater strain on the maintenance and operations budget, which is already reeling under severe stress.

(d) ***Revenue Budget.*** The distribution of revenue expenditure under various heads has also undergone a change. Pay and Allowances and Stores are the two major heads of expenditure. Pay and Allowances being the first charge, the impact of slower rate of budgetary growth has had to be absorbed be the Stores budget that provides resources for the maintenance of weapon systems and platforms. The details of the share of various heads of revenue budget in each service from the 9th to the current (12th) plan are tabulated below. The actual impact is harder as a major portion of the spares; consumables and services have a linkage with the rate of exchange, which has also been adverse in the recent past. There is no doubt that the P&A in the Defence services have to be commensurate with

Figure 18: Per cent Share of the Modernisation Expenditure of the Army/Navy/Air Force and the Distribution Pattern of this with in the Respective Budgets

Plan Period	*ARMY*					*NAVY*						*AIR FORCE*			
	Share of Modernisation Exp	*Aircraft & Aero Engines*	*Heavy & Medium Vehicles*	*Other Equipment*	*Rolling Stock*	*Share of Modernisation Exp*	*Aircraft & Aero Engines*	*Heavy & Medium Vehicles*	*Other Equipment*	*Naval Fleet*	*Naval Dock Yards*	*Share of Modernisation Exp*	*Aircraft & Aero Engines*	*Heavy & Medium Vehicles*	*Other Equipment*
12th plan	21.2	13.4	12.8	73.0	0.8	29.1	21.6	0.1	16.7	56.6	5.0	49.8	69.2	0.3	30.5
11th plan	24.1	7.8	15.7	76.5	0.0	30.7	18.7	0.1	12.3	62.9	6.1	45.2	74.6	0.2	25.2
10th plan	24.1	11.8	7.6	80.6	0.0	30.2	14.9	0.0	15.1	62.9	7.1	45.6	88.6	0.0	11.4
9th plan	30.5	6.6	14.4	77.9	1.0	32.4	11.2	0.1	7.8	73.8	7.0	37.1	80.2	0.0	19.8
From 1997-98 to 2014-15	23.7	10.2	13.1	76.4	0.4	30.2	18.2	0.1	13.9	61.8	6.0	46.1	75.6	0.2	24.2
Share of total Modernisation Expenditure		2.4	3.1	18			5.5		4.2	19	1.8		35		11

Figure 19: Army, Navy and Air Force Revenue Expenditure Under Revenue Heads as a per cent of their Revenue Budget Over Plan Periods

	Plan Period	*Pay and Allow*	*Trans-portation*	*Military Farms*	*Stores*	*Repair and Refits**	*Works*	*Rashtriya Rifles*	*Other Expendi-ture**	*Of The Total Defence Revenue Budget*	*Of The Total Defence Budget*
Army	3 yrs of 12th plan	**64.8**	2.8	0.5	**16.9**		7.4	5.3	2.2	**69.0**	41.9
	11th plan	60.5	3.1	0.4	19.8		8.6	5.0	2.6	65.6	40.7
	10th plan	47.5	4.0	0.5	31.6		9.4	4.2	2.7	64.9	41.4
	9th plan	**47.6**	3.4	0.6	**36.6**		7.5	2.3	2.1	**65.8**	49.0
	97-98 To 14-15	56.7	3.3	0.5	24.3		8.3	4.5	2.4	66.5	42.2
Navy	3 yrs of 12th plan	**43.0**	3.2		**37.9**	4.8	8.1		3.1	**10.1**	5.9
	11th plan	39.4	2.8		39.4	7.6	7.8		3	10.1	6.3
	10th plan	26.7	2.6		45.4	12.2	7.8		5.6	11.6	7.4
	9th plan	**33.4**	2.5		**36.8**	**	8.71		18.6	**9.8**	7.3
	97-98 To 14-15	36.1	2.8		40.1	7.0	8		5.9	10.4	6.6
Air Force	3 yrs of 12th plan	**46**	3.4		**38.9**		9.7		2	**16.9**	10.0
	11th plan	40.7	3.1		44.1		10.6		1.5	17	10.6
	10th plan	27	2.06		60.4		9		1.4	19.0	12.1
	9th plan	**29.4**	2.2		**59.3**		7.5		1.5	**18.9**	14.0
	97-98 To 14-15	36.6	2.8		49.5		9.5		1.6	17.7	11.2

*Repair and Refit expenditure of Navy till 2002-03 was included in the head 'OTHER EXPENDITURE'.

aspirations of the young manpower that the Defence services need to attract and have to be periodically revised as for other Govt employees and this aspect is not at issue. The binding constraint of resources and the increasing share of these resources being earmarked for P&A have resulted in adversely impacting the maintenance budget which has a direct bearing on the serviceability and the effectiveness of the weapon systems and platforms. In addition to the P&A, the manpower base also draws from the stores budget for expenditure on account of Ration Stores, Clothing Stores and Medical Stores. It also has an impact on the revenue expenditure under the heads Transportation (on account of travel), Works (on account of housing). The impact is not restricted to the Defence Budget alone, The Defence Pension expenditure does not get included in the defence budget. However, this expenditure is sizable and growing and is part of the govt. revenue expenditure.

(e) ***New Schemes.*** For acquisition to be a continuous activity there needs to be a balance between what is needed to meet committed liabilities (stage payments due for contracts concluded in the previous years) and payments that would become due on signing of new contracts and create liabilities for future. The figure of committed liabilities in periods of falling value of Rupee is understated. In the absence of a SOP committed liabilities are estimated at a rate of exchange at the time of signing of the contract. Signing of the new schemes becomes dependent on the hope that there may be slippages in the on going schemes and the Rupee will remain stable or appreciate. As may be seen below against a sum of over Rs 11000 Crs in each of the years, the amount available for new schemes in 2012-13 was Rs 5320.82 and 2013-14 Rs 2955.59 Crs at BE stage.

Figure 20

	Committed Liabilities	*New Schemes*	*Total*
2009-10	*26565.73*	*11861.27*	*38427.00*
2010-11	*28408.67*	*17278.10*	*45686.77*
2011-12	*39095.48*	*11628.49*	*50723.97*

	ARMY		*NAVY*		*AIR FORCE*	
All Rs in Crores	*Committed Liabilities*	*New Schemes*	*Committed Liabilities*	*New Schemes*	*Committed Liabilities*	*New Schemes*
2012-13	5552.63	2500.00	22531.89	720.82	26433.00	2100.00
2013-14	7024.31	493.98	22295.84	442.86	35038.62	2010.44
Total	12576.94	2993.98	44827.73	1163.68	61471.62	4110.44
% of New Schemes to Committed Liabilities		23.81		2.60		6.69

Data based on 20th report of the Parliament Standing Committee presented in Apr 2013 and presentation of FA (Acq) at IDSA in Apr 2013.

A reduction in the modernisation budget by Rs. 8,663.2 Crs and Rs 7868 Crs in 2012-13 and 2013-14 at Revised Estimates (RE) stage (dollar appreciation in the years was 5.2 per cent and 13.7 per cent respectively) means that either there were major slippages in the achievement of milestones of on-going schemes and hence stage payments did not take place or no major new schemes were signed in these two years or payments due to DPSU's and Ordnance factories may have been carried forward.

Restraint: The FRBM Act was enacted to ensure fiscal discipline. The Govt introduced the concept of effective revenue deficit, which excludes from the conventional revenue deficit, grants for the creation of capital assets (Defence capital expenditure comes under this category). With this amendment, the endeavour of the government under the FRBM Act would be to eliminate the effective revenue deficit. The Non Plan Expenditure (Defence Budget Forms a part of this expenditure) constitutes about 70 per cent of the Total Government expenditure. Items of Expenditure included in this are summarized under major categories and tabulated in the Budget document presented in parliament in the Annexures III to volume II of the expenditure budget. The percentage share of each category of expenditure to the total Non Plan Expenditure is tabulated below. The consistently major items of expenditure are Interest Payments, Defence Expenditure, Subsidies, Grants to State and UT Governments, Pensions (a major part of this is Defence Pensions) and Other Non-Plan Revenue Expenditure (This comprises the Non Plan Budget of all the ministries other than Defence Services and Police).

The three major items of expenditure, which constitute 70 to 75 per cent of the Non-Plan Expenditure, are Interest Payments, Subsidies and Defence Expenditure. The absolute figures of the Non-Plan Expenditure, Interest + Subsidies, Defence Expenditure (Capital and Revenue) and their percentage to the Non Plan Expenditure for the last 14 years are tabulated below.

From 2011-12 onwards Interest Payment and Subsidies have been above 55 per cent of the Non Plan Expenditure. The Interest Payment may gradually come down in the long term with better fiscal management, the subsidies will need political will to be contained and moderated in paediatric doses and this situation will continue to put the pressure on the Defence Budget. Defence Revenue budget has been under constant strain ever since the FRBM Act became effective. The spike of the per cent in 2008-09 and 2009-10 were only to disburse Pay Commission arrears. While the long-term hope can be that the economy will recover and achieve a GDP growth rate of 8 to 9 per cent, an immediate intervention is needed to ensure that the defence capability is sustained and the maintenance needs met. The FRBM Act was amended to introduce the concept of 'effective revenue deficit', which excludes the expenditure for creation of capital

Figure 21: Trends in Expenditure as a per cent of Non-Plan Expenditure (Annexure 3 of 2014-15 budget document)

	2005-06	*2006-07*	*2007-08*	*2008-09*	*2009-10*	*2010-11*	*2011-12*	*2012-13*	*2013-14*	*2014-15*
Interest Payments	36.33	36.34	33.69	31.58	29.55	28.60	30.62	31.42	34.09	35.53
Defence Expenditure	22.06	20.68	18.06	18.76	19.66	18.83	19.16	18.24	18.27	18.64
Subsidies	13.02	13.81	13.97	21.31	19.60	21.19	24.43	25.79	22.92	21.28
Grants to State and UT Government	8.35	8.64	7.05	6.27	6.37	6.08	5.78	4.82	5.53	5.78
Grants to Foreign Govts	0.33	0.31	0.27	0.24	0.22	0.28	0.24	0.32	0.38	0.36
Pensions	5.55	5.35	4.78	5.41	7.79	7.02	6.86	6.97	6.64	6.74
Police	3.39	3.27	2.74	3.27	3.61	3.34	3.71	3.74	3.87	3.86
Other Non-Plan Revenue Expenditure	**8.91**	**9.24**	**9.28**	**11.21**	**11.07**	**10.56**	**7.41**	**7.08**	**7.16**	**7.07**
Non-Plan Capital Exp (Excl Defence)	0.92	1.50	9.43	1.19	1.52	2.89	1.29	0.77	0.70	0.83
Loans and Advances to State and U.T. Governments	0.02	0.02	0.02	0.01	0.01	0.01	0.01	0.34	0.01	0.01
Loans to Foreign Governments	0.04	0.02	0.01	0.14	0.02		0.03	0.07	0.01	0.01
Other Loans	0.49	0.31	0.29	0.13	0.13	0.77	0.03	0.03	0.03	0.03
Non-Plan Expenditure of UTs without Legislature	0.60	0.50	0.41	0.48	0.46	0.43	0.42	0.42	0.39	0.37

Figure 22: Interest Payments Subsidies and Defence Expenditure as a per cent of Non-Plan Expenditure

Fin year	*Non-Plan Expenditure*	*Interest Payments + Subsidies*	*% of Interest+ Subsidies of the Non-Plan expenditure*	*Defence Budget*		*Capital Expenditure as a % of Non-Plan Expenditure*	*Revenue Expenditure as a % of Non-Plan Expenditure*	*Defence Expenditure as a % of Non-Plan Expenditure*	*Interest + Defence + Subsidies as a % of Non-Plan Expenditure*
				Capital	*Revenue*				
2014-15	1201892	682719	56.80	89588	134412	7.45	11.18	18.64	75.44
2013-14	1114902	635582	57.01	78872	124800	7.07	11.19	18.27	75.28
2012-13	996742	570248	57.21	70499	111277	7.07	11.16	18.24	75.45
2011-12	891990	491091	55.06	67902	103011	7.61	11.55	19.16	74.22
2010-11	818299	407442	49.79	62056	92061	7.58	11.25	18.83	68.63
2009-10	721096	354444	49.15	51112	90669	7.09	12.57	19.66	68.82
2008-09	608721	321912	52.88	40918	73305	6.72	12.04	18.76	71.65
2007-08	507589	241956	47.67	37462	54219	7.38	10.68	18.06	65.73
2006-07	413527	207397	50.15	33826	51669	8.18	12.49	20.67	70.83
2005-06	365100	180152	49.34	32338	48211	8.86	13.20	22.06	71.41
2004-05	365960	172891	47.24	31994	43862	**8.74**	11.99	20.73	67.97
2003-04	348923	168411	48.27	16863	43203	4.83	12.38	17.21	65.48
2002-03	301778	161337	53.46	14953	40709	4.95	13.49	18.44	71.91
2001-02	261116	138670	53.11	16207	38059	6.21	14.58	20.78	73.89
2000-01	242923	126152	51.93	12384	37238	5.10	15.33	20.43	72.36

assets. A major portion of 'Defence Expenditure' is for capability building and this is not restricted to only items acquired through capital budget. E.g. Ammunition is a consumable item but provides the capability to exploit the weapon platforms (when needed) acquired at considerable cost. It would be a difficult task to identify expenditure for capability building, instead it may be desirable to broadly categorise a specific percentage of Defence Budget for capability building and exclude this for arriving at the figure of effective revenue deficit. This would need the Parliament to amend the FRBM Act.

Resistance: The Parliament Standing Committee on Defence has in all their reports of the immediate past been asking MoD to prepare an 'Outcome Budget'. Despite the committee having termed this 'non preparation of outcome budget' as disturbing, the same has not being complied with. As brought out earlier, 'Selection and Maintenance of Political Aim' is the most important principle of war. The political establishment needs to have a clear appreciation of the 'capabilities' of its defence services while deciding the aim. The knowledge about the capabilities can't be acquired through a last minute briefing, but needs to be acquired through regular annual inputs. They need to be provided inputs about the current capabilities, the threat perception, the capability gaps, the plan to fill up these gaps and the resources needed for the same. The outcome budget requires projection of outlays and the projected out put. E.g. there exists a government-approved task (number of hours to be flown per month per aircraft). The approved task is different for combat aircraft, combat trainer aircraft, helicopters, transport aircraft and trainer aircraft. The Parliament Standing Committee on Defence of the 15th Lok Sabha in its 20th report has brought out that it was informed, "**the fleet serviceability in Air Force is 60 or 65 per cent** and **if the spares were available they would be able to push it to 77-80 per cent**". Instead, if the committee was apprised, that the approved annual task for the combat squadrons is xxxx no of hours. We have been able to achieve only xx per cent of the approved task. The reason for the shortfall is that because of budgetary constraints we have a serviceability of 60 per cent. If an additional annual budget of yyy Crs is provided, we will be able to build the serviceability to 80 per cent in years. This will help us generate xxx additional hours of flying which will enable us to deploy xxx no of aircraft with fully operational aircrew, duly supported by qualified ground crew. This would have given the committee clarity on the existing capability, the potential for improvement, the resources needed and enabled them to monitor both the political executives actions and follow with the Air Force. This illustration indicates that the 'Outcome' Budgets can be prepared for the defence forces. Each service for each type of formation/equipment would have to identify the primary 'capability drivers'. It would have to fix optimal level of the annual task (out put) and measure the achievement with reference to the 'outcome' (RM's

Op directive). It would take a sustained effort on the part of each service to address and identify quantifiable out put drivers and this challenge would need to be taken to provide the political establishment with objective measure of the existing capabilities, lest it adversely affects the capability building.

Review: A large amount of national resources are needed and allocated for building 'Defence Capability'. The greater the efficiency in utilisation, the better it will be for the cause of 'Defence capability' building. There should be a continuous effort for review of strategy, tactics, SOPs, policy, procedures and systems so as to be constantly addressing improvements. Given the unique domain that defence and each of its service is, the best-informed changes can be brought out through in-house reviews, which must constantly challenge the status quo. The tribal wisdom of Dakota Indians, passed on from generation to generation, says that, when you discover that you are riding a dead horse, the best strategy is to dismount. Why is Planning (LTIPP, Five years Plan, Biannual, Roll on Plan and Annual Acquisition Plan) only for capital acquisition and not for 'Capability Building'? Should we only have a Defence Acquisition Council (DAC) or why not a 'Defence Capability Council (DCC) which will be the Apex body to monitor and direct all aspects of 'Capability Building'.

12

Financial Management in Defence

Amit Cowshish

Financial Management refers to handling of all core activities of a financial nature that an organisation must undertake in order to achieve its objectives. Primarily, these activities revolve around generation and application of resources for achieving pre-determined objectives of the organisation.

The objectives of any organisation are both the beginning point and the end result of the planning process. The process of planning cannot start without an organisational vision of the objectives to be achieved. These initial objectives are refined in the course of planning so that the final plan is focussed on clearly articulated and achievable objectives within a specific timeframe. The plan itself needs to be broken down into short term and long term goals and a strategy evolved to achieve those goals. This has to be done collectively by the entire top management of the organisation.

An important aspect of planning is astute assessment of resources required for achieving the goals. A plan is as good as the resources that the organisation is able to raise to sustain the plan. The plan must, therefore, be based on a realistic assessment of resources that could be raised for implementing it.

Financial management also entails judicious application of funds in accordance with a carefully crafted business plan and established procedures to achieve the specified goals, continuous review of the organisation's performance to ensure that it remains on course and carrying out mid-course correction if the things do not appear to be going as per the plan. This process must be subjected to an honest appraisal of the outcomes at regular intervals.

It would be evident that financial management, when viewed in its entirety, is not just the responsibility of the finance managers. Much like the process of planning, financial management is also the collective responsibility of the entire top management of the organisation.

These fundamental principles of financial management are applicable to governmental organisations as much as they apply to the private business enterprises, though the manner in which these principles are applied may differ from one organisation to the other. On all these counts, financial management poses a challenge in defence.

Generation of Resources

Constraints in Generation of Resources

Generation of resources by ministries and departments of the government is very different from the way it is done by the private enterprises. While the latter are free to raise resources they require subject to the national laws and regulations, individual ministries and departments do not enjoy the same freedom. Whatever revenue they generate goes to the Consolidated Fund of India or the Public Fund,[1] as the case may be, and the resources required by them are made available to them by way of budgetary allocations approved by the parliament. The role of the Ministry of Finance (MoF) is central to this annual exercise. Therefore, 'resources' are a given factor in the financial management matrix of individual ministries and departments.

The entire expenditure on defence is borne by the central government in India. There is a limit to how much resources the government, as indeed the private enterprises, could generate. In so far as the central government is concerned, its revenue income comprises direct and indirect taxes, as well as non-tax revenue, primarily from interest, dividends and profits. The capital receipts accrue from non-debt receipts, which are basically recoveries of loans and advances, as well as debt receipts in the form of loans, borrowings and provident fund. Capital receipts also include proceeds from disinvestment of government equity in public enterprises. There are, of course, miscellaneous receipts both under the revenue and capital segments.

Article 265 of the Constitution of India prohibits the government from levying or collecting any tax, except by the authority of law. The law governing direct and indirect taxes, which are the primary sources of revenue, is laid down by the parliament. No government can consider going to the parliament with the proposal to raise these taxes beyond the limits of political expediency.

In a written reply to a question, the then Finance Minister informed *Rajya Sabha*, the upper house of the Indian parliament, in August 2013 that the number of effective income tax payers was only 2.77 per cent of the entire population as on March 31, 2011.[2] This is indicative of the serious political constraints in enlarging the tax base, especially by imposing tax on agricultural income. The constant clamour for more and more tax exemptions threaten to erode the tax-to-Gross Domestic Product (GDP) ratio which, at 15.5 per cent, is one of the lowest in the world according to a 2013 study by the Centre for Budget and Governance Accountability[3] (CBGA).

Raising resources beyond a point is not the only challenge. Reducing the burden of interest payment and subsidies is equally exacting. There is also an ever increasing demand from various sectors. The need to spend on health, education, infrastructure and internal security, etc. cannot be seen as any less important than the need to spend on defence.

Inadequacy of the Defence Budget

This mismatch between aspirations—not just of the defence establishment but practically all other sectors—and inability of the government to raise resources required for meeting those aspirations is at the root of many a problem faced by practically all departments, including defence. At the macro level, adequacy of annual defence budget is generally measured by applying three indicators: how much it amounts to in terms of percentage of the GDP, what proportion it constitutes of the Central Government Expenditure (CGE) and what has been the Year-on-Year (YoY) growth.

The allocation for defence has been declining both in terms of percentage of GDP and CGE, as also in terms of YoY growth.

Table 1

Year	*YoY Inc (%)*	*% of CGE*	*% of GDP*	*Rev: Cap*
2004-05	26.29	15.24	2.34	57:43
2005-06	6.19	15.91	2.18	59:41
2006-07	6.14	14.65	1.99	58:42
2007-08	7.23	12.86	1.84	56:44
2008-09	24.59	12.20	2.03	55:45
2009-10	24.13	13.84	2.20	61:39
2010-11	8.70	12.87	2.01	59:41
2011-12	10.90	12.96	1.92	58:42
2012-13	6.36	12.97	1.90	59:41
2013-14	11.95	12.23	1.79	57:43

Source: Author's Database.

Should Defence Budget be Pegged at 3 per cent of GDP?

This declining trend has been a source of great concern. There is a view that defence budget should be pegged at 3 per cent of the GDP. The basis of this argument is unclear. There seems to be no empirical study to support it. Even as a theoretical construct, this argument needs to be re-visited for various reasons. First of all, GDP of a country is not synonymous with resources in the hands of the government which it could allocate to various sectors.

Secondly, fixing defence budget in terms of percentage of GDP could cause volatility in annual allocation depending on how the economy performs in a given year. In a country like India, where, after a spell of sustained high growth rates touching an average of 8 per cent per annum during the eleventh plan period (2007-12),[4] it has plummeted to less than five per cent in the year 2013-14,[5] it would make it more difficult for the defence establishment to cope with reduced levels of allocation during the years the economy does not perform well, which will be inevitable if it is linked to GDP. This would also imply delinking the allocation for defence from the actual requirement in a given year.

Thirdly, had this principle been followed, allocation for defence during certain years would have been much higher than the requirement projected by Ministry of Defence (MoD). For example, for the year 2013-14, MoD has asked for a total allocation of INR 2,80,341.11 crore but got INR 2,03,672.12 crore only, thus leaving a gap of INR 76,668.99 crore. The allocation for 2013-14 was 1.79 per cent of the GDP. Had the allocation been equal to 3 per cent of the GDP, it would have worked out to INR 3,49,450 crore in absolute terms, which would have been a good INR 61,009 crore more than what the MoD had asked for.[6]

Fourthly, if allocation of higher percentage of GDP alone could secure a country militarily, countries like Pakistan should be much more secure than a country like Japan as the former spends several times more than what Japan spends on defence in terms of percentage of GDP.[7] It is a no brainer that several other factors, such as the strategic environment, military alliances, threat perception and military capability of the potential adversaries, have a bearing on the strategic security of a country and, consequently, on the budgetary requirement for maintaining an appropriate defence capability. The fact that the defence budget in India has generally been lower than 3 per cent of the GDP is, therefore, not necessarily a true measure of its inadequacy.

The Year-on-Year Growth and Defence Expenditure as Percentage of CGE

Even the YoY growth could be misleading. The budget for 2010-11 grew by 8.7 per cent over the previous year but the growth during the previous two years was close to 25 per cent (See Table 1). Seen in this perspective the growth of 8.7 per cent on the expanded base of the previous year does not appear to be too bad. But a closer examination would reveal that close to 25 per cent growth during 2008-09 and 2009-10 was primarily on account of increase in allocation for pay and allowances which became necessary following acceptance of the recommendations of the sixth Central Pay Commission (CPC) by the government. In fact, there was a jump of approximately 15 per cent in the share of pay and allowances in the revenue budget after the sixth pay commission. Thus, substantial

YoY growth may not necessarily result in any qualitative change in the state of defence preparedness.

The most significant of the three indicators is the proportion of estimated defence expenditure in the total CGE. It has declined by about 3 per cent over a ten year period starting from 2004-05 (See Table 1). It is significant because it indicates that the government is either not able to, or not willing to, spend as much as it had been spending on defence earlier. Theoretically, it could also be on account of the requirement coming down over the years, but this possibility rules itself out as there has not been a year when the MoD had not asked for far more than what was eventually allocated to it.

Impact of Inadequate Funding

The mismatch between requirement of funds projected by MoD and the actual budgetary allocation has been a recurring feature (See Table 2) but this mismatch has impacted revenue budget much more than the capital budget. With more than two-third of the revenue budget being spent on pay and allowances, and most of the balance allocation being spent on other inescapable objects of expenditure—ration, clothing, Petrol, Oil and Lubricants (POL), etc.—the funds available for buying ammunition, spares, and maintenance of infrastructure, are becoming scarce by the year. The impact of scarcity of funds gets automatically passed on to these objects of expenditure as the consequences of inadequate allocation are not immediately visible and, in any case, do not create an immediate crisis.[8]

Table 2

(INR in crore)

Year	*Revenue*			*Capital*		
	Projection	*Allocation*	*Shortfall*	*Projection*	*Allocation*	*Shortfall*
2009-10	92761.76	86879.00	5882.76	61394.66	54824.00	6570.66
2010-11	97349.97	87344.00	10005.97	75243.73	60000.00	15243.73
2011-12	118305.14	95216.68	23088.46	96709.94	69198.81	27511.13
2012-13	126939.92	113828.66	13111.26	101934.61	79578.63	22355.98
2013-14	146271.03	116931.31	29339.72	134070.18	86740.71	47329.47
Total	581627.82	500199.65	81428.17	469353.12	350342.15	119010.97

Source: Twentieth Report of the Standing Committee on Defence, Fifteenth Lok Sabha.

The capital budget, especially its capital acquisition segment which accounts for more than three-fourth of the total capital budget, presents a different picture. The allocation is regularly underutilised.[9] It is true that MoF has been reducing the allocation at the Revised Estimate (RE) stage (some time at the end of the third quarter/beginning of the fourth quarter of the financial year) but this is done after a realistic assessment of how much MoD will finally be able to spend during the remaining months of the financial year. Therefore, underutilisation is not the result of withdrawal of funds by MoF.

This problem is partly on account of the goal MoD has set for itself of maintaining a ratio of 60:40 between the revenue and capital expenditure. Probably this is dictated by the government's obligation to eliminate the revenue deficit and contain the fiscal deficit as required by the Fiscal Responsibility and Budget Management Act (FRBMA), 2003. Whatever be the reason, this ratio is now being maintained by MoD to a considerable extent (See Table 1)without any assessment of its impact on, among other things, maintenance and serviceability level of the equipment and weapons systems as well as the stock of ammunition, all of which has a bearing on defence preparedness.

What emerges from this narrative is that judging adequacy of defence budget solely on the basis of its proportion to GDP or total CGE, or even in terms of YoY growth, could be misleading. It is also evident that while allocation for defence has generally been less than the requirement projected by MoD (see Table 2), the extent of the mismatch between the projection and the allocation does not necessarily represent the actual extent of inadequacy of defence budget. The pattern of utilisation of budgetary allocations (See Table 3) shows that the revenue budget is under greater strain than the capital budget. This is the position at present but in the years to come the capital budget could also come as much under strain as the revenue budget.

Challenges in Budgeting

MoF is generally wary of the projections made by all ministries and departments. There is an assumption that the requirement is deliberately over pitched. The challenge that MoD, as indeed other ministries and departments face, is to convince MoF that the projections are realistic. Though, even that may not result in a department's requirement being met in full, realistic projections minimise the chances of arbitrary reduction by MoF. But, realistic budgeting is not possible unless the requirement is worked out based on accurate costing of all activities/ programmes proposed to be undertaken in a given year, as also the capacity to spend the money, which, in turn, is largely related to the capacity of the suppliers to deliver.

The fact of the matter, however, is that costing is one of the weakest links in the process of defence budgeting. Budget formulation is totally decentralised as the requirement is worked out by services and other departments individually. It is also unregulated as the MoD plays very little, if any, role in setting the annual targets. There are no policy directions or standard guidelines from MoD for formulation of budget. There is no uniformity in approach to budget formulation or application of standard costing techniques for working out the

Table 3

(INR in crore)

	Revenue			*Capital*			*Total*			*Under-Utilisation*		
Year	*BE*	*RE*	*Actual*	*BE*	*RE*	*Actual*	*BE*	*RE*	*Actual*	*Revenue*	*Capital*	*Total*
2002-03	**43589**	41088	**40709**	21411	14912	14953	65000	56000	55662	**2880**	6458	9338
2003-04	**44347**	43394	**43203**	20953	16906	16863	65300	60300	60066	**1144**	4090	5234
2004-05	**43517**	44852	**43862**	33483	32148	31994	77000	77000	75856	**-345**	1489	1144
2005-06	**48625**	48625	**48462**	34375	33075	32338	83000	81700	80800	**162**	2037	2200
2006-07	**51542**	51542	**51934**	37458	34458	33828	89000	86000	85762	**-392**	3630	3238
Total	231621	229501	228170	147679	131499	129975	379300	361000	358146	3450	17704	21154
2007-08	**54078**	54795	**54456**	41922	37705	37462	96000	92500	91918	**-378**	4460	4082
2008-09	**57593**	73600	**73581**	48007	41000	40918	105600	114600	114499	**-15988**	7089	-8899
2009-10	**86879**	88440	**90669**	54824	47824	51112	141703	136264	141781	**-3790**	3712	-78
2010-11	**87344**	90748	**92061**	60000	60833	62056	147344	151582	154117	**-4717**	-2056	-6773
2011-12	**95217**	104793	**103011**	69199	66144	67902	164415	170937	170913	**-7794**	1296	-6498
Total	381111	412376	413777	273952	253506	259451	655062	665883	673228	-32667	14501	-18166
2012-13	113829	108925	**111277**	79579	69579	70499	193407	178504	181776	**2552**	9080	11631
G. Total	726560	750803	753225	501210	454583	459925	1227770	1205386	1213150	-26665	41285	14620

budget estimates. Scrutiny of the estimates projected by the services and other departments to MoD is, at best, perfunctory.

Thus, generation of resources is a big challenge in defence. MoD has no option but to make do with whatever budgetary allocations are made. As mentioned earlier, allocations are invariably less than what MoD asks for. While, this has created pressure on revenue budget, full utilisation of the capital budget continues to be a challenge. This situation has come about largely on account of the problems associated with defence planning, ambiguity about short term and long term goals, absence of a strategy to achieve those goals, imprecise forecasting of budgetary requirements, and a tenuous system of outcome appraisal for carrying out mid-course correction.

Defence Planning

It is often argued that the problems besetting defence planning in India stem from the absence of National Security Objectives and Strategy and a number of other downstream documents, which renders defence planning rudderless. This may well be a valid perspective but the fact remains that even if the government lays down the National Security Objectives and Strategy, a different set of objectives and strategy will have to be formulated for defence. It is the latter which alone can serve as the immediate starting point for defence planning.

The Operational Directives by *Raksha Mantri* (Defence Minister) provide that starting point to the defence planners in India. In the run up to the 12th Five-Year Defence Plan (FYDP) (2012-17), MoD had asked the services if the Operational Directives were a good enough basis for preparing the plan. Everyone said that it was.[10] Therefore, while one may argue that there is a disconnect between the 12th FYDP, prepared by the services and approved by the Defence Acquisition Council (DAC) on April 2, 2012, and the imperatives of the (undocumented) national security objectives, there cannot be any doubt about the Plan document being a valid reference point for those responsible for implementing the plan.

The problem with defence planning arises not so much from the fact that it is not based on clearly defined (at least, publicly) broader national security objectives and strategy as it does from the problems arising from conceptual, organisational and procedural issues related to defence planning.[11] Conceptually, defence plans are confined to the activities of the three services and the Integrated Defence Staff (IDS). These plans do not cover activities of the Indian Coast Guard (ICG), the Defence Public Sector Undertakings (DPSUs) and the Ordnance Factories (OFs). The Border Roads Organisation (BRO), responsible for construction and maintenance of strategic roads in the border areas, does not figure anywhere in the scheme of things. Thus, the element of 'jointness' is missing from the defence plans.

The organisational weakness stems from the fact that there is no exclusive setup within the MoD for defence planning. Headquarters IDS is charged with the responsibility of preparing the defence plans but the plans so prepared are seldom more than an amalgamation of the individual plans prepared by the Service Headquarters. The procedural issues are far too many to be narrated here but fundamentally all these issues arise from MoD's non-involvement in the process of planning right from the inception stage and the plans being formulated by the services on unrealistic assumptions about the likely availability of funds.[12]

Mitigation of Pressure on Resources

Three other points need to be made in the context of the challenges related to generation of resources. First, little attention is being paid to exploring the possibility of cutting down expenditure and making optimum use of the budgetary allocations. While there may be a limited scope for cutting down expenditure, the potential for making better use of budgetary outlays is quite evident. Joint logistics, outsourcing, pooling of resources, more extensive use of Information Technology (IT), greater use of simulators for training and a number of other steps could cumulatively make a great impact.

Second, adequate attention is not being paid to receipts and recoveries, probably because the amount so realised does not directly get ploughed back into the defence budget. Recovery of amounts due from other departments, such as railways, as well as from state governments for providing aid to the civil power, needs to be pursued. Rates, issue price of stores, rents and tariffs also need to be fixed realistically, revised regularly and recovered in right earnest.

Third, the potential for earning revenue for the central government by making use of the idle capacity of assets and facilities under the administrative control of MoD largely remains untapped, probably has no direct bearing on the defence budget. But it is in MoD's interest to take steps that add to the central government's earnings as it is out of these earnings that the defence budget is carved out.

The pressure on defence budget can also be mitigated through offsets, foreign direct investment, lease/credit financing, disinvestment, soft loans, exports, defence surcharge, adoption of government-controlled-company-operated model for running a number of establishments, etc. This would require cooperation of and coordination with other ministries and departments. The challenge for MoD would be to formulate workable plans to give effect to these bold initiatives.

Application of Resources

Making do with Paucity of Funds

As a part of the annual exercise of budget formulation, MoF fixes the ceiling for defence expenditure after consulting MoD. This consultation is mostly at the bureaucratic level. Consulting MoD, however, does not mean that the budgetary allocation is fixed with MoD's consent. Resource allocation, particularly when the resources are scarce, is an unenviable task. As mentioned earlier, MoD routinely gets much less than what it projects (which is the sum total of projections made by services and other departments). This creates an immediate challenge for MoD.

This challenge arises from the need to determine the budgetary ceiling for the services and other departments. As per practice, MoF only fixes the macro-ceilings for revenue and capital budget and passes on the 'envelope' to MoD. In recent years, however, it has gone a step further. It now fixes the overall ceilings separately for salary and other-than-salary segments of the revenue budget, and capital acquisition and other-than-capital acquisition segments of the capital budget.

The responsibility of deciding the share of individual services and departments in the pie thus falls on MoD's shoulders. Since it invariably gets less than what it asks for, it cannot meet the requirement of services and departments in full. What makes it worse for MoD is that the services and other departments have no Plan 'B', which could be activated to make do with lesser allocation vis-a-vis what they had demanded. In the circumstances, MoD generally imposes the same cut on the projections made by the services and other departments which MoF imposes on the overall projection made by MoD. This has led to the tendency on the part of the services to over pitch the demand so that after the inevitable cut it would still get close to what it actually requires.

The buck eventually stops with the Services Headquarters (SHQs) as they are the ones who have to factorise the budget fixed for them by MoD into allocations under various budget heads. The budget head wise allocation proposed by them is routinely accepted by MoD and conveyed to MoF for incorporation in the union budget and subsequently in the Detailed Demands for Grant (DDG) presented by MoD to the parliament in accordance with Articles 112 (1) and 113 (2) respectively of the Constitution of India.

MoD's Demands for Grant

The following eight DDGs are submitted by MoD to *Lok Sabha*, the lower house of the parliament:

(a) Defence Services, Army
(b) Defence Services, Navy
(c) Defence Services, Air Force
(d) Defence Ordnance Factories
(e) Defence Services, Research and Development
(f) Capital Outlay on Defence Services
(g) Ministry of Defence (Civil)
(h) Defence Pensions

The first six DDGs are clubbed together and published as a single document called the Defence Services Estimates (DSE). The total allocation (net of receipts and recoveries) made under these DDGs is collectively referred to as the 'defence budget'. The first five DDGs provide for revenue expenditure of the three services, OFs and Defence Research and Development Organisation DRDO, and the sixth DDG provides for capital expenditure in respect of all of them.

The DDG for MoD (Civil)—hereafter referred to as civil budget—provides for revenue and capital expenditure of the following:

(a) Armed Forces Tribunal
(b) Coast Guard Organisation
(c) Secretariat of the Departments of Defence (DoD) (including the Finance Division), Defence Production, Research and Development (R&D) and Ex-servicemen Welfare
(d) Defence Accounts Department
(e) Defence Estates Organisation
(f) Jammu & Kashmir Light Infantry (JAKLI)
(g) Canteen Stores Department
(h) Chief Directorate of Purchase
(i) Public Sector Undertakings (investments, subsidies, loans and advances)

The way defence budget and the civil budget of MoD are structured presents a somewhat misleading picture of budgetary allocations and makes their management needlessly cumbersome. This would be evident from the following:

(a) The DDG for Army includes allocation for Military Farms, Ex-servicemen Health Scheme (ECHS), Inspection Organisation, Rashtriya Rifles (RR) and National Cadet Corps (NCC). The services provided by the Military Farms are not limited to the Indian Army. ECHS is a health scheme meant for retired personnel of the armed forces and their families. The scheme is administered by the Department of Ex-servicemen Welfare. Inspection Organisation provides quality assurance services to the Indian Army but this organisation is under the administrative control of the Department of Defence Production (DDP) and not of the Indian Army. Rashtriya Rifles are involved in counter-insurgency operations, much like many other para-military forces, except for the purpose of command and control. The aim of NCC is to create an environment in schools and colleges which would motivate the youth to join the armed forces.

(b) While allocation for the aforesaid organisations, whose activities are not germane to the functioning of the Indian Army, with the possible exception of RR to some extent, are included in the DDG for Army, allocation for JAKLI forms part of the civil budget of MoD, although JAKLI is now a regular regiment of the Indian Army.[13]

(c) The activities of even the RR are not integral to the role of the Indian Army. Since this force, though manned by the officers and personnel of the Indian Army, is primarily engaged in counter-insurgency operations, its expenditure should more appropriately be borne by the Ministry of Home Affairs (MHA), which is responsible for internal security of the country.

(d) Inclusion of budgetary allocation for the organisations and activities mentioned in (a) above and exclusion of JAKLI from the DDG for Army creates a misleading impression about Army's budget, apart from making its management cumbersome.

(e) The DDG for Navy includes the budgetary allocation for IDS, which is not under the command and control of the Chief of Naval Staff (CNS). In fact, the IDS budget includes allocations for the integrated tri-services Andaman and Nicobar Island Command (ANC) and the Strategic Forces Command (SFC), neither of which is under the command and control of the Chief of Integrated Defence Staff (IDS) to the Chairman, Chiefs of Staff Committee (CISC), who heads the IDS.

(f) Expenditure on pay and allowances of the personnel serving with the aforesaid commands is debited to the budget of the service they belong to rather than to the Joint Staff budget.

(g) The budgetary allocation for ICG is not a part of the defence budget, although it is the fourth branch of the armed forces of India and responsible for protection of India's maritime interests as well as enforcement of maritime law with its jurisdiction extending over India's territorial waters, contiguous zone and the Exclusive Economic Zone (EEZ).

(h) The budgetary allocation for BRO, responsible for construction and maintenance of strategic roads in the border areas, is not a part of either the defence budget or the civil budget of MoD. In fact, the budgetary allocation for BRO is made in the DDG for the Ministry of Road Transport and Highways, though the organisation is under the administrative control of Border Roads Development Board (BRDB), which is a part of MoD.

It is not just the structure of the defence budget but the scheme of budgetary heads, under which the allocations are made, that adds to the difficulty of managing the defence budget. Under the revenue segment, while some minor budget heads relate to objects of expenditure, such as pay and allowances, transportation and stores, some other minor heads relate to organisations, such as the Military Farms, Inspection Organisation, NCC and Joint Staff. Under each of the latter minor heads, there are sub-heads that relate to pay and allowances, transportation, stores etc., which are also minor heads in their own right.

There is a similar problem under the capital segment. While some minor heads relate to objects of expenditure, such as aircraft and aero-engine, (acquisition of) land and (execution of) works, some others relate to organisations, such as the Military Farms and NCC. In the case of Navy, allocation is indicated project-wise under the minor head 'naval dockyards/projects' but no such details are indicated in respect of projects of the Indian Army, Joint Staff, Indian Air Force (IAF) and the other organisations.[14]

There is also a lack of transparency about the expenditure incurred on certain services. For example, while the approximate expenditure on medical services is shown in one of the appendices to the DSE, the document provides no clue to how this expenditure is worked out and what is the service-wise break up. Similarly, it is not possible to make out from the budget document how much is spent on equipping contingents going on UN missions, which is important from the point of view of claiming re-imbursement.

Absence of Outcome-orientation

The biggest drawback with the existing structure of the defence budget is its lack of outcome-orientation. Though under pressure from the parliamentary Standing Committee on Defence, MoD made a modest beginning by presenting Outcome Budget for 2013-14 in respect of the NCC and the Married Accommodation Project (MAP) to the parliament, the fact remains that this was done more for the sake of keeping a promise made to the Standing Committee than to bring about a paradigm shift in management of defence budget.

It is significant that instructions issued by MoF do not require MoD to present Outcome Budget to the parliament, probably because it is realised that there are serious difficulties in preparing an overarching Outcome Budget covering the entire defence budget. Identification and measurability of tangible outcomes is an essential pre-requisite for preparing an Outcome Budget. Both of these pose a big challenge in defence but what really frustrates a serious attempt at preparing an Outcome Budget is the very structure of the defence budget which is not conducive to outcome budgeting.

Be that as it may, some options are worth considering. Approximately one-third of the defence budget is spent on pay and allowances. One way of preparing an outcome budget covering this segment of the budget is to identify a specified teeth-to-tail ratio as the desired outcome of the budget spent on manpower. This outcome can be measured by restructuring of the budget in such a way that it provides a clear indication of how much is spent on maintaining the combat capability of the armed forces and how much is spent on the manpower providing support services.

Another one-third of the defence budget is generally spent on capital acquisitions. Outcome budgeting is possible in respect of this segment of expenditure also if capital acquisitions are conceptualised as distinct projects (as in the case of naval projects) and the allocation is made separately for each project, linking it with the outcome to be achieved during the year.

Out of the remaining one third of the defence budget, a substantial proportion is spent on 'stores' required for maintenance and repair of equipment and weapon systems which, in turn, has a direct bearing on their serviceability. Through a suitable restructuring of the defence budget, outcome budget could be prepared in respect of the allocations made for serviceability of equipment and weapon systems. Identification and measurability of such an outcome would not pose any insurmountable problem, considering that this task is performed to a large extent by Workshops, Base Repair Depots (BRDs) and Dockyards, all of which have clearly identifiable and measurable responsibilities.

DSE Volume II

Since 2002-03, MoD has been publishing a document called Defence Services Estimates Vol II for internal use by MoD and the services. This is an expanded form of DSE. While DSE is presented to the parliament, DSE Vol II is not. The budget allocations are shown in DSE Vol II up to the sub-head/detailed head level. The document also includes budget holder-wise summary. It was expected that the details furnished therein would facilitate better monitoring of expenditure vis-a-vis the budget allocation and enhance accountability and transparency in budgetary allocation. It was also expected that this document would facilitate outcome budgeting. However, none of this happened.

Utilisation of Budget

Competent Financial Authority

With some exceptions, utilisation and micro-management of budget is the responsibility of the Competent Financial Authorities (CFA) who have the power to sanction expenditure, the Integrated Financial Advisers (IFA) whose concurrence is required for incurring the expenditure, and the paying authorities, who are responsible for making sure that the allocation is not exceeded while making payment in respect of each transaction sanctioned by the CFA. Complete real-time information about allocation, amount already utilised and the committed liabilities is not available to all three of them, as there is no overall computerised budget management system covering the entire defence budget.

Delegation of Financial Powers

There is a large scale delegation of financial powers in defence, especially in regard to the revenue expenditure. The revenue procurement powers were reviewed in

2002 and then again in 2006. An internal committee of the MoD had recommended enhancement of the delegated powers in 2010. The committee had also made several recommendations for strengthening the oversight mechanism. However, the recommendations, though accepted by the minister, were never notified. The efforts made subsequently by MoD to review the financial powers have not fructified so far.[15]

One of the reasons for not notifying enhanced powers was the apprehension that there is a large scale misuse, or at least the potential for misuse, of these delegated powers which are exercised by CFAs from the apex to the lowest echelons in the armed forces. Another apprehension was as regards enhancement of powers which are exercisable without the concurrence of the IFAs.

These apprehensions are misplaced. There is no evidence of a large-scale misuse of powers. Most of the powers are exercisable with the prior concurrence of the IFAs and the payments are mostly subject to pre-audit by the paying authorities. The Defence Accounts Department (DAD), which is responsible for internal audit of the entire defence expenditure, generates various reports, such as the half-yearly Internal Audit Report and the Report of Major Financial and Accounting Irregularities based on the outcome of internal audit. The audit findings reflected in these reports do not support the view that there has been large-scale misuse of the delegated financial powers.

The view that the powers exercisable without the concurrence of the IFAs should not be enhanced is impractical. The General Financial Rules (GFRs), 2005, which are the mother rules for financial management, provide for procurement of goods up to INR 15,000 on each occasion without calling for quotations and up to INR 1,00,000 through Purchase Committees to be constituted by the competent authorities. Going by the spirit of these rules, powers up to INR 15,000 could straightaway be made exercisable without the concurrence of IFAs. These transactions, in any case, will continue to be subject to audit by the paying authority. This will also free the IFA set up from having to deal with a large number of small value transactions and focus on larger cases.[16]

It is not just this stalemate on review of delegated powers which is creating a hindrance in efficient utilisation of the budgetary allocation. The need of the hour is to bring about a paradigm shift in the way the powers are delegated. Those who are entrusted with responsibilities must also be given full authority to utilise the allocation made to them for discharging those responsibilities. This calls for selective delegation of full financial powers, at least to commanders of the organisations, such as the workshops, repair depots and dockyards, while at the same time making it mandatory for them to prepare outcome budgets. There is not much risk involved in such delegation as exercise of those powers will be subject to availability of funds, adherence to prescribed procedure, concurrence of the IFAs and audit by DAD.

Delegation of financial powers is not a problem in respect of capital acquisitions. The powers delegated to the services have gone up from INR 10 crore to INR 150 crore between 2006 and 2013.[17] Beyond this, the powers are exercised by the Defence Minister up to INR 500 crore, Finance Minister up to INR 1,000 crore and by the CCS for all proposals exceeding INR 1,000 crore.

Procedural Framework

The delegation of power, however liberal or pragmatic it might be, will not work if the procedural framework is not conducive to efficient exercise of those powers. The procedures followed by the armed forces and the Indian Coast Guard are contained in (a) DPP, 2013 for all capital acquisitions, and (b) Defence Procurement Manual (DPM), 2009 for procurement of goods and services from the revenue budget. The OFs and DRDO follow their own procedures for capital and revenue procurements. The Defence Works Procedure (DWP), 2007 is followed for civil works executed by the Military Engineer Service (MES) but DRDO has its own separate procedure for execution of civil works. In addition to this, there are a few assorted procedures for specific functions.

Simplification of Procedures

More than half of the entire defence budget is spent in accordance with the procedures laid down in DPP and DPM. Although, these documents, especially DPP, have been revised several times, the procedures continue to be viewed as cumbersome and even archaic, hindering expeditious procurement. It is difficult to accept that despite several reviews, provisions that make the procedures cumbersome and archaic have not got deleted and provisions that bring about efficiency have not got incorporated in DPP, DPM and other procedural documents. How to make the procedures simpler and more efficient, assuming that there is a scope for doing so, is an area which requires greater attention than has been the case so far.

While simplification of procedures is an on-going process, two systemic problems have been hindering this process. First, there is no dedicated organisation within MoD to review the procedures, with the possible exception of DPP, which is periodically reviewed by the Capital Acquisition Wing. However, even in respect of DPP, which has had the most number of reviews and revisions since the first version was promulgated in 2002, the responsibility is shared by the Capital Acquisition Wing with Defence Offset Management Wing (DOMW), which functions under administrative control of the Department of Defence Production (DDP). DOMW is responsible for formulation and review of the offset guidelines, which are otherwise a part of DPP.

More importantly, the process of review has not been as interactive and transparent as it should be. To illustrate, the Indian industry has been asking for provision of Exchange Rate Variation (ERV) in capital acquisition contracts. The GFR, 2005 permit inclusion of not only ERV but also the Price Variation (PV) clause in contracts, subject to certain conditions. However, these provisions continue to be absent from DPP. There is no gainsaying that genuine concerns of the industry must be addressed.

The incremental approach to review of DPP has made it difficult to demystify many a concept used in DPP. For example, it prohibits transhipment but what constitutes transhipment is not defined. In fact, addition of a section in DPP which defines various terms used therein would go a long way in demystifying the procedure.

Review of DPM has proved to be a more difficult task. The last time it was reviewed was in 2009, after a year-long exercise by a committee set up for the purpose. Though, a supplement was brought out in 2010, there has been no further review since then. It is not as if no review is needed. The problem has been the absence of a permanent agency within MoD to manage this task. It is much the same when it comes to the Defence Works Procedure (DWP) which was last reviewed in 2007.

The second systemic problem arises from inability of the bureaucracy in MoD to ensure expeditious processing of the cases which are beyond the delegated powers and, therefore, get referred to the ministry. Considering that MoD enjoys full powers for revenue procurement and no case has to go beyond the Defence Minister, one would have thought that revenue procurement cases would move very fast. That, however, is not the case. It is difficult to say whether this is on account of lacunae in the proposals forwarded by the services to MoD, lack of procedural clarity within MoD, multiple layers of processing, officers being picked up to man higher echelons of MoD without suitable background, general reluctance to take decisions because of the fear of getting into trouble at some subsequent stage or because of some other reason(s).

This is not to say that the cases under the delegated powers get processed faster. The general impression is that it takes equally long, if not longer, for cases under the delegated powers to reach finality and that the sole cause for this is the intransigent attitude of the IFAs. This is somewhat strange, considering that CFAs have the power to overrule the advice of the IFAs.

Whatever be the reason(s), the way cases get processed in the MoD or under the delegated powers is a big hindrance in efficient management of financial resources with delay in decision making resulting in cost and time overruns. Therefore, some remedy has to be found urgently. It is difficult to say whether 'integration' of services with MoD, recommended by various committees and task forces, will solve this problem. For one thing, not much thought seems to have been given to how 'integration' of services with MoD will play out.

A more practical and acceptable idea could be to set up a Revenue Procurement Board to sanction all revenue procurement proposals referred to the Ministry, much the same way all capital procurement proposals are considered by the Defence Procurement Board (DPB) or the Defence Acquisition Council (DAC). There will, of course, be a difference in that the proposed Revenue Procurement Board would function as a committee CFA. This will relieve MoD officials from the pressure of approving procurement proposals in their individual capacity as the CFA. A similar system could be put in place for dealing with the cases under the delegated powers.

Monitoring

While it is important to create conditions conducive for utilisation of budgetary allocation through appropriate changes in the scheme of delegation of financial powers and the procedural framework, utilisation of funds cannot be the end in itself. There is a need to put in place an effective system of monitoring and oversight, resulting in mid-course corrections, whenever and wherever called for.

Sub-optimal Use of ICT for Monitoring

There are two inter-related big challenges in so far as the task of monitoring is concerned. First, monitoring of expenditure by MoD is unsystematic and it is based on statistical analysis rather than being focussed on outcomes. Second, the problem is exacerbated by sub-optimum or, at best, disjointed use of Information and Communication Technology (ICT) across the entire defence establishment for the purpose of financial management.

The monitoring system in MoD, and arguably at the lower levels, is either non-existent or not very efficient. At the apex level in MoD, the focus is almost entirely on utilisation of the capital acquisition budget. This does not help in monitoring the progress made by the spending authorities towards achieving the targeted outcomes even in respect of capital acquisitions. There are a few project-specific monitoring committees but they are not a part of a well thought out system of monitoring.

Sub-optimal Use of ICT

What perhaps comes in the way of comprehensive analytical monitoring is the absence of a single financial management system in defence which integrates the Ministry, Services and other departments with DAD, which is responsible for compiling the accounts for MoD. An amazing range of information and data flows into DAD and so is the fact that it is put to little use for the purpose of monitoring. Every single *paise* that is spent from the defence budget, civil budget, defence pensions budget, and even the BRO budget is accounted for by DAD which places it in an ideal position to create myriad databases for use by the decision-makers.

A project called Mission Excel-IT was undertaken by DAD in 2001 to create the widest-possible and diversified databases, as well as a common network that could be made use of for generating real time MIS reports by everyone from the lowest level budget holder to the highest echelons in MoD. However, the department, which pioneered computerisation in government accounts by bringing in Hollerith machines in 1960s, was unable to carry the process through. In the event, DAD, as also services and other departments of MoD, continue to manage finances through their own fragmented computerised Financial Management Systems.

The advantage of a common ICT financial management programme will not be limited to monitoring of expenditure. There are other aspects of financial management which are equally important and can be better managed through such a programme. It could be a useful tool for keeping a tab on the committed liabilities, making accurate budget forecasts, timely re-appropriation of funds, tracking life-cycle costs, accrual accounting, recovery of dues from individual consumers and other agencies, capturing cost of various goods and services, and a wide range of other useful applications.

Application of ICT for Pension Disbursement

The potential of ICT has also not been fully exploited for disbursement of pension. Presently, pension is sanctioned by the Principal Controller of Defence Accounts (PCDA) (Pensions) Allahabad, PCDA (Navy) Mumbai, Joint Controller of Defence Accounts (Air Force) New Delhi and some other Pension Sanctioning Authorities (PSAs). The Pension Payment Orders (PPOs) are then transmitted to the Pension Disbursing Authorities (PDAs)—in some cases directly and in some other through intermediary offices. The first payment, which includes lump sum payment on account of commuted value of pension, and the monthly payments are made by the PDAs. Pension is disbursed primarily through banks and the Defence Pension Disbursement Offices (DPDOs) across the length and breadth of the country. The monthly payments are then compiled and audited by the PCDA, Allahabad.

There are frequent complaints of the payments, especially the first payment, getting delayed. There is a time lag between disbursement of pension and compilation of this expenditure. Audit of pension disbursed by the PDAs is a mammoth job which does not receive adequate attention, resulting in over or under payments. All this can be taken care of through a better use of ICT. Since pension sanction is now computerised, the PSAs can themselves generate monthly entitlements and transfer the amount through National Electronic Funds Transfer (NEFT)/Real Time Gross Settlement (RTGS) to the pensioners' accounts. This will cut the delays and the need for post-audit of pension disbursement accounts, apart from ensuring accurate payments, real time compilation of expenditure and immediate revision of pension whenever any such revision is ordered by the government.

Oversight

Oversight is an important facet of financial management. The oversight mechanism in defence comprises internal audit by the network of Local Audit Officers (LAOs) of the DAD. It is one of the oldest and the most extensive systems of audit. However, over the years it has lost its efficacy as internal auditors have not been very successful in discovering aberrations and irregularities that often come to light through statutory audit.[18]

There are many reasons for this. First, there is very little, if any, involvement of the higher level officers in internal audit. Consequently, most of the audit observations relate to routine matters; very few systemic issues get thrown up in internal audit. Second, internal audit is hardly ever concurrent. It does not help much if some irregularity is noticed several years after it is committed as by that time it has either been already rectified or is beyond rectification. Third, DAD has not been able to modernise the tools and techniques of carrying out internal audit. There is hardly any use of ICT in this area. Fourth, audit is limited to the list of 'auditable documents'. The list is seldom updated and often there is lack of cooperation from the units in producing all relevant documents to the visiting audit teams.

Fifth, DAD has not been able to activate 'audit of sanctions' accorded by the CFAs. Sixth, even at the higher levels there is lack of enthusiasm in looking into the audit findings. This also has to do with most of the audit observations being comparatively trivial in nature and the incidence of systemic issues coming to light in internal audit being quite rare. The 'audit committees' at the Command, Service Headquarters and MoD levels, which were set up/supposed to be set up several years back to look into the audit findings and take corrective measures hardly ever became functional. Seventh, there is little recognition of DAD's mandate to carry out financial and performance audit. Eighth, quite possibly, some amount of corruption at the lower level comes in the way of serious aberrations and irregularities being reported.

Oversight mechanism is one of the most important tools in financial management. Its weaknesses make the task of financial management that much more difficult. Much of the problem arises from DAD's inability to improve the systems and procedure, make greater use of ICT and provide useful inputs to the decision makers. However, failure on the part of MoD to recognise the importance of internal audit as a means of oversight and the general indifference to the need for a robust internal audit mechanism poses a big challenge.

Regular Appraisal and Mid-course Correction

To complete a somewhat worrisome picture, there is no system in MoD of carrying out regular appraisals of whether things are progressing as envisaged in the plan documents and to carry out mid-course corrections. Consequently, pressing issues remain adrift. Take for example, the night blindness of the armed forces or deficiency of ammunition, which have a direct bearing on defence preparedness. Had such a system been in place, it would perhaps have been possible to fix these two problems making use of the sum of INR 70,000 crore which MoD has been unable to utilise out of the allocations made since 2002-03 for capital acquisitions.

Summing Up

Given the conditions in its neighbourhood and the aspiration of becoming a global power, India has no option but to continue to spend substantial amount on defence. However, how much it is able to spend is directly linked with the state of economy which circumscribes government's ability to raise resources for allocation to defence and other sectors. The allocation for defence has been, and is likely to continue to be, frugal when viewed with reference to the requirement projected by MoD. This calls for astute management of available financial resources.

Preparation of realistic defence plans, which take into account the strategic but also fiscal realities, is an essential pre-requisite for astute financial management. The conceptual, organisational and procedural aspects of defence planning require immediate attention. However, this alone will not help. The budgeting process also needs to be reformed, with the objective of giving it an outcome orientation. The desired results cannot be achieved without involvement of MoD in planning and budgeting right from the beginning till the end.

Since the availability of funds is likely to continue to be a problem, possibility of mitigating the pressure on defence budget need to be explored. This would require exploring the possibility of economising by resorting to joint logistics, outsourcing, pooling of resources, more extensive use of IT, greater use of simulators for training and a number of other steps that could cumulatively make a great impact. It would also require paying greater attention to receipts and recoveries and the potential for earning revenue for the central government by making use of the idle capacity of assets and facilities under the administrative control of MoD.

Pressure on defence budget can also be mitigated through offsets, foreign direct investment, lease/credit financing, disinvestment, soft loans, exports, defence surcharge, adoption of government-controlled-company-operated model for running a number of establishments, etc. Since it is in MoD's interest, it must assume the leadership role in setting up joint working groups with other ministries and departments without whose cooperation these measures cannot be taken.

There has to be a paradigm shift in the way the financial powers are delegated for revenue expenditure. The quantum of delegation should be linked with the extent of responsibility. The tendency to pander to the hierarchy of the armed forces in the matter of delegation of financial powers needs to be curbed. The reluctance to delegate full powers wherever needed must be overcome.

The delegation of power will not work unless the procedures are reviewed regularly and concerns of all stakeholders addressed. The impediments in decision-making within the MoD, as well as the services, will need to be identified and effective measures taken to remove them.

Projects that have a direct bearing on defence preparedness will need to be undertaken in a mission-mode. These could range from building up the stock of ammunition to making up the required squadron strength of IAF. The monitoring system will have to shift its focus from statistical review of utilisation of budget to analytical review of outcomes. The monitoring system must also have the inbuilt ability to give directions and remove hurdles causing time and cost overruns.

The system of internal audit requires a thorough revamp. It needs to be made officer-oriented with its focus being on systemic issues. The system of audit of sanctions needs to be activated. The audit drill for carrying out the audit of sanctions needs to be evolved with a lot of care. All this requires immediate attention not only of the department responsible for carrying out audit but also of the MoD and services. They will have to recognise the multiple benefits of internal audit. It could provide invaluable inputs for carrying out mid-course corrections in policy and procedures, apart from serving as an oversight mechanism.

None of this is, however, possible unless the potential of ICT is exploited more imaginatively by all concerned. To begin with, DAD needs to create a wide range of databases to cater to the needs of all stakeholders in MoD, other departments and services. This solitary step could provide the necessary launch pad for a robust financial management system for defence.

NOTES

1. See Article 266 of the Constitution of India
2. "Only 2.77 percent of India's population pay income tax", The *Deccan Herald*, August 31, 2013, http://www.deccanherald.com/content/187531/only-277-percent-indias-population.html
3. "India's tax-GDP ratio one of the lowest", The *Business Standard*, March 26, 2013, http://www.business-standard.com/article/economy-policy/india-s-tax-gdp-ratio-one-of-the-lowest-113032500376_1.html
4. Budget Speech for the year 2013-14 by the Union Finance Minister, accessible at http://indiabudget.nic.in/budget2013-2014/ub2013-14/bs/bs.pdf
5. Macro-economic Framework Statement 2014-15, accessible at http://indiabudget.nic.in/ub2014-15/frbm/frbm1.pdf

6. Based on the data available in the 20th report of the Standing Committee on Defence (15th Lok Sabha), accessible at http://164.100.47.134/lsscommittee/Defence/15_Defence_20.pdf
7. See "Military Expenditure (% of GDP)", The World Bank, http://data.worldbank.org/indicator/MS.MIL.XPND.GD.ZS
8. For a more detailed analysis, see author's "What is choking the Indian Defence Budget", *IDSA Comment,* February 14, 2014, http://idsa.in/idsacomments/WhatischokingtheIndiandefencebudget_acowshish_140214, and "Running Low on Ammunition", *IDSA Comment,* April 3, 2014, http://idsa.in/idsacomments/RunningLowonAmmunition_acowshish_030414
9. For a detailed account of this argument, see author's "Assessing Modernisation of the Indian Armed Forces through Budgetary Allocations", the *Journal of Defence Studies,* January 2014, 8(1), http://idsa.in/system/files/8_1_2014_AssessingModernisationoftheIAF.pdf
10. The author was associated with this exercise.
11. For a detailed analysis of the subject, see author's "A Perspective on Defence Planning in India", *Strategic Analysis,* July 2012, 36(4), http://www.idsa.in/strategicanalysis/36_4/APerspectiveonDefencePlanninginIndia_AmitCowshish
12. For a detailed discussion on this subject, see the chapter on Defence Planning, Programming and Budgeting an Agenda for Reform in this book.
13. JAKLI is the successor of JAK Militia which was not a regular regiment of the Indian Army.
14. For a detailed discussion on this subject, see author's 'Potential Improvements in the Defence Services Estimates', *Journal of Defence Studies,* 3(2), 2009 accessible at http://idsa.in/system/files/jds_3_2_acowshish.pdf
15. See the author's 'Delegation of Powers to the Armed Forces in a Time Warp', *IDSA Comment,* December 26, 2013, accessible at http://idsa.in/idsacomments/DelegationofPowerstotheArmedForces_acowshish_261213
16. See the author's 'Unshackling the Armed Forces—Need for Greater Delegation of Financial Powers', *IDSA Comment,* March 25, 2014, accessible at http://www.idsa.in/idsacomments/UnshacklingtheArmedForces_acowshish_250314
17. The Vice Chiefs of Army and Naval Staff, Deputy Chief of Air Staff, CISC and the Director General Coast Guard have financial powers to sanction individual capital acquisition proposals up to Rs 150 Crore each with the concurrence of the IFAs.
18. The internal audit is different from, and more extensive than, the statutory audit carried out by the CAG of India, whose reports are submitted to the parliament.

13

Defence Manpower

Satish Nambiar

Security Perspective

In any analysis of India's defence requirements, capabilities and preparedness, including that of manpower, the first set of issues that must necessarily be factored in, are the internal security dynamics, sub-regional and regional threats, both existential and potential, and the global security situation. To that extent, notwithstanding the internal security challenges India faces, and the imperative need to primarily focus on economic growth and social development, it would be prudent for the governing establishment and the strategic community in the country to recognise the fact that in the prevailing regional and global security scenario, besides dealing with the overt military stand-off on the Line of Control (LoC) in Jammu and Kashmir (J&K) and the proxy war being waged against India by Pakistan, as also the possibility of confrontation with China over the unresolved boundary dispute, India will be increasingly called upon to play a role in the extended region from the Persian Gulf and the East Coast of Africa in the West, to the Malacca Straits and the South China Sea in the East, as also from the Central Asian region in the North to the Southern Indian Ocean. A role imposed on us by a number of factors: the size of the country; its geo-strategic location straddling the Indian Ocean; the population of a billion and a quarter people (and growing) with a demographic dividend in its favour; its established democratic credentials; a significant capability in information technology; a large reservoir of scientific talent including in space technology; acknowledged management expertise; proven military capability; and the large market for consumer goods and services. Hence, in addressing India's defence requirements, there is no place for the "guns versus butter" debate. India requires both "guns' and "butter"; in fact the latter will be seriously jeopardised if the former is not in place.

Manpower Perspective

The second aspect that needs to be made in the particular context of defence manpower (which term for the purpose of this paper includes women), is that as we move forward in the 21st Century, with all the promise of technological revolutions in modern warfare, there are some who suggest that the nature of military leadership, and the way military personnel are asked to respond, will need to change. They believe that technological innovation will replace military leadership and the individual as the driving force behind military effectiveness. According to them, the technological evolution engenders a fundamental change in human nature; that the old days of leading by 'dash and bravado' are over; that the 'specialist' will replace the 'warrior' in overseeing and executing the conduct of military combat operations. The abiding truth is however, that wars will always be won by men (and women); weapons may change, but not human nature. If human nature remains the same despite technological advances, then motivating human beings and getting the appropriate response from them, must also have an enduring quality. The fundamental patterns of behaviour adopted by hunting apes millions of years ago still shine through the affairs of modern man. We did not evolve to live in huge conglomerations of tens of thousands of individuals. Our basic behaviour is still in many ways designed to operate in the hunting group, or as part of a tribe limited to hundreds—not thousands—of members. Loyalty to, and dependence on, the hunting group, and subsequently the tribe, are expressed in the military as loyalty to the platoon, the company, and the battalion or the regiment; the ship; the squadron. That being so, the effectiveness of the military will always depend on the quality of the personnel who form part of it. This aspect assumes added importance in the Indian scenario as, for many years to come, manning the LoC in J&K including the Actual Ground Position Line (AGPL) in the Glaciers area, the Line of Actual Control (LoAC) in Ladakh and Arunachal Pradesh, and the borders in the West and North, translates into manpower intensive deployment. Hence, the importance of adequately addressing this basic pillar of the Indian defence establishment, in order to rectify shortcomings that exist, and make it stronger and more responsive to the increasing demands that are likely to be placed on it. Equally, the compelling need to ensure security of the sea lanes of communication in the Indian Ocean Region (IOR) for trade and commerce, calls for the maintenance of a credible surface and sub-surface maritime capability.

Government Expenditure on Manpower

The impact of defence manpower costs on government expenditure is the subject of debate and analysis in every country from time to time in the efforts to manage security requirements within acceptable financial outlays. India is no exception, though in our case the subject assumes greater relevance in context of the need to maintain a relatively large military within the constraints of limited financial resources. The expenditure on pay and allowances in the Budget Estimates for 2013-14 is apparently about 66 per cent of the revenue budget and about 38 per cent of the total defence budget. Add to this the costs of food and clothing for the personnel, accommodation and related costs, personal equipment, transportation, etc. Though, expenditure on defence pensions (which apparently works out to almost three quarters of the pay and allowances outlay in the case of the Army), is not included within the Defence Budget, it has to met from the overall financial resources available to the Government of India. Hence, the imperative need to prune expenditure to the extent feasible, by addressing the important aspect of Defence Manpower.

It is possibly appropriate at this stage to clarify that nothing in the analysis that follows or the recommendations made, are original. Almost every recommendation in this paper has been made at one time or another in the last few decades or more. However, given the indifference (or unwillingness) of the political leadership to address matters military, the resistance of sections in the civilian bureaucracy to giving the military-man his due, and the unforgivable self-centred approach of sections of the military leadership, requisite action has not been initiated and pursued. Leaving us with the uncomfortable dilemma of making the same points all over again in the hope that some day, "the Sun in all its glory, may rise in the West".

Personnel Below Officer Rank (PBOR)

There can be no gainsaying the fact that the quality of manpower inducted into the Indian Armed Forces must always be maintained at the highest levels possible. To that extent, entry level educational, physical and psychological standards cannot be compromised. Equally, pay and allowances offered should, while not necessarily attempting to match levels in the corporate sector, be attractive enough to draw acceptable material. Similarly, terms and conditions of service including avenues for employment on leaving service should be attractive. As things stand, it appears that for entry at levels below officer rank, there is no serious problem, including for higher grade technical entry in the three Services. However, given the operational imperative for a youthful profile, recommendations have been made in the past for implementing an arrangement for a specified period of colour service together with an appropriate reserve liability period, for PBOR. Such an arrangement presupposes that those who complete the period of colour service are afforded the following options; subject of course, to reserve liability:

- Pursue a choice of their own; in which case the government has no further role to play, other than continuing to provide such personnel with Canteen Stores Department (CSD) facilities.

- Service upto the retirement age (of 60 or as determined from time to time) in the para-military forces, Central or State police, public sector undertakings, etc.
- Those who wish to continue and are considered fit for promotion to the ranks of non-commissioned and junior-commissioned officers should be absorbed for retention for appropriate periods after which they should be entitled to pensionary benefits, free medical treatment for themselves and families, and other facilities.

The above options are without prejudice to the avenues available to personnel below officer rank to prepare themselves for, and try for entry into, the officer ranks through the respective officer training academies by going through the appropriate selection processes.

Officer Level Entry

In so far as commissioned officers in the Armed Forces are concerned, there is need for a variation in approach. The first point that needs to be made is that the pyramid structure of the Armed Forces hierarchy imposes on the organisation the requirement to have a largely short service cadre of officers who serve for about five to ten years at the junior level of captains and majors that form the base of the structure, and then move out into other areas of employment. Complementing this is a regular cadre that provides the frame and the hierarchy. With the current scales of pay and allowances, it is probably fair to state that there are few problems of getting appropriate volunteers for entry into the regular cadre through the National Defence Academy (NDA) and direct entry at the respective Service academies. The existing shortfall of about 13,000 officers is at the level of captains and majors due to the fact that the establishment has not been able to attract the youth of the country into the short service category in adequate numbers. This is unsurprising as the terms and conditions are rather unattractive to an aspiring youngster. The question the "powers-that-be" should ask themselves is: why should a bright young person who has just graduated from college at the age of 22 or so, aspiring to do well for himself or herself, join the ranks of short service commissioned officers in the Indian Armed Forces, serve for five or 10 years, quite often under inhospitable conditions, and then, at the age of 27 or 32, set out all over again to look for a place in the highly competitive market place where there is already so much unemployment? *The answer to this rather depressing outlook lies in providing those, who after completing the terms of short service engagement are interested, with scope for lateral movement into the central and state government services including the para-military, central and state police forces, public sector undertakings, and others with an opportunity to obtain desired skills through management courses or information technology courses, etc, at government expense either before leaving the Service or after.* Needless to say, those who are interested in continuing in the Service, should be screened for the purpose and given regular commissions provided they qualify.

The measures suggested in preceding paragraphs both for PBOR and for commissioned officers, if implemented, will not only ensure a youthful profile in the Services, and significantly reduce the Government's pension liability, but make available to the wider community in the country, well-disciplined, well-trained and physically and mentally fit personnel with a capacity to deal with difficult and dangerous situations when the need arises. This will be of particular value in terms of trained manpower to the para-military and police forces dealing with insurgency and left wing extremism.

Lateral Induction

In this context, it is important to stress that the recommendation made in the Group of Ministers' Report of February 2001 based on the Kargil Review Committee (KRC) Report, for the lateral induction of trained Armed Forces personnel into State Police, Central Police Forces and Para Military Forces (PMF) like the Assam Rifles, SSB and the Coast Guard should be pursued with some vigour. The Thirty Second Report of the Standing Committee on Defence that was presented to the Lok Sabha on December 18, 2008 and laid in the Rajya Sabha the same day, had stressed the need for immediate implementation of the recommendation for "lateral movement" of Armed Forces personnel into the para military, central and state police forces. It went on to state that implementation had been stalled over the years by vested interests that should not be allowed to call the shots any longer and that its implementation will not only bring in "*some Armed Forces ethos and culture into the police forces, but also conserve state resources on training. Laterally inducted Armed Forces personnel will benefit by serving longer and in many cases within their own state. The Armed Forces will benefit significantly by retaining a younger age profile*". The Committee had further stated that the members are not satisfied with the replies given by the Ministry of Defence (MoD) that the issue of lateral entry of Armed Forces personnel remains contentious and intractable due to factors relating to fixation of inter-se seniority and disparity of pay and allowances between transfers vis-à-vis original inductees in the Central Para Military Forces. Although, the Working Group constituted by the Government for the purpose had submitted its report way back in March, 2002, the Committee found it distressing that the issues remain unresolved and precious time had been lost in deliberations without arriving at a final decision. Considering the fact that even Sixth Central Pay Commission, in their report, had made recommendations for a scheme of lateral transfer of defence personnel to Central Police Organisations etc., the Committee had tried to impress upon the Government to make concerted efforts to arrive at positive conclusions without any further loss of time. The Committee also found it rather strange that the MoD had termed induction of Ex-Servicemen in the Central Para Military Forces as a complex issue. In the light of the fact that retirement age in Central Police Forces is higher than that in the Armed Forces. The Committee expressed its inability to comprehend the plea then put forth by the Ministry that Central Armed Police Forces (CAPF) are also experiencing adverse fall out of higher age profile in the case of large number of battalions raised in recent years. Astonishingly, the Ministry had also tried to explain away that there are certain other factors like no reservation for SC, ST, and OBCs in the Army which has constitutional implications; need to modify recruitment rules; promotion avenues of CPF personnel etc., which need to be considered for coming to a decision. The Committee was not inclined to accept the reasons as convincing enough for the delay in settling this issue and felt that rather than finding excuses, the Government should examine this issue in its entirety and take concrete steps in the right direction in a time bound manner.

Misperceptions and Myths

At this stage it may be useful to dispel a couple of misperceptions or myths about the quality of personnel in the Indian Armed Forces in some sections of the strategic community including, unfortunately, some elements in the senior military leadership. That the personnel entering the Indian Armed Forces in recent years do not match the quality that was forthcoming in the years gone by.

Let us first deal with the personnel below officer. The author will attempt to do so in context of his own experience in the Indian Army that he joined in the mid 1950s; and that too the infantry. It cannot be denied that in those days the large percentage of the rank and file were drawn from the rural countryside (as is so even today), and relatively illiterate, some having dropped out of school at class two or three level. A composite bunch of individuals who followed our commands and instructions without question or the slightest disinclination. They reposed complete trust in the officer class, their commanders, in peace time and in war. In recent years, the intake into the rank and file even in the infantry, is at an education level of at least class ten; that is high school; some are even graduates. With their exposure to the ubiquitous print and electronic media on a more or less daily basis, and the capacity to communicate instantly with friends and relatives through the mobile telephone, the jawan of today is a person conscious of his rights and privileges, who needs to be convinced that his commanders are worthy of his trust, confidence and unquestioning obedience in operational situations. And, I dare say, rightly so. This of course requires a quality of leadership at the officer level well above that our generation was required to provide.

Which leads on to discussion pertaining to the commissioned officers of the Indian Armed Forces. There is often much comment by retired senior officers, as also unfortunately by some senior serving military officers, about the quality of officer material entering the Indian Armed Forces today. That the "cream of youth" are not joining the forces; that a large number of entrants are the offspring of junior commissioned officers; or from the less privileged sections of society; and so on. This sort of comment is not only extremely patronising but downright unforgivable for a number of reasons. As mentioned earlier, the author entered the Indian Military Academy (IMA) in the then "Direct Entry" category while studying for a Bachelor of Science (BSc) degree at St Xavier's College in Mumbai (recently in the news for quite the wrong reasons). One thing that can be stated clearly based on his experience is that the Armed Forces were not the preferred choice of the so-called "cream of the youth" even at that time; the corporate world was. Service as a commissioned officer in the Indian Armed Forces was the preferred choice of those looking for adventure, outdoor activity and service to the Nation. The Indian Armed Forces then, as today, offer a quality of life that is quite unique, provided one is prepared for the difficult and sometimes unsettled conditions of service. In so far as the family background of the entrants is concerned, one can only agonise over the fact that even 67 years after Independence and exposure to global trends, many of our thoughts and actions indicate adherence to age old feudal attitudes. It should be a matter of great satisfaction to all of us that the offspring of less privileged sections of our society are availing of the educational opportunities afforded to them and are competing on equal terms with counterparts from the so-called privileged sections to secure entry into institutions like the Armed Forces academies and become commissioned officers in command of troops. It is indeed a matter of great pride that one can state today without fear of contradiction, that the young officers of the Armed Forces, irrespective of their origins, place their lives on the line by leading from the front, as always; most recently proved by their performance during the Kargil conflict; and continue to do so in the conduct of operations on the LoC in J&K and in counter-insurgency operations.

Selective Compulsory Military Service

For a country like India with its huge population, it makes little sense to have universal compulsory national service in the military. There is in fact no shortage of aspirants for entry at the level of PBOR. Even so, in making a case for induction of quality personnel into the military and to promote better understanding of matters military within the governing establishment, it may be appropriate to suggest that we put in place institutional arrangements for ensuring that all entry into Central and State Government employment including into public sector undertakings, be made contingent on two/three years of compulsory service in the Armed Forces; a "***selective compulsory military service***" concept. This recommendation should apply for induction of personnel into the IAS, IFS, IPS, etc, as well as entry at lower levels including into the state police, CPOs, the para-military and public sector undertakings. Such a measure will not only address the shortage of officers in units of the Armed Forces at the junior level but also ensure ready availability of trained manpower in civilian establishments to deal with internal security situations that often call for coordinated 'muscular' response.

Professionalism of the Indian Armed Forces: Achieved Through High Quality Training

The author can state without fear of contradiction that *the professional standards of personnel of the Indian Armed Forces match the best in the world.* We may not match some countries of the developed world in terms of the quality of weapons and equipment. But *our soldiers, sailors and airmen are 'second to none' in terms of individual and collective military professionalism.* The author's credentials for making such a categorical statement stems from the fact that he has seen many militaries around the world: having done the Staff College course in Australia as a young major; was part of an Indian Army training team in Iraq as a lieutenant colonel; served as Military Adviser at the High Commission of India in the United Kingdom as a brigadier; and, as the first Force Commander and Head of Mission of the United Nations forces in the former Yugoslavia in the rank of lieutenant general, in which capacity, he had the honour and privilege of having under his command, uniformed personnel from 34 countries of the world, besides civilian personnel from many more.

It is important to recognise that these high standards of professionalism are the result of many factors, such as:

- Proper screening of prospective candidates for entry into the Armed Forces at PBOR levels; in terms of basic educational qualifications, minimum acceptable physical standards, mental aptitude, etc.
- Competitive written examinations for entry at officer level, followed by well-established comprehensive physical activity, group activity and psychological tests for successful candidates at selection boards manned by personnel qualified and trained for the purpose.
- Training for varying periods at training establishments and regimental/ corps training centres to prepare PBOR for the rigours of service; including where applicable, specialised training for different trades.
- Aspirants for commission as officers in the Armed Forces are put through rigorous educational and training schedules at the NDA, Officers Training Academy (OTA) (for short service) and respective Service Academies to acquire and master professional skills, and more importantly, leadership traits.

- Leadership and professional skills are honed through periodic attendance on courses conducted at various instructional establishments at varying stages of service.

The purpose of dwelling on the above aspect of professionalism is to stress that the high standards of professionalism attained by personnel of the Indian Armed Forces are the result of proper screening of personnel for entry, the top quality training imparted to recruits and cadets after induction into the forces, and the well-conceived, organised, and conducted, training courses at various stages of service. Hence, it is vital that in our efforts at reducing what may be perceived as redundant manpower, we should avoid tinkering with those training organisations and establishments that are the pillars of the high standards of professionalism the Indian Armed Forces can be proud of.

Status in Society, Izzat and Self Respect

Based on one's personal experience while in Indian Army uniform for just under four decades and out of it for the last two decades, it is possible to state with some conviction that those who choose to join the profession of arms do not do so for monetary reasons, as all are aware that this profession is not a place for 'making money' as it were. People do so because it is perceived as a honourable profession that provides a certain quality of life, a status in society with a degree of security, and an opportunity to serve the nation. Hence, after joining the Armed Forces, they seek that status in society the profession merits, and the "Izzat" and self respect that goes with it. There is little doubt that the people at large treat personnel from the Indian Armed Forces with great respect and admiration; not only in times of war or natural disasters, but also in the normal course. The same does not however apply to the political leadership and sections of the civilian bureaucracy including the police. The political leadership is generally indifferent except for the occasional platitudes. And the civilian bureaucracy has unfortunately, over the years, done its utmost to degrade the status of personnel of the Armed Forces in one way or another to the extent that the "Izzat" and self-respect the military-man and his kin value have been seriously dented. Some of the aspects that merit the attention of the establishment in this regard, particularly at district administration level including police, are as follows: facilitation of the process of admission of children of Servicemen to schools and other educational institutions of their choice; assistance of local authorities to the families of Servicemen in the resolution of disputes particularly pertaining to land wrongfully taken over in villages; medical attention of families where military facilities are not easily accessible; care of war widows, orphans, battle casualties, ex-Servicemen, etc. *If the Indian Armed Forces are to retain the high standards of professionalism that are recognised and respected by the international community and by the Indian people at large, a concerted effort will need to be made to restore to the military-man the status in society, "Izzat" and self-respect the profession of arms merits. Only then will the quality of intake and its retention be credible and worthy of the nation and its people. This aspect is without doubt as important, if not more so, than the aspect of pay and allowances.*

Women in the Armed Forces

It is intriguing that all discussion in recent years on the subject of induction of women in the Indian Armed Forces and an appropriate role for them has centred on their induction as commissioned officers. In context of the theme of this paper, the need to widen the base of quality material available to the Armed Forces, as also to meet the growing social demand for gender equality, it is time that recruitment of PBOR be opened up for women who are interested in joining the forces. Till there is unanimity, or at least some consensus, on whether or not, women should also perform combat related tasks, their induction could be encouraged in all other trades and categories on the same terms as their male counterparts.

In so far as the ranks of commissioned officers are concerned, it is time that the age-old chauvinistic attitudes are set aside and induction in this category be opened up for women on the same terms and conditions as their male counterparts. This means affording women the scope for entry into the regular cadre of commissioned officers through the NDA and respective Service Academies, as also the scope to be considered for regular commission on completing short service terms.

While on the subject of women in the Armed Forces it may be useful to make a point that is perhaps outside the specific scope of this paper, but is relevant in the overall context of defence manpower management; at least within the Indian Army. In the last couple of decades, the role of wives of senior officers at various levels of command as part of the ubiquitous Army Wives Welfare Association (AWWA) has assumed proportions that are not necessarily in total conformity with the customs and traditions of the Service and are probably beginning to have adverse effects at lower levels. *Welfare of personnel and their families has always been, and must continue to be a "command" responsibility; that of commanders at all levels. This cannot and must not be delegated to, or allowed to be assumed by, individuals who are not bound by the Army, Navy and Air Force Acts, and the Defence Services Regulations. Army wives no doubt have a role to play at unit and formation level, but this role needs to be undertaken within the time-tested norms of complementing the command functions, and NOT assuming them.*

Training and Logistics: Scope for Jointness and Outsourcing

As mentioned earlier, training is one of the essential components of the organisational programme that ensures aspirants (the "raw material") seeking careers in the Armed Forces are properly moulded, and mentally, physically, psychologically and professionally equipped, to become assets that are capable of producing the desired results for the country when called upon to do so; namely, in time of war or in aid to civil authorities including disaster relief. This is without doubt being done by the plethora of training establishments that have been set up for the purpose. However, there is little doubt that, over the years, there has been much duplication, triplication and possibly more, in terms of basic training of personnel for various trades that have much in common between the three Services, as also the Coast Guard and the Para Military forces; as for example, drivers, clerks, cooks, mechanics, signallers, and many other such trades. It is no doubt possible to rationalise the existing establishments into joint ones that can meet the requirement thus saving on manpower. Such rationalisation will also contribute towards achieving a greater degree of "jointness" that will go a long way in promoting this philosophy in the wider arena. There is also no doubt considerable scope for outsourcing certain general aspects of trade training to recognised civilian institutions thus saving on manpower and infra-structure costs.

Similarly, there is much scope for jointness in logistics; namely, in the areas of provisioning of rations, clothing, vehicles and common items of equipment. Equally there is a strong case for outsourcing many of the logistics functions to civilian agencies that have well established infra-structure to meet the requirements. This aspect would have been dealt with in a separate chapter in detail. But the point that merits emphasis is that efforts for implementation of such a philosophy of jointness and outsourcing of some aspects to civilian agencies both in the fields of training and logistics will encounter determined resistance from vested interests of "empires" that have been built up over the years. "Empires" that will face dis-integration and dissolution should such a philosophy be put in place. It will therefore need bold decision making and equally determined implementation measures.

Rashtriya Rifles

As the then Additional Director General Military Operations (DGMO) in 1990, the author was part of the process of drafting the first Cabinet Committee on Political Affairs (CCPA) paper on the subject of formation of the Rashtriya Rifles, and later in 1994 was the Deputy Chief of the Army Staff when the force commenced raising after the issue of Government of India executive orders to the effect. The concept on which the raising of the force was premised was that it would be a para-military force like the Assam Rifles which would undertake counter-insurgency operations thus releasing regular Army units from that commitment, and in times of war, provide security of the lines of communication in insurgency affected areas. In the last two decades, the Rashtriya Rifles has developed into a force of over 65,000 personnel that has more than fulfilled the tasks it was intended to perform. When the concept was evolved and accepted, it was intended that the force would be manned by personnel comprising a percentage of regular Army volunteers on deputation, ex-servicemen and lateral inductees from various para-military forces and central police organisations, and that the expenditure on pay and allowances of personnel, equipment, maintenance, transport costs, etc. would be borne by the Ministry of Home Affairs (MHA).

However, for various reasons, this has not happened, and the force as it exists today, comprises only regular Army personnel primarily from the Infantry, supplemented by volunteers from other arms and services, who benefit from operational experience they would not otherwise be exposed to. Personnel from the regular Army, both at the level of commissioned officers and PBOR, are sent on deputation to the Rashtriya Rifles for periods ranging from two to three years. Such personnel are entitled to an attractive deputation allowance that is well received and serves as an incentive for service under adverse conditions.

Unfortunately, a Government of India decision taken some time back that all expenditure on the Rashtriya Rifles would be borne by the MHA has not yet been implemented, apparently due to bureaucratic manipulation or lethargy, or both. It is time that the decision is implemented with immediate effect thus removing the burden on the defence budget.

Summary of Recommendations

The various recommendations made in preceding pages on rationalisation of defence manpower to meet the security requirements of the country and attempting to prune expenditure in this regard to the extent feasible, including on pensions for defence personnel, are summarised as follows:

- Given India's security commitments and the emerging regional and global scenario there is no scope for a "guns versus butter" debate; in order to ensure "butter" for its large population, India requires "guns" also.
- Notwithstanding all the technological advancements in weapons and equipment, victory in war will continue to depend on the "individual"; hence the importance of defence manpower including top quality military leadership, cannot be discounted.
- The commitments on the LoC in J&K including the Actual Ground Position Line (AGPL) in the Glaciers area, the LoAC in Ladakh and Arunachal Pradesh, and the borders in the West and North, call for manpower intensive deployment. Equally, the compelling need to ensure

security of the sea lanes of communication in the IOR for trade and commerce, calls for the maintenance of a credible surface and sub-surface maritime capability.

- The existing parameters for the induction of quality personnel into the Armed Forces, namely the educational standards for entry, physical fitness levels and aptitude or psychological tests must continue; there should not be any dilution in this regard. Together with this, the prevailing high standards of professionalism in the Indian Armed Forces must be maintained by imparting top quality training to the inductees at PBOR and officer level, at the various training establishments and academies.
- The imperative need for putting in place attractive avenues of employment for those personnel who are required to leave and desire to do so after completion of the laid down terms of 'colour' service for PBOR, and short service commission at officer level, must be immediately addressed if the 'youthful' profile of the Armed Forces is to be ensured and quality of intake is to be retained at the desired level. In this context the long-standing recommendation of lateral induction of Armed Forces personnel into the central and state civil services, para-military forces, central and state police, and public sector undertakings, etc must be implemented without further procrastination. This aspect had been included in the recommendations made in the Group of Ministers' Report of 2001 and has been repeatedly reiterated by the Parliamentary Standing Committee on Defence, as also by the Sixth Pay Commission.
- This may be an appropriate time to put in place institutional arrangements for ensuring that all entry into Central and State Government employment including into public sector undertakings, be made contingent on two/three years of compulsory military service in the Armed Forces; *a "selective compulsory military service"* concept. To include personnel seeking entry into the IAS, IFS, IPS, etc, as well as entry at lower levels including into the state police, CPOs, the para-military and Public Sector Undertakings (PSUs). Such a measure will not only appropriately address the shortage of officers in units of the Armed Forces at the junior level but also provide much needed knowledge on matters military to administrators and police, and ensure the availability of trained manpower in civilian establishments that are required to deal with internal security situations that often call for coordinated 'muscular' response.
- In our efforts at reducing what may be perceived as redundant manpower, it is vitally important that we avoid tinkering with those training organisations and establishments that are the pillars of the high standards of professionalism the Indian Armed Forces can be proud of.

- If the Indian Armed Forces are to retain the high standards of professionalism that are recognised and respected by the international community and by the Indian people at large, a concerted effort must be made to restore to the military-man the status in society, "Izzat" and self-respect the profession of arms merits. Only then will the quality of intake and its retention be credible and worthy of the nation and its people. This aspect is without doubt as important, if not more so, than the aspect of pay and allowances.
- Induction of women at all levels in the Indian Armed Forces, including at levels below officer rank, should be encouraged on the same terms and conditions as for their male counterparts. Till there is some consensus on the desirability or otherwise of having women in combat roles, their induction may be restricted to trades and categories in non-combat roles.
- Welfare of personnel and their families has always been, and must continue to remain a "command" responsibility; that of commanders at all levels. This cannot and must not be delegated to, or allowed to be assumed by, individuals who are not bound by the Army, Navy and Air Force Acts, and the Defence Services Regulations (DSR). Army wives no doubt have a role to play at unit and formation level, but this role needs to be undertaken within the time-tested norms of complementing the command functions, and NOT assuming them.
- Jointness and outsourcing in some areas of training, and in the field of logistics, needs to be addressed and implemented on priority. Resistance from vested interest must be ruthlessly dealt with.
- The Rashtriya Rifles should be designated as a para-military force under the MHA which should bear all expenditure on pay and allowances of defence personnel on deputation, as also on weapons and equipment, their maintenance costs, and all other associated costs such as on provisions, clothing, transportation, etc. No further delay in implementation should be permitted.

14

Logistics and Supply Chain Management

Pramod Vasant Athawale

Background

'Military Logistics' covers a far wider scope of functions as compared to the term's interpretation in the civil world. At the outset, it is essential to understand this fact to be able to carry out a purposeful analysis for suggesting reforms. It is important to know that logistics in civil usually implies actions pertaining and limited to Supply Chain Management (SCM), unlike a whole array of functions in the military. The scope of logistics in the military includes design, development, acquisition, maintenance, modification, upgrade, storage, distribution and disposal. Most military leadership may hesitate to agree that everything outside actual operations, Op plans (strategy & tactics) and Op training is a part of logistical functions.

> *"I am tempted to make a slightly exaggerated statement that logistics is all of war-making except shooting guns, releasing bombs and firing the torpedoes."*
> *—Adm Lynde D. McCormick, US Navy*

It is therefore apt that logistics and SCM, which is sometimes an afterthought in military strategies and acquisitions, has been included as a separate chapter within this treatise. In consonance with Adm McCormick, I would go further to say that logistics and supply chain issues are at the core of a combat force; without these no analysis can ever be comprehensive.

One common factor among all proposed reforms is that the suggestions are based predominantly on either of the two aspects, viz. technological solutions or organisational structural changes. The human aspect usually gets buried under the pile of bureaucratic procedures and more rules defined as a part of reforms.

Consequently, the big picture conceived by the committee for reforms gets diffused before moving on to implementation stage.

> *"We cannot solve our problems by the same level of thinking that created them."*
>
> —***Albert Einstein***

The fact that many a reform has failed to produce the intended outcome need not deter us from continuing the endeavour. However, treading the beaten track is sure to disappoint. Instead of following a strictly formal approach of listing out inconsistencies, a different approach has therefore been attempted here. The following popular methods have to be avoided:

(a) The obsession of subdividing a system in an attempt to optimise parts with a belief that the system shall consequently improve.
(b) Going through the same process over and over again hoping to find a different (expected) answer this time.

Think Systemic

The theme of this book is systemic. An attempt at systemic treading through various elements at higher levels including planning, budgeting, acquisition, Research and development (R&D) and industry is therefore a must. Systemic thinking and systems approach bring to mind two of the most valuable works, '*Fifth Discipline*' *by Peter Senge*[1] and '*Theory of Constraints*' *by E.U. Goldratt.*[2] I will base most of my thoughts on these two concepts. It will be useful to remember the following precepts.

(a) *Don't optimise parts,* implement global measures.
(b) *Areas of maximum leverage are often obscure*—identification is important.
(c) *Organisation Structure determines behaviour*—Field level constraints often point to causes at policy level.
(d) *Cause and Effect* are *often not related in time* and *space.*
(e) *There is no blame—people are good, our assumptions are bad.*

The reader may need a little introduction to Theory of Constraints. Elliyahu M. Goldratt developed the 'Theory of Constraints (TOC)' as a management and improvement philosophy. His books including The Goal,[3] The Goal II—It's Not Luck[4] have illustrated the philosophy in an interesting story like style. The simplicity of approach in problem solving is the defining feature of TOC.

At the root of the TOC thinking process lies a conflict resolution approach called *Evaporating Cloud* (of conflict). The systemic cloud is drawn as shown in Fig. 1 to represent real life situations and solving conflict surrounding a given problem. The prerequisite is an objective (block **A**), which is a positive systemic

Figure 1: The Cloud

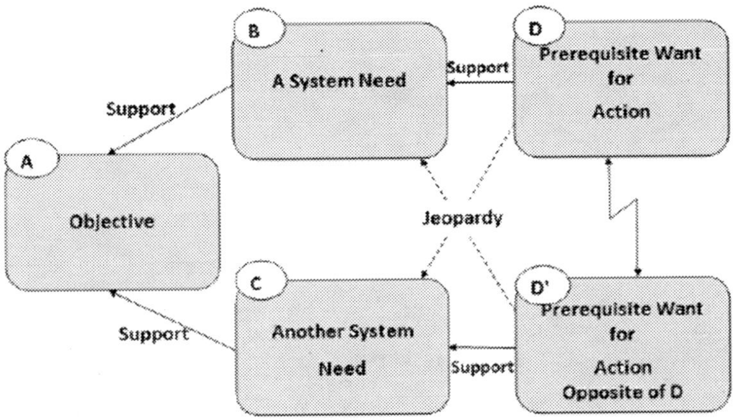

objective. **B** and **C** are needs; both are positive and supportive of the objective. The actions and wants at **D** and **D'** individually supporting the needs at **B** and C respectively are, however, conflicting with each other and cannot exist together. Also that **D** jeopardises the need at **C** while **D'** jeopardises the need at **B**; this is what makes the conflict really tight. The TOC paradigm that ***people are all good; only our assumptions are bad***—brings out the power of conflict resolution. The assumptions are verbalised for each of the links AB, BD, AC, CD', D'B and DC as shown below:

- In order to have **A**, we must have the requirement **B** because *<reason 1>*
  -
  -
  In order to have **A**, we must have the requirement **B** because *<reason m>*
- And similar verbalisation for links **AC, BD**, and **CD'**.
  Then
- If action **D** is carried out then we cannot get C because *<reason 1>*
  -
  -
  If action **D** is carried out then we cannot get C because *<reason r>*
- And similar verbalisation for the link **D'B.**

Lieutenant's Cloud. We will use the evaporating clouds method to visualise conflicts in various situations. Detailed verbalisation to validate or invalidate assumptions will however be left out of this work. Kelvyn Youngman [5] has called the conflict shown here in Fig. 2 as '*The Lieutenant's Cloud*'. Here the lieutenant wishes to perform a task but is stopped by a rule which prohibits him. At **D** is a rule that we have, but we don't want. And at **D'** is an action that we cannot, but do wish to take. It is quite amazing then that there is something negative in

Figure 2: The Lieutenant's Cloud

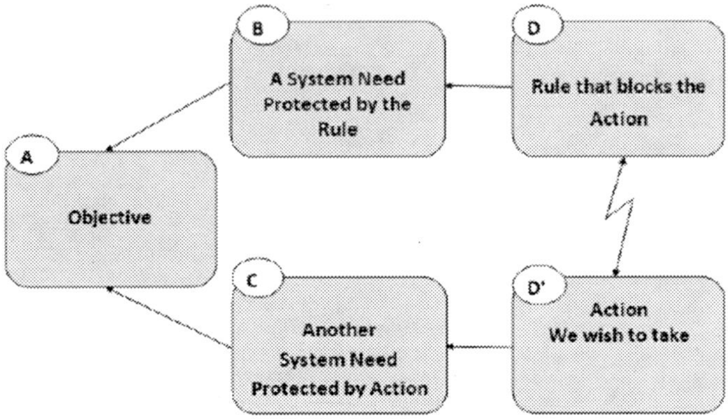

D, but we carry on suffering from it because that also satisfies a positive need (or so we feel) towards the achievement of the *Goal.* At the same time it is intriguing that knowing well about the good outcome of a positive change or action in **D'**, we continue to be paralysed and fail to change. The result is a status quo because of our fear that if we take action at **D'** (and change) then it will jeopardise the need at **B** and the *Goal.* It is here that verbalisation of our assumptions question and validates beliefs. In some cases where an argument is only vaguely perceived can be clearly understood and strengthened through this process.

> *"Systemic thinking is a difficult task in the bureaucratic environment where there is a strong drive to hold on to turf and protect domains."*
>
> *—Jeremy Rifkin*

What's Military Logistics: Whose Job is It?

We had acknowledged a far wider scope of military logistics compared to its civil counterpart. Besides design, development, acquisition, maintenance, modification, upgrade, storage, distribution and disposal of material, in fact, logistics in the context of military also includes functions related to infrastructure, healthcare and personnel. No wonder the realisation that besides war fighting strategy and tactics, every other function could be termed as logistics gives an uncomfortable feeling to some—so aptly expressed as follows:

> *"In peace, Generals stride confidently and can invade a world simply by sweeping their hands grandly over a map. In war they must stride more slowly .... Generals fear logisticians in war, Generals try to forget logisticians in peace."*
>
> ***—Anonymous***

Logistics holistically connecting with operations can be represented as shown in Fig. 3. At this stage let us take a look at the genesis of the logistics functions and

Figure 3

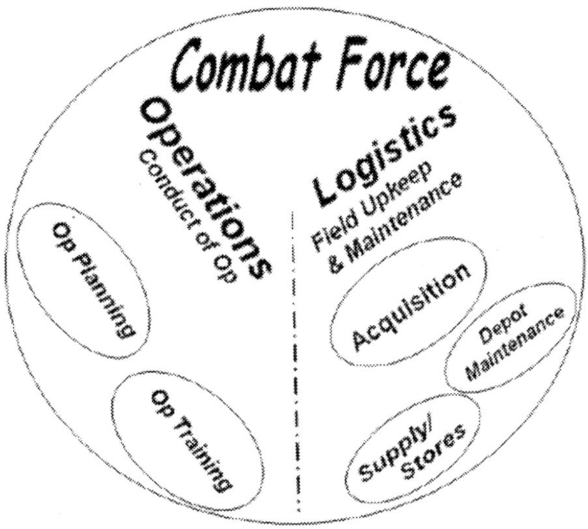

cadres that perform these. Army, Navy and Air Force inherited different legacies at independence and have thence continued to evolve somewhat differently in spite of a common Indian military character. However, all the three services have the roots of what is today called logistics, in the ordnance/supply/stores/equipment cadres somewhat owning similar functional responsibilities.

Ordnance in the Army was reorganised in the early 20th century into three separate departments viz. factories, stores and inspection, all under the Director General of Ordnance. In due course, through the war and later in independent India, the manufacture of stores and munitions by Ordnance Factories moved under civilian control and the Quality Assurance (QA) (beginning as inspection) raised an Army of its own with a huge department, leaving primarily the stores function alone under the control of Army Ordnance Corps (AOC). Talk of logistics today and the first mention is about Ordnance Corps, although these functions are squarely placed on Director General OP Logistics (DG OL), Adjutant General (AG), Quarter Master General (QMG) and Master General Ordnance (MGO). Incidentally, the tri-service tasks performed by Director General Armed Forces Medical Services (DGAFMS) and Engineer-in-Chief (E-in-C) for healthcare and civil works respectively are also logistics functions. Eventually the responsibility of logistics as a comprehensive military function is undertaken together by many while the Ordnance man is seen as the logistician of the Army.

Indian Navy had its Directorate of Stores formed out of Directorate of Supplies shortly after independence. This was renamed as Directorate of Logistics Support (DLS) in early seventies. The Supply & Secretariat branch was first merged with the Executive branch before a specialist Logistics cadre was created in the Executive branch in 1989. The logistics function for stores (victualing, clothing, etc.);

personnel administration and material management are performed under different heads at the top management. However, the working level base is provided by the logistics branch officers who specialise besides personnel administration, primarily in stores and supply.

Among Indian Armed Forces, the *Air Force* is arguably credited with having the most well integrated logistics system. Right at the birth of the Air Force, one of the first six officers commissioned was in the Equipment branch, albeit by chance because he could not qualify as a pilot for reasons of shorter leg length. Keeping abreast with global trends in the seventies, the branch was renamed 'Logistics', notwithstanding the fact that its functional purview remained the same. With technological sophistication and the growth of the Air Force, ever so gradually, the logistics responsibility has increasingly been undertaken by the engineers while pilots focus on sophisticated flying/operational functions.

The field logistics can be attended to only by those close to the fleet—the combat men. There has, however, been a distinction between pilots and all other combat men in terms of the training requirements for individual skills. Towards development and maintenance of individual skill, till the levels of commanding a squadron, the pilot has to devote huge time and effort, which are unmatched by any other combatant. Therefore, a pilot-engineer arrangement has evolved best described by "*engineer getting on the cockpit ladder as the pilot comes off it*". The buddy engineer takes on all responsibilities ranging from transportation of squadron men/material and general upkeep of aircraft & systems, to the highest levels of maintenance. Therefore, corresponding to the operations men from the Army and Navy, here is a duo in the Air Force that together attends to the field logistics and logistical planning while a specific entity looks after the storage and supply support needs.

The Global View

Semantics do play an important role. Logistics as the title name for a set of people without adequate authority, ownership and consequent responsibility for comprehensive logistic management can get confusing. This can lead to inappropriate commitments within and inter services matters. In international cooperation and joint exercises, we have had experiences where logistics exchange programmes represented from our side by supply/stores personnel have been found to be woefully inadequate to deal with the holistic fleet support issues including life cycle maintenance.

How does the world understand the terms *'logistics'* and *'logisticians'*? It may be good to maintain that we go by our original thinking and not get tempted to copy models. However, more damaging it is when we end up adopting parts without understanding the whole concept. Let us see the top level of understanding of the terms logistics, logisticians and globally held expectations.

UK. The available, open literature indicates that UK had a Defence Logistics Organisation (DLO), which maintained and upgraded military equipment and coordinated its storage and distribution. UK Ministry of Defence (MoD) also had an executive agency named Defence Procurement Agency (DPA), which was responsible for acquisition of material, equipment and services for British armed forces. Both these merged together in 2007 to form a new organisation called Defence Equipment and Support, whose chief is called Chief of Defence Material (CDM). Under the purview of CDM, the three chiefs of material for services (Fleet, Land and Air) function besides other branches for resources. Three main points emerge:

(a) The interpretation of logistics is comprehensive, ranging from maintenance and upgrade extending to storage and distribution.
(b) Acquisition and maintenance/logistics go hand in hand.
(c) Integration at the highest level is vital.

USA: The US Department of Defence (DoD) has three Departments, one each for Army, Navy and Air Force. Among many agencies under the DoD, one is Defence Logistics Agency (DLA), which provides supplies to military services. Each of the three departments (Army, Navy and Air Force) for itself has a Command for logistics. While the Navy has it called '*Naval Supply Systems* Command' Army and Air Force have these named as Material Commands. A look at one of these would be of interest here. The Air Force Material Command (AFMC) was created in 1992 by reintegrating the two earlier split up Commands, Air Force Logistics Command (AFLC) and Air Force Systems Command (AFSC). The Systems Command component provided for engineering and research labs, flight test & evaluation centres, and acquisition management for all Air Force requirements. The Logistics Command component was for maintenance/overhaul, upgrades, repairs, storage, supply chain and disposal (including scientific research before retirement). The Systems Command's functions of '*Research & Development and Acquisitions*' were thus integrated with the '*Logistics*' functions to provide '*cradle to grave*' oversight to all aircraft and systems. The highlights of the organisation structure are:

(a) Their structures provide for integrated function of logistics.
(b) The term Logistics is neither interpreted nor semantically tagged with the elements dealing with only storage/supply/distribution—it means holistic support.
(c) The structures are well integrated at the highest levels of the organisation also.

The Services' Common Precept

In comparison to the global affairs and understanding, we may now appreciate the muddle that our services are in. Some of the following problems are of concern:

(a) The semantic confusion created by adoption of the name *logistics* for a smaller part function (as in Navy and Air Force).
(b) Vertical isolation among different elements contributing towards comprehensive logistics.
(c) Structural inefficacy caused by inadequate authority with the elements ultimately responsible for the fleet upkeep.
(d) Non-integration of the function at the higher levels within forces as well as at joint services levels.

Life Cycle Management

A weapon system or sub-system life cycle goes through the phases viz. acquisition, induction, usage, expansion, major repairs/overhauls, modifications, upgrades/re-fits, obsolescence, removal from service and disposal. I have included expansion here, as this is the most common happening in our defence services. Contrary to original plans, with changing scenarios we have found merits in expanding in-use fleets of weapon systems/platforms to replace life expired/retiring inventories. Steadily rising number of SU-30 MKI after the initial acquisition is a pertinent example.

Now, what exactly is Life Cycle Management? Life Cycle Management, in logistics parlance, is usually seen from the point of view of the supplier, to deal with issues ranging from market needs through manufacture, sales, to supply chain collaboration and contract management. However, Life Cycle management from the users' perspective in military is entirely different and challenging. Compared to any civil organisation, defence forces have huge inventories in much wider variety to be managed over far greater life cycles of the order of up to 40 years or so. Then, would independent actions concerned with managing material, technology, infrastructure, storage, distribution, personnel, training, etc. in all phases of life of a weapon system be called life cycle management? Partly yes, and holistically no! We would then deal with parts only without looking at the system as a whole—and may I remind the reader *not to attempt optimisation of parts* as a solution. This is what exactly we have been doing, dealing with parts as they came, because we have not made efforts to develop a *Life Cycle Management Tool* despite immense software potential within the country, defence services own skills, and Defence Research and Development Organisation (DRDO) running several labs engaged primarily in simulation software work.

The Services have recently come up with the concept of Life Cycle Costing (LCC) for comparative evaluation of weapon systems before acquisition. Yet, none has a life cycle fleet management tool to play around with the outcome as one or more of the hundreds of parametres change. As we go along the usage of a newly acquired system, we won't even know whether the system follows the trends, which qualified it for acquisition. More worthy would be the benefits to planning as we ride on the life cycle progression curve and tweak the governing variables to optimise. The life cycle management software would be a visualisation tool that would connect different phases of transition of material or weapon systems right from acquisition to disposal thus providing a framework for logistics planning while enabling refinements in estimations for forecasting in future.

A good Life Cycle Management Tool will connect various determining factors through all phases. An example would help in appreciation. An aircraft fleet gets inducted and we wish to establish indigenous overhaul facilities for aero engines. The Manufacturer's prescribed Total Technical Life (TTL) is 2000 hrs and the Time Between Overhauls (TBO) is 1,000 hrs. It would mean that *for every 2,000 hrs of aero engines usage, we would need to carry out one overhaul.* The total aero engine usage will depend on the fleet size and the average utilisation rate per aircraft. The estimated requirement of infrastructure would be accordingly based on these calculations. Now, as is common, after confidence generation and relevant tests, the manufacturer may increase the TTL. As an example, consider a TTL raise to 3,000 hrs while keeping the TBO fixed at 1000 hrs. The arising will increase by a ratio of 2/3000:1/2000, i.e. 1.33 times. This would mean that a facility established for 50 would need to stretch to accept 66 aero engines. If, over a period, the fleet size is increased to thrice the original plan, we can see that the rise will be of the order of $1.33 \times 3 = 3.99$, i.e. 200 aero engines instead of 50.

Aero engines and major sub systems themselves have a large number of parts. Aircraft and weapon systems like ships, submarines and tanks have parts and variables that cannot be even counted easily leave alone kept track of for interdependence without a management tool. The effect of management decisions based on even a few variables, which depended on just one assumption, could go widely wrong with a small change in that assumption. The effect could be turbulent and realised late enough to take a call in absence of a Life Cycle Management Tool.

The Life Cycle Management Tool will effectively connect with *life cycle costing* besides just being an evaluation tool for use during acquisition phase. Not only for material, the tool would relate to manpower planning and training also. This can help in evaluation of the sustainment cost advantage in view of commonalities or with intended reduction in variety. Life Cycle Management Tool can also be configured to deal with a group of systems or a system of systems—it would then be delightful for the top management and finance to visualise deeper insights as they consider a few services together to derive advantages of commonality.

The Life Cycle Management Tool threads through the whole logistics arena. The development of life cycle management software is therefore a must today to envisage needs ranging from budgeting, manpower and infrastructure planning, costing, sustainment, to life extensions and replacements. All services are on their way to develop Enterprise Resource Planning (ERPs) not only to include the processes relating to demand/supply/disposal transactions, but also their state transition during field usage/maintenance, repair, overhauls and upgrades. The icing on the cake will however be when the Life Cycle Management Tools integrated with material management ERPs will provide for holistic logistics planning.

Access to a Life Cycle Management Tool would be a delight to one and all; operations, administrative and acquisition wings, finance (both at MoD and Service HQs), and eventually for the logistics management and maintenance.

The Acquisition, Maintenance and Disposal Loop

The life of material flows from the requirements conception stage leading to acquisitions into maintenance and upkeep in service leading back to conceptualising replacements alongside disposal of obsolete material. Logistics is all about working through the life cycles of material (and also men). In short, the chain of activities effectively executed to link acquisition, maintenance (including supply chain) and disposal means good logistics.

Acquisition logistics would include an assessment of all activities through the life cycle beginning with envisaging the size (numbers) of acquisition and estimation of cost. The determining factors are listed below:

- Assessment of possible indigenous content.
- Maintenance support plans, including establishment of indigenous facilities (in-house as well as with industry).
- Operational support needs and field maintenance requirements (infrastructural and material).
- Time schedules for arising needs for various maintenance requirements.
- Spares requirement depending upon all the above.
- Storage, handling and distribution requirements for main equipment/ systems/sub-systems/as well as spares.
- Requirement of personnel and training.
- Technical publications.
- Commonality of parts, support equipment, skills, and sources of supply with other systems and also user services; existent and planned in future.

This flow of life of material is often restrained because of the absence of a firm handshake between the acquisition and maintenance. Even within the maintenance phase, the inappropriately perceived *purchase specialisation* tends to further separate the two parts. The predicament can be viewed by the following two expressions:

Acquisition → Maintenance: "*We buy, you maintain*"

Maintenance ← Supply: "Tell *us the specs and we shall buy what you need*"

Each one of the above three parts intends to do good (*people are all good*), but, they end up optimising their own parts as *maintenance and upkeep* gets squeezed from the two sides. *The first of the possible reforms could be to consider merging the three functions together* as is the case within US Defence services Material Commands—*'structure determines behaviour'*.

Figure 4 shows the conflict between the responsibilities and authority of Purchase Manager and Maintenance Manager as presented in '*Deming and Goldratt*' by Lepore and Cohen.[6] The *Maintenance Manager is measured by the 'uptime'* of his production infrastructure. But, he does not have the authority to buy requisite spares. The spares are purchased by the *Purchase Manager*, who is *measured by the least expenditure on purchases.* Accordingly, he laid down following rules for purchase of *cheapest available spares.*

Figure 4: The Maintenance Manager

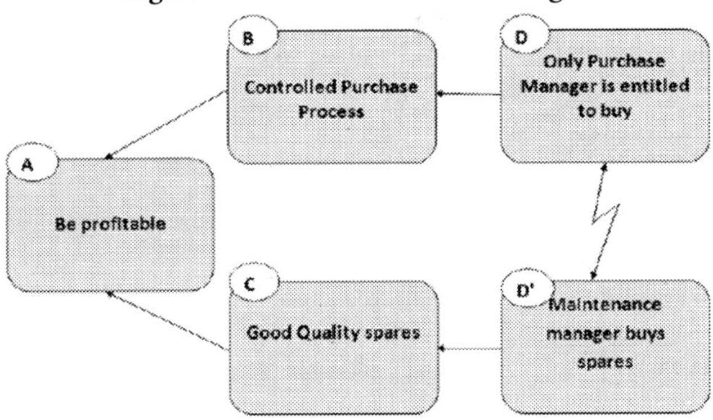

The dependencies and assumptions are verbalised as given below:

AB. In order to have the company to be profitable (**A**) we need control on the purchase process (**B**), because increased purchase costs would reduce profits.

BD. In order to have control on purchase process (**B**) we have to authorise only Purchase Manager to buy (**D**), because only he can strike the best deal following laid down norms.

BD'. If maintenance Manager buys spares (**D'**), accountability would be lost and we cannot (**jeopardy**) exercise control over purchase process (**B**).

BD'. If maintenance Manager buys spares (**D'**), he would wish to buy costly spares for his perceived reasons of reliability of spares and the control would be lost (**jeopardy**) on purchase process (**B**).

AC. In order to have the company to be profitable (**A**) we need to have good quality spares (**C**) because good spares will give us high uptime and consequently higher production and profits.

CD'. In order to have good quality spares (**C**) maintenance Manager must buy spares (**D'**) because only he can assess the quality.
CD. If Purchase Manager buys spares (**D**), we cannot (**jeopardy**) be assured of quality (**C**), because he would go for least price.

The assumptions can now be examined.

- Is it true that only purchase manager can strike the best deal?
- *If Maintenance manager* ***advises*** *Purchase manager for spares*(instead of himself buying), will the control on Purchase Process still be lost?
- If the Maintenance *Manager buys spares*, which are not the cheapest, will it really end up in costs going up such as ***to bring profits down***?

The first two questions throw up a solution that if Maintenance manager advises on spares purchase, purchase process can be controlled by the Purchase Manager. Also that good quality spares can be purchased with the intervention of the Maintenance Manager. However, even if the Maintenance Manager advises Purchase Manager for spares, the *accountability of both remains substantially diluted*, as the responsibility gets divided. The answer to this negativity can be provided by breaking the logical separation between **D** and **D'**. Now, the question (iii) also needs to be answered about profit really reducing if Maintenance Manager advises spares, which are not the cheapest. The answer therefore lies in *throughput accounting* for the system rather than local optimisation for individual performances measures. In this case especially it turns up as given below:

- Good quality spares may increase cost of spares.
- But, good quality spares will enhance uptime and reduce breakdowns.
- Good quality spares will need fewer replacements.
- Enhanced uptime will increase throughput of the system.
- With increased throughput (T), enhancement of profits can be ensured even if the operating cost (OE) goes up marginally (Profit = T – OE).

The change shown in Fig. 5 enables Maintenance Manager extend advice for spares purchase. But, he is now responsible for the throughput, which is systemic rather than uptime of machines. And in the purchase process, instead of only purchase cost being of concern, operating expense, which again is a systemic parametre, now becomes the measure. So, the *Maintenance Manager* while *advising for spares* can be made responsible for *both, maintaining high throughput as well as controlling operating expense.* The Purchase Manager moves conveniently out of the conflict.

There are several other areas for improvement besides just procurements. These are issues related to mind-set. Oversight or deliberate compromises due to budget or time constraints during acquisitions are often blamed for maintenance nightmares later on. Procedural compulsions weigh so heavily on the staff at Service HQs that conclusion of contracts itself is considered a great achievement

Figure 5

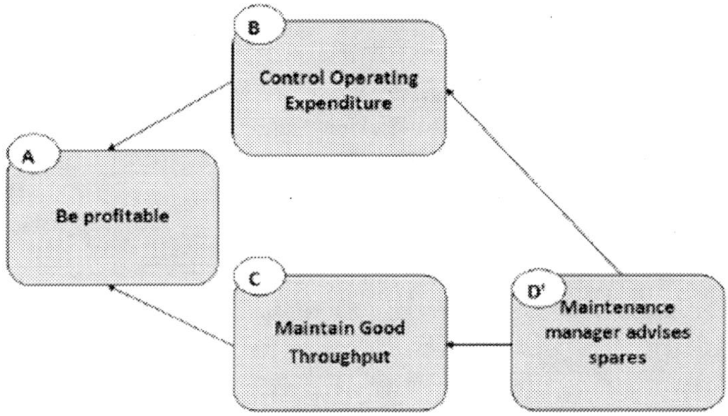

(in a struggle with the bureaucracy) in contrast with the fulfilment of holistic needs for maintenance support.

The above example has shown inappropriateness of measure of performance as *'Down time'* and *'Least expenditure'* for Maintenance and Purchase functions respectively. These measures were required to be changed to *'throughput'* and *'operating expense'*. Similarly, all elements involved in acquisition, as in all other activities, have to be measured in global units. The procurement rules are backed by great wisdom and all sincerity to provide a framework to bring transparency and avoid arbitrariness. However, one part cannot only look at procedures alone while the other focuses on operational requirements. We have to remind ourselves that the *obsession with rules* on one part of the group restrains the other from logical interpretation in favour of task execution (refer Lieutenant's Cloud). The clouds shown in Fig. 6 and Fig. 7 will serve as food for thought.

Figure 6: The Acquisition Cloud

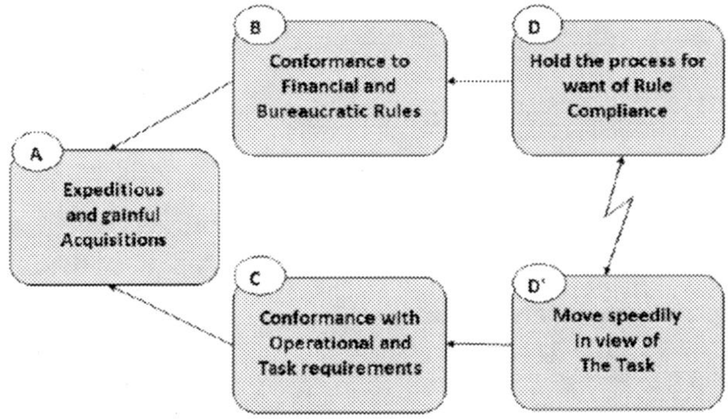

Figure 7: The Acquisition Cloud

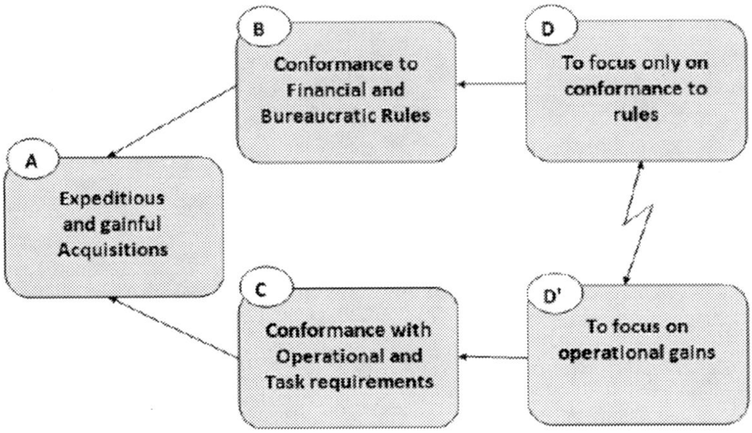

The outcome of *maintenance philosophies* depends on vital parametres like *war reserves, scales of holding spares for units/depots and repair tasks* on Defence Public Sector Undertaking *(DPSUs)* or *depots.* MTBFs are not held, repair yields vary, ageing fleets need unprecedented spares and maintenance! These situations need dynamic actions, but we get bogged down by the procedures. Theoretically, we have mechanisms to periodically review once in three years or every year, etc. But the only 10 per cent parts which severely affect are not reviewed separately—we follow procedures!

A word about disposal is extremely important. Every service suffers from enormous delays in approvals for obsolete inventories to be disposed off purely on account of procedural requirements. There are too many agencies involved; none really worth adding much value while entitled to ask questions and taking its own sweet time without accountability for delays. The cost of carrying obsolete inventories is exorbitant although not ever estimated well because of lack of a life cycle management tool. The procedures for disposals need a comprehensive review to lay down timeframes for approval within six months so that obsolete inventories can be disposed off within a period of about two years. Does the two years period seem long? Today, it takes indefinite amount of time—10 to 15 years is usual.

Provisioning and Procurement

Provisioning is the lead in activity before procurement of material to keep the inventory levels up to what is called the stockage objective. Provisioning and forecasting are activities, which are considered most challenging and therefore of great interest to all logisticians. There are two distinct elements involved here—one of forecasting the needs for a specific period, and the other of procurements of necessary quantities of material to last that period of forecast.

Forecast requirements bring back memories of grandmother days. Once a year, she got the food grains purchased. These were procured at the best prices in season, then cleaned, processed and stored at home under large storage created for the purpose. During the year, the availability usually fluctuated heavily with the corresponding variations in prices as well as the quality of grains. Not so affluent homes had smaller storage to last only for a few months, which also took care of smaller ups and downs in availability in local market. However, the poor had to contend with their purchases every day or even for every meal. The poor had to take a bigger brunt of the non-availabilities and corresponding steep price shoot up—but they had no choice. Unaffected by the market uncertainties, an affluent grandma stored enough to see through the year and a little more. Today, better storage facilities and changed doctrines have smoothened market variations. Long-term storage philosophy in every household has therefore been rendered old fashioned.

However, storage of spare parts for a long forecast military requirement does not seem to go out of fashion at all. A few norms associated with the military have resulted in *rules that bind the Lieutenant* (ref TOC example). We have for long believed that we needed to write unique specs for our needs (military is different from the civil world!). Most proven Commercial Off-The-Shelf (COTS) products needed alterations for us—we did however instantly lose the COTS advantage of cost, lead time, wide support, life cycle upgrades etc. Even more damaging has been the blind acceptance of archaic rules of provisioning and forecasting, *called myths by my former colleague Wg Cdr Kaushik Das.*[7] Some of the norms followed for determining the forecast requirements could only be termed as ludicrous. It is time for a big shake up to question the following norms:

- To forecast and provision for a period of the order of three to five years.
- Long processing delays before placement of orders and even longer supply lead-time.
- Supply lead-time of the order of 18 months and above even for PSUs.
- PSUs do not forecast by themselves—Time starts for them only after Service HQ orders.
- The agreed timeframes are routinely exceeded by big margins.

When we face some of these questions squarely, we begin to wonder WHY! Why is it that we need a change and we can't make it? Why is it that respective PSUs cannot be made to partner in the provisioning process so that they have a fair idea of our requirements well before orders placement? Most weapon systems, even from foreign sources, are supported by someone known as Original Equipment Manufacturer (OEM). If not, then why don't we identify the single supply agency with the help of the country's government? Why do we hesitate partnering with even the foreign supplier despite knowing well that we are wedded for as many as 25 to 40 years? Yes, we are obsessed with rules and in absence of a life cycle management tool; we have no way of assessing the damage. We are unable to get an appreciation of cost comparison (cost of delays) making justification with finance very vary cumbersome. *The cost world remains dominant over the throughput world in absence of a measure for war potential.* The procurement cloud shown in Fig. 8 indicates the conflict.

Figure 8: Purchase vs Life Cycle Cost Dilemma

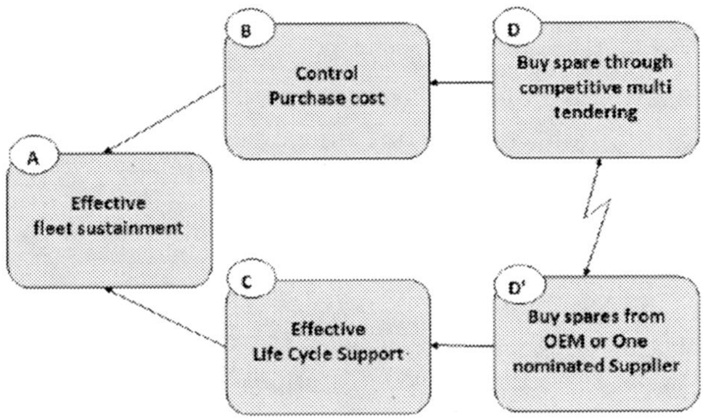

As we verbalise assumptions, a few facts emerge clearly.

- In order to have effective fleet sustainment we need to control purchase cost because reduced cost means potential retained for sustainment.
- But, the questions to ask are:
  - If inadequate spares were purchased, or purchases delayed in search of lowest cost, what are the operational losses?
  - Is purchase cost a global measure?
  - Can we look for a global measure like maintaining low life cycle maintenance cost?
  - Can we further modify the need (at 'B') as '*low life cycle maintenance cost per available system*'?

With those questions for validation, we can now modify the block ***B*** to carry the need as "Low life cycle cost per available aircraft or weapon system"—and surely a lot of intelligence begins to filter in. Now, least cost spares in individual deals are not good enough if the deals make us wait indefinitely or the fill rates remain less than 100 per cent. The modified cloud can then be drawn as shown in Fig. 9.

A partnership model with OEMs for win-win solutions to logistics support issues is the only answer. However, as explained earlier in introduction to TOC, *a perpetual and undue fear that the situation will get worse (cost will shoot up)* if we share information with the supplier keeps us paralysed in the present.

Figure 9

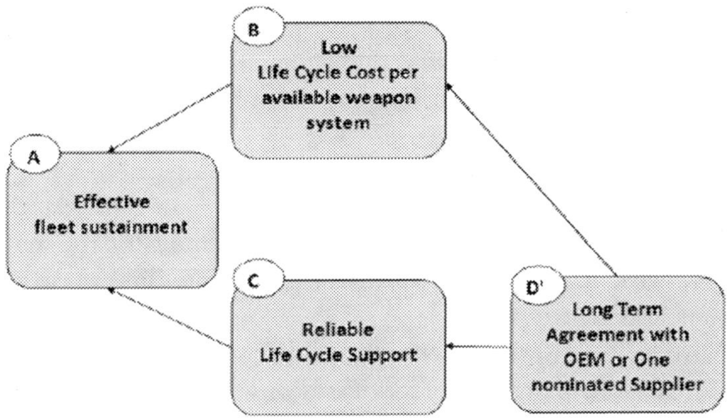

The procurements are also affected by the following two distinct factors:

(a) The most common factor is the involvement of too many agencies, which incidentally has been a master bureaucratic stroke that ensures non-accountability of any one. A number of agencies like user, indenter, purchaser, technical evaluator, cost accounting specialist, Deputy Competent Financial Authority (CFA), financial advisor and the CFA make a long list. It is therefore essential that the list be kept down to a *maximum of three* besides the CFA.

(b) The second vital factor is the distance of the purchaser from fleet appreciation and knowledge. The purchaser, carrying out a support activity, should not begin to dominate with the rulebook. The dynamics of maintenance and usage (operation) determining the requirements over a long life cycle are often overlooked by those who don't see beyond procedures and part numbers. The result has been the use of statistics of fill rates etc. as measures of satisfaction while critical spares remain unsupplied year after year.

Outsourcing and Performance Based Logistics

A call for outsourcing various functional responsibilities within the defence services, alongside defence PSUs and Ordnance Factories has got intensified in the last one decade. It picked up momentum especially after the Kelkar committee recommendations on the subject of strengthening 'Self Reliance in Defence Preparedness'. It is however no surprise that, in USA the Performance Based Logistics (PBL) had been mandated a few years before that as a follow up on the outsourcing, which had found favour with most companies besides the government. Before we go long into this section, I must clarify that the intention of putting up the two terms, outsourcing and PBL together in the title is not because these are synonyms. In fact *PBL is not outsourcing of logistics functions.* Both relate closely to effectiveness of logistics support and are also commonly misunderstood. We will discuss these one by one keeping in mind the associated myths like '*no need for tech acumen*' *when outsourcing* and '*no work requirement by customers*' *in PBL.*

The concept of outsourcing the Maintenance, Repair & Overhaul (MRO) activities globally gained popularity with the booming of civil aviation industry. However, in absence of a well-grouped civil aviation industry, the well-organised MoD framework has attracted industry attention for potential business development in defence.

Outsourcing as an option has been considered favourably by business houses from the developed countries more for the reasons of off shoring to take advantage of the cheaper labour available in countries like China, India and Sri Lanka. Outsourcing within the country is however not favourable for that reason. Yet, a few organisations have jumped in to join the outsourcing as a fad without looking into the advantages and disadvantages. Outsourcing, if not directly advantageous in terms of cost, would be preferable for giving away *non-core activities* or work that is of *high and narrow specialisation* for which infrastructure and manpower expenditure and effort would be better avoided.

Outsourcing by the government is usually recommended with the intention of cutting bureaucracy and bringing in agility in functioning. Defence forces, although a part of the government, are not typically the offices of the government. Routine outsourcing is therefore not appropriate, except for a few administrative support functions. The downside of outsourcing has to be kept in mind, viz. loss of in-house expertise, inability to meet the unprecedented and unforeseen wartime surge requirements, and a significant loss of control. At the same time, it is important to note that *shifting work from military depots to public sector units cannot be considered as outsourcing.* In recent years, we have seen a spate of outsourcing most of the maintenance activities to Defence Public Sector Undertakings (DPSUs). Compared to in-house depots, these have never been cost effective while adding an unnecessary layer of bureaucracy to make logistical responses excessively sluggish.

Notwithstanding all the above, outsourcing should be undertaken in a fair measure as the services doing everything in-house will never bring worthy return on investment even from the point of effort on manpower and infrastructure. *It is however not recommended to engage PSUs, who need to be left alone and held accountable for design, development and indigenous manufacture.* Besides private sector bringing the much-needed agility in response, it will also help in spreading the industrialisation base for defence systems and hardware. A classical conflict remains with us—we find private companies not yet well entrenched in defence production and therefore unreliable; at the same time, unless given defence contracts, how will they ever get experienced and rooted to provide us confidence. The conflict can be understood as shown in Fig. 10. By now, the reader would be capable of verbalising assumptions, check for validation and challenge to find injections or answers.

Figure 10: The Public Private Dilemma

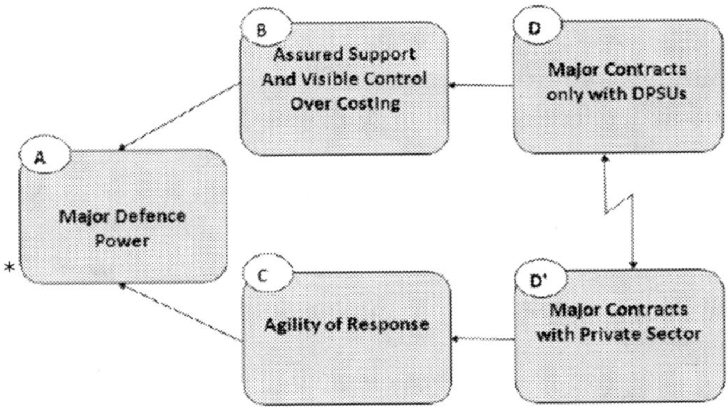

PBL took roots in around 2001 when the US DoD declared PBL as a preferred approach and asked for the development and implementation of PBL strategies. These strategies were to include best use of public and private sector capabilities through partnership. The intention in PBL is to move away from functionality oriented support programmes to seeking operational readiness, reliability and maintainability. Here we buy an integrated performance package instead of contracting for spares, repair technology, data, tools and licenses.

With the above explanation it would be clear that PBL is entirely different from outsourcing depot maintenance i.e. MRO. Although, it involves the whole range of logistics activities, it is not the same as contracting out logistics despite the fact that PBL switches most of the supply chain's risk and responsibility from customer to the supplier. The defining reality is that PBL requires committed and balanced contribution from both the parties. In our case, there have been a few half-hearted attempts to contract PBL without having made the commitments and including only part responsibilities. Long term repair or maintenance agreements have been considered as PBL, while many a contract has been undertaken without adequate study on our part as we remained satisfied with foreign vendors passing on imported *hearsay knowledge,* usually advantageous to them.

Logistics engineering and PBL are parts of graduate courses abroad. Along with late Air Cmde Jasjit Singh's anguish over the lack of strategic education in national universities, this lack of logistics education also remains a surprise. Perhaps the reasons are lack of attention and importance to logistics by professional organisations and also the fact that logistics by avoidance of a qualification is considered a non-engineering domain. Engineers on the other hand find it convenient to twist the term itself and call it 'Performance Based Maintenance'.

Like the outsourced MRO, PBL also would be essential for adoption by defence services, but in a suitably small measure to begin with indigenous fleet. A start with indigenously developed systems and also those manufactured under foreign licenses by our PSUs would be best for developing concepts in the next few years. PSUs, which lay back without concern as services struggle, with indigenisation and substitution of difficult to procure foreign components, surely need to be tasked better and contracted for PBL. It is only natural that academic studies and research in most institutions can begin after a reasonable success and commercialisation of the PBL in industry. However, the development of concepts for defence can preferably be carried out with the help of think tanks like Centre for Land Warfare Studies (CLAWS), National Maritime Foundation (NMF) and Centre for Air Power Studies (CAPS). The design and development (specification) of performance requirements, performance metrics and the contractual framework would call for defence and industrial experience and acumen.

In the two models discussed above, either the customer or the supplier carries all the ultimate responsibility. However, a third model of arrangement has been emerging to enable offsetting the disadvantages to the customer. This is a partnership, which would apply to all support arrangements, viz. totally in-house maintenance including depot overhaul, outsourced MRO, and PBL. I wish to call it the Customer Supplier Partnership (CSP) model. According to this model, the human resource is always put together by both, the customer and the supplier. With totally in-house facilities, a small (about five to 10 per cent) workforce can be contributed by the contractor to maintain currency on licensing, updates, modification etc. The composition is reversed in facilities completely owned by the supplier, where the customer contributes a small part of the work force (10 to 20 per cent) to cater for the negative effects of loss of expertise, loss of control, and to maintain surge capacity. It may be noted that the supplier need not necessarily be a private company. And therefore, the model is named CSP and not Public Private Partnership (PPP).

It is no secret, and in fact a matter of regret that deputations from the services are not quite kindly taken by even DRDO and DPSUs. The loss has been immense, especially in the last three decades. I would even recommend mandatory deputations in the opposite direction into services, which have a tremendous potential for logistics innovations. The fact of the matter is that controlling a mix of human resource does not seem to be in our comfort zones. Therefore, with regard to *CSP,* I reckon that the most difficult aspect would be the specification of contract and consequent sincere honouring of commitments. Honouring the partnership with shared responsibilities will remain the most challenging and sensitive element of these contracts.

Standardisation

An Army officer moves out of his unit always with a movement order. A Naval officer is recognised outside his parent ship with the information provided on the Gen Form carried by him. And in contrast, the Air Force officer on temporary duties just moves and reports to the destination without even carrying authorising signals. Each one of the procedures has its own information closing in loops and cross check mechanisms. If one looks at the data requirements for an officer's temporary move from a unit to another, these would be very similar for Army, Navy and Air Force personnel. But, each service is happy, and rather proud about its own distinct service procedures. A joint services unit has to however keep all the three provisions.

This is not all. A simple spark plug of a motor vehicle commonly used by all three services is recognised by three different part numbers in the three respective inventory systems. Inventory codification schemes, data structures, forms and procedures for issue, receipt and transfer of items of inventory are entirely different for all three services. Tri services commands and units, which seem to be joint when viewed from outside are actually considerably disjointed in low-level procedures despite honourable intentions. As discussed earlier, the dissimilarities have come up through the legacies adopted along with the genesis of each service.

The scope of operations has expanded well into the joint regime. We won't make effective use of resources if we only appear to be joint despite having Headquarters Integrated Defence Staff (HQ IDS) and also a few Joint Services Commands. Army, Navy and Air Force have a large number of common items of inventory. Most of these are held under different part numbers, names and descriptions, as the classification systems are quite different in the three services. The result is despite the commonality of parts no exchange or sharing of resources is possible in times of need during joint operations. Standardisation is not only useful for joint operations but also for mutual transfers of inventory items in need by one service when the other can share. Each service maintains reasonably good inventory Data Base Management Systems (DBMS), but these can't be joined together because of lack of a common code. When a service is ready to dispose off inventories of a weapon system and the other service holds systems in use of similar origin, it is a fair guess that many sub components could possibly be made use of instead of being sold as scrap. But, in absence of a common picture, technicians can only be tasked to carry out cumbersome physical inspections. The predicament is not limited to situations of need across two services—suppliers often deliver items common to two fleets within the same service without ensuring uniqueness of part numbers.

Well, the standardisation in military is not something new. The need for military standards was realised during the World War II when the allied forces could not even share small items as bullets. In India also the Directorate of

Standardisation (for military) was established as early as 1962. The Standardisation Committee, with SA to RM as its head was set up just a couple of years before that. The Directorate of Standardisation carries out the following functions:

- In case of common interest to more than one service, lay down standards for the following:
  - Specifications for products, interfaces, and services.
  - Guidelines for procedures and practices.
- Lay down codification scheme and implement a standard codification for defence inventories.
  - The robust and scientific North Atlantic Treaty Organisation (NATO) system of codification has been adopted.
  - Codification of inventories is given priority for those systems, which are common to two or more services.
- Recommend rationalisation of inventories through variety reduction.
- Effect entry control during induction of systems/components in services.
- Guide in identification of alternative utilisation of inventories under disposal, and also verify plans for replacements.

In over five decades, the Directorate of Standardisation has received significant acknowledgement at the national level. Efforts have been put in by its zestful staff. However, if one looks back with introspection, there has been little accomplishment, which could be marked as noteworthy or gainful for defence services. I would tend to agree that a large part of contribution towards this lack of achievement has also been from the services because the directorate has not been able to project itself as a part of them. The Directorate of Standardisation has been seen by the services as only a necessary bureaucratic step in acquisition and disposal processes consuming its own given wasteful time. On its own part the Directorate of Standardisation has been satisfied in being a part of MoD, Department of Production and Supply, and not technically answerable to Service HQs. As a result, there has never been a review of its functional efficacy in five decades—*organisation structure does determine behaviour.*

Standardisation affects the status of logistics preparedness in a major way. The subject is too vital to be neglected for any longer than the five decades of sluggish bureaucratic approach. The following few actions are recommended for immediate consideration:

- A functional review of Directorate of Standardisation by a joint services team.
- Organisational restructuring to place Directorate of Standardisation within HQ Integrated Defence Staff (HQ IDS).
- To ensure greater connect of Directorate of Standardisation with Services.
- The services logistical requirements should drive the defence R&D and industry from the standardisation point of view.

IT Enablement for an Integrated Approach to Logistics

Inventory management along with accounting functions was the first to get the benefit of IT (then better known as computer technology) in defence services. After the initial COBOL based programmes the inventory DBMS continued to be developed in-house in all services. New systems replaced the older hardware/ software combinations almost at the rate of one every five or six years because of the fast change of computer systems. These DBMS packages called Management Information Systems (MIS) required huge effort in off-line data entry, which always lagged behind the work processes besides requiring specialist (according to the then standards) data-entry-operators. Consequently these MIS packages produced limited success for statistical analysis and were useful as intermediate steps in further progress of info technology.

To most Indians the term IT appears to be synonymous with the Indian character. However, it would be surprising to realise that most dollar earning Indian IT business has been of sub-contracts for parts of application and not total systemic solutions. Justifiably, the services have not been quite keen to adopt and totally depend on foreign made systems like Systems Applications Products (SAP). The leveraging of IT even with the help of industry for organisation wide '*Enterprise Resource Planning*' logistical solutions have therefore fallen short of expectations. The other fact is that some of the extra ordinary in-house efforts in all the three services could not mature more on account of technological limitations of communication and networking than computing ability or resources. This would perhaps explain why networked inventory management systems came up sequentially in time for Navy (Integrated Logistics Management System (ILMS) and Air Force (Integrated Material Management On Line System (IMMOLS) before the Army, i.e. geographically smaller to larger scope.

While the Air Force's IMMOLS has all inventory transaction provisions including provisioning, and it also has online equipment accounting and audit facilities, all services need to go well beyond that. Operations on material are not only transactions through storage, distribution and disposal. Comprehensively tracking material through its usage, maintenance, upgrade, disposal and replacement would be essential enterprise wide. Accordingly, every process acting upon material will have to be taken into account.

Network enablement with a view to facilitate Network Centric Warfare (NCW) has been in progress in all three services. Network enablement is not only connecting communication networks—it would amount to designing networks and processes in a way to provide for Network Centric Operations (NCO) with a collaborative concept. Forces operate with men and material. The two vital parts of the whole database are therefore *operational data and formats* and *material* data. The services are working towards establishment of their large network under the Network For Spectrum (NFS) project. In the meanwhile, it would be of paramount importance for all three services to individually and collectively devise data structures and formats for all material on inventory and processes that operate on material. Eventually all processes will need to talk to each other to enable entities on the network to seamlessly communicate with each other. The design of interfaces and interface standards is also vital not only within the material domain but also across domains to and fro operational processes. All legacy software without Service Oriented Architecture (SOA) needs diligent effort to provide for interfacing layers to enable process-to-process communication. Comprehensive work in that area must begin while all new add-ons are made rigorously SOA compliant.

The stability of IT specific human resource among military cadres remains uncertain. Therefore, partnership with industry is recommended for the development of not only software systems but also the standards.

A truly integrated approach to logistics management will emerge when the logistics information will seem intrinsic to the operational processes. The war fighter will not require to ask for logistics information.

Conclusion

Robust logistics groundwork translates into military capability. A measure of military capability is however elusive. If forces made money instead of an abstract thing as *war potential*, it would have been a simple matter to evaluate the accomplishments of a military outfit in terms of money made in relation to money put in. In absence of that, it is impossible to relate every Rupee put in with the generated potential. Conversely, every Rupee cut out (inappropriately termed as saved) from the expenditure appears to increase efficiency as we consider output as fixed. Under such assumptions, a delayed process would always appear to cut cost and improve efficiency. I would recommend *study and research* on the subject of quantification and transformation of units of the output war potential as a measure of throughput generated by the armed forces. Only then can we measure effectiveness and worth of all logistics.

> *The World we have created is a process of our thinking. It cannot be changed unless we change our thinking.*
>
> —***Albert Einstein***

Logistics is not about spare parts storage and distribution alone. It runs through all parts of military organisations and systems. Often looked at from a parts view, the supply/stores departmental logic dominates. Our characteristic attempts for improvements in logistics by parts have not borne satisfactory results. A shift in thinking to get off the beaten track would be necessary. We have to identify maximum leverage points (core constraints) within each vital area discussed above for exploitation through systemic measures to remove clouds of conflict.

In each discussed area of activity *a combined study would be recommended* to work out the action roadmap starting with the core constraints in each specific field. A few concluding points for consideration are summarised:

- Review logistics organisation structures within services.
- Create a higher-level logistics structure over and above service HQs.
- Emphasise on life cycle management concepts. Mandate the development of a visualisation tool to enable *cost per available system per day* to become the determining factor in decision-making.
- Carry out a total review of stockage objectives and forecasting norms for provisioning. *Reduce the acceptable delays to absolute minimum.*
- Move to a partnership model with all suppliers.
- Outsource maintenance with care within a defined level. Develop outsourcing models with private enterprises.
- PBL is initially recommended in cases of indigenous design/development or license manufacturer by DPSUs. Mandate about three major PBL contracts by each arm in the next two years.
- Mandate a review of the functioning of Directorate of Standardisation, and assess the requirement of restructuring.
- Leverage IT for integrating logistics with operational processes.
- Engage services associated think tanks for development of specifically mandated concepts. Standardisation, provisioning/forecasting, PBL, partnership models, org structure and throughput measurement (logistical war potential) are vital issues.
- Encourage task orientation over rules to enable systemic measures determine decisions.

REFERENCES

1. Fifth Discipline by Peter Senge, 1996, 2006; Random House Business Books: US.
2. 'Theory of Constraints' by Goldratt EM (1999), The North River Press: Great Barrington, MA 'The Goal' by Goldratt EM and Cox J (1984) The North River Press; Reprint by Productivity & Quality Publishing: Great Barrington, MA.
3. 'Goal II—It's not Luck' by Goldratt EM (1994), The North River Press; Reprint by Productivity & Quality Publishing: Great Barrington, MA
4. On line guide in implementing, TOC 2008-09 by Dr. Kelvyn Youngman.
5. Deming and Goldratt by Domenico Lepore and Oded Cohen; Reprint (2010) by Productivity & Quality Publishing.
6. Myth called MPE: A service paper by Wg Cdr Kaushik Das.

15

INDIA'S OFFSET POLICY: THE WAY FORWARD

Satya Narayan Misra

Introduction

Offsets are a range of industrial and commercial compensation practices required as a condition of the purchase of defence articles and services through co-production, license production, sub-contractorisation, Foreign Direct Investment (FDI) and technology transfer.

It runs counter to the conventional logic of neo-classical economics of perfect competition driving optimal pricing. WTO guidelines also frown upon such restrictive trade arrangements like offsets. In the conventional trade literature, therefore, there is scant reference to offset policy by trade theorists like Prof. Bhagwati, Krugman, Stiglitzand Rodik.

However, we do not straddle an optimal world in global arms purchase. It's circumscribed by oligopolies, particularly in high technology aerospace and ship building products where second best outcomes and proliferation of agents rule the roost.

Offsets have witnessed significant adherents. Niche technology transfers have taken place between USA and Japan in the mid 1950s and with South Korea and Brazil under the aegis of offset arrangement. The global evidence shows a marked predilection for indirect offset (61 per cent) flowing to non defence sectors like education, health and infrastructure with outsourcing contributing 50 per cent of direct offsets due to labour arbitrage. The cost and employment benefits have been generally illusory or debatable with supporting data rather wafer-thin.

Nevertheless, offset policy has come to stay in a large number of countries with political objective often obfuscating the economic advantages that flow out of this opaque arrangement. India, a late entrant into the offset club, tried to leverage its huge arms import to bolster its military industry capability by announcing its offset policy in 2005. This was in line with Kelkar Committee's recommendations for ushering in vibrant public private partnership to ramp-up India's indigenous defence manufacturing capability.

There have been four revisions in the policy since then with the latest being in August 2012. The substantive leitmotif of the changes seek to **foster internationally competitive defence enterprise, encourage capacity for defence related R&D products and services**, and encourage synergy in sectors like aerospace and internal security. The major highlights of the August 2012 policy include, **multipliers up to three to incentivise investment in Micro, Small and Medium Enterprises (MSMEs), facilitate technology acquisition by the Defence Research and Development Organisation (DRDO) and allowing Transfer of Technologies (ToT) as valid mode of offset discharge.** The other changes include extending the banking period to seven years, expanding the list of eligible product/ services for discharge of offset obligation and extending the period of execution of offset contracts by two years beyond the period of main procurement contract. Further, taking note of the general dissatisfaction with the functioning of Defence Offset Facilitation Agency (DOFA), Defence Offset Monitoring Wing (DOMW) has been reconstituted with more powers to hopefully anchor and supervise the process effectively by hand-holding all stakeholders.

This paper attempts to critically examine adequacy of the policy as it has evolved so far in **achieving the expected momentum in self reliance**, and improvement in value addition in India's Defence Industrial Base (DIB), **analyse areas where the policy options can be further improved** and to suggest a possible **road map** in-order to **realize the full potential of offset policy to make India a global defence manufacturing hub.**

India's Military Industry Complex

In-order to have a proper appreciation of the enormous potential that India has to become a global defence manufacturing hub, it would be necessary to have an insight into India's Military Industry Complex (MIC), take stock of its capability and value addition and the role that the private sector plays in this palimpsest.

India's military industrial complex consists of nine DPSUs, 40 OFs, 50 DRDO labs, 140 private defence companies and 5000 Small and Medium Enterprises (SMEs) who are involved in production of around 450 items.

The nine Defence Public Sector Undertakings (DPSUs) are engaged in manufacture of a wide range of products like helicopters, fighters, warships, submarines, patrol vessels, heavy vehicles and earthmovers, missiles and a variety of electronic devices, alloys, and special purpose steel. The 40 Ordnance Factories (OFs) are engaged in production of small arms and ammunition of all the weapon systems, clothing, armoured and transport vehicles.

The OFs have achieved a very high degree of self reliance in small arms and ammunition while in the longer range artillery guns of 155 mm calibre the Army is still groping to fill up the void; thanks to the Bofors imbroglio.

The DPSUs and OFs have built substantial production capability largely through license agreements ('Buy and Make') for a variety of platforms like tanks, Infantry Combat Vehicles (ICVs), vehicles, missiles, frigates, submarines, aircrafts, missiles and electronic devices.

An overview of the performance of the DPSUs and OFs in terms of Value of Production (VoP), Value of Sales (VoS), Profit after Tax (PAT) and Value Addition is placed below as Table 1.

Table 1: Financial Performance of DPSUs/OFs (2009-10) (Rs. in Crs.)

DPSU	*VOP*	*VOS*	*PAT*	*Value Addition*
HAL	13489	11456	1967.4	39%
BEL	5247	5219	720.8	41%
BEML	3708	3537	222.8	39%
MDL	2856	3150	240.1	23%
GRSE	870.7	424.2	114.8	35%
GSL	866	472.9	130.7	37%
MIDHANI	373	371	44.6	57%
BDL	631.6	627	33.7	50%
HSL	608	618	2.3	-
TOTAL (DPSUs)	*28649.3*	*25893.1*	*3477.2*	*38%*
OFS	11817	8715	—	85%
Grand Total	**40466.3**	**34610.1**	3477.2	

Source: Annual Report, MOD.

It would thus be seen that while the **OFs** have a **very high value addition (85 per cent),** it's **quite lowin** case of the **defence PSUs (38 per cent)**, except for Midhani which is remarkably fleet footed in indigenising super-alloys and manufacturing steel for strategic sectors.

Private Sector

Consequent on opening up of the defence industry sector in May 2001 allowing full Indian private sector participation with a FDI cap of 26 per cent, a number of Joint Ventures (JVs) have mushroomed between Indian and foreign companies.

Major private sector industries like Tata's, L&T, Mahindra & Mahindra and SMEs are actively engaged in software development, engineering services, manufacturing and sub-assemblies, accounting for 25per cent supply of components to DPSUs & OFs. The private sector in India is still at a nascent stage compared to other developed countries. The private sector companies are, however, closely associated with national and strategic programmes like Light

Combat Aircraft (LCA), Main Battle Tank (MBT), Pinaka, Arihant, Dhanush and Brahmos. Many of them have excellent facilities but display significant limitation in terms of design capability and system integration as they were not recipients of technology transfers in the past. The **'Buy and Make' (Indian) option in 2009 provide the private sector for the first time a window to technology transfer** which was the exclusive preserve of DPSUs/OFs earlier.

The private sector is now into production of fast patrol vessels and IPVs by out competing defence shipyards—in terms of cost and delivery commitments; thanks to the **level playing field provided in Ship Building Procedure-2010**. In the aerospace sector also, Tatas have ventured into manufacture of aero-structures and cabins. Foreign Original Equipment Manufacturer (OEMs) like Lockheed Martin and Sikorsky show distinct predilection to partner with the Tatas instead of Hindustan Aeronautics Limited (HAL). Unmanned Aerial Vehicles (UAVs) is another area where Tatas foresee an excellent opportunity to partner with M/S IAI, Israel to meet the large requirement of the three services for air surveillance.

Self-Reliance

A key concern in India's Military Industrial Complex is the high and unremitting dependence on imports for critical items which accounts for nearly 70 per cent of our acquisition budget. Noting this concern, a review committee headed by Dr. Kalam, the then SA to RM, with participation of all the Services and the DPSUs brought out in 1993 the uncertainties in supply of defence systems by countries of the former Soviet Union, mounting pressure of embargo on critical technologies from developed nations and **set a goal of enhancing the indigenous content in the defence inventory from 30 per cent (1995) to a possible 70 per cent by 2005**. Self-Reliance Index was defined as the **ratio of Indigenous Systems Procurement Cost to Total System Procurement Cost of the year**. The Committee identified the future systems requirements as under.

Table 2: Future Systems Required

- Automated Air Defence System
- Satellite Based Navigation System
- Air and Space Based Early Warning System
- C4 I System
- Under Water Sensors and Weapons
- Medium and Long Range Guided Missile System with Launching from Multiple Platforms
- Unmanned Air Vehicles (UAVs)
- Stealth Air Craft
- Air Borne Electronic Warning System, Electronic Counter Measure (ECM and ECCM)
- Very small Aperture Terminals for Satellite Communication GPS (Global Positioning System) Receiver

Despite the substantial investment made by the DPSUs and OFs over the year and an assured order book from the services, the **SRI quotient remains stagnant at 30**per cent **even now**. *The major reasons in the aerospace sector can be summed up as under:*

The predominant reliance on licensed manufacturing without taking adequate steps to bolster design and development capability is indeed a major cause in the fighter aircraft segment. According to (Late) Air Commodore Jasjit Singh, the vertical disjunction between design, development and production agencies has also contributed significantly to tardy delivery and poor quality of aircraft production.

It would be interesting to mention that the Soviet Union brought the production agencies directly under the design bureau and such an arrangement has shown remarkable results. Discerning observers like Tony Saich mention that the major organisational problem with S&T System is the lack of linkage across vertical structure; particularly between the research and production sectors.

The above observations hold important lessons for India where the DRDO and the production agencies do not operate in an integrated manner. The Rama Rao Committee, noting with concern the interminable delays in Kaveri, LCA and MBT programmes strongly recommended that R&D must function as part of a production agency who have a commitment to deliver in time and as per services quality requirements.

Critical Technology Areas

Self-Reliance is linked to our capability to design and produce critical subsystems like **propulsion, weapon,** and **sensors** of major platforms. Areas identified by Dr. Kalam Committee 18 years back remain largely unchanged even today.

Table 3: Areas of Critical Technology

1	Gas Turbine Engine	Single Crystal and Special Coating for turbine blades
2	Missile	Un-cooled FPA seekers
3	Aeronautics	Smart Aero structures Stealth Technology
4	Material	Nano Material, Carbon Fibres
5	Naval Systems	Super Cavitating Technology
6	Sensors	AESA, Radar, RLG, INGPS
7	Communication	Software Defined Radio
8	Avionics	Gen III, II Tubes
9	Surveillance	UAVs, Satellites

Even in aero-grade material used for fuselage by fighters and high quality steel required by frigates, submarines and aircraft carriers our dependence on imports is around 90 per cent. Composites which are required in substantial measure for producing helicopters need carbon fibres which are yet to be indigenously sourced.

License agreements in the past have **only fostered "Know Hows" and not the keys to Know Why**. Our poor design capability in HAL and BEL and DRDO's endemic time overrun to design critical sub systems like **Focal Plane Arrays (FPAs), passive seekers, RLGs & GPS and Gas Turbine Engines have contributed to this** impasse. Inadequate investments by the private sector in R&D and lack of Joint Technology development arrangements with major design houses have not helped matters either.

Major Areas of Offset Realisation

Since the initiation of the Offset Policy in 2005, the MoD has signed nearly 20 offset contracts worth over $4.5billion. From the experience of offset realised so far, the major areas are (a) Sub contractorisation (58 per cent) involving supply of fuselage, cabins, radome, tail cone, data link, and other products, (b) Engineering projects, project management, (c) Overhaul and repair facilities (16 per cent), (d) Various types of training facilities, simulators and (e) Ground handling and support equipments. Further, the disaggregation in different categories can be summarized as under:

Manufactured final assembly	58%
Simulators, Training Centre	18%
MRO	16%
GHE/GSE (Ground Handling & Support)	8%

Source: DOFA, MoD.

The types of work realised through offset arrangement in HAL, a prime player for offset realisation are as under:

Table 4: Types of Offsets in Aerospace Sector

1.	Build to Print	32%
2.	Design to Build	21%
3.	MRO Facilities	27%
4.	Software Packages	12%
5.	Design Packages	8%

Source: HAL.

In the defence sector it is contended that Maintenance Repair Overhaul (MRO) is the most basic level of capability. In Malaysia, offsets have contributed handsomely to local MRO capacity/capability.

The offset contracts for MIG 29 upgrade and VVIP helicopters will help HAL to bolster its MRO capability. In the 'Globe Master' contract also HAL is likely to benefit in terms of Repair Overhaul (ROH) facilities through offset. Presently, North America and Europe contribute with more than 60 per cent of global MRO market. Singapore is also an emerging MRO hub. Substantial amount is spent by organisations in MRO compared to acquisition. This could be a thrust area where HAL in partnership with global companies and private sector can be a global hub for MRO, providing a cost effective option.

Technology Development Capability

It would be useful at this stage to take note of India's capability in different areas.

Capability	*R&D*	*Design*	*Manufacture*	*MRO/Overhaul*
Aerospace	Low	Low	Medium	Medium
Armed Vehicle	Low	Low	Medium	Medium
Marine	Low	Low	Medium	Medium
Weapon	Low	Low	Medium	Medium
ICT	Low	Medium	Medium	Medium

It would be important to mention that technology transfers in the past to DPSUs like HAL, BEL, BDL, MDL & Midhani has ensured that a high degree of indigenisation and cost savings has been achieved as the following table would reveal.

Table 5: Indigenisation and Its Impact on Cost
Indigenisation Profile of DPSUs/OFs

DPSU	*Product*	*Indigenisation*	*Cost savings*
BDL	Milan	71%	60%
	Konkur	97%	30%
HAL	SU30 (Air Frame)	55%	45%
	AL31FP (SU30 Engine)	65%	45%
	HAWK	40%	18%
Medak	ICV	90%	50%
Midhani	Titanium alloys	60%	15%
BEL	Sonobuoys	70%	30%

Source: CMDs, DPSUs.

However, technology transfers provide **know how** and **not the 'knowledge base'** and requisite skill personnel to **Design & Build**. Therefore, **substantial investment in R&D both** by the **public sector and private sector players would be the key to India's ability to** build, design and create manufacturing capability of critical subsystems. Significantly, many SMEs of late, are investing handsomely in R&D making them technically fleet footed and more confident of absorbing leading edge technology. They are leaner, more agile, have low setup cost, high level of skills, and cost effective production of smaller systems compared to many larger private sector companies.

Big private Indian companies, therefore, need to invest more in R&D to encourage foreign OEMs to collaborate in high technology products. The private sector companies like Tatas, L&T, and Pipavav, despite having excellent facilities, have inherent limitations in terms of design development capability and system integration. Japan's success in fast technology absorption was largely due to its highly skilled personnel and low cost of labour. This holds an important lesson for major private players and SMEs in India. HAL and BEL also need to up-scale their R&D investment to around 10 per cent from the present allocation of around six per cent if they intend to successfully absorb technology in major programmes like the Fifth Generation Fighter Aircraft (FGFA), Multirole Transport Air Craft (MRTA) and Tactical Communication System (TCS).

In countries like France, R&D activities absorb more than 15 per cent of the turnover of aerospace companies. French research excels in propulsion and combustion, composite materials, aerodynamics, acoustics, and embedded electronics making France a leading player in the aerospace and defence sector.

It's also important to note that military technologies have excellent spin offs to the civilian and commercial segment. Some of them can be identified as under:

- Air breathing Propulsion.
- Semi Conductor Material and very high speed ICs based on Gallium Arsenide or Silicon chips will have application in automotive, telecom & industrial robotics.
- Composite material.
- Passive sensors—Medicine, Satellites for remote sensing, Communication and Weather application.
- Photonics.
- Computational fluid dynamics.

Prof. Rama Rao strongly advocates dual use technology in areas like Aircraft Control, Imaging for Agriculture, Water & Mineral resources, flight display and avionics. MoD, instead of its **present obsession with arms acquisition** approach, needs to **develop a military technology capability building approach, where dual use technology becomes a part of our offset realisation and has excellent commercial spin off.**

Cost Effectiveness of Offset Contracts

It's unlikely that the offset arrangement will lead to cost reduction, based on current trends. Offsets are generally considered economically inefficient and welfare diminishing, reflecting trade diversion rather than trade creation.

Economists like Prof. Paul Dunne aver that economic benefits of offsets are simply an excuse and unproven. Prof. Brauer calls for full audit of each offset contract. It is also important to define methods to monitor, control and document offset accounting process, as well as the audit process should be identified. Brauer and Dunne, in fact, contend that offsets do not result in cost reduction; neither do they create sustained jobs. Experience of a few countries in this regard can be summarised as under:

Australia has a no cost premium expectation; but this is not borne by facts. The administrative cost of offset alone is expected to cost arms sellers anywhere from seven-10 per cent of contract value. UK's participation in the US dominated JSF (Joint Strike Fighter) programme is estimated to be four per cent more expensive than outright purchase. Denmark acknowledges that offsets result in added cost and Finland estimates 10-15 per cent added cost per offset contract. Skons reports that in the Finnish F/A-18 Hornet deal, the administrative cost was three-six per cent of contract value. For Belgium, Struys' contends that offset related costs are 20-30 per cent of imported item.

Prof. Eriksson, based on a study on the effect of offsets on European defence industry, reports that five-10 per cent is a reasonable range for the **direct cost of offset**. However, Prof. Hartley observes that in the procurement of F-16 by a consortium of European Countries, the respondents were of the view that it led to lower costs. Germany asked for 100 per cent offset during its rearmament period and accepted additional cost if it led to transfer of key technology.

The offset claims of the vendors need to be properly evaluated, as they do have a tendency to inflate them. Both overseas firms bidding for defence contracts and national defence ministries have also exaggerated the benefits of offsets.

Based on a study of offset contract for acquisition of fleet tanker from M/s Fincantieri, it was noticed that:

- Though, the first Fleet tanker has been delivered, only 50 per cent offset obligation was yet to be discharged and OEM has been asking for change of offset partners.
- There has been inordinate delay by OFB to supply the Kavach System.
- Offsets had a cost penalty of at least 10 per cent

Based on the broad international experience consensus seems to be that:

- The defence offsets are more expensive than off the shelf purchase.
- They create little by way of new or sustainable employment
- They do not make substantive contribution to the general economic development.
- No significant technology transfer takes place to either civilian or military sector.

Policy Changes (2005-12)

Several major policy initiatives and guidelines have been issued by Government of India to provide greater clarity and direction. Some of them pertain to guidelines on JV arrangements, and by a significant pronouncement like National Manufacturing Policy (2011) by National Manufacturing Zones (NMZs). These initiatives have been further bolstered by the recent spate of liberalisation in the FDI in the retail sector. These policies have been particularly MSME friendly who account for 40 per cent of industrial output and 60 per cent of India's export. They are being provided a multiplier upto three when JVs are established with them. Besides, in the retail sector 30 per cent sourcing from SSI by MNC is being made mandatory.

The other major policy is the Defence Production Policy (DPP) (2010) reiterates the concern for higher Self Reliance Index (SRI) in tandem with all stake holders. A significant suggestion is for a National Technology fund which will provide financial assistance to **academia, institutions of national importance and the private sector** with a view to galvanising R&D activity in niche areas and improve our design capability in critical technology.

The National Manufacturing Policy (2010) aims at a 25 per cent share for the manufacturing sector by creating NMZs. This is expected to generate additional employment of around 100 million in the next decade. Since additional employment generation has been one of the weakest area in our five year plan achievements so far, manufacturing is a potent candidate for bolstering employment provided properly supported by the state governments in terms of provision of land, water and electricity.

Both the Economic Survey (2012-13) and the 12th plan document flags manufacturing as the sunshine sector going by experience of China which has become a global hub in manufacturing contributing nearly 35 per cent of their GDP. Defence manufacturing must be considered a subset of the national concern for manufacturing and any attempt to disentangle defence manufacturing from national manufacturing would be a serious policy error.

Comment on Policy Changes

It would be necessary to evaluate the likely impact of major policy changes made in DPP, 2012.

Technology Transfer

The DPP provides for various windows for technology transfer through the 'Buy and Make' option to the DPSUs and OFs. DPP-2009 included the Buy and Make (Indian) option which provided a window to the private sector as technology recipient. Inclusion of technology in the 'Buy' option through offset routes is an added option now.

It would be necessary for the Services, DPSUs/OFs and DRDO to identify not only the priority areas for technology transfer but also make a clear choice of technology which should be leveraged through the 'Buy and Make' as well as the 'Buy' option. Otherwise, it's likely that outdated technology would be palmed off in the 'Buy' option unless the RFP clearly identifies the targeted technology and its currency.

Technology is often linked to export promotion and offset credit is predicated on its impact on exports. This is a very effective strategy adapted by Turkey. Israel has become a major defence exporter by targeting key technologies such as FPA, Seekers, Communication equipments and UAVs from the USA. These are useful templates for India.

In the mother of all contracts, the 'Medium Multi Role Combat Aircraft' (MMRCA) where 50 per cent offsets are expected (approximately $10 billion), efforts should be made to get key technologies like Active Electronically Scanned Array (AESA) Radar, Single Crystal Blade and Special coatings. India must not miss out this opportunity; now that technology transfer is part of the Offset Credit.

Multiplier

Providing higher credit for preferred technology, skill up-gradation and training is practiced by every country. This has to be worked out by an Empowered Committee representing the DRDO, Services and DPSU/OFs as they would be able to identify the serious gaps in our design and manufacturing capability.

At present, the Civil Aviation industry provides multiplier in its offset arrangements for Boeing and Airbus. Since both the civil aviation and military aviation sectors would be looked at in a holistic manner, a coordinated effort is needed to rationalise the application of multiplier in this sector.

Policy Changes not Covered

What is disconcerting is our inability to grapple with a few major policy issues and set up a clear road map to implement them. They are as under:

Non-inclusion of Ship Building

The previous policy measures included aerospace and homeland security product qualifying for offset as they are considered synergistic sector. It is patently surprising that commercial shipbuilding has not been included in the policy changes so far, though it's a major synergistic sector. The Krishnamurthi Committee (2007) appointed by the Government to suggest ways and means to bolster manufacturing capability had flagged the need to look at both commercial and warship building in unison.

In fact, with the increased focus on coastal surveillance, a large number of patrolling vessels are being ordered by the Navy, the Indian Coast Guard as well as the state government authorities. Besides, a large number of tankers and Landing Platform Dock (LPDs) are on order. The capacity of India's shipbuilding, both in the Public and Private sector is almost 50 per cent of the large orders in the pipeline. Countries such as South Korea and China have had a real head start in the shipbuilding sector by focusing on manufacturing and design capability.

For the offset policy to be successful in the commercial shipbuilding sector, the subsidy scheme must be revived immediately as implication of removal of such subsidies has led to disastrous consequences as the following Table would reveal.

New Orders Declined after Removal of Subsidy

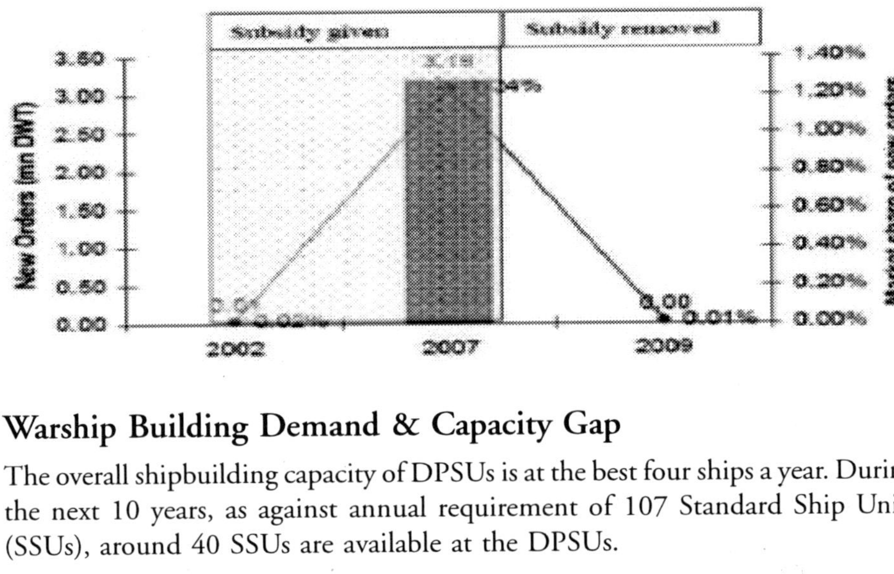

Warship Building Demand & Capacity Gap

The overall shipbuilding capacity of DPSUs is at the best four ships a year. During the next 10 years, as against annual requirement of 107 Standard Ship Units (SSUs), around 40 SSUs are available at the DPSUs.

International Experience

At the end of year 2010, world market stood at 261 million GT in terms of order book position, 77 million GT in terms of new orders and 96 million GT in terms of completion of order. Growth of world market has been very erratic since 2009 in terms of order book and new orders while it has been stable as far as completions are concerned. The fluctuations in the world market are captured in the following graph:

World Shipbuilding Market

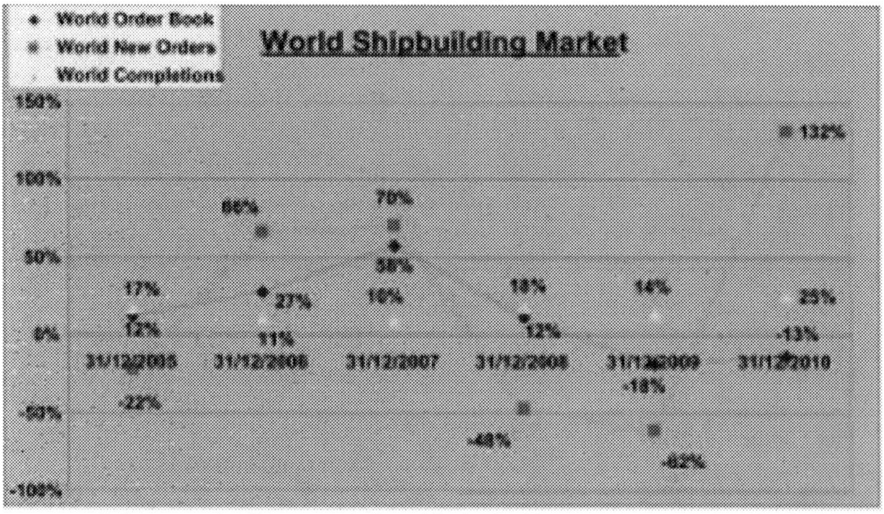

Source: HIS (Former Lloyd's Register) "World Shipbuilding Statistics" year and (Shipbuilding Statistics: Shipbuilding Association of Japan-March 2011).

The world market in shipbuilding is dominated by three Asian countries namely China, South Korea and Japan which together account for approximately 90 percent of world market in terms of existing order book at the end of year 2010. The emergence of these countries in the second half of the last century is a lesson for other countries such as India. Among the three nations, China has seen some spectacular growth in the industry since 1990s while South Korea usurped Japan as the world leader in 1999.

Table 6: Share in World's Order for Shipbuilding

Country	*2004*	*2009*	*2010*
Japan	34	17.3	16.3
South Korea	37.2	34.7	34.3
China	14.0	37.0	39.5
Europe	5.2	2.2	1.6
Others	0.5	1.1	0.9

The National Manufacturing Council (NMCC) in its report to PMO (2009) made the following recommendations for developing Indian shipbuilding Industry.

- Prepare on an urgent basis a comprehensive plan to enhance domestic ship building capabilities and building large new shipyards.
- Adopt a Mission Mode Approach for the purpose. In this context, the examples of both Korea and China be studies; and
- A continuing mechanism be evolved to synergise the efforts of the naval authorities under Ministry of Defence and the Ministry of Shipping for meeting long term requirements of the country.

Capacity expansion in the commercial sector will have a positive spin off for the warship construction activity as it will allow shipyard to focus more on complex warship construction activity. In that sense, the policy facilitation of level playing field to private sector players in Shipbuilding Procedure 2011 is really welcome.

FDI Policy: Still Half Hearted

The FDI cap in India remains at 26 per cent attracting measly investment into the defence sector as the following table will show.

Table 7: FDI Inflow—2000-2010 (Million $)

Sector	*% share*	*Amount of Inflow*
Service Sector	21%	24227
Computer S/W & H/W	8.8%	10168
Telecom	8.5%	9821
Housing & Real Estate	8.1%	8519
Construction	8%	8190
Defence	-	0.15
		120155

It would be seen that sectors like IT, Telecom and Infrastructure which qualify for 100 per cent, FDI have shown remarkable inflow of FDI into India while Defence remains an unattractive proposition.

Global experience in this regard shows that countries such as China and Malaysia have shown a high degree of pragmatism by allowing high FDI in their major manufacturing projects. China permitted FDI of 76 per cent in its JV to M/s Embraer. Malaysia also increased its FDI substantially in the manufacturing sector. This has enabled these countries to have substantial manufacturing base in the aircraft Industry and increase their global share in manufacturing.

It would not be out of place to mention that, the JV for the Brahmos cruise missile programme with 50:50 partnership between India and Russia has witnessed significant order book potential. In the newly forged JV for the Multi Role Transport Programme between HAL and SDB, Russian Prime Minister Putin, in a recent address to the industries, highlighted the significant role of their partnership with India with excellent export potential. Therefore, there is a strong case for increasing our FDI cap in defence above 50 per cent.

The success of a liberal FDI policy is critically dependent on how it is managed for the benefit of the domestic industry. Some lessons in this regard can be drawn from the practices of countries, like China which has used FDI as an instrument for developing its strategic industries.

- Enabling its industries to integrate into the global value-chain to accelerate its industrial and technological transformation (while avoiding reinvention) of the technological wheel.

- China is quite "explicit in the type of foreign investment that is 'prohibited', 'permitted', or 'encouraged', with the latter category focusing on advanced technologies." To induce foreign investors into its high-tech industries China provides various incentives such as tax rebates and lower tariff rates.

Indirect Offsets: Non Inclusion

The other disappointment in the new policy is non inclusion of indirect offset benefits as the following table would show, most of the countries have a combination of both civil and defence sectors in their offset policy. Besides, the minimum value of contract for offsets is far lower than the threshold in vogue in India's offset policy.

Table 8: Offset Policies of Selected Countries

Sl.No.	*Country*	*Minimum Value of Defence Contract*	*Minimum Offset Required*	*Offset Sector*
1	Australia	US $3.75 million	No Specific Min or Max	Defence
2	Canada	-	100%	Defence & Civilian
3	Finland	10€ million	100%	Defence
4	Greece	10€ million	120%	Defence
5	Israel	US $0.5 million	35%	Defence & Civilian
6	Italy	US $6.6 million	Not less than 70%	Defence
7	Netherlands	5€ million	100%	Defence & Civilian
8	Norway	US $6.7 million	100%	Defence & Civilian
9	Poland	5€ million	100% (defence 50% min)	Defence & Civilian
10	South Korea	US $10 million	30%	Defence
11	Spain	NA	100%, but may vary	Defence & Civilian
12	Switzerland	US $17 million (may vary)	100%	Defence & Civilian
13	Taiwan	US $10 million	70%	Defence
14	Turkey	US $10 million	50%	Defence & Civilian
15	UK	US $17.2 million, £50 million for French & German Companies	100%	Defence
16	Austria	$1 million	100%	Defence & Civilian
17	Brazil	$5 million	10%	Defence & Civilian
18	South Africa	$2 million	50%	Defence & Civilian
19	UAE	$10 million	60%	Civilian
20	Germany	$5 million	Negotiable	Defence & Civilian

Source: Adapted from US Department of Commerce, Bureau of Industry and Security, "Offsets in Defence Trade: Twelfth Report to congress", December 2007.

It would thus be seen that 60 per cent of the countries opt for both direct and indirect offsets, while the rest target defence-specific or civil sector benefits. In the USA, from 1993 to 2009, the total contract value of offsets was $76 billion with 46 countries. Of these, 37 per cent was direct and 63 per cent, indirect. Prof. Eriksson, in his study of European defence industries observes that between 2000 and 2005, direct offsets were of the order of 40 per cent, while indirect defence offsets and civil indirect offsets were 35 per cent and 25 per cent respectively.

As per the Twelfth Plan (2012-17), India's total fund requirement for infrastructure development will be around $1,025 billion. Such massive funding requirement is proposed through 50:50 public partnerships.

Besides, the social sector is an underdeveloped segment in India, as India ranks 119 out of 169 countries with a score of 0.519 in the Human Development Index (HDI). Prof. Amartya Sen, in his latest book "Uncertain Glory" brings-out the performance of India as compared to countries like China and South Korea on various parameters in the following table. What clearly comes out is our poor track record in the social sector.

Table 9: Overview of Growth and Development Parameters

Sl.No.	*Parameters*	*India*	*Pakistan*	*China*	*Sri Lanka*	*South Korea*
1	GDP (PPP)$	3203	2424	7418	4929	27,541
2	GDP (Annual Growth)	3.6	1.3	8.6	4.1	5.5
3	% Below Poverty Line (2010) $2	68.7	60.2	29.8	29	-
4	Gross Domestic Saving	31	8	53	15	31
5	FDI as % GDP	1.7	1.6	3.0	1.6	0.4
6	Export as % GDP	31	8	53	18	34
7	IMR (1000)	47	59	13	11	4
8	% Low Birth Weight Babies	28	32	3	17	-
9	MMR (1 Lakh)	200	260	37	35	16
10	Female Literacy	51	40	91	90	90
11	Mean Years of Schooling	4.4	4.9	7.5	9.3	11.6

Source: Human Development Report & World Development Indicators.

National Offset Policy

A discussion paper was mooted in October 2006 for having a National Offset Policy under Ministry of Commerce. It preferred direct offsets by availing of high end technology through ToT and Co-production. It also recommended indirect offsets by way of investment in IT, Telecom, Bio Technology, Agricultural research and export promotion. The cabinet paper did not meet the enthusiastic response needed from other Ministries and faced severe resistance of Ministry of Defence apprehending that such nodal responsibility will be dilatory.

Level Playing Field

A minor irritant in offset policy is the lack of level playing field in areas like taxes and duties. The offset benefit reduces from 30 per cent to 21 per cent because of the present structure of taxes and duties. This is an anomalous situation as in the Buy (Global) category the ED, ST element of the Indian competitor is ignored while foreign supplier's CIF cost is taken into account for determining L_1. However, for an Indian partner discharging offset commitment for an Indian programme, all these demands including CD on import elements are charged. Tables placed below will explain this position.

Order on Indian Industry (Direct): Tax Implication

Taxes & Duties	*%*	*Inputs*		*Value Addition*	*Product Cost*
		Import	*Local*		
%		20	30	50	100
Custom Duty	Nil	0	-	-	-
CVD	Nil	0	-	-	-
ED	16.48	-	5	-	-
CST	3	-	1	-	-
Total Tax			6	-	-
Total Cost of Product		20	36	50	106
Taxes on Finished Products					
ED	-				
VAT	12.5				13
MODVAT	-				
Deliverable Product Cost with Taxes					119

Offset order on Indian Industry: Tax Implication

Taxes & Duties	*Inputs*		*Value Addition*	*Product Cost*
	Import	*Local*		
%	**20**	**30**	**50**	**100**
CD (20%)	4	-	-	-
CVD (16.48%)	3	-	-	-
ED (16.48%)	-	5	-	-
CST (3%)	-	1	-	-
Total Tax	7	6	-	-
Total Cost of Product	27	36	50	113
Taxes on Finished Products				
ED (16.48%)	-	-	-	19
VAT (12.5%)	-	-	-	16
CENVAT	-	-	-	8
Net ED	-	-	-	11
Deliverable Product Cost with Taxes	-	-	-	140

Similarly in the case of Exchange Rate Variation (ERV), such benefits presently denied to the private sector needs to be extended to them at par with the Defence PSUs.

Suggestions from Major Stakeholders

It would be worthwhile to reflect the viewpoint of the major stakeholders viz. the Services, Private Sector & OEM to make our offset policy more effective: They are as under:

Services

- **HQRs IDS,** is of the view that DRDO functions in isolation from user requirement and suffers from endemic cost and time overrun. Therefore technology absorption by DRDO with reference to end users is likely to be self defeating.
  This was also the considered view of the Dr. Rama Rao Committee, which wants closer association with the end users.
- **Indian Air Force** (IAF) is of the view that FDI caps needs to be revised upwards. The confidence that the OEM will have from a greater share in manufacturing and profit will be a good stimulus for them to invest in India. It would be also in our interest to allow indirect offset in areas like infrastructure.
- **Navy**—While DRDO has sound capabilities in the science of critical technologies like GPS and RLG, the key problem seems to be converting these capabilities to a product.

Private Sector

- **L&T**—The private sector should be allowed to be system integrators and made a partner instead of being a mere Tier I supplier.
- **Tatas**—Tatas are of the view that offsets should include a wider spectrum like medical equipments, energy production and environment.

OEMs

- **BAE Systems**—Makes a strong case for allowing credit transfer between sub-contractors and prime contractors. Further, they pitch for indirect offset and draw reference to the network of smart schools and teacher training programme successfully implemented in Thailand by opting for indirect offsets.
- **GE Aviation**—makes a strong pitch for offset trading and allowing dual use technology as part of offsets.

- **Lockheed Martin US**—Is extremely critical of our tardy progress in operationalising various policy announcements like credit banking.

Concluding Thoughts

India embarked on the liberalisation path in 1991 by dismantling the license and quota-permit-Raj. In the defence sector, the wave of liberalisation came a decade later by encouraging 100 per cent private sector participation and allowing 26 per cent FDI. The half-baked policy of 2005 has now embraced a larger canvas by including technology transfer, multiplier and civil aerospace, homeland security and civil shipbuilding sectors in its ambit. However, the expectation of critical technology inflow and concomitant improvement in SRI in critical sub systems like weapons, propulsion and sensors are unlikely to materialize unless the FDI policy is further liberalised. Defence industrialisation strategy must be made a part of the overall national manufacturing capability strategy. The social sector and infrastructure improvement will serve as a potent prelude for overall development strategy. Accordingly, indirect offsets must be part of the offset policy with a mix of direct and indirect offset options. The services and private sector also strongly pitch for it.

India can be a preferred destination for foreign investment with its strong democratic roots and impartial legal, banking and regulatory frame work. The private sector must be treated as 'partners' and potential system integrators. However, such partnership to be effective must have a strong resolve to improve Our Total Factor Productivity (TFP). Prof. Hu and Khan (1979) using Cobb-Douglas production function show that China's fast growth in the 90's was contributed significantly by TFP (41.6 per cent).

We need to learn from best global practices. Brazil has demonstrated it through production of Embraer Aircraft, South Korea as a major Ship building nation and China as a global manufacturing hub. Their liberal and pragmatic FDI policy, strong political mentoring through a holistic national approach has ensured their global footprint.

It's time India eschews its protectionist bias towards In-house production agencies and genuinely fosters a PPP initiative with Private Sector, OEMs and Design houses. A more pragmatic offset policy can be a major catalyst to this potent synergistic process.

16

ARMS TRADE OFFSET: GLOBAL TREND AND 'BEST' PRACTICES

Laxman Kumar Behera

Global arms trade is increasingly becoming a two-way process. Instead of the traditional off-the-shelf procurement involving goods/services being exchanged for money, more and more arms buyers are now demanding some form of work directly flowing from the contracts they sign with foreign entities. The flow back arrangement in the contract, widely known as offsets, is usually demanded as a certain percentage of the contract value. They are also demanded in various forms ranging from traditional counter trade practices (purchase, buy-back or counter purchase) to the modern-day practices such as license production, co-production, investment, and technology transfer. The purpose for demanding offset also varies from country to country depending upon their priorities. While some countries ask offsets in the form of foreign investment and the like for general economic development, others demand a definite work share in the items being procured. Offsets can therefore be of two types: direct and indirect.[1]

The widely accepted practice of offsets can be gauged from the fact that presently around 120-130 countries have offset requirements in some form or other, compared to some 15 countries that had such requirement in early seventies.[2] The popularity of offsets notwithstanding, there is a wide divergence in the way offsets are practised by several countries. Usually offsets demanding countries have formal policy framework, although some countries like China and Japan do not have such framework to practice offsets. Within the policy framework, countries also differ in terms of threshold, percentage and scope of offsets. Difference is also observed in the way countries pursue their offsets objectives, particularly with respect to valuation of offset credit, establishing long-term relationship with offset provider and promoting defence industrialisation.

Besides, countries also differ with respect to institutional mechanisms to implement and monitor offset programmes.

The chapter examines, in some details, the offset policies of six countries: Canada, Israel, Malaysia, South Korea, Turkey and UAE which not only have had a declared policy on offsets but have also undertaken periodic revisions based on the experience gained over a period of time. Occasional reference to Indian offset policy is also made to highlight its convergence and divergence with the policies of countries surveyed in this paper.

The chapter is divided into two parts. Part I of the paper surveys global offset volume, trend and emerging issues. Part-II surveys offset policies followed by the above mentioned countries.

PART I

Global Offsets: Volume, Trends and Emerging Issues

Although, a large number of countries demand offsets in their foreign purchase, not all countries reveal any meaningful official data, preventing an authentic estimate of the magnitude of offset transactions at the global level. The lack of official data has however led to estimates by various agencies. For instance, Avascent, a consulting firm, estimates that offsets obligations worth $214 billion were generated world-wide during the seven year period, 2005-2011. The firm also estimates an additional $225 billion offset obligations by 2016. Based on the Avascent's estimates, on an average, offsets of $37 billion are generated annually.[3]

Avascent's estimates may not necessarily reflect the true value of offsets as industry's estimates tend to be lower.[4] Besides, Avascent does not distinguish between the defence offsets and civil offsets. This makes it difficult to arrive at the precise volume of offsets in arms trade.

Given the lack of comprehensive official data on arms trade offsets, the statistics provided by the Bureau of Industry and Security (BIS) of the US Department of Commerce remains the only official source for any meaningful analysis. The BIS data is not only defence specific, but also captures value of offsets and its percentage share in US's total arms export, and offset transaction by type (direct and indirect) and category (co-production, licensed production, technology transfer etc.).[5] The BIS data is however restricted to the US companies which are mandated to report to the US government on any defence export which entails an offset requirement exceeding $5.0 million. The US companies are also required to intimate "offset transactions completed in performance of existing offset commitments for which offset credits $250,000 or more has been claimed from foreign representative."[6]

Assuming that the US is the largest offset provider (by virtue of being the largest arms exporter in the world), and that countries asking offsets from the US companies also demand similar arrangements with other arms suppliers, the BIS data can be used to generalise at the global level.

As per the 17th BIS report, during 1993-2011, 53 US defence companies signed 830offset-related defence export contracts with 47 countries. The value of associated offsets was $83.73 billion, representing 68.28 per cent of total arms export value of $122.67 billion. In 2011 alone, nine US companies signed 59 offset-related defence agreements valued $10.76 billion with 27 countries. The offset value of these contracts was $5.48 billion or 50.92 per cent of total export value.[7]

The BIS report notes that during 1993-2011, direct offsets accounted for 40.8 per cent of all offset transactions, in comparison to 58.8 per cent for indirect offsets.[8] In 2011, however, the share of direct offsets was higher at 48.7 per cent (the share of indirect offset was 51.1 per cent). Among all the offset categories reported by the US companies, three categories—purchases, subcontracting and technology transfer—stood out as the most preferred offset transactions. Between 1993 and 2011, they together represented 81.1 per cent of all offset transactions by number, 77 per cent by actual transaction value and 72.6 per cent by credit value.[9]

A key aspect of BIS report pertains to annual variation of percentage of offsets in the US's arms exports. During the 19 reporting years, for which the BIS provides year-wise statistics, the offset percentage has fluctuated from the lowest 34 per cent in 1993 to the highest 125 per cent in 2003. The Figure 1 provides a smoother trend line by way of plotting a 3-year moving average of the BIS statistics. As the figure illustrates, there are clearly two distinct periods, with the cut-off period being 2003-05. In the first period, the demand for offset (in percentage terms) is more or less on an upward trajectory. The second phase is characterised by a persistent decline.

Figure 1: Offset Percentage in US's Defence Trade, 1993-2011 (3-Year Moving Average)

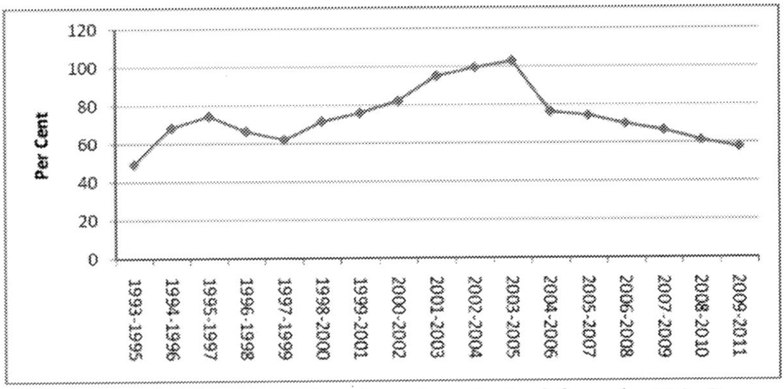

Source: Figure extrapolated by the author from data obtained from the U.S. Department of Commerce, Bureau of Industry and Security, *Offsets in Defence Trade: Seventeenth Study*, February 2013, p. 3.

The persistent decline in offset percentage post 2003-05 raises a vital question as to whether the trend reflects a gradually declining emphasis on the use of offset. While a definite answer lies in the examination of policy of all the countries asking for offsets, an early explanation could be made in the context of the official policies and positions of the US and Europe, two major players in the international offset trade.

The US, which is by far the largest offset provider, has always been worried about the negative impact of offsets on its economy, industrial and technological base. Officially, the US government views offsets as "economically inefficient and trade-distorting", and prohibits its government agencies from being directly involved in offset related activities.[10] To limit the adverse impact of offsets, the US government has undertaken two crucial measures. First, it has authorised its government agency to prepare an annual report to enable the US Congress to assess the magnitude of impact of offsets in defence trade. The BIS report, 17th in the series, is the outcome of such mandate. Second, the US government has set up an interagency team (comprising Secretaries of Commerce, Defense, Labour, and State, and the United States Trade Representative) to engage foreign governments bilaterally and multilaterally to "limit the adverse effects of offsets in defence procurement". By January 2012, the interagency team has submitted five reports to the Congress. The report of the interagency team is, however, silent as to what extent the body has been successful in convincing the US arms buyers to limit the use of offsets. Given the clout of the US in global arms trade, it won't be surprising if buyers of American weapons have paid heed to the US agency. However, as mentioned earlier, it needs to be probed in great details as there is opposing evidence to this effect. On one hand, there are countries like Malaysia and South Korea who have progressively increased the percentage of offsets. On the other hand, the European countries, which had traditionally high offset percentage requirements, have started lowering the demand.

EDA's Code of Conduct on Offsets

Parallel to the US efforts to curb impact of offset is the similar effort in the Europe. It is noteworthy that historically, Europe had a very high rate of offset requirement, often exceeding 100 per cent of the contract value. For instance, a 2007 European Defence Agency (EDA)-sponsored study found an average offset per cent of 135 per cent among the European countries during 2000-2006. The offset percentage was also found to be much higher for countries like Finland, Greece, Poland and Spain which demanded an average of 145 per cent offsets during the study period.[11] Another example of high offset demand is also evident from the UK's contract with Boeing in which the American company was asked to provide offset of 130 per cent.[12] It is also noteworthy that high offset demand was prevalent despite the European Union (EU) Defence Procurement Directive, prohibiting offset like practices in procurement. Nonetheless the countries resorted to offsets by way of invoking the Article 346 of the Directive that gives exemption on national security ground.

The excessively high demand for offsets led to a concern that it might erode the competitiveness of the European defence and technologies base. In a significant development, the EDA, a group of 27 EU member countries, announced a voluntary, non-legally-binding Code of Conduct on Offsets, which came into force on July 01, 2009.[13] The 'ultimate aim' of the Code is to "create the market conditions ... in which offset may no longer be needed."[14] It however acknowledges that "today's defence market is not perfect" and there exists a scope for offsets, at least in the short-run.

The EDA's code of conduct lays down broad principles to the subscribing member states. Among others, the Code caps the offset requirement at no more than the value of the main contract, meaning offset of maximum 100 per cent is permissible in defence trade. It also stipulates that when offset is used as a factor in the selection of bids, its weight age should be less significant so as to ensure procurement of the best available system at most economically competitive price. In an attempt to do away with the practice in which specific offsets were being asked by the buyers, the code provides freedom to the bidder to choose the cost effective options for discharge of offset obligations. In other words, the suppliers are required to be given freedom to choose their supply chain partners from the buying countries through a fair and open competition. The code finally binds the subscriber members to "mutual abatements to reduce reciprocal offset commitments."

Although the Code of Conduct is voluntary and legally non-binding, subscriber members have either aligned, or in the process of aligning, their respective offset policies with the Code's broad principles. For instance, the UK, a key EDA member, has abolished its Industrial Participation (IP) policy which was the hallmark of its high demand for offsets. On the other hand, it has adopted, since March 2012, a liberal Defence and Security Industrial Engagement Policy (DSIEP). The DSIEP seeks voluntary participation of the foreign companies to do business with the UK MoD, as opposed to the practice under the previous IP regime under which the UK insisted on offsets of 100 per cent or more on contracts exceeding $16 million.[15] Given the compliance of the UK and several other European countries with the principle of the Code of Conduct, particularly with respect to the limiting offsets to maximum 100 per cent, it is not surprising to see a downward trend in the global offset demand, as is reflected in the US BIS data.

PART II

Offsets: Threshold, Percentage and Multiplier

As a common practice, countries often define the threshold limit of the main arms contract beyond which offsets are mandatorily applicable. Countries also define the precise offset requirement by way of specifying a certain percentage of the main contract value to be mandatorily ploughed back to the domestic industry. Beyond these, countries also have a multiplier provision in their offset policy. While the threshold limit determines the scope of offsets, the latter two provisions (offset percentage and multiplier) determine the size of the offsets that can flow from the main contract. The Table 1 summarises these conditions for a select number of countries studied in the chapter. As can be seen, except for Canada, India has the highest threshold limit. This means, unlike most other countries which demand offsets in contracts valued as low as $5-15 million, Indian industry cannot benefit from such smaller contracts unless the contact value reaches $55 million.

Table 1: Offset: Threshold, Percentage and Multiplier

Country	*Threshold Limit (US$ Million)*	*Offset Requirement (%)*	*Multiplier*
Canada	100*	100	4-9
India	55	30	1.5-3
Israel	5	50	1.5
Malaysia	15	100	No multiplier**
South Korea	10	50	No multiplier
Turkey	No Threshold***	70	2-8
UAE	10	60	1.5-5

*: Canada has however the option of asking for offsets in contracts valued between $2 million and $100 million. The demand for offsets in such cases is determined by three factors: "(1) Is the procurement strategic to Canadian industry?, (2) Are the potential bidding companies of interest to Canadian industry and are they capable of fulfilling [offset] obligation?, and (3) Is the project a smaller part of a larger one?"
**: Although, Malaysia does not allow multiplier as a general rule, it however considers it on "exceptional circumstances such as when the offset programme can lead to high-end technology acquisition or maximisation of FDI into Malaysia."
***: In its revised policy of 2011, Turkey abolished its earlier threshold limit of $10 million, virtually giving it the power to ask for offsets irrespective of the value of contract.
Source: Author's database.

India has also the lowest offset percentage requirement among the listed countries. This means, given the value of an arms contract, the size of offsets that the Indian industry can get is lower than that for the other listed countries. However, this may not be true if one is to factor in multiplier which ranges between 1.5 and nine for these select countries. Given the wide variation in the value of the multiplier, the actual transaction value of offset can logically be different for countries having different offset percentage requirement. For instance, 100 per cent offset with a multiplier of nine (as is the case with Canada) in a procurement contract valued, say $900 million, results in lower offset transaction value ($100 million) than a similar contract with 60 per cent offset with a multiplier of 5 (as is the case of UAE). In case of UAE, the actual value of offset transaction would be $108 million.

From the above discussion, it appears that a lower offset percentage requirement with a lower multiplier is technically same as proportionately higher offset percentage requirement with higher multiplier. However, this logic hides a critical dimension that goes beyond the simple mathematical calculation. It is noteworthy that multiplier is used for specific areas of activities such as investment on R&D (as is the case in Israel), platform exports, technological cooperation and enabling technology specifically asked (Turkey), and high-end technology transfer (India). However, in most of the cases, the vendors have the discretion to choose those activities for fulfilling their offset obligations. In practice what one notices is that very few vendors choose these specific areas, because the nature of transactions is considered to be too beneficial to the buyers. This is the reason why multiplier has been of little relevance in offset transactions at the global level. This is amply illustrated in the 17th BIS Report which notes that out of 12,100 offset transactions made between 1993 and 2012; only 12 per cent transactions had a multiplier of greater than one. The average value of multiplier of these transactions was found to be a mere 1.2.[16]

Since multiplier is of lesser use, what becomes significant from a buyer's point of view is the percentage of offset requirement that determines the size of offsets that can flow to the domestic industry. This is perhaps the reason why countries like Malaysia and South Korea do not have multiplier provision in their policies, yet have a high offset percentage requirement. India on the other hand persists with a 30 per cent offset requirement since the policy was first announced in 2005.

Hybrid Input-Output Model for Calculation of Offset Credit

Many countries including India allow investment as one of the means for discharge of supplier's offset obligations. However, few countries bother to see if such investment, for which the foreign vendors earn offset credits, is having any real impact on the domestic economy. In this regard, the UAE's revised offset policy brought out in 2010 is an exception. The revised offset policy has incorporated a 'hybrid' model for calculation of offset credit that virtually puts onus on the foreign suppliers to ensure that a part of the offset inflows brings real benefits to the UAE economy.[17] As per the model, total offset credit is divided into two categories: inputs credits and output credits. A foreign company earns input credits when it makes an investment in UAE. The investment can take place in three broad forms: industry enablers, knowledge empowerment and equity contribution. The maximum that the foreign company is allowed to earn input credit is 30 per cent of its total obligations. In other words, minimum 70 per cent credits are to be earned through output credits, which are given when such investment leads to export sales, net profit of the ventures in which investment is made and generates incomes (salary) for UAE nationals. Evidently, the UAE model of calculating offset credit ensures that the flow of investment leads to measurable outcome rather than being an end in itself. This model could be useful for other countries which want foreign investment but have no clue as to how to ensure measuring outcomes flowing from such investments.

Value Addition

Many countries apply the principle of value addition for the purpose of estimating the true value of offset credit which can be claimed by the foreign vendors. The value-add principle ensures that the foreign vendors get their due offset credit for the local content they are able to achieve in the buying country. Normally, the value of offset credit is equal to the value addition of a product, although some countries allow 100 per cent credit beyond a certain localisation level. For instance, Norway's 2004 policy provides 100 per cent offset credit if 80 per cent localisation or more is ensured by the foreign vendors.[18]

Many countries have formulated detailed guidelines for estimating value addition in offset transaction. The Industrial and Regional Benefits (IRB) policy of Canada, which seeks offset benefits from the government's defence and security procurement, provides two methods—Net Selling Price method and the Cost Aggregate Method—to estimate the Canadian Content Value (CCV). The underlying principle of both the methodologies is to ensure that "only the Canadian labour and materials of a particular work package is counted toward an IRB contractor's obligation; all foreign overhead, labour and materials for any particular transaction is excluded from CCV."[19]

In India, value addition is determined "by subtracting (i) value of imported components (i.e.) import content in the product and (ii) any fees/royalty paid" from the final purchase/export price of the eligible products.[20] It is however to be noted that unlike Canada which applies the value addition principle for both products and services, India policy is only restricted to the products. In other words, under the Indian offset guidelines, foreign vendors can claim full credit for a services related transaction which may have 100 per cent import content. This not only gives an undue advantage to the foreign suppliers but also distorts the level playing field to the disadvantage of the manufacturing sector.

Principle of Additionality and Causality

As Hartley and Martin rightly note, an offset agreement "oblige[s] the foreign supplier and its sub-contractors to buy goods and services over and above what they would have bought from firms in the purchaser's economy in the absence of the offset agreement."[21] In other words, offsets involve transactions that are in addition to the transactions made under the normal market forces and are purely caused by the new contractual obligations. The idea of offsets is therefore to create new market opportunities which would not have been possible without an offset contract. However, the principle of additionality and causality is often overlooked while awarding offset contracts by many countries, including India which does not have any provision in its offset guidelines to this effect. Consequently, the foreign vendors are free to claim credits for the transactions (say for purchase of goods and services) which they normally do as part of their commercial activities under the normal market forces.

Compared to India, Canada, Malaysia and UAE emphasise on additionality and causality in their offset contracts. For the additionality point of view, the Malaysian policy categorically states that "all new proposals or activities must reflect visible increment of value-add on top of the basic/mandatory needs of the main procurement contract through direct offsets and present offset recipient's capability/capacity through indirect offsets in order to be considered for offset credits. For the purpose of causality, the Malaysian policy states that "all offset programmes must result directly from the procurement contract."[22] The UAE policy also talks of "expansion of existing business" and "causality (causing business to happen)" as the minimum criteria for offset activities in order to be considered for credits.[23]

Compared to Malaysia and the UAE, Canada offers a better scientific approach to additionality and causality. For the additionality point of view, Canada applies the following methodology for purchase of goods and services which are made from the existing Canadian vendors:

- The average of three-year purchases immediately preceding the date of identification of offset transaction by the Canadian offset authority;
- Offset credit would be awarded in each of the reporting periods, based on those purchase value which exceed the three year average.

The above methodology for calculation does not, however, apply if the product/service being purchased:

- Involves a direct work;
- Is substantially different than what was previously purchased;
- Involves a different end use (market sale, application, etc.) than what was previously purchased; or,
- Follows a competitive process to re-select the Canadian supplier.

To establish the causality factor, Canadian policy provides detailed guidelines that require the bidder to submit as documentary evidence, the "internal emails, official correspondence, meeting notes, corporate presentations or other complete or redacted documents", to prove that transaction are influenced by the offset requirement. It is noteworthy that while the responsibility for demonstrating causality lies with the bidder, the acceptance of such claim is with Canadian offset authorities. Among other factors, the Canadian authorities assess the causality claims based on the following three key factors:

- Market share: What is the market share held by an offset recipient for a particular product or service?
- Business History: What is the nature, intensity and longevity of any existing business relationship between the offset supplier and the offset recipient?
- Intellectual Property: Are there any intellectual property considerations that impact on the offset provider's choice of the offset recipient?

Banking and Offset Trading

Among the seven countries studied in the paper, except for the UAE, others have a banking provision in their respective offset policies, although they differ in terms of the kind of transactions allowed for banking, the extent to which banking is allowed, the validly period of banked credits and the flexibility in the use of banked credit (Table 3). Among the six countries which have banking provision, except for South Korea, which allows banking only for the excess transactions generated by vendors from their ongoing offset programmes, others allow banking in anticipation of future procurement programmes as well as in the event of overachievement of credits from the on-going programmes. The freedom to bank is unlimited in all countries except for Canada, which requires the vendors to identify a future procurement project against which the banked credits would be used; and stipulates a cap for banking amount. As per the Canadian policy, vendors are allowed to bank a maximum 15 per cent of their bid price of a future contract it wishes to participate in. In case of overachievement, the vendors are allowed to bank a maximum of 10 percent of total obligation value of an ongoing offset project, subject to a maximum of $100 million.[24] Canada also follows a stringent methodology for the purpose of the validity of banked offset credit. Unlike others which allow the entire value of banked credit to remain valid for a certain fixed period (three to seven years), Canada follows a 'depreciation schedule' that reduce the value of banked credit over a period of time. As per the Canadian policy, 100 per cent of value of the banked credit remains valid for first three years, followed by 75 per cent of value between third and fourth year and 50 per cent of value between fourth and fifth year (the validity lapses after the fifth year).

Table 2: Offset Banking and Trading

Country	*Validity of Banking Period (Years)*	*Trading*
Canada	5	Not Permitted
India	7	Permitted within the scope of the same contract between the main contractors and its Tier-I sub-contractors
Israel[25]	Not less than 5	Permitted among the supplier's corporate divisions and subsidiaries
Malaysia	5	Permitted subject to a limit of 50 per cent of the new obligations
South Korea	3	The banked offset credit of subcontractors can be utilised by the main contractors provided the former participate in the "identical main acquisition programme"
Turkey	5	Permitted to a limited extent
UAE	No provision	No provision

The freedom to use banked credit differs from country to country. Israel and Malaysia have a liberal policy that allows the vendors to use the entire banked credit for future use. Canada, India and South Korea however allow a limited use of banked credit. Canada puts a "limit of 50 percent of the total obligation that can be met using banked transactions." India allows full use of banked credits, but requires minimum two contracts for utilising the entire banked credit. In South Korea, the "ratio upon which the contractor may utilise the banked offset value against the obligations will be determined within 50 per cent by the Defence Acquisition Programme Administration (DAPA)."

Trading of banked offset credit does not seem to be a popular option among the countries. For instance, Canada, which allows banking for up to five years, clearly prohibits trading of banked transaction between the companies.[26] Malaysia, on the other hand, allows trading, but subject to a limit of 50 per cent of the new obligations.[27]

Offset Obligations on Domestic Enterprises

In an emerging trend, some countries such as Canada, India, Turkey and the UAE subject their own companies to offset conditions when the product offered by the domestic companies includes a certain percentage of import elements. The idea behind subjecting domestic industry to offset conditions is to prevent the local companies from acting as the front organisations of foreign companies; and force them to develop sub-suppliers of parts and components through compulsory subcontracting. However, there is a difference in the way various countries stipulate offset requirement for their own countries. Among the countries which require their own industry to provide offsets, Canada is a useful case study.

The Canadian policy does not distinguish between foreign and domestic companies as far as procurement contracts are concerned. The IRB, Canada's official offset policy categorically states that "any company that wins a specific Government of Canada procurement that has an Industrial and Regional Benefits requirement must fulfil the IRB obligation."[28] Since Canada stipulates 100 per cent offsets, the local companies winning contracts are also required to place business activities in the domestic industry valued at 100 per cent of the contract value. Like any other foreign companies having offset obligations, the Canadian companies are also required to meet the same set of criteria in order to become eligible. For instance, the Canadian company has to demonstrate that its offset proposals are compatible with the criteria of causality, incrementality and Canadian Content Value (CCV).

As per the Defence Offset Guidelines (DOG), Indian companies participating in 'Buy (Global)' contracts valued Rs 300 crore or more are required to provide offset if the indigenous content of their offered product is less than 50 per cent.[29] However unlike Canada the Indian policy does not provide a clear framework for the local companies to discharge their offset obligations. Of the seven different avenues that the DOG provides for discharge of offset obligations, the local industry can at best use only one avenue (i.e., executing export orders) to discharge their obligations. Suffice to mention that unlike the foreign companies which can earn offset credit for the investment in Indian enterprises or for the purchase order placed on the Indian companies, the Indian companies cannot take credit for such types of transactions. Evidently, the Indian companies having an offset liability would have a disadvantage vis-à-vis their foreign counterparts.

Apart from the offset avenue-related disadvantage, the Indian companies also face discrimination on account of indigenisation requirement. As mentioned earlier, Indian companies participating in 'Buy (Global)' procurement contracts are subject to offset liability if the indigenous content is less than 50 per cent. The offset liability is to be discharged at the rate of 30 per cent of the foreign exchange component of the procurement contract. From the outside it appears that Indian companies have lesser obligations than the foreign companies. However, a deeper examination would show that Indian company has to bear more burden than its foreign counterparts. Unlike the foreign companies which are free to supply the final product based on parts and components sourced from anywhere in the world, the Indian company has to undertake a certain level of indigenisation, which is nothing but direct offsets that it has to bear apart from the offset liability arising out of the import content. Moreover, the direct offsets, indicating the level of indigenisation, are to be proved at the time of field evaluation trials[30] On the other hand, the entire 30 per cent offset liability of the foreign supplies can be discharged indirectly in the areas totally unrelated to the procured item, and the time period for discharge can exceed two years beyond the warranty period of main procurement contract.

The discrimination of time period apart, the degree of indigenisation associated with direct offsets combined with the offset liability arising out of import content distort the level playing field against the domestic suppliers. The distortion is so much so that except for zero indigenisation (a theoretical possibility in which case the Indian company is a mere trader), at all other level of indigenisation, the burden on Indian company is more than 30 per cent which is the total offset obligations for the foreign company. This is illustrated in the Table 3 which shows the nature of burden on Indian companies at varying rate of indigenisation.

Table 3: Burden on Indian Companies under 'Buy (Global)' Contract

Indigenous Content (%)	*Offset Liability, % (30% of Import content)*	*Total Burden, % (indigenous Content plus Offset liability)*
0	30	30
10	27	37
15	25.5	40.5
20	24	44
25	22.5	47.5
30	21	51
35	19.5	54.5
40	18	58
45	16.5	61.5
49.9	15	65
50	0	50
>50	0	>50

Note: It is unlikely that an Indian company offering a product with less than 30 per cent indigenous content would be issued a 'Buy (Global)' tender to respond. In that case the indigenous content between zero and 30 per cent (as shown in column 1 of the Table) is a mere theoretical possibility.

Channelling Offset

While discharging the offset obligations, the foreign companies tend to choose certain business activities which may be cost-effective for them but are of little value from the buyer's point of view. This occurs primarily due to the design of policy that gives complete freedom to the foreign OEMs in choosing offsets. To guard against this, countries like Turkey, Canada and South Korea have reserved a right to ask specific offsets. Turkey, which is more concerned about boosting arms exports, specifically asks foreign vendors through the RFP to buy local made defence items through offset route.[31] Turkey's focus on arms exports through offsets seems to be yielding rich dividend. In 2012, its total arms exports were valued at $1.2 billion, placing the country among the world's 20 biggest arms exporters. It is believed that around 80 per cent of the arms exports are offset-induced.[32]

In its policy improvement carried out in December 2011, Canada has for the first time stipulated an Enhanced Priority Technology List (EPTL), for which a minimum five per cent offsets is to be reserved. The List, to be stated upfront in the RFP, is intended to encourage the development of advanced technologies in the aerospace and defence sector.[33]

In South Korea, offsets are channelled in two ways: influencing the source selection and reserving the right to nominate local companies to partner with the foreign companies for discharge of latter's offset obligations. The source selection is influenced by way of stating upfront in the RFP the offsets required in each acquisition. The required offsets are divided into a number of categories with each category having an assigned numerical value. The categories then become the basis for selecting the winner. Presently, South Korea has six categories of offsets with 'Category A' having the highest value of 6 and the 'Category E' lowest value of 1 (Table 4). DAPA has also the provision of giving 10 points provided a foreign company agrees to give state of the art technology that can be utilised in the R&D projects.

Table 4: South Korean Offset Category and Weighted Value

Category	*A*	*B*	*C*	*D*	*E*
Weighted Value	6	4	3	2	1

Source: Defence Acquisition Programme Administration (DAPA), Republic of Korea, *Defence Offset Programme Guidelines*, January 2012, p. 9.

South Korea reserves the right to select the local companies, known as Korean Industry Participant (KIP), who would partner with foreign companies for discharge of offset obligations. In those cases where the foreign vendors are allowed to suggest KIP, DAPA has also the final say. By reserving the right to select KIP, the DAPA ensures that right kind of domestic industry players get the opportunity which is in the interest of the Korean industry.

Establishing Long Term Relationship through Offsets

Many countries use their offset policies to force foreign companies to resort to business activities in the buyer's country through legally binding contracts, the violation of which warrants penalties. However, many a time such legally-binding offset-induced activities are of short duration and are not necessarily beneficial for the buyer's country in the long term. This is because the business arrangement is not often based on competitiveness to sustain the viability of the offset-induced-projects after the transaction period is over. A case in point is Malaysia, which witnessed closure of certain projects after the supplier's offset obligation was over. Two such projects related to Malaysia's foreign purchase of modular suspension bridge and ACV300 Armoured Personnel Carriers (APCs). As part of modular suspension composite bridges, an offset investment of $1.5 million was spent on a Malaysian firm, CTRM, by way of training the company's workers and investing in the factory's jigs and fixtures. The CTRM's role was to provide carbon composite launch rails for the bridges. However, once the offset period was over, the Malaysian firm received no further orders and consequently it was forced to shut down its factory. In the case of APC procurement, Malaysia's experience was similar. The APC deal involved off-the-shelf procurement of 146 APCs from a Turkish firm followed by license production of 65 vehicles through Completely Knocked-Down (CKD) kits by a local firm, DEFTECH. A total of $17.5 million offset credit was claimed by the Turkish supplier for providing license and for its investment on infrastructure, jigs, tools and a test track at the Pekan facility. Like in the CTRM's case, the Pekan facility also did not received much work to sustain its activities beyond the offset period.[34]

To prevent recurrence of past experience, Malaysia now emphasises on long-term viability of offset-induced projects. Its revised policy, announced in March 2011, categorically states that offset "programmes proposed must be economically and operationally sustainable after the [offset] discharge period." Post 2011 revision, it is now the responsibility of the vendors to justify to the Malaysian offset authorities the sustainability of the projects they propose to undertake through the offset route.

The offset policy followed by Israel emphasises heavily on establishing long term partnership with foreign companies. To build such long-run partnership, the policy focuses on two broad principles: proactive guidance by the Israel offset authority and competitiveness of Israeli industry to work with foreign companies. Unlike offset authorities of many countries, the Industrial Cooperation Authority (ICA)—the offset agency under the Ministry of Economy—takes extra care in facilitating offset-related interaction between the domestic industry and foreign companies. The idea is to identify areas of cooperation and the best Israeli companies which can work on offset projects efficiently. Some of the roles that ICA plays include:

- Assistance to overseas companies in identifying and locating suitable Israeli manufacturers and partners for joint ventures, outsourcing, R&D and other modes of cooperation and strategic partnerships with Israeli industry.
- Providing information about Israeli industry.
- Conducting surveys related to Israeli industry.
- Coordinating visits by representatives of Israeli industry to foreign companies.
- Coordinating visits by representatives of foreign companies to Israel in order to survey local industry.
- Organising conferences between foreign companies and Israeli industry.

Israel acknowledges that any long-term relationship with foreign companies cannot sustain without the best Israeli company being in the loop.[35] Accordingly, it allows a competition within the domestic industry so as to allow the best company to partner in an offset project with a foreign company. Israel's stated policy seems to be yielding long-term value for the domestic industry. As stated by the outgoing chief of the Israel's offset authority, "on each $1 of [offset] obligation, we tend to secure about $3 or even $4."[36]

The ICA's model for establishing long-term partnership, especially through a proactive role in cementing domestic industry's long-term relationship could be a lesson for other countries which despite having a dedicated offset authority are often found constrained to play the role of a true facilitator. For instance, India's Defence Offset Facilitation Agency (DOFA), or its successor, the Defence Offset Management Wing (DOMW), are never heard of performing the functions that ICA does.

Offset Swapping

In an emerging trend, South Korea is one of the few countries which allow offset swapping. The swapping is allowed to support the domestic industry with offset obligations in a foreign country. Under the swapping provision, either the domestic industry or the foreign partner having an offset obligation in South Korea can approach DAPA to consider a swapping proposal.[37]

Beyond Defence: Offset Policy at National Level

Some countries including India operate offset policy in the narrow prism of defence procurement only. In other words, the offset requirement is not applicable for non-defence sector. South Korea and Israel are, however, among those countries whose offset policy is applicable at the national level for both defence and civil procurement. In case of Israel, the offset requirements, enshrined in its official Industrial Cooperation (IC) guidelines, is applicable for any procurement by the State, Government Corporations and Public Agencies when their value of purchase of foreign goods or services exceeds $5 million. Moreover, Israel is in the process of bringing municipal authorities under the offset purview. This would subject contracts for sewage treatment projects, water treatment, power systems, etc. to mandatory industrial cooperation conditions.[38]

Israel's (and for that matter any country's) offset policy at the national level however brings out a critical issue which merits some explanation. The issue is related to the international norms set out by the 159-member trade group, the World Trade Organisation (WTO). It is noteworthy that Israel is one of the signatories to the WTO's Government Procurement Agreement (GPA).[39] The GPA, which is in force since January 1996, is a legally binding agreement among tasks including offsets, these agencies are believed to be ...n decision making.

...owever, there is no single agency for managing offsets. The ...itation Agency (DOFA) or its successor the Defenc... ...ent Wing (DOMW), which functions under the Indi... ...ent of Defence Production performs a part of the functions, ...iffused among the service headquarters and the Acquisition W... ...rtment of Defence (DoD). Evidently there is no single point of acc...

Conclusion

Notwithstanding the efforts by the US and several European cou... the perceived 'adverse impact' of offsets, the role of offsets in arm... to stay, at least for a foreseeable period. There is also every likelih... the shrinking military spending in advanced arms manufacturin... the simultaneous increase in defence expenditure by big arms imp... in Asia and others parts of the world, offsets would play an ev... in the international arms trade. In a buyers dominating global armament ... countries, which have declared offset policy, would try to improvise their existing policies to maximise their arms import. India being one of the biggest arms importers in the world, and having a declared offset policy since 2005, it is vital that its policy is not only dynamic and but takes into account some of the fundamental practices followed by others countries. Presently, the Indian offset policy, despite having gone through several rounds of revisions still remains a conservative one and lacks some of the fundamental principles adopted by others. Given that offset has a cost premium loaded into the main contract, it is high time that Indian policy makers took a serious look at the policy.

NOTES

1. Direct offsets are related to the system being procured and are typically in the form of co-production, subcontracting, licensed production, technology transfer. On the other hand, indirect offsets are unrelated to the items imported by the buyer. Such offsets usually include counter trade transactions, investment, financing activities, export related assistance, and technology transfer.
2. Peter Hall and Stefan Markowski, "On the Normality and Abnormality of Offsets Obligations" *Defence and Peace Economics*, 5, 1994, p. 173.
3. "The Half Trillion Dollar Challenge: Designing Offset Strategies to Build Reputation, Promote Development", July 2012, http://www.avascent.com/wp-content/uploads/2013/02/Avascent-Offsets-2-White-Paper.pdf (Accessed November 08, 2013)
4. "The Defence Industry: Guns and Sugar", *The Economist*, May 25, 2013, http://www.economist.com/news/business/21578400-more-governments-are-insisting-weapons-sellers-invest-side-deals-help-them-develop.
5. It is however to be noted that the pubic version of BIS data does not include country-wise offset.

the signatory members (42 as of 2013) to promote cross borde... procurement of goods and services. The Agreement prohibits di...ment against foreign suppliers in the government procurement. In this regard, ...ion 16 of the GPA specifically forbids use of offsets for "qualification and ...le of suppliers." However, an exception to the Agreement is provided und... Article 23 on national security ground, which allows virtually unrestricted us... offsets in military contracts.

It is to be noted that the GPA is plurilateral in nature, meaning its applicability is limited to the GPA signatories only. In other words, the GPA is not legally binding on the remaining 117 members of the WTO (including India[40]) who are not signatories of GPA.

It is also to be noted that although Article 16 of the GPA prohibits offsets in government procurement, it still gives special exemption to the developing countries to "negotiate [at the time of accession] conditions for the use of offsets, such as the requirements for incorporation of domestic content." However, such offset "requirement shall be used only for qualification to participate in the procurement process and not as criteria for awarding contracts."[41]

Although Israel is a developed country, it has managed to retain the rights to demand offset in civil contracts also. Israel's offset rights seem to have been allowed under the window of negotiation provided for negotiation for each party within the GPA group. The negotiation allows a party to negotiate the list of the government agencies and the goods and services which are open to bidding by all the GPA members. Since the list is agreeable to all the parties, asking offsets from others also mean giving the same rights to others. Keeping this in view, Israel's offset threshold for civil contracts within the GPA framework is different from the threshold limits for the non-GPA members and for the military contracts. These are mentioned below:

- Defence and security purchases require an undertaking of at least 50 percent of the foreign content value.
- Civil procurements from countries that are signatories to the GPA of the WTO will be subject to a requirement of 20 percent of the foreign content value.
- Civil purchases from non-GPA countries are subject to Industrial Cooperation amounting to 35 percent of foreign content valu...

Israel's dynamic threshold limits for offsets could be a usef... for countries like India which aspire to becom... contemplating a national offset policy[42]... its offsets requirement as en... (DPP) would b...

6. P. 2.
7. Bureau of Commerce and Security, US I
17th Study, February 2013, pp. 2-3.
8. The summation of direct and indire
small number of offsets transactio
either category.
9. In 2011, of the total number of transactions
cent were technology transfer.
10. The US government does not however prevent its
offset activities. As per the US government policy,
offsets, and the responsibility for negotiating and imp
with the companies involved". See "1990 Presidential
/www.bis.doc.gov/index.php/other-areas/strategic-ir
offsets-in-defense-trade (Accessed November 13, 20
11. E. Anders Eriksson et al., "Study on the Effects of Offs
Defence Industry and Market", July 2007.
12. Stephen Martin and Keith Hartley, "UK Firms' Ex
Offsets: Survey Results", *Defence and Peace Econom*
13. Brooks Tigner, "Briefing: EU Offset Policy Efforts St
Defence Weekly, November 22, 2012.
14. European Defence Agency, "Code of Conduct on Of
Participating in the European Defence Agency Versio
/www.eda.europa.eu/docs/default-source/documents/T
15. Guy Anderson, "Four companies now subscribe to
Engagement Policy", *Jane's Defence Weekly*, October
16. Bureau of Commerce and Security, US Department
17th Study, February 2013, pp. 4, 21.
17. Offset Programme Bureau of United Arab Emirates, "
http://www.idp.ae/en/agreements/Offset%20Policy%
18. Norwegian Ministry of Defence, "Guidelines for Es
connection with Procurement of Defence Material fro
p. 4.
19. Industry Canada, "IRB Eligibility Criteria", http
h_00043.html
20. Indian Ministry of Defence, *Defence Procurement I*
21. Stephen Martin and Keith Hartley, "UK Firms' E
Offsets: Survey Results", *Defence and Peace Econom*
22. Malaysian Ministry of Finance, "Policy and Guideline
Procurement (2nd Edition), March 2011, p.4.
23. UAE Offset Programme Bureau, Defence Contra
Edition, p. 9.
24. Industry Canada, "Banking of Industrial and R
www.ic.gc.ca/eic/site/042.nsf/eng/00035.html
25. Industrial Cooperation Authority, Israeli Ministry
Cooperation in Israel", http://www.moital.gov.il/NR
78B6CC5F6E7E.htm
26. Industry Canada, Industrial and Regional Benefits:
3.0, 2013, p. 31.

list which it wants to...
ment.

...plementation and Monitoring

One of the trickiest issues associated with offsets is related to management of offsets particularly with respect of implementation and monitoring. Loopholes in these twoareas could be counterproductive as has been found by the Comptroller and Auditor General of India (CAG), which undertook a critical study of 16 offset contacts (valued Rs 18,444.6 crore) signed by India between 2007 and 2011. The CAG had observed: invalid selection of Indian Offset Partners (IOP); zero value addition by the IOP; award of the offset contract in violation of the stipulated provisions; and weak monitoring of offset projects. Interestingly, the CAG's observations were attributed, to a large extent, to weak management of offsets.[43]

To manage offsets, Canada has set up an IRB directorate within the Aerospace, Defence and Marine Branch of Industry Canada. The directorate is the single-window agency for managing offsets. The management responsibility includes deciding the applicability of offsets, evaluating the offset proposal, giving credit for offsets discharged. Evidently, power to implement and monitor is at one place, even though the main procurement contract is signed by another agency.

Like Canada, Israel has also a similar organisational structure for managing offsets. The ICA of Israel which is under the Ministry of Economy is the nodal agency for management of offset. Under the Israeli law, the ICA is authorised to ensure that the foreign procurement (valued $5 million or more) undertaken by any government entity is in compliance with the mandatory offset requirement. Although, the ICA is not directly responsible for signing the contract, it has the responsibility, as a first step in managing offsets, to vet the offset undertaking form which is part of the tender document. Post-signing of the main contract, the ICA is completely responsible for enforcement of the foreign vendors' obligation as per the undertaking signed by the vendors. The ICA's functions include all communication with the foreign suppliers; receiving periodic reports from the vendors and assigning credits based on the progress in implementation; granting extension of time period if required.[44] Evidently, the ICA acts as a single-window agency for everything related to offsets.

Turkey and South Korea have also dedicated agencies for offsets. They are: the Under secretariat for Defence Industries (SSM in Turkish abbreviation) of Turkey and the DAPA of South Korea. However, unlike the IRB and ICA, both the SSM and DAPA are not only placed within the defence ministries of these countries but their role goes beyond offsets to include defence industrial development, acquisition and R&D management. Being the single agency for

27. Malaysian Ministry of Finance, *Policy and Guideline on Offset Programmes in Government Procurement* (2nd Edition), March 2011, p. 8, http://mides.mod.gov.my/index.php/info/pekeliling/pekeliling-offset; Defence Acquisition Programme Administration (DAPA), Republic of Korea, *Defence Offset Programme Guidelines*, January 2012, p. 18
28. Industry Canada, "Frequently Asked Questions" http://www.ic.gc.ca/eic/site/042.nsf/eng/00015.html#q14
29. Ministry of Defence, Government of India, *Defence Procurement Procedure 2013: Capital Procurement*, p. 46.
30. It is however to be noted that the DPP is not clear as to how and when the Indian companies would show the indigenous content.
31. Undersecretariat for Defence Industries, Ministry of National Defence, *Industrial Participation/Offset Guidelines*, April 2011, p. 9.
32. Carola Hoyos and Antoine Amann, "Turkey Builds Domestic Defence Industry", *Financial Times*, October 09, 2013, http://www.ft.com/intl/cms/s/0/837ef75a-1980-11e3-afc2-00144feab7de.html.
33. Industry Canada, "New Approach: Enhanced Priority Technology List", http://www.ic.gc.ca/eic/site/042.nsf/eng/00062.html
34. Kogila Balakrishnan, "Evaluating the Role of Offsets in Creating a Sustainable Defence Industrial Base: The Case of Malaysia", *The Journal of Defence and Security*, 1, No. 1, 2000.
35. Israeli Ministry of Economy, "Industrial Cooperation in Israel", http://www.moital.gov.il/NR/exeres/B204AC95-046B-4458-ACF3-41F965386044.htm
36. Barbara Opall-Rome, "Israel's Offsets Soar; More Local Firms Earn a Share", *Defense News*, January 19, 2013
37. Defence Acquisition Programme Administration (DAPA), Republic of Korea, *Defence Offset Programme Guidelines*, January 2012, p. 18
38. Israeli Ministry of Economy, "Guidelines for Industrial Cooperation in Israel", http://www.moital.gov.il/NR/exeres/85C96324-328D-40FC-9E8A-78B6CC5F6E7E.htm
39. World Trade Organisation, "Parties and observers to the GPA", http://www.wto.org/english/tratop_e/gproc_e/memobs_e.htm
40. India has got an observer status in the GPA
41. See Article XVI of World Trade Organisation, "Agreement on Government Procurement", http://www.wto.org/english/docs_e/legal_e/gpr-94_e.pdf
42. Amit Sen, "Govt Mulls Offset Policy for Purchases from Foreign Firms", *The Hindu Business Line*, November 18, 2013.
43. Report of the Comptroller and Auditor General of India for the year Ended March 2011, Union Government (Defence Services): Air Force and Navy, Compliance Audit, No 17 of 2012-13, pp. 17-25.
44. Israeli Ministry of Economy, "Industrial Cooperation in Israel", http://www.moital.gov.il/NR/exeres/B204AC95-046B-4458-ACF3-41F965386044.htm

17

Oversight in Defence

Vinod Rai

The Ministry of Defence (MoD) and the armed forces are the big ticket expending department in the Union government. Invariably the procedures guiding major administrative decisions in the ministry do come up for scrutiny time and again. This ministry, despite it's rather well architectured procedures involving a dedicated Defence Accounts Department (DAD), often comes up for adverse notice whenever some unforeseen event takes place in the Armed Forces. It has to be recognised that by its very nature, the methodology adopted for administrative approvals in the defense units have to be such as to ensure timeliness and have an inbuilt mechanism for flexibility in procedural prescription when urgency requires, such that outcomes are achieved without any relaxation in core parametres governing procurements in routine times. Unless a certain element of flexibility is built into the mechanism the debate or criticism of procedure dominating every activity and thereby stymying the very nature of urgency/secrecy of the objective will always leave a smacking of dissatisfaction among all the agencies involved. Nevertheless, by the very nature of the fact that the armed forces are big ticket spenders, unless an element of oversighting is built into the process there would be contention, speculation of wrongdoing and inevitably over caution among the bureaucracy leading to avoidable delays. Thus, any mechanism devised must have the right mix of caution and adherence to tight time lines.

It has also to be recognised that the framers of the constitution have provided for a civil bureaucracy as a buffer between the uniformed bureaucracy and the political executive. Hence, policy decisions or large procurements programmes have necessarily to pass through and thereby withstand the scrutiny of the civilian bureaucracy. This is to ensure that the decisions are above board and meet with the broad objectives for which they are taken. Let me put it in common parlance —the underlying philosophy is that multiple heads of different hues are better than singular administrative set ups. The earlier that the uniformed bureaucracy and the civilian bureaucracy align themselves to the fact that they are working towards a common goal, the better it is for the country. Neither is subservient to the other. Both have to work in tandem as what is at stake is the operational preparedness of the armed forces which is of paramount importance to the country. This issue can hardly ever be over emphasised.

It has also to be recognised that no procedure put in place at any point of time is static. Defence requirements are dynamic. Situations at any point of time will demand different approaches. Hence, it will be very inadvisable to have a ' one size fits all ' kind of an approach. There are certain issues which should necessarily be delegated to the service headquarters. I do not propose to indicate the type and nature of these issues as they will need to be decided by the service headquarters and the MoD sitting together and deliberating them. It will however have to be ensured that the concurrent or internal controls are in place to provide confidence to the decision makers as well as those finally giving the overall go ahead. Any such system devised, will have to provide for a well designed internal audit structure reporting directly to the Chief Accounting Authority of the ministry who would invariably be the Secretary.

The operational preparedness of the Armed Forces and a recent spate of unfortunate events have indeed thrown up some very basic concerns regarding the extent to which the present day structure and system of ensuring that the Forces are well provided for and are in a situation where they can be relied upon to fulfil the call of duty. These concerns are not of a passing or transient nature. They are deep seated and in view of the fact that decisions concerning the security forces have a long gestation period, the urgency to resolve them is imperative. We are at an inflexion point where tinkering at the periphery is not going to deliver. The decisions to be taken have to be radical and must ensure long term sustainability. The irony is that there is no dearth of committees, task forces and Groups of Ministers (GoM) who appear to have deliberated on these aspects. One severe failing in our obsession with secrecy or confidentiality is that none of the recommendations of these groups ever come out into public domain. The other is the action that follows the recommendation of these groups and whether any sufficiently high authority monitors the action and whether at any point of time we decide that action is indeed complete and that that particular chapter be closed. It is in this background that a firm and final decision will have to be taken to ensure that there is an urgent need for reforms in the Defence space. The reforms will have to be over the entire gamut of activities. It should cover a total revamp of systems and practices within the Service headquarter establishment and that within the MoD and other departments of government. These reforms will have to ensure that they encompass a long term perspective and that they permit sufficient flexibility to meet with contingencies that arise from time to time. In other words they will have to possess a dynamic paradigm.

Our policies have had the tag of being largely reactive, rather than proactive and well thought out in advance. How much our intelligence inputs and our own national cyber strength appear to be effective, is debatable. We need a structural change to ensure a more integrated and holistic approach to the entire issue of national security planning where all the state players come onto a common platform for the designing of the security policy. While no doubt fire walls are required for maintenance of intelligence data, the process of each force sharing inputs for an integrated approach is of prime importance. Quite often individual services have been found to be not so cooperative in sharing information into a common pool.

In this entire process the overarching objective will have to be to ensure that the Services are a fighting fit unit which are well provided for and wherein the morale of the men is at the highest. This objective will have a twofold approach:

> *One,* as internal to the services. Such an approach can best be left to the uniformed bureaucracy albeit with the caveat that insular organisations breed dissatisfaction and that no security establishment can afford such dissatisfaction. Respect and loyalty to the leadership comes only voluntarily and cannot be enforced by discipline alone. To what extent the present leadership is able to lead from the front and by example is a debateable issue.
>
> *Second,* the other aspect of the reform process concerns the MoD and the Civilian setup. This set up will have to devise structures and systems in close coordination with the Service headquarters to ensure that their aspirational needs, to the limit of budgetary limitations are met. No such reforms can be devised which have government procedures dominate all other objectives. They will have to be outcome based and that too, outcome within the limited time span that the need of the hour dictates. This brings me to the methodology part of things.

The methodology has to be devised to deliver rapid results and facilitate flexibility with sufficient decentralisation and trust built in. No doubt, accountability has to be a watchword as in govt transparency has to necessarily be given a very high priority. The Oversight mechanism both internal and external has to be built into the structure. Internal controls on a concurrent basis are a key to ensuring oversight and that procedures can withstand intense scrutiny. Unfortunately these mechanisms are not sufficiently well placed leading to avoidable glitches. Following the post-Kargil review of higher defence management systems by a GoM, new processes and institutional mechanisms have been put in place and defence expenditure has shown significant increase after 2004. In nominal terms, Defence capital expenditure has doubled over previously incurred capital expenditure since independence but this does not necessarily mean concomitant doubling of defence capability. Firstly, due to price inflation more rupees are spent for buying comparable capability than before. Secondly, earlier the payment schedules of Defence contracts were staggered over a long time period under Russian lines of credit. Now the payments under contracts are compressed to much shorter time frames and are usually front loaded with sizeable advance payments. Thus, there is more cash outgo, more defence capital expenditure in nominal terms, without matching deliveries or increase in defence capability. Nevertheless, it is undeniable that there has been increase in pace of acquisition, particularly by Navy and Air Force.

In terms of procurement systems, major institutional changes post—GoM include revamping of procedures under Defence Procurement Manual (DPM) for Revenue expenditure and Defence Procurement Procedure (DPP) for Capital expenditure, enhancement in delegation of financial powers of both MoD and Services Headquarters. The DPP has been frequently revised. Provisions regarding offsets expected from foreign suppliers of major defence equipment under acquisition contracts have been fine-tuned and system of pre-bid Integrity Pact and oversight of tendering procedure by observers from a panel approved by Central Vigilance Commission (CVC) have been introduced. Defence Acquisition Council (DAC) headed by the Defence Minister has built up a large portfolio of sanctioned acquisition programmes which of course are lagging behind both due to budgetary constraints as well as delays at various stages of tendering and field trials.

It is difficult to pass a summary judgement on whether these changes have all been helpful and implemented well. The results are mixed for different types of procurements and different Services. Some critics believe that the MoD has become too process-oriented to the detriment of intended outcomes. However, due diligence has its own short-term costs and long-term benefits and cannot be dismissed as unnecessary. The difficulty has been in designating a single point of responsibility for different activities both in the service headquarters and the MoD. As a consequence proposals tend to get tossed between the two with no one functionary willing to 'father' it.

So many defence acquisitions/procurements are stalled due to procedural wrangles. MoD should not tie itself in knots and render its working to be too process centric, irrespective of outcome. There should be accountability for results, not for blind compliance to rules and procedures borrowed from General Financial Rules (GFRs) though the nature of civilian market is totally different from defence market. Government's general procurement procedures are designed on the presumption that the government can dictate terms. The defence market is quite often a sellers' market whereas most segments of the civilian market are buyers' markets. In the domestic market, the government can afford to dictate terms, prescribe procedural formalities, ask for any type of guarantee and conclude contracts which, at least, on paper, seem to be loaded in favour of government but the same template does not apply for Defence contracts especially with foreign suppliers. Defence Suppliers dictate terms, which the government is forced to accept. Since bureaucrats do not want to deviate from Procurement Manuals, delays and problems ensue.

Government needs to recognise this harsh reality and design more flexible rules for defence procurement and take decision making to higher levels. In the Civil sector, one often finds Ministers, Empowered Group of Ministers (eGoMs) or Committee of Secretaries deciding crucial issues wherever financial stakes are high. They deliberate on price at which say PSU shares or national resources would be sold but in MoD, all negotiations from Rs.100 crore onward are done by Joint Secretary level committees. Naturally they ensure that all procedures are compiled with to the dot. The system becomes process-centric, not outcome-centric. Following rules and regulations takes time. To speed up delivery, core corners cannot be cut. The acquisition time must be reduced by careful planning and better project management. Requirements must be carefully thought out and clearly defined to meet overall objectives. The bidding process must be fair and open. The key principles of contracting viz., competition, fairness and transparency must be consistently incorporated in each transaction. There should be an effective contract review process to provide reasonable assurance that high value contracts are undertaken in accordance with established rules. Important and critical risks must be clearly identified and managed. Government buyers must equip themselves with skills to identify and assess risks commensurate with significance of purchase. The procurement framework must operate with clearly defined accountabilities, open and competitive processes and highest standards of professionalism. Maintaining best practice procurement requires continuous improvement. Immediate attention and focus must be given to achieve excellence in procurement, in substance and not only as a formality. The primary responsibility of designing and implementing various delivery systems vests with the executive. It is for the executive to ensure that the delivery mechanisms are efficient and effective with robust internal control mechanisms. Other agencies including Audit, of course, play a very important role in ensuring probity, transparency and accountability in the governance of various delivery systems but that is only as an oversight function.

Ministers/CCS/eGOM, do not play any role in Defence acquisitions beyond sanctioning the need and budget. Should we not explore importing some of the procurement and financial decision making systems from the Civil sector to the Defence sector? Another important import from civil side could be the idea of various models of auctions, which bring down risks in multi-round bidding instead of single stage L1 procedure. High value complex procurements need special procedures. General template of single stage L1 is not suitable for procuring very high-value, complex systems by MoD. We need to switch over to alternative bidding systems like multi-stage bidding/reverse auction/Swiss challenge, T1/L1 or other systems of assigning weightage to quality edge in price bids etc. The Cabinet Secretariat has started a consultation process and the auction models could come into play in defence sector after the Public Procurement Law stabilises.

It is so easy to derail defence procurement process. All that interests adversarial to us have to do is to plant some allegations, file some anonymous/pseudonymous complaint. The MoD gets jittery, and cancels or freezes the supply contract even before an FIR is registered, charge sheet is filed or charges are proved. That is what our adversaries want! Disproportionate and self-hurting retaliation against perceived bribe givers (foreigners) but little action against Indian nationals perceived to be bribe-receivers. They get all protection of Fundamental Rights, innocent-until-proved-guilty treatment but the same logic is not extended to foreign suppliers!! Result: Even more limited competition in an already uncompetitive market imposing unacceptable costs.

The spate of recent accidents point to an unhealthy trend towards too much attention to capital acquisitions and relative neglect of maintenance and upkeep. New acquisitions are planned without factoring possible recurring impact on Revenue budgets. In the last five to seven years, the MoD's capital expenditure appears to be numerically higher than prior cumulative defence capex since independence. But a lot of this expenditure is merely advance release of funds under multi-year contracts to Defence PSUs and foreign suppliers against which deliverables will take years to materialise.

Defence Planning

In the context of capital acquisitions a severe constraint in planning of future acquisitions or indigenous production programmes of the MoD is that its Five Year Plans (FYPs) never get approved in time. This creates an inherent handicap in the procurement process. It makes prioritisation difficult. It makes it difficult for project managers or planners to take advantage of floating RFP's or proposing supply programmes when the time is ripe for it as later there are cost over runs and other debilitating factors. Invariably, unplanned and ad hoc acquisitions are undertaken. This, in turn, impacts the training schedule of the field level operators leading to a classic 'cart before the horse' situation. More than any other factor, the nation suffers as there then comes about a capability gap in the operational preparedness of the force.

Defence budgeting and accounting is still traditional line-item budgeting whereas Civil ministries have moved to performance and outcome budgeting. Capability based planning and budgeting in defence has to be introduced. What is the intended outcome of defence expenditure? Having a fleet of a certain size or capability to neutralise threat XYZ with a combination of options ABC? If we want to protect our airspace against intrusion, we should aim at some target capability say detection of intrusion within a defined time period. Having set such a target, one can seek to work backwards and work out what combination of satellites, static and mobile radars we need to install. We must set a target capability of being able to mobilise XYZ number of troops at border ABC and then work backwards to see what vehicles, trains, aircraft we need, what roads/ bridges you need to be built or upgraded. Apparently, such capability based planning system does not exist. Planning outcome is merely a Perspective Plan which eventually turns out to be a compilation of the wish list of respective Services for acquiring various equipment, with no documented synergy between one acquisition proposal to another within Service or intra-Service synergy. Tri-Service capability builds up needs to be comprehensively dovetailed so that the acquisitions and preparedness complement each other producing synergies.

Consistency and freezing of qualitative requirements is a very critical feature of defence planning. The fact that the supply line takes a long time to deliver and that mid course corrections delay the process even further does seem to get adequate attention and we suffer at the hands of changes in heads of services leading to a relook at the Q R's thereby introducing uncertainity. Unless Q R's are frozen, unless some serious consequences merits their reopening, we should follow a tradition of having them written in stone once they are formalised. Quite often, formulating them narrowly also leads to various other tradeoffs which have consequences of their own. Certain times there have been situations where the equipment to be procured cannot even be tested at our own testing sites and we have to rely upon the facilities available with the supplier. This is a direct consequence of unimaginative planning, unrealistic time frames and aspiring for equipment which is still in the development stage.

If the perspective plans become a mere compilation of respective Services' wish lists of hardware, rather than a prioritised and resource-backed list, the acquisition process focuses on what can be procured within available budgetary resources readily. This is an issue which does not seem to have been given a considerable thought and needs to be undertaken in a comprehensive manner where tri-service consultation is also factored in. The methodology has to be inclusive rather than compartmentalised. Planning cannot be done in silos. Since no service operates independent of support and cooperation of the other, it is all the more essential than the prioritisation and acquisitions are complementary to each other's functioning.

Need for greater delegation to Services for Revenue expenditure: While acquisition/replacement of defence systems should continue to be of prime concern to the MoD, there is a case for enhanced delegation to Services for maintenance and upkeep of existing defence systems. The delegation structure should be based on the principle of subsidiarity as per the recommendations of the 2nd Administrative Reforms Commission (ARC). Decisions should be taken at levels most appropriate to take them. We need to put in place procedures which are sensitive to urgent and immediate needs for maintaining the preparedness at desired levels. Such operational preparedness is squarely the responsibility of the Chief's of each service. It is only a corollary of this fact that the chiefs are then given the freedom to make timely acquisition of spares or stores of daily requirement. This will enhance efficiency and entail greater accountability. Not providing such decentralisation leads to delays and hence consequent non fixation of responsibility.

There cannot however be total abdication on the part of MoD because the Civilian leadership is responsible to Parliament. An adequate oversight system has to be the foundation of a logical and systematised framework of delegation of financial powers. MoD has so far been reluctant to enhanced delegation on two considerations:

(i) A certain top percentile cases should come to MoD, and
(ii) Absence of robust internal audit system.

The main instruments of controls by higher formations in a hierarchy are typically as follows:

- Control through rationing of budgetary resources for specific purposes and power to re-appropriate them for different purposes
- Fixing Scales of authorisation
- Internal Audit
- Exception reporting ex post through a well-calibrated Management Information System (MIS)
- Reviews and Inspections

It is understood that an exercise to review the delegation of powers to Service Hqrs and subordinate formations was pre-conditioned by MoD by an intensive Internal Audit. Apparently the findings in this Special Internal Audit ordered by the Defence Minister were cause for concern. In the absence of consensus on the contours of an internal audit system acceptable to all stakeholders, there has been no progress either in enhancing the delegation of powers or in addressing the objections raised in the Internal Audit reports.

Defence Budget

In their projections to the 13th Finance Commission on Defence Budget, the Ministry of Finance has projected a growth rate of seven per cent per annum for defence revenue expenditure and 10 per annum for defence Capital expenditure. The resultant projection for the overall annual growth rate of defence expenditure works out to 8.33 per cent. Due to compression of payment schedules, front loading of payments under defence contracts and discontinuance of Russian lines of credit to finance, the historical trends are not good enough indicator for defence budget growth. It is likely to be much more skewed upwards in the years to come. Exchange rate fluctuations are a matter of great concern to MoD as a sizeable expenditure eventually goes out in foreign currency, directly or through imports by Indian vendors'. One major problem affecting operational preparedness has been relatively lower allocation of Revenue budget, which is largely pre-empted by pay and allowances leaving insufficient funds for ammunition, maintenance and overhaul. A Committee on Defence Budget, chaired by Secretary Defence Finance was set up in 2011 by MoD.

Pitfalls of institutionalised divide between systems for Revenue and Capital expenditure viz buying new vs extracting more juice out of existing equipment are a perennial dilemma. Maintenance costs are increasing. Major upgrades/ refurbishments are required in legacy equipment. The system does not institutionalise the debate on conflict between new acquisition and maintenance of old equipment, both pursued almost independently. Holistic appraisal is missing due to institutional Revenue/Capital divide from planning stage downwards. This also needs critical review. Deliberations of most of the Steering Committees/ Project Management Boards, which could focus on thematic issues or projects are either dysfunctional or engaged in somewhat superficial reviews with no regular feedback mechanism. The Ministry apparently operates without the benefit of full background information. The single file system is not backed by strong MIS. Selective amnesia/disclosure appears to be omnipresent due to oversight. With meaningful MIS and backgrounders apparently missing, institutional memory is not built up leaving the system exposed to the risk of "suggestiofalsi, suppressioveri". Information is all scattered and hence not retrievable, not usable. All resource planning is incremental: whether manpower, budget or equipments— no zero based budgeting, no zero based manpower review; No review of basic authorisations in ages. Financial planning is largely acquisition planning rather than capability oriented planning. Financial planning and defence capability planning need to be dovetailed for a more holistic appraisal of our requirements and the road map to procure them. Process of QRs formulation and vetting needs to be more democratic, more inclusive even if the Services retain the final say. QRs are sometimes framed by combining the best features of competing systems often resulting in a mere wishlist.

Budgetary devolutions for Defence and GDP do influence each other. Adequate expenditure on security is also a pre-requisite for economic growth. Also, expenditure on security builds up and systems contribute to industrial development and job creation. Ideally the real determinants of a defence budget should be the capacity voids vis-a-vis that of potential adversaries rather than a percentage of GDP or share of other Ministries or tax collection in total budget. Defence budget size is a compromise between what we aspire and what we can afford at current state of development. However, a realistic view will have to be taken in the sense that as a part of a parliamentary democracy, the needs of the rural sector such as primary health, primary education, water, rural employment and infrastructure, do get precedence at times. Hence, there are always severe competing demands on the budgetary devolution to different sectors. Defence will have to compete with these too. Neutralising security threats is a vital input to building the nation's prosperity and Defence needs are important but we also need resources to build the country to be defended! We need to catch up with arrears of social and physical infrastructure in the country. So the issue of affordable cost of security becomes important. The Finance Ministry's hands are tied by the increasing burden of subsidies and concomitant increase in fiscal deficit. Hence, there is an inevitability in the question mark on the availability of resources for defence unless there is radical shift in fiscal planning.

Defence production capability: Unlike Civilian producers, production for defence usually commences only after receipt of firm orders. Since inventory carrying costs are huge and risk of obsolescence very high, there are very few things of interest to Defence Forces available off-the-shelf. The factories face serious constraints as ordering has been erratic in the past. Even the production lines of foreign suppliers need restart, modernisation and augmentation in many cases. There are no ready solutions except to have a credible, finance-backed acquisition plan and steady pace ordering. While we are trying to enforce offset obligations on overseas defence suppliers to leverage our acquisitions for augmenting domestic industrial capability, sobering reality is that the Indian 'defence' industry lacks capability to absorb the offsets. The acquisition levels are probably not sufficient leverage to induce foreign OEMs to part with crucial technology. At best some low-end, bulk manufacturing alone will come to India but for that we don't need the leverage of offsets. It can come on its own commercial logic. It is possible to scale up our production capacity if a clearer policy on defence exports emerges. Also, offset scope can be widened to cover IT & Telecom for faster defence procurement and national interest. We need to critically review our policy of offsets in defence sector.

The basic fact that we need to come to terms with is that public sector manufacturing or productionising systems are not the most efficient. This fact has been well accepted in the civilian PSU's. Considering the fact that the culture of PSU's whether in the defence units or in others have the same legacy issues. Time has come to rethink the logic of limiting defence equipment production only to the public sector or government departmental production units. History is witness to the fact that the advent of new generation private sector banks enthused a whole new competitive culture among the public sector banking set up. Similarly, an 'open skies' policy permitting private airlines not only led to competition and thereby revolutionised air travel totally to the convenience of the travelling public, but also enthused professionalism in the public sector Air

India. Unless we recognise these realities and gradually start opening up the defence production also to private sector the benefits of competition and tight time schedules will never be realised. Today, a cost plus ship building programme does not enthuse the requirement of efficiency or achieving time and cost schedules. There is also no incentive to innovate or modernise. In the US and other democracies most of the defence related equipment is manufactured in the private sector and there obviously is no security breach or leak. Hence, there is no reason why the Indian defence forces should continue to suffer under the vicissitudes and mercy of the departmental and public sector units. This philosophy will require an entire new rethink. It is time we started thinking in that direction if we have to ensure timely and efficient supply to the armed forces.

The need to develop alternate sources of supply from the private sector will definitely revolutionise the existing public sector units as also introduce a whole new work culture which has become necessary to make these units survive. The private sector does possess better and cutting edge technology. It will also help in the process of price discovery which totally eludes policy planners and budget formulations. Quite often, in the absence of an alternate production source the price bench marking of equipment is done totally in the dark. Having an alternate source, will give better orientation to planners towards timelines, prices and introduction of latest technology besides bringing in a whole new paradigm of modernisation. It will be beneficial to build bridges and set up private public partnership ventures which can draw upon the benefits of both. This will require a road map to be put in place at the earliest.

The make versus buy decision is as old as the nation. No doubt self reliance is the best policy. However, we cannot subordinate national defence preparedness to indigenous production programmes having infinite timelines. 30 years for the development of a combat aircraft or a submarine is not a very desirable experiment for any country. Indigenisation needs to be pursued with accountability as a cost benefit approach, where time is a major variable. The DRDO is a very large and well structured department. However, it always appears to be on the wrong side of the service headquarters in terms of timelines in its development or research processes. There certainly is some element of fact in this criticism. However, the only way such criticism can be stemmed is by performance, indeed timely performance and setting a culture of it for the future.

I had mentioned at the beginning itself that the Defence forces have a dedicated defence account department which is totally in sync with its practices and procedures. This department provides all the necessary accounting and auditing support and guidance. There is need to design, in accordance with international internal auditing standards, an internal audit framework and organisation by restructuring the existing resources available with the ministry or the controller general of defence accounts. Internal audit is the only mechanism by which the secretary of the department will get real time information on stages of implementation and the compliance of procedures of all the activities taking place in the department. It is a very powerful medium of ensuring accountability and transparency in the entire process. Going forward, there will be greater demands on the transparency of government decision making processes. It is not for long that the defence sector can take protection under secrecy or sensitive matters clause. Most of these issues will have to be put out in the public domain very soon. So the earlier that we cater for it and take advance preparatory action the better advised that we will be. A good and effective internal audit framework also lessens the burden on external audit thereby ensuring timely resolution of issues.

A major reason for poor financial accountability is the weak internal controls in financial management of the Government. Internal controls serve to provide assurances on proper financial reporting, safeguarding of assets and achievement of organisational objective with due regard to economy, efficiency and effectiveness. Very importantly, it is the foundation of accountability. Unlike most countries in the world, India is yet to formally embrace a modern framework of internal control. A comprehensive framework for establishing and maintaining internal control needs to be developed. The MoD must take effective steps to ensure that their organisational structures are robust and that public funds are not prone to misuse, waste and fraud. The departments must upgrade their control environment and plug weaknesses in key procurement control activities. Establishing effective internal control involves an assessment of the risks that a government agency faces. Government departments lack a proper risk assessment framework for identifying and managing procurement activities that are vulnerable to fraud, waste and abuse. Hence, development of risk management skills in defence agencies would be necessary. Government has to bring themselves up to the task of formalising their risk assessment and control processes in the interest of better financial management. The way forward would be to sensitise the Ministry/ Department on the need for risk management and initiate development of skills for risk management. The objective should be to ensure that risk management becomes a standard feature of the way department carry out their activities. Without a risk management strategy for procurement, the Government would not be fully equipped to identify areas that would require stronger oversight.

At this stage it is very important for me to introduce the role of the Comptroller and Auditor General (CAG) and the rationale for having an oversight mechanism at such a high constitutional level. In a parliamentary democracy of the kind that we practice and which has delivered us near to double digit growth, it is very essential for government to not only be acting transparently on behalf of the people but also seen to be doing so. All governments fulfil a fiduciary responsibility. In doing so they spend the public's money, obviously for the good of the people or the nation. It is inevitable that in a democratic system where each pillar has a role to perform there is introduced an independent authority to authenticate the working of the executive. This has to be an agency at a high level and be created at an arms length distance from government and independent of it. It is for this reason that in democracies world wide the institution of the auditor general has been accorded constitutional status. It would be inappropriate to presume that this institution is a mere accounting body meant to validate the accounts of the govt only. As has been recently clarified by the Supreme Court, the National Auditor has been mandated to hold the govt financially accountable to the legislature. So in the case of the MoD or indeed any other ministry. The CAG has to ensure that the budget as passed by parliament and with the appropriations as passed by it is actually expended in the same manner. Thus, it would not only suffice for the CAG to do a compliance or Financial audit to merely ascertain that rules and procedures have been followed or expenditure has been booked under the relevant head of account. The CAG has to do performance audit, where required, to ensure that moneys have actually been expended in an effective, efficient and economic manner. This is to ascertain the quality of govt spending and to assure the parliament that the outcomes as desired by it have actually been achieved. It is in this positive role that the oversight mechanism of the CAG is meant to operate. Since the MoD is a big ticket spender it must use the experience and observations of this audit to reform procedures and improve the quality of spending by undertaking mid course corrections. Such positive and well conceived action would indeed act as an efficiency upgrade. It would be a waste of effort to have this role lost by taking a contrarian or adversarial view. There is no 'we-they' relationship between audit and the executive depts. Both are on the same side of the table. The objective of both being to upgrade the working of government departments and improve the delivery of services to the public and the nation.

The Indian defence establishment faces the oft repeated innuendos of being insular, opaque and procedure driven. These in fact are the more charitable interpretations. There are references to the department ensuring, or in fact resisting, attempts to open up with obviously ulterior motives. What is required is a total paradigm change, a quantum improvement in our preparedness and innovation capabilities. We cannot afford to be inflicting roadblocks onto ourselves such that we have set backs at every stage. Poor governance procedures and out dated practices cannot be allowed to debilitate our state of defence preparedness. The need is to build up our capability, overcome tardiness which has held back the sector from surging ahead and ensure that the benefit of technology and efficient resource management accrues to us. The task is not all that difficult. It only requires a determined mind set and the sincerity of purpose.

18

Oversight for Defence: Mechanism, Objectives and Methodology

Pratyush Sinha

Any discussion on a defence oversight body must necessarily answer a number of questions spread over several issues. The first issue obviously concerns its reach and how it would accommodate the existing oversight bodies. Second would be the comparative advantages of a single overarching body versus a group of entities tasked with the oversight functions of the different wings of the defence establishment. Third would be its powers in relation to the individual services. Fourth would be defining oversight itself in terms of the subjects that would be under the purview of the proposed body. Its location—whether in the Ministry of Defence (MoD) or outside of it could be another issue. Finally and critical to the entire discussion is the equation that is likely to evolve between any suggested oversight mechanism and certain privileged bodies like the Cabinet Committee on Security (CCS), parliamentary committees and now the Lok Pal.

Before we start raising and then answering the questions on the aforesaid issues it may be germane to the subject to briefly outline the present oversight scenario in India and also to survey the relevant best global practices.

Before we do that it is important to define some of the parameters against which to judge the effectiveness of the oversight or its concerns. It must ensure integrity, fair play, objectivity and transparency in the system. In addition it should demand accountability from each stake holder and value for money from every spender of Government money.

There already exist a slew of organisations that can be said to be a part of the oversight mechanism of Indian defence establishment, specially its acquisition system. The parliamentary committees, the Comptroller and Auditor General of India (C&AG) and the Central Vigilance Commission (CVC) have a more direct role in this process of accountability. While the parliamentary committees can and do look into all aspects of defence planning, deployment and preparedness, the C&AG is the premier audit institution and closely examines the propriety and efficiency of expenditure in the sector. CVC is charged with overseeing the maintenance and enforcement of integrity and ethical behaviour on the part of decision makers. On paper these three separate bodies appear adequate as far as the structural needs go. But in practice gaps have been found and serious doubts remain in public mind about the fairness and objectivity of many decisions in the defence sector. While misgivings occasionally arise in all spheres of defence, the most controversial have been those that relate to the acquisition of weapon systems. Both C&AG and to a large extent the CVC can do little to prevent a wrong doing from taking place except by way of establishing guilt of individuals later, suggesting action against those individuals and recommending such systemic changes as would lessen the chances of such an occurrence in future. CVC in particular has been issuing detailed procurement guidelines in order to ensure transparency and fairness in Govt. purchases. CVC has also sometimes intervened in an ongoing acquisition when serious complaints were made but such incidents are rare. The C&AG and the parliamentary committees similarly have taken note of various lapses and criticised the way decisions were taken. Both have also given advice for improvements in the system. Some sections of civil society keep close watch over defence acquisitions and in several instances have gone to courts seeking independent enquiry/investigation if they smelt any malfeasance. As a matter of fact the decision makers whether in uniform or without it, often complain about too much oversight leading to a paralysis in decision making—the curse of three Cs as it were.

In general any oversight should concern all aspects of an organisation. This though may not work in the case of defence because of how powers and responsibilities are distributed within the various wings that together constitute the defence establishment. A large part of expenditure and personnel matters are determined at the level of the military or the public sector or the organisation like DRDO. Then there are concerns regarding national security and 'need to know' context that may restrict the access of oversight. The military hierarchies and the concept of discipline within it further complicate the matter as issues of manpower deployment, recruitment, promotions and lack of moral scruples although within the realm of oversight may be in conflict with the existing mechanism if taken up by an oversight body. So we may have to draw the line between what is desirable and what is feasible. To begin with there should be some clarity about what within defence cries out for an effective oversight. Going by the number of controversies surrounding it procurement is what shapes the public perception about transparency, accountability and integrity of defence establishment in India. Promotions and postings of senior military officers have lately become controversial but with the setting up of a tribunal attempts have been made to ensure fairness and accountability in the system. Even after several attempts at streamlining the procedures and make them more transparent, equitable and competitive, defence procurement remains the Achilles heel of decision making and expenditure in defence. So this essay will mainly concentrate on suggesting measures for improving oversight in this area without adversely affecting speed and flexibility of decision making.

Defence procurement, capital items in particular, has remained mired in delays, u-turns, controversy and a general public perception about rampant corruption in high value defence purchases. This is so despite several attempts in the past several years to streamline the defence procurement procedure and internal organisational changes. A separate multi-disciplinary wing headed by a very senior officer within the MoD, constitution of a Defence Minister led acquisition council and the abolition of middlemen in the system, all of them have failed to bring about a qualitative change or reduce the controversy or delays. This has cost the nation enormously in terms of both defence preparedness and a ballooning of price for the same weapons system because of the delays. A number of committees and thinking heads have pondered the issues, reforms have ensued but in reality things have remained the same. Oversight cannot by itself be an answer to the problem but if combined with other measures it can be the source that supplies the arsenal for winning the war against opacity and venality in the system.

The purpose of this paper is not to suggest changes in the procurement procedures because this subject has been dealt with elsewhere in this volume. My comments on the elements of the procedures will be confined to observations on the points where the oversight and the procurement procedures would intersect.

What exists today by way of oversight, if you leave out the external bodies like the C&AG and CVC and the parliamentary committees is the departmental vigilance and the accountability enforced through the various rules in the military hierarchy. The institution of Chief Vigilance Officers (CVOs), mostly on a part time basis except in the case of PSUs, neither has the wherewithal nor the authority to run an effective and efficient oversight. The office has therefore tended to be complaint oriented and thus reactive and is seen more as a stumbling block to faster decision making than a guarantor for integrity, fair play and accountability. Many attempts at upgrading this office and to prepare it for an increasingly demanding and uncertain environment have not succeeded. It has therefore not developed the trust and efficiency required of a good oversight body. The fact that the CVOs are only partly free from internal controls has added to this predicament. The CVOs in defence PSUs suffer from a similar fate even though they are full time in the job and are externally sourced. This is in addition to the checks and balances embedded in any hierarchical system.

The constitutional and statutory bodies such as CVC, C&AG and Central Bureau of Investigation (CBI) get into the act late in the cycle of events and are seldom in the position to prevent a wrong doing. Theirs is mostly a post mortem leading to course correction in future. At best they are effective as parts of punitive vigilance. In an efficient criminal justice system where a criminal misconduct is swiftly investigated and rapidly punished this would be adequate warning to potential wrong doers and may even suffice in conjunction with normal administrative actions to keep the entire system in line and accountable. In India this has not happened mainly because of the long delays of the criminal justice system and less than satisfactory investigations. The administrative procedures too are beset with delays and are a tardy source of enforcing accountability and transparency. One would normally assume that with RTI Act, anti-corruption laws, active judiciary and civil society, there would be no need to think of further oversight. In mature democracies the criminal justice system and the parliamentary oversight together with the annual audit have proved to be efficient means of defence oversight. Can we then say that it is not so much the absence of institutional arrangements as the lack of coherence in approach, ill-defined powers and a tendency to be opaque that create the impression and also lead to unsatisfactory oversight? Or are there weaknesses in the processes of decision making that cause the problems of transparency and accountability?

We may therefore first attempt to see whether some required changes in the processes, greater clarity in the respective roles of oversight bodies and adoption of best global practices would not obviate the need for a radical overhaul of the system, more so because the latter may not always be doable. Many in the defence establishment already think that far too many oversight bodies have only contributed to delays in decision making and led to serious gaps in defence preparedness without ensuring integrity, fair play and value for money.

The starting point of any serious examination of various issues in oversight should therefore be an identification of the various factors that have remained problematic over the years. One way of identifying them would be those that attract the most allegations and disputes and so the greatest amount of unease amongst the general public. The areas of decision-making with significant discretionary powers verging on arbitrariness also pose problems of oversight. The U-turns at any stage of decision is another bane raising concerns about the motive behind the u-turns. The location of the decision makers within the system and their independence has remained a matter of difference of opinion. Sometimes this debate unfortunately is reduced to a base level as a dispute between the civil and military authorities. To me this appears to be wholly unnecessary in finding a solution and is meant to create sensationalism. I say so because the problems, as we would see, are neutrality of any such bias and inhabit both the worlds—the civil and the military.

We may also be wary of reposing too much faith in oversight alone for solving the problems in defence procurement and preparedness. Oversight can only go so far in ensuring integrity and objectivity and can not be a guarantor against all the ills of the system.

From various reports of CAG, enquiries/investigations of CVC and CBI, parliamentary debates and the recommendations of the parliamentary committees, judicial reviews and media coverage, one can get a fair picture of what are the main problem areas in defence procurement.

All procurements originate from the individual service headquarters. The qualitative requirements and essentiality of the weapon systems/platforms are based on the inputs and analysis provided by the military establishment. The actual procurement is processed by the defence acquisition wing of the MoD. Inputs are also given by the Integrated Defence Finance Wing. The acquisition wing assists the Ministry in getting various approvals including that of the Cabinet Committee on Security (CCS). Qualitative requirement is the first hurdle and is the beginning of any controversy. Complaints are frequently made about the tailoring of the qualitative requirements to suit a particular supplier. A small number of officials in the service headquarters are primarily responsible for preparing the qualitative requirements (QRs). There is no independent oversight and how and why a conclusion is reached is not always clear. Unlike many other countries the QRs in India go into minute details like the thickness of the metal to be used that deviate from the main performance criteria. Such details restrict the competition and may lean on a favoured supplier. Most countries emphasise the functionality of the weapon system and lay down rigid performance criteria, rather than the dimensions and specifications of the components used. An oversight intervention here would improve the quality and certainty of decision making. A panel of retired senior service officials may assist in formulating the QRs as part of oversight mechanism.

The defence acquisition wing is manned by civil and military personnel. It is multi-disciplinary and as such possesses the required knowledge to evaluate and vet the proposals when they arrive from the military sources. The complexity and the fast changing technology of defence sector are not amenable to understanding by someone who is on short term deputation. There is the added factor of the sense of the service loyalty that the officers on secondment generally carry. There are very few instances of the qualitative requirements undergoing a radical change at the instance of the acquisition wing in order to better reflect the strategic/tactical needs and to promote more competition. Lack of independent evaluation has opened the door for lobbying by various means. This must be thus the second point of oversight that allows an impartial and normative vetting of the QRs at the acquisition wing to make it more generic in nature and performance oriented rather than input focussed. The acquisition wing may enlist the support from a panel of experts drawn from military establishment and academia to vet the QRs.

Field trial of the short-listed weapons/platforms is a minefield of allegations and one of the main causes of delays and u-turns. Allegations fly thick and fast about rigging and the resultant bias. In a celebrated case, field trials were conducted not on the military but the civilian version of the helicopter and the decision then had to be annulled after years of preparatory work. Such examples abound. The existing in-house oversight has failed to prevent the misuse of the procedure. This is the third point of oversight. This must consist of completely independent and highly knowledgeable experts in their respective fields and unattached military veterans of sound standing to act as observers during the field trial. Their report in a structured format should be given individually to the acquisition wing and the sum of their views must be taken as the final verdict on performance.

Notices inviting tenders (NIT) and/or notices inviting expressions of interest are the most crucial documents in the procurement process. Both are vulnerable to manipulation. A bias here can completely undermine the integrity of the tender. It is therefore another point of oversight. In spite of the clear provisions in the Defence Procurement Procedure (DPP) examples can be cited where subtle tweak in the tender condition or an innocuous looking provision in the qualifying criteria or in evaluation criteria can seriously erode the competitive advantage of one or the other bidder. In the absence of an independent vetting of the proposal at this stage, these changes go unchallenged till someone sniffs a scam and then all hell breaks out putting the entire process in a reverse gear. Blame game starts and a vital piece of equipment is put on hold for several years. Clearly mere refining of the procurement procedure has not helped and so the solution has to be found outside of the guidelines. The answer is in oversight intervention at this stage. All the tender conditions including bid evaluation and qualifying criteria must be finalised before the NIT is issued and any change must be vetted by an independent body in order to ensure that the change is not meant to disturb the level playing field.

The proposals are initiated and approvals at various stages are all shrouded in great secrecy. While some confidentiality is necessary, there is no harm and definite virtue in sharing with the bidders the grounds on which bids have been accepted or rejected. The U.S.A. and many other countries do it. At this stage the concept of representation by the rejected bidders may also be introduced. 15 days time may be given for filing the representation which must be disposed of by an independent oversight body within six weeks of the filing of the representation. It should be in the form of a speaking order. The opacity that now surrounds the decision making process gives rise to innuendoes and creates doubts in the minds of the general public about the integrity of the procurement. The argument about the delays cannot wash because even at present most significant acquisitions are beset with long delays. The change is a risk worth taking. Experience of other countries with this procedure has been good.

It will be clear that this paper has so far refrained from suggesting any new organisation or major changes in the existing structures of oversight. In any case, CAG, CVC, CBI or the various parliamentary committees will be discussed only in so far as they impact on the oversight concerns of the defence procurement. The ministry vigilance of course will be discussed later once we are clear about the various oversight points.

It may be the appropriate stage in this essay to join the debate over mere procedural violations, need for short cuts and value for money in defence procurements.

It is made to look as if the above three are in opposition to each other. It need not be so. Any fair acquisition system must ensure just three things—transparency, equity and competitiveness. A tender that ensures this will be termed as ethically correct. As long as these three principles are adhered to one can be flexible. It is wrongly assumed that all the procedural violations are looked upon by the vigilance/audit organisations as fit for enquiry/investigation. The same is true of the short cuts. Problem arises because those violations are not related to any verifiable purpose and in most cases are found to be favouring a particular bidder or product. In case of defence equipment factors other than mere price may be important. Strategic considerations and/or need to match the capabilities of your main adversary may lead to a single vendor or a particular weapon but then it should be decided at the highest level and then one need not go through the drill of competitive bidding. Correct price will still be an important point for oversight.

The trickiest part of the decision making process and most susceptible to manipulation is the stage at which the proposal is ripe for approval at the Minister and the Cabinet level. Not only the failed bidders but their national governments enter the scene and new incentives, some overt but mostly covert, are offered to influence the final decision. Experience shows that a large number of cases fail to proceed further due to the external factors. Because of the position of the individuals involved in decision making at this stage the existing oversight mechanism has proved to be ineffective. In any case oversight generally has been mostly in the nature of action after the event and delays, about turns and scrapping of a proposal even at the final stage have seldom been a subject matter of vigilance enquiry or investigation by a specialised agency. This is the weakest link in the process and allegations have generally centred around activities and actions at this stage of decision making. Any oversight that can intervene at this point will have to be fully empowered and not lacking in expertise. At the same time adding another layer and permitting frequent intervention would further complicate the issues and more delays would result. How to strike a balance between objectivity and speed is therefore of critical importance.

It is clear from the discussion so far that if we want to have an efficient oversight body which at the same time is not an impediment in faster decision making then we shall have to think beyond the office of the CVO. We need not create a new body. I have introduced the concept of various oversight intervention points with each having a panel of independent individuals to oversee the needed intervention.

We have already identified a number of points for oversight interventions by a group of independent experts. That could be the starting point of reimagining the entire body to be called the oversight structure. In the first place it will not be a top down organisation. It will be more like a federated set up. Each oversight intervention point would be served by a panel of three to four people who will be drawn from the military and the finance wing of the government and will be assisted by subject matter specialists taken from reputed bodies like the IITs etc. Selection of these individuals must be carefully done and the respective service headquarters should have the power of suggestion and not veto. Their findings must be binding on decision makers. I have already suggested an appeal mechanism and that should be the only place for an aggrieved party to go. Appeal must be filed and decided within a prescribed time frame. Every decision must be put on the web-site and should give the reasons for that decision. Automatic escalation of pending decisions should also be a part of the proposed oversight mechanism. The system of seeking comments from all the related parties on the findings must go and whatever inputs are required by the independent bodies and sought to be given by others must be presented before the independent bodies before hand. If any allegation is made about unfairness at any stage before the proposal reaches the Secy/RM/CCS then it should be referred to the independent body concerned. Specific charge of bribe or any other instance of malfeasance will continue to be the responsibility of CVO/CBI/CVC or service headquarters.

The important thing is to ensure that the proposed oversight bodies are given mandatory powers for that limited scope of work. Their finding must be recorded in writing and in the form of a speaking order. They should be immediately placed on the website. Detailed Standard Operating Procedure (SOPs) and time frame will have to be laid down for each of these oversight intervention points. The members should work on sitting fee basis and must not be serving at that point in time in the government. A panel of such individuals should be prepared annually and a member may serve for three to four years or for the normal cycle of acquisition in the case of major purchases.

The real challenge is to suggest an oversight mechanism for ensuring objectivity, transparency and integrity once the proposal reaches the higher echelons of government. The permanent solution lies in creating a completely independent statutory body for defence acquisitions that takes over once the needs of the military have been identified and agreed to by the government, budget has been provided and go ahead is given to this statutory body. The statutory body will then carry out the entire exercise till it culminates in the procurement of the equipment. No outside agency including government can interfere in the process of ongoing acquisition. The independence and undivided responsibility of the organisation ensures accountability and transparency of the process. Defence acquisition wing has not been able to fulfil the expectations of expeditious acquisitions without controversy and delays. The long term solution therefore lies in creating an independent statutory body for all kinds of weapon purchase.

But short of a completely independent statutory body what oversight can be thought of in order to ensure objectivity, transparency and expedition at the last hurdle of decision making? It is common knowledge that the decisions are deliberately delayed and sometimes threat of not going ahead with the proposal after it has crossed all the barriers are the standard weapons in the armoury of those seeking a monetary advantage out of the said procurement. More often than not the interested suppliers succumb to this pressure and the proposal goes through. If a deal is not struck excuses are found to not proceed with the proposal. The nation loses both ways. As defence acquisitions have emerged as a major source of political funding in India mere tinkering with the system will not help. At the same time we cannot in our political system, at least for now, keep the political executives out of the loop of defence acquisition decision making. Even an upgraded post of CVO will not be able to oversee this level. The parliamentary committees, CAG, CVC or the CBI will come to the scene much later and their ex-facto examination cannot undo the harm done. We may have to think of a mechanism to ensure that the final proposal is not purposely enmeshed in delays/ controversies to extract advantage.

Perhaps the solution lies in extending the concept of external real time oversight to this level as well. First a time table must be laid down for the movement of file right from the stage of the finalisation of the qualitative requirements till all the bids have been evaluated. From the stage of the completion of the bid evaluation till the final approval of the winning bid again the proposal should move according to a time frame. This should include time taken for price negotiation as well. Any deviation from this should attract the attention of the proposed external oversight body. Because of the levels of the decision makers involved this external committee should comprise very senior and eminent persons.

It is suggested that it is composed of retired Supreme Court judge/C&AG/ CVC/a service Chief and an academician specialising in strategic matters. They act like an ombudsman for defence procurements. This will have to be supplemented by a rigid time frame from the day the qualitative requirements are prepared till the proposal lands in the CCS for major acquisitions and the apex decision maker in case of other procurements. Any delay outside of the time frame and any u-turns or revisions at the stage of the Secy./Minister must necessarily attract the attention of this oversight body. The members should function on a sitting fee basis and their recommendations should be binding on the decision makers.

It may be seen that I am suggesting a sort of a federation of a number of oversight bodies for the critical stages of the acquisition process. This is a radical departure from the conventional wisdom on the subject which favours a centralised body which acts on the basis of complaints and is more geared towards punitive vigilance. The office of the CVO in the MoD is organised on the same principles and has not succeeded in ensuring an efficient and clean acquisition process. CVO will continue to discharge the traditional vigilance functions but their role in the new architecture will be very limited.

The new architecture will be lean, flexible, completely independent and most important of all its oversight will be available on real time basis, the absence of which has been a bane of the procurement process. Since its response will be triggered not by a complaint but by any deviation from an agreed norm or a laid down time frame it will not be easy to manipulate it for partisan ends.

The challenge of oversight is to create an environment around the defence matters, particularly weapon procurements that sustains an atmosphere of trust and credibility in the system. At the same time it should not be so intrusive that the decision makers lose all initiative and shun action. An adhoc body of eminent persons who would act only to ensure normative behaviour when the acquisition process is in progress will not be intrusive. Elsewhere in this paper a suggestion has been made to introduce a system of appeals and for transparency of decisions at various stages. This will discourage frivolous complaints and insulate decision makers from post facto allegations for having taken a certain view in a disputed matter. The nature of engagement of the members of the committee, on sitting fee basis, will ensure that they remain independent.

The key to the success of the new arrangement will be the selection of the committee members. Once chosen their names should be displayed on the website, also giving the grounds for selection. This will facilitate exclusion of any undesirable name sneaking in because the publicity will ensure that civil society will act to block any such move.

The kind of structure suggested in this paper will in no way be in conflict with the existing constitutional and statutory bodies and not also duplicate their functions. It is in the nature of a new paradigm. It has all the elements of what is normally understood by the concept of preventive vigilance. In that sense it is like a management tool and would not be an adversary to faster decision making. At the same time it will fulfil the role expected of an effective oversight. The inputs by various committee members at different stages would serve better policy making in future. Parliamentary committees, C&AG and CVC will also benefit in their work by drawing appropriate lessons from the observations and recommendations of the oversight committees. The three service headquarters should welcome it because each committee will have fair representation of persons with a military background and so the complaint that at a higher stage of decision making service views do not always carry weight will be answered.

The complaint based CVO wing will continue as punitive vigilance has an important role in any scheme of oversight. But the wing needs to be completely overhauled, redesigned, reskilled and adequately empowered for this purpose. This can be done in consultation with the CVC. The defence PSUs and their vigilance wing will need a similar makeover in order to reflect the commercial dimensions of their work. The emphasis in both their cases must be on selecting personnel with defence expertise.

In the end I must say that any system is only as good as the individuals manning it. No amount of change, improvement or reform will work if there is lack of sincerity and dedication in those tasked with making the system work.

ANNEXURES

Capital & Revenue Budget Over the Years and the Share of Capital Budget as a % of the Budget & Actual Expenditure *(All Rs in Crs)*

	BE		*Capital Budget as % of Defence Budget*	*Actual (RE for 13-14)*		*Capital Budget as % of Total Actual Expenditure*	*Plan Period*	*Impact on Revenue Budget % of growth over1996-97 and 2007-08 on a/c of Pay Commission arrears*	*Capital Expenditure as a % of the total Defence Expenditure during the Plan period*
	Capital	*Revenue*		*Capital*	*Revenue*				
2014-15	94588	134412	41.30				**12th Plan from 2012-13 to 2016-17**		
2013-14	86741	116931	42.59	78872	124800	38.73			
2012-13	79579	113829	41.15	70499	111277	38.78			
2011-12	69148	92517	42.77	67902	103011	39.73	**XIth Defence Plan**		
2010-11	60000	87344	40.72	62056	92061	40.27			**38.57**
2009-10	54824	86879	38.69	51112	90669	36.05		**67.23**	Pay commission Arrears Payment & Revised rate of Pay(23.69% increse in Revenue Budget over previous year
2008-09	48007	57593	45.46	40918	73305	35.82		**35.20**	
2007-08	41922	54078	43.67	37462	54219	40.86			
2006-07	37458	51542	42.09	33826	51669	39.56	**Xth Defence Plan**		
2005-06	34375	48624	41.42	32338	48211	40.15			
2004-05	33483	43517	43.48	31994	43862	42.18			**36.34**
2003-04	20953	44347	32.09	16863	43203	28.07			
2002-03	21411	43589	32.94	14953	40709	26.86			
2001-02	19959	42041	32.19	16207	38059	29.87	**IXth Defence Plan**		
2000-01	17926	40661	30.60	12384	37238	24.96			
1999-00	12230	33464	26.77	11855	35216	25.19			**26.35**
1998-99	10360	30840	25.15	10036	29862	25.15		**42.22**	Pay commission Arrears Payment & Revised rate of Pay(14.09% increse in Revenue Budget over previous year
1997-98	8907	26713	25.01	9104	26174	25.81		**24.66**	
1996-97	8944	18855	32.17	8508	20997	28.84	**VIIIth Defence Plan**		
1995-96	7354	18146	28.84	8015	18241	30.53			
1994-95				6819	16426	29.34			**30.13**
1993-94				6867	14977	31.44			
1992-93				5473	12108	31.13			

Modernisation as a % of the Capital Budget & Actual Capital Expenditure Over the Years *(All Rs in Crs)*

	Budget Estimates				*Actual Expenditure (RE 13-14)*				*% Utilisation of Modernisation Budget*
	Capital	*Modernisation*	*Others (includes Land, capital works, DRDO, Ordnance Factories etc)*	*Modernisation as a % of Capital*	*Actual Capital Expenditure*	*Modernisation*	*Others (includes Land, capital works, DRDO, Ordnance Factories etc)*	*Modernisation as a % of Capital*	
2014-15	94588	75659	18929	80					
2013-14	86741	73868	12873	85	78872	66682	12190	85	90
2012-13	70499	59151	11348	84	70499	59151	11348	84	100
2011-12	69199	56625	12574	82	67902	56679	11224	83	100
2010-11	60000	47528	12472	79	62056	50314	11742	81	106
2009-10	54824	43816	11008	80	51112	42025	9087	82	96
2008-09	48007	40163	7844	84	40918	32418	8500	79	81
2007-08	41922	34515	7407	82	37462	30397	7065	81	88
2006-07	37458	31510	5948	84	33826	27818	6007	82	88
2005-06	34375	28470	5905	83	32338	26972	5365	83	95
2004-05	33483	29379	4104	88	31994	28600	3394	89	97
2003-04	20953	18067	2886	86	16863	14584	2279	86	81
2002-03	21411	18881	2530	88	14953	12938	2015	87	69
2001-02	19959	17866	2093	90	16207	14430	1777	89	81
2000-01	17926	16003	1923	89	12384	10502	1882	85	66
1999-00	12230	10570	1660	86	11855	10219	1636	86	97
1998-99	10360	8765	1595	85	10036	8663	1373	86	99
1997-98	8907	7364	1543	83	9104	7661	1443	84	104
1996-97	8944	7663	1281	86	8508	7245	1263	85	95
1995-96	7354	6136	1218	83	8015	6910	1105	86	113
Total 1995-96 to 2013-14	664551	556339	108212	1607	614904	514208	100696	84	92

Actual Expenditure on Modernisation and its Distribution Over the Years *(All Rs in Crs)*

	Actual EXP on Modernisation	Aircraft & Aero Engines	Heavy & Medium Vehicles	Other Equipment	Naval Fleet	Naval Dockyard/ Projects	Procurement of Rolling Stock	Joint Staff	Rashtriya Rifles
2014-15 (BE)	75659	21730	2921	35302	12576	1613	275	1029	213
2013-14 (RE)	66682	37190	1521	17796	8758	550	82	619	167
2012-13	59151	27575	1862	16830	11074	752		924	133
Current Plan Total	201492	86495	6304	69928	32408	2915	357	2572	513
% of Modernisation Exp		43	3.13	34.71	16.08	1.45	0.18	1.28	0.25
2011-12	56679	26215	2359	16331	10321	648	7	778	20
2010-11	50314	19343	1938	17205	10620	720	94	389	4
2009-10	42025	15838	1309	16275	7460	720	107	273	44
2008-09	32418	12408	1210	11986	5405	1164	0	219	26
2007-08	30397	13090	1400	8800	6162	668	25	224	26
XIth Plan Total	211832	86895	8217	70597	39967	3920	233	1884	121
% of Modernisation Exp		41.02	3.88	33.33	18.87	1.85	0.11	0.89	0.06
2006-07	27818	13920	686	5390	7080	465	57	198	23
2005-06	26972	12405	571	8923	4477	367	12	201	16
2004-05	28600	15986	328	6871	4645	473	33	207	55
2003-04	14584	5237	364	5555	2710	621	5	74	17
2002-03	12938	5039	74	5384	1995	438	8		
Xth Plan Total	110912	52587	2023	32124	20907	2366	115	680	112
% of Modernisation Exp		47.41	1.82	28.96	18.85	2.13	0.10	0.61	0.10
2001-02	14430	4644	1033	5312	3119	267	55		
2000-01	10502	3165	440	3951	2580	257	108		
1999-00	10219	3284	377	3766	2499	293	0	0	0

(*Contd.*)

	Actual EXP on Modernisation	*Aircraft & Aero Engines*	*Heavy & Medium Vehicles*	*Other Equipment*	*Naval Fleet*	*Naval Dockyard/ Projects*	*Procurement of Rolling Stock*	*Joint Staff*	*Rashtriya Rifles*
1998-99	8663	3272	350	2523	2323	195	0	0	0
1997-98	7661	3841	85	1776	1795	164	0	0	0
IXth Plan Total	51475	18206	2285	17328	12316	1176	164	0	0
% of Modernisation Exp		35	13	33.66	23.93	2.28	0.32	0.00	0.00
1996-97	7245	2757	199	2571	1524	189	4		0
1995-96	6910	2762	177	2350	1525	93	3	0	0
% of Modernisation Exp 95-96 to 96-97		39	3	35	22	2	3	0	0
Total 9th to the current Plan	589867	249701	19205	194898	108646	10659	876	5136	746
% of Modernisation Exp		42.33	3.26	33.04	18.42	1.81	0.15	0.87	0.13

Distribution of Capital Budget Amongst the Three Services and its Utilisation % Over the Years *(All Rs in Crs)*

	Capital Budget (BE)	*Actual Expenditure during the Year (RE for 13-14)*	*% Utilisation of BE*	*Army*			*Navy*			*Air Force*		
				BE	*Actual Expenditure*	*% Utilisation of BE*	*BE*	*Actual Expenditure*	*% Utilisation of BE*	*BE*	*Actual Expenditure*	*% Utilisation of BE*
2014-15(BE)	94588			25238			23833			33310		
2013-14(RE)	86741	78872	91	17890	14966	84	24149	20419	85	39208	37721	96
2012-13	79579	70499	89	19147	14758	77	24765	17760	72	30476	32980	108
2011-12	69198	67902	98	19151	14948	78	14658	19212	131	30224	28812	95
2010-11	60000	62056	103	17201	15796	92	12138	17140	141	25252	23604	93
2009-10	54824	51112	93	18020	14803	82	12282	13348	109	20114	18551	92
2008-09	48007	40918	85	13331	10623	80	12086	9457	78	19271	16598	86
2007-08	41922	37462	89	11634	11930	103	10561	8935	85	16829	13492	80
2006-07	37458	33826	90	10399	7251	70	9428	9486	101	15007	14627	97
2005-06	34375	32338	94	9427	9300	99	9226	7804	85	12804	12531	98
2004-05	33483	31994	96	8837	7412	84	7856	8315	106	14802	14784	100
2003-04	20953	16863	80	5682	5173	91	7030	5366	76	7095	5455	77
2002-03	21411	14953	70	7420	5291	71	5318	3805	72	7502	5017	67
2001-02	19959	16207	81	6453	5574	86	4881	4800	98	7559	4948	65
2000-01	17926	12384	69	6081	4291	71	4188	3741	89	6600	3346	51
1999-00	12230	11855	97	3746	3485	93	3401	3342	98	4236	4224	100
1998-99	10360	10036	97	2679	2748	103	3052	2973	97	3677	3658	99
1997-98	8907	9104	102	2145	2003	93	1897	2337	123	3972	3962	100
1996-97	8944	8508	95	2764	2724	99	2080	1931	93	3475	3164	91
1995-96	7354	8015	109	2446	2452	100	1855	1980	107	2417	3024	125
Utilisation 95-96 to 13-14	673629	614903	91	184453	155528	84	170850	162151	95	270520	250499	93

Distribution of Modernisation Expenditure within Each Service *(Rs in Crs)*

	Army					*Navy*						*Air Force*				
	Actual Exp on Modernisation	*Aircraft & Aero Engines*	*Heavy & Medium Vehicles*	*Other Equipment*	*Rolling Stock*	*Actual Exp on Modernisation*	*Aircraft & Aero Engines*	*Heavy & Medium Vehicles*	*Other Equipment*	*Naval Fleet*	*Naval Dock Yards*	*Actual Exp on Modernisation*	*Aircraft & Aero Engines*	*Heavy & Medium Vehicles*	*Other Equipment*	*Total Exp on Modernisation*
2014-15 (BE)	20687	2128	2692	15592	275	21912	3331	34	4358	12576	1613	31818	16271	194.29	15352	74417
2013-14 (RE)	10634	1182	1481	7889	82	19245	7418	4	2515	8758	550	36017	28589	36	7392	65895
2012-13	10739	2307	1773	6658		16302	1695	7	2773	11074	752	31053	23573	81	7399	58094
Total	42059	5617	5946	30139	357	57459	12444	46	9646	32408	2915	98887	68433	312	30142	198406
% Share	21	13	14	72	1	29	22	0	17	56	5	50	69	0	30	
2011-12	10839	1605	2274	6960		18547	4336	12	2583	10969	648	27135	20274	73	6788	56521
2010-11	11559	62	1910	9588		16108	3187	3	1579	10620	720	22160	16094	26	6039	49827
2009-10	11501	138	1274	10090		12663	3603	13	868	7460	720	17438	12097	23	5317	41602
2008-09	7689	603	1115	5971		8829	538	6	1716	5405	1164	15661	11268	89	4304	32178
2007-08	9077	1561	1379	6138		8404	410	2	1162	6162	668	12641	11119	20	1502	30122
Plan Total	50664	3968	7950	38746	0	64551	12074	35	7907	40615	3920	95035	70853	231	23950	210250
% Share	24	8	16	76	0	31	19	0	12	63	6	45	75	0	25	
2006-07	4531	640	684	3207		9099	366	1	1187	7080	465	13910	12914		996	27540
2005-06	7264	1013	570	5680		7424	1071	0	1509	4477	367	12055	10321	1	1733	26743
2004-05	6082	740	327	5016		7879	1963	1	797	4645	473	14342	13283	0	1059	28303
2003-04	4196	403	362	3431		5175	810	3	1031	2710	621	5117	4025		1092	14488
2002-03	4479	333	73	4073		3682	758	0	491	1995	438	4795	3975		821	12957
Plan Total	26552	3129	2016	21407	0	33260	4968	5	5015	20907	2366	50220	44517	1	5702	110032
% Share	24	12	8	81	0	30	15	0	15	63	7	46	89	0	11	
2001-02	5006	261	1031	3659	55	4703	809	2	505	3119	267	4721	3573		1148	14430
2000-01	3728	192	439	2990	108	3654	311	2	504	2580	257	3120	2663		457	10502

1999-00	2980	252	373	2356	0	3237	295	5	145	2499	293	4001	2737	0	1265	10219
1998-99	2352	205	346	1800	0	2869	246	4	102	2323	195	3442	2821	0	622	8663
1997-98	1634	123	79	1432	0	2225	214	2	51	1795	164	3801	3504	3	293	7661
Plan Total	15700	1033	2268	12236	164	16688	1875	14	1308	12316	1176	19086	15298	4	3784	51474
% Share	31	7	14	78	1	32	11	0	8	74	7	37	80	0	20	
1996-97	2275	80	192	2000	4	1931	172	6	39	1524	189	3039	2505	2	533	7245
1995-96	2099	54	169	1872	3	1920	287	3	12	1525	93	2891	2420	5	466	6910
Total from 1995-96 to 2014-15	139350	13881	18541	106400	528	175809	31820	109	23927	109294	10659	269157	204027	554	64577	584316
% of Total Modernisation Exp of the Respective Service Budget		9.96	13.31	76.35	0.38		18.10	0.06	13.61	62.17	6.06		75.80	0.21	23.99	0
Share of Total Modernisation Exp	23.85					30.09						46.06				
Share of Total Modernisation Exp		2.38	3.17	18.21	0.09		5.45	0.02	4.09	18.70	1.82		34.92	0.09	11.05	

Revenue Budget Allocation & Actual Expenditure in the Services over the Years *(Rs in Crs)*

	BE					Actual					Expenditure as % of BE
	BE	*Army*	*Navy*	*Air Force*	*Others*	*Expenditure (RE for 13-14)*	*Army*	*Navy*	*Air Force*	*Others*	
2014-15	134412	92669	13976	20507	7260						
2013-14	116931	81834	12194	18295	4608	124800	86283	13164	19283	6070	107
2012-13	113829	78114	12548	17706	5460	111277	77381	11834	17529	4533	98
2011-12	95217	64252	10589	15928	4448	103011	69792	11904	16773	4543	108
2010-11	87344	57327	9330	15211	5477	92061	62934	9979	14551	4596	105
2009-10	86879	58648	8322	14318	5590	94669	62737	9587	14708	7636	109
2008-09	57593	36271	7421	10856	3046	73581	47519	7791	12673	5599	128
2007-08	54078	34087	6968	10193	2830	54444	34198	6950	10102	3194	101
2006-07	51542	32299	6713	9858	2672	51933	32652	6715	9648	2919	101
2005-06	48625	31243	6027	9005	2350	48462	30492	6163	9173	2635	100
2004-05	43517	27829	5294	8468	1926	43862	28191	5214	8252	2195	101
2003-04	44347	28921	4951	8324	2152	43203	28348	4743	7732	2380	97
2002-03	43589	30691	4554	8187	158	40709	27191	4351	7369	1799	93
2001-02	42041	31103	4258	7714	-1033	38059	28221	3569	6836	-567	91
2000-01	40661	28939	4040	7896	-215	37238	26359	3643	7265	-29	92
1999-00	33464	23925	3363	6043	134	35216	26529	3495	6019	-827	105
1998-99	30840	21528	2924	5724	664	29862	21421	3043	5388	-856	97
1997-98*	26713	15585	2259	4814	435	26174	17892	2457	5164	690	100
1996-97	18855	12952	1834	3912	157	20997	14199	2046	4329	424	111
1995-96	19957	13348	1870	4058	681	18841	12936	1820	3908	178	94
Total	1056022	708894	115460	186509	41539	1088399	735274	118466	186700	47113	103
% of Revenue Budget		67.1	10.9	17.7	3.9		67.6	10.9	17.2	4.3	

DRDO Budget Expenditure *(Rs in Crs)*

Actual expenditure during the Financial Year	*Capital*	*Revenue*	*Total*	*Total Def Budget*	*DRDO Budget as a % of the Defence Budget*	*Capital*		*Revenue*							
						Mach & Equip from 04-05	*Works*	*Training*	*R&D*	*P&A Ser Per*	*P & A Civ*	*TPT*	*Stores*	*Works*	*Other Exp*
2014-15(BE)	9298	5985	15283	229000	**6.67**	8541	753	18	895	270	2025	160	1829	626	217
2013-14(RE)	5258	5673	10930	203672	**5.37**	4726	431	15	791	245	1860	123	1860	626	201
2012-13	4644	5150	9795	181776	**5.39**	4165	479	15	517	227	1694	111	1870	621	164
2011-12	4616	5278	9894	170913	**5.79**	4033	583	11	984	198	1535	108	1774	543	168
2010-11	4965	5184	10149	154117	**6.59**	4439	526	9	1218	202	1410	90	1666	492	145
2009-10	4154	4321	8475	141781	**5.98**	3802	352	8	563	220	1526	72	1454	412	101
2008-09	3859	3840	7699	114223	**6.74**	3442	417	7	697	141	1097	64	1396	375	98
2007-08	2947	3158	6105	91680	**6.66**	2412	535	5	678	83	661	68	1301	326	69
2006-07	2356	3007	5363	85495	**6.27**	1893	463	4	555	71	613	58	1369	291	68
2005-06	2506	2778	5283	80549	**6.56**	2140	366	4	497	60	591	51	1282	262	61
2004-05	1305	2410	3715	75856	**4.90**	923	381	3	486	53	542	40	1021	223	54
2003-04	743	2700	3443	60066	**5.73**		743	3	449	39	489	37	1454	186	54
2002-03	683	2325	3008	55662	**5.40**		683	0	345	44	462	34	1221	184	50
2001-02	779	2349	3128	54266	**5.76**		779								
2000-01	919	2437	3356	49622	**6.76**		919								
1999-00	714	2119	2833	47071	**6.02**		714								
1998-99	561	1739	2300	39898	**5.76**		561								
1997-98	674	1285	1958	35278	**5.55**		674								
1996-97	564	882	1446	29505	**4.90**		564								
1995-96	397	999	1396	26856	**5.20**		397								
Total	**51943**	**63616**	**115559**	**1870925**	5.95	**40517**	**11321**	**102**	**8674**	**1852**	**14505**	**1016**	**19498**	**5167**	**1449**
% Share	**44.95**	**55.05**				% of each sub head of the Revenue budget		**0.20**	**16.60**	**3.54**	**27.75**	**1.94**	**37.31**	**9.89**	**2.77**

DRDO Revenue Budget till 2002-03 was part of the ARMY REVENUE BUDGET & only from BE of 2003-04.new head was opened. The Capital budget of DRDO comprised of only the works head & funds for Machinery & Equipment was part of the Revenue Budget till 2003-04.

Share of Revenue Budget -Three Services *(Rs in Crs)*

Financial Year	*Total Actual Expenditure*				*Total Defence Revenue Budget*	*Total Defence Budget*	*% of Three Services Revenue Expenditure to Defence Revenue Budget*	*% of Three Services Revenue Expenditure to Defence Budget*
	Army	*Navy*	*Air Force*	*Total Expenditure Army, Navy & Air Force*				
2014-15 (BE)	92669	13976	20507	127152	134412	229000	94.60	55.52
2013-14 (RE)	86283	13164	19283	118730	124800	203672	95.14	58.29
2012-13	77381	11834	17529	106743	111277	181776	95.93	58.72
12th Plan	163663	24998	36812	225473	236077	385448		
% Share	**72.59**	**11.09**	**16.33**					
2011-12	69189	10844	17322	97355	103011	170913	94.51	56.96
2010-11	62683	9059	15179	86920	92061	154117	94.42	56.40
2009-10	60500	8618	14708	83827	94669	141781	88.55	59.12
2008-09	47394	7236	13243	67873	73581	114223	92.24	59.42
2007-08	34179	6620	10559	51357	54444	91680	94.33	56.02
11th Plan	273944	42377	71011	387332	417766	672715		
					83.09	**88.11**	**% Increase over 10th Plan**	
% Share	**70.73**	**10.94**	**18.33**					
2006-07	32812	6393	10064	49270	51933	85495	94.87	57.63
2005-06	30720	6073	9393	46185	48462	80549	95.30	57.34
2004-05	28687	4975	8446	42107	43862	75856	96.00	55.51
2003-04	28498	4617	7897	41012	43203	60066	94.93	68.28
2002-03	27381	4305	7562	39248	40709	55662	96.41	70.51
10th Plan	148097	26363	43363	217822	228170	357627		
					35.49	**58.15**	**% Increase over 9th Plan**	
% Share	**67.99**	**12.10**	**19.91**					
2001-02	25890	3649	7069	36608	38059	54266	96.19	67.46
2000-01	24005	3740	7485	35230	39098	49622	90.11	71.00

(Contd.)

(***Contd.***)

Financial Year	*Total Actual Expenditure*				*Total Defence Revenue Budget*	*Total Defence Budget*	*% of Three Services Revenue Expenditure to Defence Revenue Budget*	*% of Three Services Revenue Expenditure to Defence Budget*
	Army	*Navy*	*Air Force*	*Total Expenditure Army, Navy & Air Force*				
1999-00	24439	3543	6250	34232	35216	47071	97.21	72.73
1998-99	19746	3109	5615	28470	29862	39898	95.34	71.36
1997-98	16654	2477	5338	24468	26174	35278	93.48	69.36
9th Plan	110733	16518	31758	159009	168408	226134		
% Share	**69.64**	**10.39**	**19.97**					
1996-97	14199	2046	4329	20573	20997	29505	97.98	69.73
1995-96	12936	1820	3908	18664	18841	26856	99.06	69.49
Grand Total	723573	114121	191180	1028873	1090259	1698285	94.37	60.58
% share of the Revenue Expenditure of the three services	**70.33**	**11.09**	**18.58**					

Revenue Expenditure of the Army Over the Years and the Major Expenditure Heads (The Army Budget is excluding ECHS, Ins Org & NCC) *(Rs in Crs)*

Financial Year	*Pay & Allow*	*Transportation*	*Military Farms*	*Stores*	*Works*	*Rashtriya Rifles*	*Other Expenditure*	*Total Actual Expenditure*	*Total Defence Revenue Budget*	*Total Defence Budget*	*% of Army Revenue Expenditure to Defence Revenue Budget*	*% of Army Revenue Expenditure to Defence Budget*
2014-15 (BE)	59928.92	2368	428.8	15198.34	6784.55	4874.51	2481.7	92065	134412	229000	68.49	40.20
2013-14 (RE)	55030	2350	493	14663	6285	4536	1894	85251	124800	203672	68.31	41.86
2012-13	49924	2241	393	12757	5774	4078	1652	76818	108925	178504	70.52	43.03
12th Plan	164883	6959	1315	42618	18843	13488	6027	254134	368137	611176	69.03	41.58
As a % of Total Revenue exp of ARMY during the current Plan	**65**	**3**	**1**	**17**	**7**	**5**	**2**					
2011-12	43347	2173	316	12446	5666	3587	1654	69189	103011	170913	67.17	40.48
2010-11	38511	1871	255	12149	5311	3099	1486	62683	92061	154117	68.09	40.67
2009-10	40035	1792	219	9407	4610	3048	1389	60500	94669	141781	63.91	42.67
2008-09	27011	1372	216	10713	4283	2420	1378	47394	73581	114223	64.41	41.49
2007-08	16753	1312	200	9489	3649	1603	1173	34179	54444	91680	62.78	37.28
11th Plan	165657	8519	1207	54204	23518	13758	7081	273944	417766	672715	65.57	40.72
As a % of Total Revenue exp of Army during the XIth Plan	**60**	**3**	**0**	**20**	**9**	**5**	**3**					
2006-07	15611	1299	179	9934	3254	1514	1021	32812	51933	85495	63.18	38.38
2005-06	14841	1208	170	9122	3044	1365	969	30720	48462	80549	63.39	38.14
2004-05	14100	1121	154	8528	2816	1228	740	28687	43862	75856	65.40	37.82
2003-04	13017	1221	148	9779	2546	1114	673	28498	43203	60066	65.96	47.44
2002-03	12734	1146	148	9466	2240	994	652	27381	40709	55662	67.26	49.19

(Contd.)

(Contd.)

Financial Year	*Pay & Allow*	*Transportation*	*Military Farms*	*Stores*	*Works*	*Rashtriya Rifles*	*Other Expenditure*	*Total Actual Expenditure*	*Total Defence Revenue Budget*	*Total Defence Budget*	*% of Army Revenue Expenditure to Defence Revenue Budget*	*% of Army Revenue Expenditure to Defence Budget*
10th Plan	70303	5995	799	46830	13901	6215	4054	148097	228170	357627	64.91	41.41
As a % of Total Revenue exp of Army during the Xth Plan	47	4	1	32	9	4	3					
2001-02	12019	982	146	9282	2052	861	548	25890	38059	54266	68.03	47.71
2000-01	11441	841	155	8560	1855	615	539	24005	39098	49622	61.40	48.38
1999-00	10744	873	142	9990	1705	522	463	24439	35216	47071	69.40	51.92
1998-99	9831	605	126	7019	1421	337	405	19746	29862	39898	66.12	49.49
1997-98	8669	411	111	5651	1251	232	329	16654	26174	35278	63.63	47.21
9th Plan	52703	3712	679	40502	8285	2568	2284	110733	168408	226134	65.75	48.97
As a % of Total Revenue exp of Army during the IXth Plan	48	3	1	37	7	2	2					
1996-97	6590	342	91	4800	1070	166	284	13343	20997	29505	63.55	45.22
1995-96	5866	319	81	4370	988	117	301	12042	18841	26856	63.91	44.84
Total for 1995-96 & 96-97	12456	662	172	9170	2058	283	585	25386	39838			
As a % of Total Revenue exp for Two years	49	3	1	36	8	1	2					
Grand Total	466003	25847	4171	193324	66605	36312	20032	812294	1222319	1924012	66.46	42.22
As a % of Total Revenue exp of ARMY	57	3	1	24	8	4	2					

Revenue Expenditure of the Navy Over the Years and the Major Expenditure Heads (The Navy Budget excludes Joint Staff allocations) *(All Rs in Crs)*

	Pay & Allow	*Transportation*	*Repairs & Refits*	*Stores*	*Works*	*Other Expenditure*	*Total Actual Expenditure*	*Total Revenue Budget*	*Total Defence Budget*	*% of Navy Revenue Expenditure to Defence Revenue Budget*	*% of Navy Revenue Expenditure to Defence Budget*
2014-15 (BE)	5506	353	511	4929	934	355	12587	134412	229000	9.36	5.50
2013-14 (RE)	5056	353	442	4613	1069	350	11883	116931	203672	10.16	5.83
2012-13	4697	380	654	3982	760	351	10824	108925	178504	9.94	6.06
12th plan	15259	1086	1607	13523	2763	1056	35294	225856	382176	15.63	9.24
As a % of Total Revenue exp of navy during the current Plan	43	3	5	38	8	3	100				
2011-12	4508	353	768	4173	763	280	10844	103011	170913	10.53	6.35
2010-11	3731	288	606	3437	701	296	9059	92061	154117	9.84	5.88
2009-10	3972	233	572	2957	645	241	8618	94669	141781	9.10	6.08
2008-09	2714	180	525	2967	632	218	7236	73581	114223	9.83	6.34
2007-08	1784	142	735	3179	558	221	6620	54444	91680	12.16	7.22
11th Plan	16709	1195	3206	16713	3298	1257	42377	417766	672715	10.14	6.30
As a % of Total Revenue exp of navy during the XIth Plan	39	3	8	39	8	3	100				
2006-07	1615	166	1202	2718	489	203	6393	51933	85495	12.31	7.48
2005-06	1501	149	1206	2628	444	145	6073	48462	80549	12.53	7.54
2004-05	1401	125	433	2487	394	136	4975	43862	75856	11.34	6.56
2003-04	1293	124	374	2328	373	124	4617	43203	60066	10.69	7.69

(Contd.)

(Contd.)

	Pay & Allow	Transportation	Repairs & Refits	Stores	Works	Other Expenditure	Total Actual Expenditure	Total Revenue Budget	Total Defence Budget	% of Navy Revenue Expenditure to Defence Revenue Budget	% of Navy Revenue Expenditure to Defence Budget
2002-03	1234	129		1809	356	777	4305	40709	55662	10.58	7.73
10th Plan	7044	695	3215	11970	2055	1384	26363	228170	357627	11.55	7.37
As a % of Total Revenue exp of navy during the Xth Plan	27	3	12	45	8	5	100				
2001-02	1210	95		1311	339	694	3649	38059	54266	9.59	6.72
2000-01	1231	97		1384	309	719	3740	39098	49622	9.57	7.54
1999-00	1099	86		1245	290	822	3543	35216	47071	10.06	7.53
1998-99	1085	73		1163	267	521	3109	29862	39898	10.41	7.79
1997-98	896	60		972	233	316	2477	26174	35278	9.46	7.02
9th Plan	5522	410	0	6076	1439	3071	16518	168408	226134	9.81	7.30
As a % of Total Revenue exp of navy during the IXth Plan	33	2	0	37	9	19	100				
1996-97	662	48		891	180	303	2084	20997	29505	9.93	7.06
1995-96	587	45		805	163	39	1639	18841	26856		
Total for 1995-96 & 96-97	1248	93	0	1697	343	343	3723	39838	56361		
As a % of Total Revenue exp for Two years	34	2	0	46	9	9	100				
Grand Total	45781	3478	8833	49336	9774	7111	124275	1080038	1695012	11.51	7.33
As a % of Total Revenue exp	37	3	7	40	8	6	100				

Revenue Expenditure of the Air Force Over the Years and the Major Expenditure Heads *(Rs in Crs)*

	Pay & Allow	*Transportation*	*Stores*	*Works*	*Special Projects*	*Other Expenditure*	*Total Actual Expenditure*	*Total Revenue Budget*	*Total Defence Budget*	*% of Air Force Revenue Expenditure to Defence Revenue Budget*	*% of Air Force Revenue Expenditure to Defence Budget*
2014-15 (BE)	9972	824	7900	1946	0	565	21207	134412	229000	15.78	9.26
2013-14 (RE)	9155	698	7806	1910	0	414	19983	116931	203672	17.09	9.81
2012-13	8377	611	7038	1775	0	336	18138	108925	178504	16.65	10.16
12th plan	27505	2133	22744	5631	0	1316	59328	360268	611176	16.47	9.71
As a % of Total Revenue exp of AIR FORCE during the current Plan	46	4	38	9	0	2					
2011-12	7532	763	6931	1800	0	297	17322	103011	170913	16.82	10.13
2010-11	6856	620	5774	1692	0	236	15179	92061	154117	16.49	9.85
2009-10	6971	358	5640	1560	0	179	14708	94669	141781	15.54	10.37
2008-09	4681	249	6820	1318	0	176	13243	73581	114223	18.00	11.59
2007-08	2829	225	6191	1167	0	146	10559	54444	91680	19.39	11.52
11th Plan	28870	2215	31356	7536	1	1033	71011	417766	672715	17.00	10.56
As a % of Total Revenue exp of Air Force during the XIth Plan	41	3	44	11	0	1					
2006-07	2597	178	6250	909	0	130	10064	51933	85495	19.38	11.77
2005-06	2473	205	5725	841	0	149	9393	48462	80549	19.38	11.66
2004-05	2311	190	5018	805	1	121	8446	43862	75856	19.26	11.13
2003-04	2174	166	4724	714	3	117	7897	43203	60066	18.28	13.15

(Contd.)

(Contd.)

	Pay & Allow	*Transportation*	*Stores*	*Works*	*Special Projects*	*Other Expenditure*	*Total Actual Expenditure*	*Total Revenue Budget*	*Total Defence Budget*	*% of Air Force Revenue Expenditure to Defence Revenue Budget*	*% of Air Force Revenue Expenditure to Defence Budget*
2002-03	2160	156	4483	647	7	109	7562	40709	55662	18.58	13.59
10th Plan	11714	895	26200	3916	12	626	43363	228170	357627	19.00	12.13
As a % of Total Revenue exp of Air Force during the Xth Plan	27	2	60	9	0	1					
2001-02	2025	169	4170	599	8	99	7069	38059	54266	18.57	13.03
2000-01	2070	165	4607	532	9	103	7485	39098	49622	19.14	15.08
1999-00	1898	135	3634	470	8	106	6250	35216	47071	17.75	13.28
1998-99	1793	124	3172	426	8	93	5615	29862	39898	18.80	14.07
1997-98	1555	90	3255	359	7	73	5338	26174	35278	20.39	15.13
9th Plan	9340	683	18837	2386	39	472	31758	168408	226134	18.86	14.04
As a % of Total Revenue exp of Air Force during the IXth Plan	29	2	59	8	0	1					
1996-97	1145	79	2939	296	6	68	4533	20997	29505	21.59	15.36
1995-96	1026	86	2607	271	6	60	4056	18841	26856	21.53	15.10
Total for 1995-96 & 96-97	2171	165	5546	567	12	128	8588	39838	56361		
As a % of Total Revenue exp for Two years	25	2	65	7	0	1	**100**				
Grand Total	79600	6091	104683	20036	63	3575	214048	1214450	1924012	17.63	11.13
As a % of Total Revenue exp of AIR FORCE	37.19	2.85	48.91	9.36	0.03	1.67					

Army-Stores Budget Sub-Head Wise *(Rs in Crs)*

			POL					Ordnance Stores								Information Technology								
Financial Year	*Total Stores Exp/Bud*	*Provisions & G&S for animals*	*Diesel*	*ATF*	*Others*	*Total*	*Animals*	*Ordnance*	*Clothing*	*MT & Connected*	*Total*	*Medical & Vet*	*Engineer*	*AF & A Engines*	*Aviation*	*Hardware*	*Sofware*	*Maint*	*Stationery & Cons*	*Training*	*Total*	*R&D*	*Disaster Relief*	*Security Related*
2014-15 (BE)	15198	2478	1400	602	883	2886	74	6262	1279	605	8146	631	347	219	38	184	65	40	67	14	370	5		5
2013-14 (RE)	14663	2761	1428	718	308	3120	0	5792	1152	591	7536	695	156	60	66	141	14	31	72	8	265	4		
2012-13	12757	2564	745	499	661	1905	0	5552	963	654	7170	581	164	73	50	136	13	32	63	3	247	3	0	0
2011-12	12446	2256	830	583	616	2029	0	5604	659	739	7001	558	153	80	45	213	9	30	66	4	321	3	0	0
2010-11	12149	1867	786	451	543	1780	0	5929	556	790	7275	506	189	231	26	162	9	31	62	7	271	3	0	
2009-10	9407	1488	675	368	491	1534	37	4928	349	-111	5166	443	190	225	19	208	9	24	55	6	303	3	0	0
2008-09	10713	1489	697	503	504	1704	0	5228	474	559	6261	447	218	238	17	237	11	23	59	6	336	3	0	0
2007-08	9489	1263	710	454	455	1619	0	4043	472	968	5483	431	190	207	15	185	9	20	57	6	277	3	0	0
2006-07	9934	1212	782	455	396	1633	0	3776	540	1819	6136	349	152	152	8	200	8	19	59	5	290	1	0	0
2005-06	9122	1135	674	123	398	1194	0	3356	510	2125	5991	306	126	135	8	153	4	16	47	3	224	3	0	0
2004-05	8528	1079	535	121	328	984	0	3291	575	1927	5794	285	91	118	10	118	4	11	31	3	167	1	0	0
2003-04	9779	989	373	127	341	842	0	3922	484	2903	7309	259	117	101	5	120	0	10	25	1	157	0	0	0
2002-03	9467	984	383	142	383	908	0	4178	579	2251	7008	257	85	92	4						128	0	0	0
2001-02	9282	932	409	115	393	918	0	4383	469	2144	6996	180	81	62	6						107	0	0	0
2000-01	8560	887				737	0	3876	503	2218	6598	148	72	46	4						68	0	0	0
1999-00	9990	962	622		92	714		4672	517	2747	7936	145	64	114	5						50			
1998-99	7019	964	507		85	592	0	2697	245	2151	5092	111	67	169	3						21			
1997-98	5651	867	458		90	548	0	3131	247	661	4039	114	56	26	1									
1996-97	4800	712	397		90	487		2640	212	568	3420	103	62	16	0									
1995-96	4370	713	359		53	413	0	2365	194	518	3077	95	50	22	0									
TOTAL	178126	25123	11370	4660	6228	23660	38	79366	9700	26222	115288	6013	2283	2170	292						3232	27	0	0
% of Stores Budget		**14.1**				**13.3**		44.6	5.4	14.7	**64.7**	**3.4**	**1.3**	**1.2**	**0.2**						**1.8**	**0.0**		

Navy-Stores Budget Sub-Head Wise *(Rs in Crs)*

	Total Stores Exp/Bud	Naval stores	Provisions & Water	POL incl Cooking Gas	Armament	Clothing	Medical	MT	Spares incl machinery for Dockyard	Weapon Spares	Spl equp for Scientific labs	Aviation	Custom Duty	Information Technology						Indigenisation	R&D	Security Related
														Hardware	Software	Maint	Stationery & Cons	Training	Total			
2014-15 (BE)	4929	399	232	2248.7	298.2	92	100	9	780.5	312	2.75	360		40.3	9	10	6	2	68	25	2	
2013-14 (RE)	4613	367	191	2234	280	65	99	7	743	210	2.4	315		33	15	13	8	1	70	29	1	
2012-13	3982	432	158	1453	291	61	92	9	666	391	1	352		29	13	17	7	2	67	9	0	0
2011-12	4173	478	135	1632	259	61	86	8	845	269	3	312		39	14	13	9	2	75	9	0	0
2010-11	3437	397	116	1040	209	56	60	12	929	193	2	339	0	43	13	7	7	1	70	13	0	0
2009-10	2957	394	100	913	117	29	61	11	750	145	1	372	0	37	8	7	5	1	57	8	0	0
2008-09	2967	355	90	1015	162	27	49	13	624	149	2	411	0	38	11	8	5	1	63	7	0	0
2007-08	3179	321	71	1084	510	30	34	13	517	64	2	478	0	33	8	7	8	1	56	0	0	0
2006-07	2718	299	67	851	214	50	32	13	497	238	3	404	0	33	3	6	7	1	50	0	0	0
2005-06	2628	232	54	820	687	45	24	13	302	123	1	293	0	22	2	4	6	1	35	0	0	0
2004-05	2487	263	47	748	624	21	23	17	372	119	0	217	3	22	4	2	6	0	34	0	0	0
2003-04	2328	212	40	564	676	20	20	13	425	121	0	212	0	21	2	1	2	0	26	0	0	0
2002-03	1809	228	37	460	386	28	23	13	359	90	1	183	0									
2001-02	1311	216	37	446	303	21	13	8	162	52	0	54	0									
2000-01	1384	198	40	319	407	27	14	6	217	93	0	62	0									
1999-00	1245	209	39	304	344	17	12	10	154	101	0	55	0									
1998-99	1163	162	44	208	316	23	12	12	258	66	1	60	1									
1997-98	972	152	36	177	244	26	4	14	180	62	0	76	1									
1996-97	891	187	34	207	138	20	6	10	209	15	0	65	-1									
1995-96	805	209	25	115	174	23	5	3	187	11	0	52	0									
TOTAL	41219	4234	1030	11648	5188	493	542	160	6818	2147	19	3743	3	316	77	71	61	10	535	46	1	0
% of Stores Budget		**10**	**2**	**28**	**13**	**1**	**1**	**0**	**17**	**5**	**0**	**9**							**1**	**0**	**0**	

Air Force Stores Budget Sub-Head Wise *(Rs in Crs)*

												Information Technology							
Financial Year	*Total Stores Exp/Bud*	*Air Frame & Aero Engines*	*Aviation*	*MT stores*	*Provisions & LPG*	*POL*	*Ordnance*	*Clothing*	*Medical*	*Other Misc*	*R&D*	*Hardware*	*Software*	*Maint*	*Stationery & Cons*	*Training*	*Total*	*Security Related Eqp*	*Pol as a % of Stores Budget*
2014-15 (BE)	7900	1342.98	1969	70	128	3570	426	60	112	70	15	66	7	11	17	2.5	103	33	45.19
2013-14	7806	1059	1345	73	129	4183	502	140	112	74	18	84	12	11	22	3	131	38	53.59
2012-13	7038	675	1474	72	113	3768	559	79	111	66	9	74	8	9	20	2	112	0	53.53
2011-12	6931	1027	1500	78	121	3337	419	146	97	66	2	94	12	10	21	2	140	0	48.15
2010-11	5775	1139	1139	62	123	2662	264	128	80	55	6	79	9	8	16	3	116	0	46.10
2009-10	5640	1162	1439	61	88	2170	355	145	84	42	3	65	8	5	11	2	91	0	38.48
2008-09	6820	1717	1470	83	90	2876	206	171	59	65	5	58	5	4	10	2	78	0	42.18
2007-08	6191	1941	1130	92	71	2305	362	110	50	42	3	67	4	3	9	1	84	0	37.24
2006-07	6250	1946	1348	84	65	2250	312	103	37	36	2	52	3	4	7	1	67	0	36.01
2005-06	5725	2011	1118	83	63	1905	305	128	38	26	2	35	1	3	5	1	45	0	33.28
2004-05	5018	1687	1000	126	52	1557	435	57	41	33	3	17	1	3	5	1	27	0	31.02
2003-04	4724	1688	1008	79	53	1150	588	58	24	51	3	16	0	2	3	0	22	0	24.34
2002-03	4483	1868	997	79	67	973	386	33	17	47	4						12	0	21.71
2001-02	4170	1499	933	91	44	1059	431	33	21	46	2						11	0	25.40
2000-01	4607	1837	734	81	53	1254	527	38	13	61	2						8	0	27.21
1999-00	3634	1257	762	88	49	895	479	31	12	52	1						6		24.64
1998-99	3172	1228	593	54	58	948	155	44	9	34	49								29.90
1997-98	3255	1252	733	40	52	927	142	57	9	35	7								28.49
1996-97	2939	825	891	36	43	865	189	56	6	22	4								29.44
1995-96	2607	779	800	48	35	629	243	24	6	23	19								24.14
Total	96784	26598	20414	1412	1369	35717	6859	1580	825	876	146	641	65	61	129	18	949	38	36.90
% of Stores Budget		27	21	1	1	37	7	2	1	1	0.15						1.0	4	

Sales Value of Production DPSU's & Ordnance Factories (Rs in Crs)

	HAL	*BDL*	*Mazagon Docks Ltd - (value of production)*	*Goa Shipyard- value of production*	*Gardenreach - (value of production)*	*BEL*	*BEML*	*Midhani*	*Ordnance factories- value of Issuies, including civil & export**
2012-13	14324	1072	2291	507	1529	6012	3290	559	
2011-12	14204	959	2524	676	1293	5704	3648	509	10880.87
2010-11	13116	939	2611	990	1053	5530	3647	418	11215
2009-10	11457	627	2856	866	871	5220	3589	371	8715
2008-09	10373	465	2569	508	673	4624	3013	309	7229
2007-08	8625	454	2322	317	573	4103	2713	255	6938
2006-07	7784	434	1872	267	642	3953	2602	193	6197
2005-06	5342	532	518	250	662	3536	2206	153	6892
2004-05	4534	451	541	142	470	3212	1856	131	6187
2003-04	3800	525	496	201	487	2799	1766	125	6524
2002-03	3120	278	540	232	523	2508	1681	91	6508
2001-02	2775	283	583	220	489	1942	1424	104	6031

*C&AG Report No 16 of 2012-13 & Ministry of Defence, Government of India, Annual Report (relevant years), 2011-12 as per CA No. 30 of 2013 (Defence Services).

Expenditure on Works *(All Rupees in Crores)*

	Army			Navy			Air Force			Rashtriya Rifels	NCC	ECHS	Joint Staff		DRDO		Ordinance Factories		Inspection Organisation				
	Land	*Construction Works*	*Revenue Works*	*Land*	*Construction Works*	*Revenue Works*	*Land*	*Construction Works+Spl Projects*	*Revenue Works*	*Revenue Works*	*Revenue Works*	*Revenue Works*	*Land/Works*	*Revenue Works*	*Construction Works*	*Revenue Works*	*Construction Works*	*Revenue Works*	*Construction Works*	*Revenue Works*	*Total Works Expenditure*	*Total Defence Expenditure*	*Works Expenditure as a % of Defence Expenditure*
2014-15(BE)	300	4268	6785	310	582	934	76	1816	1946	57	8	15	547	143	757	626	454	142	6	70	19842	229000	8.66
2013-14(RE)	111	4039	6285	30	525	1069	3	1704	1910	52	9	10	305	143	531	626	222	104	12	67	17757	203672	8.72
2012-13	68	3814	5774	7	527	760	22	1909	1775	42	5	3	382	121	479	621	265	77	5	57	16711	193407	8.64
2011-12	17	4053	5711	18	515	763	3	1673	1800	40	5	2		123	583	543	267	76	7	57	16256	164415	9.89
2010-11	47	4080	5311	6	637	701	56	1387	1692	41	4	2		114	526	493	169	58	15	42	15381	147344	10.44
2009-10	44	3091	4610	104	308	645	73	1040	1560	39	4	1		101	352	412	157	50	16	41	12649	141703	8.93
2008-09	37	2857	4283	4	406	632	6	931	1318	33	4	1		106	417	375	107	62	29	43	11650	105600	11.03
2007-08	22	2761	3649	24	285	558	3	848	1167	24	3	1		97	535	326	87	63	7	38	10496	96000	10.93
2006-07	22	2585	3254	2	187	489	9	718	909	21	2	1		110	463	291	80	57	18	32	9252	89000	10.40
2005-06	37	1944	3044	30	149	444	3	473	841	20	2	1		77	366	262	144	59	12	33	7940	83000	9.57
2004-05	8	1223	2816	85	144	394	1	440	805	10	2	0		47	381	223	111	57	42	29	6818	77000	8.85
2003-04	14	936	2546	8	109	373	3	335	714	7	1			40	743	186	98	58	15	26	6212	65300	9.51
2002-03	16	780	2240	1	121	356	3	245	647	6	2			18	683	184	65	57	21	25	5470	65000	8.42
2001-02	14	547	2052	1	97	339	5	223	599	6	1			15	779	167	63	50	11	23	4990	62000	8.05
2000-01	19	537	1855	0	87	309	5	222	532	2	1				919	149	79	44	12	21	4794	58587	8.18
1999-00	29	469	1705	5	100	290	26	197	470		1				713	127	40	42	2	20	4236	45694	9.27
1998-99	13	379	1421	2	102	267	20	195	426		1				561	116	36	39	2	17	3598	41200	8.73
1997-98	22	345	1251	9	103	233	4	158	359		1				674	98	35	34	5	15	3345	35620	9.39
1996-97	27	417	1070	-2	77	180	0	124	296						564	78	46		6	13	2897	29505	9.82
1995-96	12	341	988	5	55	163	1	133	271		1				397	69	54		4	10	2503	26856	9.32
Grand Total	879	39466	66651	649	5115	9898	324	14771	20036	399	56	37	1234	1253	11424	5972	2580	1131	246	678	182798	1959904	9.33

Defence Expenditure-Rate of Growth versus Rate of Inflation & Budget in USD

Financial Year	*Total Defence Expenditure (Rs in Crs)*	*% Increase over previous year*	*Rate of Inflation (WPI)*	*Annual rate of US $*	*% Movement of Rs:$ exchange Rate over previous year*	*Indian Defence Budget in US $ Billion*	*% Increase over previous year*
2013-14	203672	12.05		60.5	11.19	33.66	0.77
2012-13	181776	6.36	7.37	54.41	13.54	33.41	-6.32
2011-12	170913	10.90	8.93	47.92	5.15	35.66	5.47
2010-11	154117	8.70	9.56	45.58	-3.88	33.81	13.09
2009-10	141781	24.13	3.81	47.42	3.27	29.90	20.20
2008-09	114223	24.59	8.06	45.92	14.11	24.88	9.19
2007-08	91680	7.24	4.67	40.24	-11.14	22.78	20.68
2006-07	85495	6.14	6.60	45.28	2.28	18.88	3.77
2005-06	80549	6.19	4.50	44.27	-1.46	18.19	7.76
2004-05	75856	26.29	6.48	44.93	-2.22	16.88	29.16
2003-04	60066	7.91	5.46	45.95	-5.05	13.07	13.65
2002-03	55662	2.57	3.41	48.40	1.47	11.50	1.08
2001-02	54266	9.36	3.60	47.69	4.39	11.38	4.75
2000-01	49622	5.42	7.16	45.68	5.43	10.86	-0.01
1999-00	47071	17.98	3.27	43.33	3.00	10.86	14.54
1998-99	39898	13.10	5.95	42.07	13.20	9.48	-0.09
1997-98	35278	19.57	4.40	37.16	4.69	9.49	14.21
1996-97	29505	9.86	4.61	35.50	6.13	8.31	3.52
1995-96	26856	15.53	7.99	33.45	6.53	8.03	8.45
1994-95	23245	6.41	12.60	31.40	0.11	7.40	6.30
1993-94	21845	24.25	8.35	31.37	2.34	6.96	21.41
1992-93	17582	7.55	10.06	30.65	25.23	5.74	-14.12
1991-92	16347	5.97	13.74	24.47	36.40	6.68	-22.31
1990-91	15426	7.01	10.26	17.94	7.77	8.60	-0.71
1989-90	14416	8.06	7.46	16.65	14.97	8.66	-6.01
1988-89	13341	11.48	7.46	14.48	11.69	9.21	-0.19
1987-88	11967	14.22	8.14	12.97	1.47	9.23	12.57
1986-87	10477	31.18	5.82	12.78	4.44	8.20	25.60
1985-86	7987	11.93	4.41	12.23	2.91	6.53	8.76
1984-85	7136	13.11	6.47	11.89	14.98	6.00	-1.63
1983-84	6309	16.66	7.53	10.34	6.97	6.10	9.06
1982-83	5408	16.25	4.90	9.67	7.78	5.59	7.86
1981-82	4652	20.30	9.33	8.97	13.39	5.19	6.09
1980-81	3867	15.23	18.24	7.91	-2.33	4.89	17.97
1979-80	3356	17.02	17.12	8.10	-1.57	4.14	18.88
1978-79	2868	8.88	0.00	8.23	-4.18	3.49	13.64
1977-78	2634	2.77	5.21	8.59	-4.36	3.07	7.46
1976-77	2563	3.68	2.08	8.98	3.40	2.85	0.27
1975-76	2472	17.05	-1.09	8.68	9.34	2.85	7.05
1974-75	2112	25.64	25.20	7.94	1.90	2.66	23.29
1973-74	1681	1.76	20.22	7.79	1.53	2.16	0.22
1972-73	1652	8.33	10.04	7.68	2.70	2.15	5.48
1971-72	1525	27.19	5.60	7.47	-1.12	2.04	28.63
1970-71	1199			7.56		1.59	

Exchange Rate of the Indian Rupee vis-à-vis the SDR, US Dollar, Pound Sterling, D.M. / Euro and Japanese Yen (Financial Year – Annual Average) As per Table 147 of RBI Handbook of Statistics on Indian Economy

(Rupees per unit of foreign currency)

Year	*SDR Average*	*US Dollar Average*	*Pound Sterling Average*	*Deutsche Mark/Euro Average*	*Japanese Yen Average*
2012-13	83.0262	54.4091	85.9713	70.0693	65.853
2011-12	75.3132	47.9229	76.3912	65.8939	60.7484
2010-11	69.7228	45.5768	70.8853	60.2181	53.2963
2009-10	73.7333	47.4166	75.8861	67.0843	51.1261
2008-09	71.2770	45.9170	78.4485	65.1345	46.0521
2007-08	62.6506	40.2410	80.8016	56.9906	35.2896
2006-07	67.2538	45.2849	85.7274	58.1110	38.7975
2005-06	64.4898	44.2735	79.0472	53.9124	39.1438
2004-05	66.9282	44.9315	82.8644	56.5523	41.8046
2003-04	65.6876	45.9516	77.7389	53.9896	40.7077
2002-03	64.1257	48.3953	74.8193	48.0901	39.7363
2001-02	60.2150	47.6919	68.3189	42.1811	38.1790
2000-01	59.5459	45.6844	67.5522	41.4832	41.4052
1999-00	58.9335	43.3327	69.8510	44.7909	39.0606
1998-99	57.5129	42.0706	69.5505	24.1792	33.1341
1997-98	50.6735	37.1648	61.0240	20.9613	30.2990
1996-97	50.8858	35.4999	56.3646	22.9244	31.5879
1995-96	50.4768	33.4498	52.3526	23.3993	34.8425
1994-95	45.7908	31.3986	48.8211	20.2017	31.6341
1993-94	43.8863	31.3655	47.2064	18.7403	29.1100
1992-93	37.1415	30.6488	51.6858	19.5877	24.5900
1991-92	33.4325	24.4737	42.5151	14.6248	18.4400
1990-91	24.8431	17.9428	33.1930	11.4351	12.7900
1989-90	21.3684	16.6492	26.9179	9.0922	11.6600
1988-89	19.2619	14.4817	25.5959	8.0494	11.3000
1987-88	17.1208	12.9658	22.0872	7.4004	9.4100
1986-87	15.4472	12.7782	19.0722	6.2970	8.0200
1985-86	12.9232	12.2349	16.8467	4.5553	5.6200
1984-85	11.9328	11.8886	14.8668	3.9877	4.8700
1983-84	10.9405	10.3400	15.4174	3.9402	4.3800
1982-83	10.5628	9.6660	16.1356	3.9600	3.8900
1981-82	10.3354	8.9683	17.1096	3.8607	3.9400
1980-81	10.1777	7.9092	18.5042	4.1875	3.7500
1979-80	10.4935	8.0975	17.6550	4.4717	3.5800
1978-79	10.4315	8.2267	15.9658	4.2200	4.0000
1977-78	10.1605	8.5858	15.4292	3.8358	3.3300
1976-77	10.3500	8.9775	15.5733	3.6308	3.0000
1975-76	10.3642	8.6825	18.3933	3.4458	3.0000
1974-75	9.6233	7.9408	18.8000	3.1917	3.0000
1973-74	9.3979	7.7925	18.8000	3.0075	3.0000
1972-73	8.4626	7.6750	18.8425	2.4392	3.0000
1971-72	7.6735	7.4731	18.4000	2.1974	2.0400
1970-71	7.5000	7.5578	18.0000	2.0490	2.0800

Notes:
1) The data on exchange rate for Japanese Yen is in Rupees per 100 Yen.
2) The end year rate for 1998-99 pertain to March 26, 1999 of Deutsche Mark rate.
3) Data from 1971 to1991-92 are based on official exchange rates.
4) Data from 1992-93 onwards are based on FEDAI (Foreign Exchange Dealers' Association of India) indicative rates.
5) Data from 1971 to 1972-73 for the Deutsche Mark and the Japanese Yen are cross rates with the US Dollar.
6) The Euro replaced the Deutsche Mark w.e.f. January 1, 1999.

Comparison of WPI & CPI (Index as per Table No 39 RBI & Table No 40 RBI Handbook of Statistics on Indian Economy) AND key indicators table 0.1 Economic Survey 2013-14

Financial Year	*Inflation Based on WPI All Commodities*	*Inflation Based on CPI Industrial Workers*
2013-14	5.97	9.37
2012-13	7.37	10.40
2011-12	8.93	8.33
2010-11	9.56	10.43
2009-10	3.81	12.41
2008-09	8.06	9.02
2007-08	4.67	6.40
2006-07	6.60	6.83
2005-06	4.50	4.23
2004-05	6.48	4.00
2003-04	5.46	3.73
2002-03	3.41	4.10
2001-02	3.60	4.28
2000-01	7.16	3.74
1999-00	3.27	3.38
1998-99	5.95	13.11
1997-98	4.40	7.02
1996-97	4.61	9.50
1995-96	7.99	10.21
1994-95	12.60	10.08
1993-94	8.35	7.50
1992-93	10.06	9.59
1991-92	13.74	13.47
1990-91	10.26	11.56
1989-90	7.46	6.13
1988-89	7.46	9.40
1987-88	8.14	8.76
1986-87	5.82	8.73
1985-86	4.41	6.78
1984-85	6.47	6.31
1983-84	7.53	12.55
1982-83	4.90	7.76
1981-82	9.33	12.47
1980-81	18.24	11.39
1979-80	17.12	8.76
1978-79	0.00	2.16
1977-78	5.21	7.64
1976-77	2.08	-3.83
1975-76	-1.09	-1.26
1974-75	25.20	26.80
1973-74	20.22	20.77
1972-73	10.04	7.81
1971-72	5.60	3.23

World Military Expenditure, 1988-2013
In US$ billion at constant (2011) Price

Year	*US$ Billion*	*Year*	*US$ Billion*
1988	1619	2001	1144.3
1989	1562	2002	1213
1990	1534.4	2003	1286.3
1991	...	2004	1358.8
1992	1198.6	2005	1416.5
1993	1156.4	2006	1463.4
1994	1126	2007	1520.2
1995	1072.8	2008	1598.1
1996	1053.1	2009	1705.1
1997	1063.3	2010	1731.8
1998	1052.4	2011	1739.3
1999	1078	2012	1736.3
2000	1118.8	2013	1701.7

Note: ... Data not available

Source: SIPRI Military Expenditure Database, http://milexdata.sipri.org/files/?file=SIPRI+milex+data+1988-2013+v2.xlsx (accessed on May 21, 2014)

Top 10 Military Spender (As % of GDP), 2010

Rank	*Country*	*Military Expenditure as % of GDP*
1	Oman	11.3
2	Saudi Arabia	9.3
3	Afghanistan	6.3
4	Israel	[5.6]
5	Algeria	4.8
6	Angola	4.8
7	Azerbaijan	4.7
8	Myanmar	4.5
9	Lebanon	[4.4]
10	Russia	[4.1]

Notes: 1. [ ]: estimated figure
Source: SIPRI Military Expenditure Database, http://milexdata.sipri.org/files/?file=SIPRI+military+expenditure+database+1988-2013.xlsx (accessed on May 21, 2014).

Top 10 Military Spenders, 2013-In Constant US$ Billion

Rank	*Country*	*Military Spending ($ Billon)*	*Military Spending as % of GDP*	*World Share (%)*
1	US	640	3.8	37
2	China	[188]	[2.0]	11
3	Russia	[87.8]	[4.1]	5
4	Saudi Arabia	67	9.3	3.8
5	France	61.2	2.2	3.5
6	UK	57.9	2.3	3.3
7	Germany	48.8	1.4	2.8
8	Japan	48.6	1	2.8
9	India	47.4	2.5	2.7
10	South Korea	33.9	2.8	1.9

Notes: 1. [ ]: estimated figure
2. Figures for India include expenditure on paramilitary forces
Source: Sam Perlo-Freeman and Carina Solmirano, "Trends in World Military Expenditure, 2013", SIPRI Fact Sheet, April 2014

Top-10 Arms Producer, 2012

Rank	*Company*	*Country*	*Defence Revenue (In US$ Million)*	*Total Revenue (In US$ Million)*	*Defence (%)*	*Rank*	*Company*	*Country*	*Defence Revenue (In US$ Million)*	*Total Revenue (In US$ Million)*	*Defence (%)*
1	Lockheed Martin	US	44883	47182	95.1	6	Northrop Grumman	US	20600	25218	81.7
2	Boeing	US	31378	81698	38.4	7	EADS	Netherlands	14912.96	72636.4	20.5
3	BAE	UK	26813.12	28255.2	94.9	8	Finmeccanica	Italy	12528.67	22135.47	56.6
4	Raytheon	US	22705.02	24414	93	9	United Technologies	US	12117	57700	21
5	General Dynamics	US	21023	31513	66.7	10	L-3 Communications	US	10839	13146	82.5

Note: HAL, India's biggest defence company ranks 37th
Source: Defense News, "Defense News top 100 for 2013", http://special.defensenews.com/top-100/charts/rank_2013.php (accessed on July 28, 2013)

Arms Export, by Supplier, 2004-2011 (Current US$ Billion)

	2004	*2005*	*2006*	*2007*	*2008*	*2009*	*2010*	*2011*	*Total 2004-2011*
US	11.61	11.77	12.3	12.3	11.92	14.22	11.97	16.16	102.24
Russia	5.6	3.9	6.3	5.2	6.6	5.6	6.9	8.7	48.8
France	5.6	2.7	1.8	2.5	1.8	1.3	1.7	1.7	19.1
UK	3.2	3.7	4.9	2.2	2.3	2.5	2.8	3	24.6
China	0.9	1	1.5	1.7	2.2	1.7	2.9	1.3	13.2
Germany	2	1.9	2.4	3	3.7	3	2.5	1.6	20.1
Italy	0.2	1	0.4	0.7	0.8	0.8	1.2	1.7	6.8
All other European	2.4	3.1	3.3	4	5.6	6.1	5.7	6.2	36.4
All Others	3.1	2.8	2.2	3.2	3.2	4.8	5	3.9	28.2
Total	34.61	31.87	35.1	34.8	38.12	40.02	40.67	44.26	299.44

Source: Richard F. Grimmett and Paul K. Kerr, Conventional Arms Transfers to Developing Nations, 2004-2011, CRS Report for Congress, August 24, 2012, p. 76.

Defence Budget Over the Years and its Relationship with the Central Government Expenditure and GDP at Market Prices

(*All Rs in Crores*)

Financial Year	*Defence Budget BE*	*Defence Budget (BE) Growth Over Previous Year*	*Actual Defence Expenditure (RE for 13-14)*	*Actual Defence Expenditure Growth Over Previous Year*	*Actual Expenditure as a %age of the BE*	*Expenditure of the Central Govt*	*Central Govt Expenditure Growth Over the Previous Year*	*Defence Expenditure as a % of the Central Govt Expenditure*	*GDP at Market Prices (Economic survey 2013-14 (DEA, MoF) GDP figures of 13-14 & 14-15 are as per Budget 2014-15 (presented on 10 Jul 14)*	*GDP at Market Prices Growth Over the Previous Year*	*Defence Expenditure as a % of the GDP at Market Prices*	*Exchange Rate US $ (Annual Average Rate as per RBI)*	*Indian Defence Budget in US $ Billion*
2014-15 (BE)	229000	12.47				1794892	12.9	12.8	12876653	13.4	1.78		
2013-14 (RE)	203672	5.3	203672	12.0	100	1590434	12.8	12.8	11355073	12.3	1.79	60.50	33.67
2012-13	193407	17.6	181776	6.4	94.0	1410372	9.4	12.9	10113281	12.2	1.80	54.41	33.41
2011-12	164415	11.6	170913	10.9	104.0	1288763	10.6	13.3	9009722	15.7	1.90	47.92	35.66
2010-11	147344	4.0	154117	8.7	104.6	1164727	17.4	13.2	7784115	20.2	1.98	45.58	33.81
2009-10	141703	34.2	141781	24.1	100.1	992440	14.8	14.3	6477827	15.1	2.19	47.42	29.90
2008-09	105600	10.0	114223	24.6	108.2	864530	25.5	13.2	5630063	12.9	2.03	45.92	24.88
2007-08	96000	7.9	91680	7.2	95.5	688909	20.8	13.3	4987090	16.1	1.84	40.24	22.78
2006-07	89000	7.2	85495	6.1	96.1	570185	13.8	15.0	42 94706	16.3	1.99	45.28	18.88
2005-06	83000	7.8	80549	6.2	97.0	501083	8.0	16.1	3693369	13.9	2.18	44.27	18.19
2004-05	77000	17.9	75856	26.3	98.5	463831	8.8	16.4	3242209	14.2	2.34	44.93	16.88
2003-04	65300	0.5	60066	7.9	92.0	426132	6.8	14.1	2837900	12.1	2.12	45.95	13.07
2002-03	65000	4.8	55662	2.6	85.5	398879	10.6	14.0	2530663	7.8	2.20	48.40	11.50
2001-02	62000	5.8	54266	9.4	87.5	360616	9.9	15.0	2348330	8.3	2.31	47.69	11.38
2000-01	58587	28.2	49622	5.4	84.7	328265	6.7	15.1	2168652	7.8	2.29	45.68	10.86
1999-00	45694	10.9	47071	18.0	103.0	307509	16.6	15.3	2012198	11.6	2.34	43.33	10.86
1998-99	41200	15.7	39898	13.1	96.8	263755	17.3	15.1	1803378	14.7	2.21	42.07	9.48
1997-98	35620	28.1	35278	19.6	99.0	224866	6.4	15.7	1572394	10.8	2.24	37.16	9.49

1996-97	27798	9.0	29505	9.9	106.1	211260	14.1	14.0	1419277	15.7	2.08	35.50	8.31
1995-96	25500	-1.9	26856	15.5	105.3	185233	10.9	14.5	1226725	17.3	2.19	33.45	8.03
1994-95	26000	35.6	23245	6.4	89.4	166998	14.5	13.9	1045590	17.3	2.22	31.40	7.40
1993-94	19180	9.6	21845	24.2	113.9	145788	15.8	15.0	891335	15.1	2.45	31.37	6.96
1992-93	17500	7.0	17582	7.6	100.5	125927	11.7	14.0	774545	14.9	2.27	30.65	5.74
1991-92	16350	3.8	16347	6.0	100.0	112731	7.4	14.5	673875	15.0	2.43	24.47	6.68
1990-91	15750	21.2	15426	7.0	97.9	104973	10.4	14.7	586212	16.8	2.63	17.94	8.60
1989-90	13000	0.0	14416	8.1	110.9	95049	16.8	15.2	501928	14.9	2.87	16.65	8.66
1988-89	13000	3.9	13341	11.5	102.6	81402	15.8	16.4	436893	18.7	3.05	14.48	9.21
1987-88	12512	43.4	11967	14.2	95.6	70305	9.8	17.0	368211	13.7	3.25	12.97	9.23
1986-87	8728	13.6	10477	31.2	120.0	64023	20.5	16.4	323949	11.9	3.23	12.78	8.20
1985-86	7686	13.0	7987	11.9	103.9	53112	21.0	15.0	289524	12.8	2.76	12.23	6.53
1984-85	6800	13.9	7136	13.1	104.9	43879	21.9	16.3	256611	12.0	2.78	11.89	6.00
1983-84	5971	17.1	6309	16.7	105.7	35988	18.0	17.5	229021	16.5	2.75	10.34	6.10
1982-83	5100	21.4	5408	16.3	106.0	30494	20.1	17.7	196644	11.9	2.75	9.67	5.59
1981-82	4200	16.7	4652	20.3	110.8	25401	12.9	18.3	175805	17.5	2.65	8.97	5.19
1980-81	3600	18.0	3867	15.2	107.4	22495	21.6	17.2	149642	19.0	2.58	7.91	4.89
1979-80	3050	3.6	3356	17.0	110.0	18504	4.4	18.1	125729	9.7	2.67	8.10	4.14
1978-79	2945	7.0	2868	8.9	97.4	17717	18.2	16.2	114647	8.3	2.50	8.23	3.49
1977-78	2752	8.2	2634	2.8	95.7	14986	14.0	17.6	105848	13.3	2.49	8.59	3.07
1976-77	2544	11.9	2563	3.7	100.7	13150	9.2	19.5	93422	7.7	2.74	8.98	2.85
1975-76	2274	18.7	2472	17.0	108.7	12037		20.5	86707	7.4	2.85	8.68	2.85
1974-75	1915	19.7	2112	25.6	110.3				80770	18.1	2.61	7.94	2.66
1973-74	1600	13.6	1681	1.8	105.1				68420	21.7	2.46	7.79	2.16
1972-73	1408	13.4	1652	8.3	117.3				56214	10.2	2.94	7.68	2.15
1971-72	1242	7.8	1525	27.2	122.8				50999	7.1	2.99	7.47	2.04
1970-71	1152	3.8	1199	8.9	104.1	5577		21.5	47638	6.8	2.52	7.56	1.59
1969-70	1110	9.4	1101	6.6	99.2				44605	10.1	2.47		

(Contd.)

1968-69	1015	4.7	1033	6.7	101.8			40512	5.9	2.55
1967-68	969	5.6	968	6.5	99.9			38261	17.1	2.53
1966-67	918	4.4	909	2.7	99.0			32669	13.2	2.78
1965-66	879	2.9	885	9.8	100.7	3940	22.5	28857	5.4	3.07
1964-65	854	-1.5	806	-12.0	94.4			27367	16.6	2.95
1963-64	867	133.1	916	93.2	105.7			23462	14.8	3.90
1962-63	372	18.1	474	50.5	127.4			20429	7.5	2.32
1961-62	315	1.6	315	12.1	100.0			19010	6.0	1.66
1960-61	310	12.7	281	2.2	90.6	1806	15.6	17942	9.5	1.57
1959-60	275	-9.8	275	-2.5	100.0			16384	5.4	1.68
1958-59	305	10.5	282	0.7	92.5			15551	11.5	1.81
1957-58	276	20.0	280	32.1	101.4			13951	3.0	2.01
1956-57	230	2.2	212	11.6	92.2			13547	19.1	1.56
1955-56	225	0.9	190	-2.6	84.4	975	19.5	11371	1.8	1.67
1954-55	223	3.7	195	-0.5	87.4			11170	-5.4	1.75
1953-54	215	0.0	196	5.9	91.2			11810	8.8	1.66
1952-53	215	11.4	185	2.2	86.0			10850	-1.8	1.71
1951-52	193		181					11054		1.64

The data compiled above has been taken from the Defence Budget- A Statistical Digest, printed by Finance Division of Ministry of Defence, December 2006, Defence Service Estimates , Economic Survey 2013-14 and Union Budget Presented in Parliament on 10 JUL 2014. The actual expenditure for 13-14 is the RE figure and GDP for 2013-14 & 2014-15 is the figures in the Budget at a glance 2014-15 based on advance estimates of 2013-14 released by CSO. The Defence expenditure & its ratio between central Govt Expenditure /GDP for 2014-15 are based on the BE figures of Defence budget and central Government expenditure as per union budget 2014-15.

INDEX

A&N Command, 42-43, 45, 49-50
Acquisition, 33, 47, 60-61, 70, 74, 82, 90, 93, 115, 143-55, 167-69, 183, 187-88, 207, 212, 217, 221, 223-25, 245-46, 248, 251-54, 299, 302, 307, 313-19, 323-25, 327, 329, 331-32
    Cloud, 257
Act, 98, 183, 185, 187, 198, 203, 206
Active Electronically Scanned Array (AESA), 274, 280
Additional Director Generals Weapons & Equipment, 14
Adjutant General, 249
Adm Lynde D. McCormick, US Navy, 245
Advanced Light Helicopter, 128
Agni missile, 2
AGPL, 232, 242
AHQ, 31
Air Based Early Warning System, 273
Air Borne Electronic Warning System, 273
Air Commodore Jasjit Singh, 263, 274
Air Force Logistics Command, 251
Air Force Material Command, 251
Air Force Stores Budget Sub-Head Wise, 185
Air Force Systems Command, 251
Air Force, 189, 250, 267
Air HQ, 31
Aircraft & Aero Engines, 185
Aircraft carrier, 133
Ajay Vikram Singh Committee, 42
Al Qaida, 5
ANURAG, 125
AoB Rules, 30
Arjun, 129
Armed Forces Medical Services, 45
Armoured Personnel Carriers (APCs), 166, 178, 302
Army Medical Corps, 49
Army Ordnance Corps, 249
ARTRAC, 66
ASAT, 140
ASEAN Regional Forum, 7
Assam Rifles, 235, 241
ATF, 178, 179
Automated Air Defence System, 273

BAE Systems, 287
BAFO, 145
Bangladesh War, 25
Bangladesh, 1, 6
Bangladesh-China-India-Myanmar corridor, 6
Banking, 299
Base Repair Depots, 221
BHEEMA, 125
BHEL, 165
Bially, Janice, 190
Border Roads Development Board, 219
Border Roads Organisation (BRO), 116, 215, 219
    budget, 225
Bose, Subhash Chandra, 24
Bottom-Up Review, 84-85
BRAHMOS cruise missile, 142
    programme, 283
Budget Control Act, 85
Budget, 132, 175, 188, 317-22
    and State Economy, 182
    Capital, 185, 187
    Challenges, 213
    Inadequacy, 210, 212
    Performance, 175
    Process, 112
    Revenue, 199
Bureau of Industry and Security (BIS), 290, 291, 295
Buy and Make, 149, 272, 279-280
    Global, 154, 167
    Indian, 167, 169
Buy, 280, 286
    Global, 154, 286, 300-1

C4ISR, 96, 97, 273
Network, 127
Cabinet Committee of Political Affairs, 76, 241
Cabinet Committee on Security (CCS), 28, 58, 62, 63, 75, 81, 104, 111, 314, 323, 331
CAG, 88, 306, 321-22, 327, 329, 331
Canadian Content Value (CCV), 296, 300
Capability Based Planning (CBP), 94, 95, 96, 97
Capability, 207
Political Awareness, 193-94
Capital Acquisition Wing, 223
Central Armed Police Forces, 236
Central Bureau of Investigation (CBI), 153, 326, 327, 329, 331
Central Command, 69
Central Government Expenditure, 210
Central Police Forces, 235
Central Vigilance Commission (CVC), 153, 313, 323-27, 329, 331, 333
Centre for Budget and Governance Accountability, 210
Challenge, 185
Chief of Defence Staff (CDS), 56-57, 61, 65, 67, 70, 72, 104
Chief of Integrated Defence Staff, 104
Chief of Integrated Staff to the Chairman, 219
Chief of Joint Staff (CJS), 44-45, 48-50-51
Chief of Naval Staff, 219
Chief Vigilance Officer (CVO), 325, 330-33
Chiefs of Staff, 50
China, 1-8, 11, 39, 67, 73, 132-33, 195, 231, 262, 279, 281-85, 288-89, 363
Maritime strategy, 6
Circular Error Probability, 193
Civil Aviation industry, 280
Civil-military
Equation, 19
Evolution of, 26-28
Integration, 34
Mix, 13
Relations, 19-20, 24-26, 35, 107, 109
Structure, 10
Clausewitz, Carl von, 22
CLAWS, 264
Coast Guard vessels, 166
Coast Guard, 235
COBOL, 267
Cold War, 11
Combat surface vessels, 133
Commander-in-Chief (C-in-C), 22, 26, 41, 42, 46, 59, 249
Communication, 274
Competent Financial Authority (CFA), 221, 261
Completely Knocked Down (CKD), 149, 303
Comptroller and Auditor General (C&AG), 153, 323-26, 331, 333
Computational Fluid Dynamics, 125
Confederation of Indian Industry, 169
Constitution of India
Article 265, 209
Consumer Price Index, 180
Contract, 278
COSC, 57, 59, 66, 109
Cost of ownership, 187
COTS, 144, 163, 259
CRAY
Supercomputer, 124-25
Credits, 295
CRISIL, 166
CRPF, 27
Customer Supplier Partnership, 264
Cyber, 47, 48, 69
Security, 127
Space, 126
Threat, 126
Warfare, 68, 72, 190

Database Management Systems (DBMS), 265, 267
Davis, Paul K., 94, 108, 182
DDGs, 115-18, 217
Defence Accounts Department (DAD), 222, 227, 313
Defence Acquisition Council (DAC), 75, 76, 79, 81, 154, 207, 215, 225, 313
Defence Acquisition Programme Administration (DAPA), 299, 306
Defence and Security Industrial Engagement Policy, 293
Defence Committee of the Cabinet, 207
Defence Green Paper, 105
Defence Minister, Bartles, 88
Defence Procurement Procedure (DPP), 89, 138, 279, 305, 313, 328
Defence production capability, 319
Defence Public Sector Undertakings (DPSUs), 81, 150-51, 157, 158, 159, 160, 165, 168, 215, 258, 262, 264, 269, 271-74, 279-80
Defence Review, 96

Defence Services Estimates, 218, 221
Defence Staff Headquarters, 31
Defence Strategy Review, 98
Defence Works Procedure, 223-24
DEFTECH, 303
Delegation of Financial Powers, 221
Department of Defence Production (DDP), 30, 76, 103, 154, 157, 170, 218, 223
Department of Ex-Servicemen Welfare, 30
Department of Industrial Policy and Promotion, guidelines, 162
Direct cost, 278
Direct Entry, 237
Director General Armed Forces Medical Services, 249
Directorate of Standardisation, 266
Distribution of Capital Expenditure, 198
DoD, 27, 30-31, 91, 102, 113, 218, 251, 307
DOFA, 271, 304, 307
DOMW, 223, 271, 304, 307
DOTMLPF, 95
Down time, 257
DPC, 76, 103
DPG, 83, 105
DPM, 102, 223, 224, 313
Dr. Kalam Committee, 274
Dr. Kalam, 273
Dr. Rama Rao Committee, 287
DRDO, 32, 42, 63, 76, 81, 103, 114, 121-22, 124, 128-30, 139-40, 149-51, 154, 157, 164, 167, 170, 223, 252, 264, 271, 274, 280, 287, 320, 324
DSR, 244
Dunne, Prof. Paul, 278

East Asia, 163
East China Sea, 2
Eastern Command, 69
Economic Survey, 279
eGOM, 314
Eighth Defence Plan, 77
E-in-C, 249
Einstein, Albert, 246, 268
Electrical and Mechanical Engineers, 24
Electronic Counter Measure, 273
Electronic Warfare (EW), 123, 128
  systems, 132
Electronic Warfare Systems, 130
Eleventh, Five Year Plan, 60, 71, 79,81
Enterprise Resource Planning, 254, 267
EPTL, 302
ERV, 224, 287
Estimates Committee, 91
EU, 292-93
Euro-Atlantic region, 7
Europe, 26, 39, 48, 171, 276, 282, 292
European Defence Agency, 292
European Defence Industry, 278, 285
Exclusive Economic Zone, 219
Expeditionary Force, 39
Expenditure, 206, 211
Exports
  Need for, 163-64
Exservicemen Health Scheme, 218

Fifth Generation Fighter Aircraft, 277
Financial Accountability and Control, 47
Financial management, 208
Finland, 284
FIR, 315
First Five Year Defence Plan, 103
Fiscal Responsibility and Budget Management, 78, 213
Fissile Material Cut-off Treaty, 4
Five year Defence Plan (FYDP), 92, 93, 94, 98, 103, 111, 215
Five-Year Rolling Programme, 91
Focal Plane Arrays, 275, 280
Forces, 39
Foreign Direct Investment (FDI), 8, 152, 216, 228, 272, 279, 287, 288
  Inflow, 283
  Policy, 283
Foreign Military Sales, 147
Forward Observation Officer, 9
France, 106, 124, 157, 277
Free Indian Legion, 24

G-7, 124
Garrison Engineer, 46
Gas Turbine Engine, 274-75
Gen. Cariappa, 24
General Financial Rules, 2005, 172
General JJ Singh (Retd), 176
GFRs, 222, 313
Ghosh, A.K., 108
Global War On Terror, 85
Global, 290-93
Goldwater Nichols Act, 18, 65
Government Procurement Agreement, 304
GPS, 273, 275
Green Revolution, 131

Group of Ministers (GoM), 28, 31, 90, 104, 311, 312, 313
Guided Missiles, 123

HAL, 39, 272-73, 275-77, 283, 357
Head Quarters (HQs), 28, 30, 31, 35, 45, 46, 175, 184, 188, 265-66
Higher Defence Organisation, 57
 Structures for, 58
Hitch, Charles J., 102
HS Code 88, 161
Huntington, Samuel, 20-21, 106

ICRA, 166
Improvised Explosive Devices, 95
India's Military Industrial Complex, 273
India-Japan-US cooperation, 7
Indian Air Force (IAF), 39, 133, 177, 220, 287
Indian Armed Forces, 243-44, 250
 Professionalism, 238-39
Indian Coast Guard, 215
Indian Defence Review, 82
Indian Institute of Foreign Trade, 165
Indian Meteorological Department, 125
Indian Military Academy, 237
Indian National Army, 24
Indian Ocean Region (IOR), 11, 232, 243
Indian Offset Partner, 306
Indian Space Research Organisation (ISRO), 9
India-Pakistan War, 9, 103
India-Tibet border, 2
Indirect, 284
Industrial Cooperation, 304-5
Industrial Participation (IP), 293
Industries (Development and Regulation) Act, 1951, 168
Infantry Combat Vehicles (ICVs), 272
Information and Communication Technology (ICT), 131, 155, 162, 225, 227, 229, 276
Information Technology (IT), 130, 267, 268, 269, 283
Integrated Defence Staff (IDS), 14, 55, 76, 79, 109, 116, 154, 215, 219, 265, 266
Integrated Financial Advisor, 221-22
Integrated Guided Missile Development Programme, 128
Integrated Logistics Management System, 267
Integrated Material Management Online System, 267
Intellectual Property Rights (IPR), 164
Intellectual Property, 298
Inter-Governmental Agreement, 147
IRBM, 125
Israel, 273, 280, 284, 290, 294-95, 299, 303-06
Itemised Spares Parts Price List, 145
Izzat, 239-40, 244

Jammu and Kashmir (J&K), 1, 3, 69, 231-32, 237, 242
Jammu and Kashmir Light Infantry (JAKLI), 116, 218, 219
Japan, 7, 41, 107, 124, 160, 211, 270, 277, 282, 289, 363
Joint Capability Assets, 48
Joint Ventures (JVs), 63, 121, 135, 138-39, 141, 160, 167, 272, 279, 283
Jointness, 15, 34, 46, 52, 63-65, 67, 70, 72, 73, 111, 215, 241, 244

Kargil Review Committee (KRC), 28, 42, 55, 57, 59, 235
Kelkar Committee, 160, 164-66, 261, 271
Kothari, Prof DS, 121
Krishnamurthi Committee, 280

Layne,Christopher, 190
Lewis, Kevin , 182
Life Cycle Cost (LCC), 145, 146, 252
 principles, 147
Life Cycle Cost Dilemma, 187, 253, 260
Life Cycle Management, 252
 Tool, 252, 253, 254
Light Combat Aircraft (LCA), 125, 128, 273-74
Light Combat Helicopter, 128
Line of Actual Control (LoAC), 2, 232
Line of Control (LoC), 1, 231-32, 242
Long Range Agni-5, 121
Long Term Integrated Perspective Plan (LTIPP), 61, 70, 75-77, 79-82, 89, 94, 96, 126, 143, 154, 207

Main Battle Tank (MBT), 129, 273, 274
Maintenance Repair and Overhaul (MRO), 150, 152, 171, 262-64, 275
 activities, 171
 facilities, 171
 market, 171
Maj Gen Len Le Roux, 92
Malacca Straits, 6-7, 133, 231

Management Information System (MIS), 267, 317, 318
Married Accommodation Project (MAP), 119, 220
McNamara, Robert, 102
Mean Time Between Failures (MTBF), 145, 148, 155, 258
Mean Time to Repair (MTTR), 145, 148
Medium Multi-Role Combat Aircraft (MMRCA), 280
Meilissa McPherson, 190
Melvin R. Laird, 102
Menon, Krishna, 54
MHA, 62, 219, 242
MIC, 141-42, 271
Micro, Small and Medium Enterprises (MSMEs), 150, 151, 271, 279
MIG 29, 276
Military
    Cantonments, 46
    Capability, 189-90
    Expenditure, 49
    Farms, 220
Ministry of Defence (MoD), 9, 12, 14, 17, 27, 29, 53, 58, 59-61, 63, 71-72, 74-75, 78-81, 87-88, 91-92, 101-3, 109-15, 117-19, 146, 151, 155, 161, 165, 167, 170, 175, 185, 187-88, 206, 211-13, 215-22, 224-25, 227-28, 231, 235-36, 251, 254, 262, 266, 277, 305, 307, 310-13, 315-18, 321-23, 325, 327, 332
    civil-servant, 33
Demands for Grant, 217
Ministry of External Affairs (MEA), 16, 62, 63
Ministry of Finance (MoF), 75, 78, 92, 112-14, 209, 213, 220
Missile Technology Control Regime (MTCR), 124, 162, 168
Missile, 139, 274
MMRCA, 187, 280
Multi Role Transport Programme, 283

Nakra, D.S., 75
National Association of Defence Industries, 167
National Cadet Corps (NCC), 116, 119, 218, 219, 220
National Capability, 190
National Defence Academy, 234
National Electronic Fund Transfers, 226
National Industrial Classification (NIC), 105
    Code, 161
National Offset Policy, 285
National Security Advisor (NSA), 9, 81, 109
National Security Advisory Board, 71
National Security Council (NSC), 71, 81, 106, 107
National Security Objectives and Strategy, 215
National Security Strategy (NSS), 57-58, 80
National Security, 12-13, 15, 18, 104, 106
    Compulsions of, 22-24
    Reform, 28
NATO, 96, 266
    Alliance, 94
    Defence organisations, 97
Navy, 189, 267, 281, 287
Nehru, Jawaharlal, former Prime Minister, 53
Net-Centric Operations, 47
Netherlands, 284
Network for Spectrum, 268
Ninth Defence Plan, 78
No Cost No Commitment, 170
Northern Command, 69
Nuclear Suppliers Group (NSG), 4, 162, 168
Nuclear, 131
Nuclear, Biological and Chemical, 127

OEMs, 144-49, 152-53, 167, 168, 259-60, 273, 277-78, 301
Officers Training Academy, 238
Offset, 294
Op Parakram, 40, 42
Operations Research, 108
Ordnance Factories (OFs), 114-15, 139, 151, 157-60, 170, 215, 223, 261, 271, 272, 274, 279, 280
Organisation of Islamic Cooperation, 3
Outcome Budget, 206, 220-21
    2005-06, 175
Outsourcing, 151, 164, 170, 216, 228, 241, 261-64, 269-70, 303
Overhaul and repair facilities, 275
Oversight mechanism, 312
Oversight, 227

Parliament Standing Committee, 206
Parliamentary committees, 333
Pay and Allowances (P&A), 88, 180, 183, 185, 199
Pay and Allowances, 88
PBL, 149, 261, 262, 263, 269
PBOR, 233, 235, 237, 242

Percentage, 294
Performance Based Maintenance, 264
Permanent Chairman Chiefs of Staff, 50
Plan, 76, 92, 111, 215
Planning Commission, 184
Planning, Programming, and Budgeting System (PPBS), 90, 93, 94, 101-03, 112, 116
Policy at National Level, 281, 303, 304
PPB model, 114, 115
Prime Minister Nehru, 24
Product, 161
Prof. Eriksson, 278
Prof. Rama Rao, 277
Professional Officers' Valuation, 146
PSUs, 128, 139, 148, 170, 243, 261, 262, 264, 315, 319, 325, 333
Public Expenditure Survey Committee, 91
Public Private Partnership (PPP), 151, 264

QDR, 83, 86, 94, 105
Qualitative Requirement (QR), 18, 139, 144, 154, 318, 327, 328
Quality Assurance, 249

R&D, 164, 166, 218, 274, 276-77, 306
Raksha Udyog Ratna, 164-66
Rama Rao Committee, 274
Rashtriya Rifles, 218-19
Realisation, 275
Reconnaissance, 47, 62, 111, 134
Reforming the National Security System, 28, 90, 104
Repair and Overhaul, 276
Request for Information (RFI), 145, 148, 167
Request for Proposal (RFP), 145, 154, 167, 187, 302
Revolution in Military Affairs, 40
Rifkin, Jeremy, 248

SCOMET, 162
Second Administrative Reforms Commission, 316
Seekers, 280
Selective compulsory military service, 237, 243
Self Reliance, 274
Self-Reliance Index (SRI), 274, 279
Sen, Prof. Amartya, 285
Sengupta, Shri Probir, 165
Service Head Quarter (SHQ), 27, 30, 31, 33-34, 53-54, 217
Service Oriented Architecture (SOA), 268
Services, 109, 117, 148, 151, 154, 190, 217
Estimates, 115
Singh, Manmohan, Former Prime Minister, 36
SIPRI Military Expenditure Database, 194
Sixth Defence Plan, 76-77
SMEs, 169, 271, 276
Snyder, Glenn, 106
South Eastern Command, 69
South Korea, 282, 284, 290, 299, 301, 306
South Western Command, 69
Southern Command, 69
Southern Indian Ocean, 231
Special Economic Zone, 152
Standardisation Committee, 266
Standardisation, 265-66
Standing Committee, 104
Strategic Defence Review, 58, 105
Strategic Forces Command (SFC), 42, 55, 66, 69, 219
SU-30 MKI, 139, 252
Submarine Launched Ballistic Missile B-05, 121
Subrahmanyam, K., 13
Surveillance, 47, 68, 274
Swapping, 304

T-90S, 139
Tactical Communication System, 277
Tactical Systems, 130
Tanham, George, 23
Targeting, 47
Technology Perspective Capability Roadmap, 81
Tellis, Ashley J., 190
Tenth Defence Plan, 60, 71, 78
Theatre Commands, 45
Theory of Constraints (TOC), 246, 247, 260
Thirteenth Finance Commission, 98, 317
Threshold, 294
Time Between Overhaul, 253
ToB Rules, 30
Trading, 298-99
Transfer of Technology (ToT), 139, 149, 170, 271, 285
Trishul Missile, 129
TSR Subramnian, 190
TTL, 253
Turkey, 284, 290, 295, 299, 301, 306
Turn Around Time, 145, 148
Twelfth Plan, 285

Twelfth, Defence Plans, 75, 79, 81
Types in Aerospace Sector, 275

UK Strategic Review, 98
Unmanned Aerial Vehicle (UAV), 96-97, 123, 166, 273, 280

War Wastage Reserves (WWR), 179, 192-93
Wassenaar Arrangement, 162
Weapon systems, 149
Weapon, 274, 276
Weapons of Mass Destruction, 124
Western Command, 69
Wholesale Price Index, 180
Wipro, 165
World Trade Organisation (WTO), 160, 270, 304-5
World War II, 21, 24, 10, 103, 265